European Community Law

Josephine Shaw
Senior Lecturer in Law, Keele University

Law series editor: Marise Cremona
Senior Fellow, Centre for Commercial Law Studies
Queen Mary and Westfield College, University of London

MACMILLAN

First published 1993 by
THE MACMILLAN PRESS LTD
Houndmills, Basingstoke, Hampshire RG21 2XS
and London
Companies and representatives
throughout the world

ISBN 0-333-58527-5

A catalogue record for this book is available
from the British Library.

Copy-edited and typeset by Povey–Edmondson
Okehampton and Rochdale, England

Printed in China

10	9	8	7	6	5	4	3	2	
02	01	00	99	98	97	96	95	94	93

Contents

also p220

Part IV THE CONTROL OF THE COMMUNITY INSTITUTIONS

Part VI   THE SOCIAL DIMENSION OF THE EUROPEAN COMMUNITY

16   The basic framework of Community social policy   323

Preface and Acknowledgements

This book aims to provide a general introduction to European Community, suitable for use on the type of course or module at undergraduate level on Community law which matches the requirements of the Law Society's document on 'Fundamental Principles' in the Academic Stage of Legal Education. It aims to give students a firm grounding in the institutional background and the constitutional fundamentals of the Community, and to give them a reasonably detailed knowledge of the legal framework of the internal market. I shall doubtless be accused of tokenism for including just one chapter in Part VI on Social Policy. That is included both to give students some idea of the non-economic aspects of Community law, and in order to emphasise that not all the Community's legislative programmes have proceeded as (relatively) smoothly as the project to complete the internal market.

All law books face the difficulty of following a moving target. Few targets have been as mobile as Community law during the summer, autumn and winter of 1992, when considerable doubts arose in some Member States about the desirability of ratifying the Treaty on European Union, or Treaty of Maastricht. After the Edinburgh Summit in December 1992, it appeared more likely that the Treaty would be duly ratified by all Member States, and accordingly this book has gone to press based on the assumption that the Treaty will be adopted and come into force during the course of 1993.

Thanks are due to all those who have helped me in any way with this book. I owe a debt in particular to those who endured rather strained domestic arrangements and relations during the summer and autumn of 1992, especially Leo Shaw and Amanda Godfrey. My thanks go to the series editor, Marise Cremona, who encouraged me to write this book, and offered useful advice and constructive criticisms of earlier drafts, and to the publishers. I acknowledge also the contribution of successive cohorts of undergraduate and postgraduate students of Community law at the Universities of Exeter and Keele who suffered my early attempts to render the mass of material which comprises Community law moderately pedagogically digestible. I cannot, alas, record that my illegible hand-writing was transformed into perfect typescript by willing and cheerful helpers. That kind of secretarial assistance is simply not now available in the University of the 1990s. I can, however, record a flawless performance by my Keele-supplied Elonex and associated software, without which I, like many academics who have grown up during the wordprocessor age, would be unable to string more than two sentences together. Finally, thanks are due in large measure to Sally Wheeler for encouragement and help – both practical and emotional – throughout the period when this book was written.

I alone, however, remain responsible for any errors.

JOSEPHINE SHAW

Table of Cases

A: Cases before the European Court of Justice

1 By Case Number (in year order)

2   Alphabetical list

B: Cases before the Court of First Instance

C: Cases before National Courts

1 English Courts

2   German Courts

3   Irish Courts

4   Belgian Courts

5   French Courts

Table of Treaties Establishing the European Communities and the European Union

Table of UK Statutes

List of Abbreviations

CAP	Common Agricultural Policy
CCP	Common Commercial Policy
CCT	Common Customs Tariff
CE	Compulsory expenditure
CEE	Charge having an equivalent effect
CFSP	Common Foreign and Security Policy
COREPER	Committee of Permanent Representatives
DG	Directorate-General
DTEU	Draft Treaty of European Union
EEA	European Economic Area
ECB	European Central Bank
ECHR	European Convention on Human Rights
ECOSOC	Economic and Social Committee
ECSC	European Coal and Steel Community
EDC	European Defence Community
EEC	European Economic Community
EEIG	European Economic Interest Group
EFTA	European Free Trade Area
EMS	European Monetary System
EMU	European Monetary Union
ERM	Exchange Rate Mechanism
ESCB	European System of Central Banks
Euratom	European Atomic Energy Authority
GATT	General Agreement on Tariffs and Trade
MEEQR	Measure having equivalent effect to quantitative restrictions
MEP	Member of the European Parliament
NCE	Non-compulsory expenditure
OECD	Organisation for European Cooperation and Development
OEEC	Organisation for European Cooperation
SEA	Single European Act
SPA	Social Policy Agreement
TEU	Treaty on European Union
WEU	Western European Union

Part I

Introduction

1 Studying European Community Law

1.1 Beginning European Community Law

The purpose of this introductory chapter is to equip you, the reader, with the basic tools you need to embark upon the study of European Community law, a subject which has something of a reputation for being impenetrable. It assumes that you have some knowledge of the basic components of a legal system, but very little knowledge of what the European Community can do, what it cannot do, and why it is important in a specifically legal sense. It offers in 1.5 a brief overview of the Community legal system, containing basic pointers on to which more detailed study can be grafted, which highlights the pivotal role of the Court of Justice in the system of integration as set up by the Treaties of Rome and Paris in the 1950s and as evolved through the Single European Act (SEA) and the Treaty of Maastricht or Treaty of European Union (TEU) in the 1980s and 1990s.

The Community is not just a new type of legal order – one which can only be understood if certain basic precepts of the study of national law are set aside; it is also a legal order in which a very specific and clear purpose is dominant. This is the promotion of a process of integration, leading towards the union of European states. This purpose operates at a number of different levels, including the economic (breaking down the barriers to trade between states) and the political (creating a common political identity for the Community), but it is ever present. The Court of Justice never loses sight of the aim of integration when it is interpreting Community law, and nor should those who study it. 1.3 contains an outline sketch of this aim, and the concept of 'integration' is one of those which receives attention in 1.4, which attempts to demystify certain aspects of the language of the European Community.

In comparison to most national legal systems, and certainly in comparison to the legal systems of the states which form its constituent members, the legal system of the European Community is particularly unstable and in a state of constant flux and change. Changes come about either because of a dynamic intervention on the part of the Court of Justice in the interpretation of Community law, or because the Member States have negotiated further amendments to the Community's constitution – its basic Treaties. Since the reasons for these changes lie more frequently in the field of politics than law, it will be apparent that Community law can only properly be understood in its wider political and economic context, and that the successful study of Community law presupposes the acquisition of a substantial body of contextual knowledge. Some guidance on acquiring that knowledge is offered in 1.7. 1.6

offers assistance in locating the Community treaties, legislation and official documentation, and in making a basic selection from amongst the voluminous legal literature available. We begin, however, with some basic facts about the European Community.

1.2   The European Community: The Basic Facts

The European Community started out as a Community of six: France, the Federal Republic of Germany, Italy, Belgium, Luxembourg and the Netherlands. In 1973 Denmark, Ireland and the UK acceded; Norway signed a Treaty of Accession, but did not join when membership was rejected by popular vote in a referendum. Further expansion occurred in 1980 with the accession of Greece, and in 1986 with the accession of Spain and Portugal, creating a Community of twelve. *De facto* expansion occurred once again in 1990, with the unification of Germany having the effect of bringing the former German Democratic Republic into the Community although not as a separate member. Following the collapse of Communism in central and eastern Europe, and with the ever closer trading links between the various European countries, membership of the European Community has become an increasingly coveted prize. Candidates for membership at present include countries as varied as Austria, Sweden, Turkey, Malta and Morocco (the last is probably ruled out because it is not a European country).

The 'European Community' has in fact been the commonly used designation for a political entity, composed of a number of distinct legal entities with separate international legal personality, which are generally identified as a single unit. These are the three Communities, of which two are confined in their application to particular sectors of the economy: the European Coal and Steel Community (ECSC), formed by the Treaty of Paris concluded in 1951 which came into force on July 25 1952, and the European Atomic Energy Community (Euratom), formed by the Treaty of Rome concluded in 1957 which came into force on January 1 1958. Also created in 1958 by a second Treaty of Rome 1957 was the European Economic Community (EEC), the 'everything else' Community, which has acquired a hegemonic position within the political and legal framework of the Community. Confusingly, Article G of the Treaty on European Union redesignates the European Economic Community as the 'European Community', leaving the other two sectoral Communities with their existing titles. The Articles of what must now be termed the 'EC Treaty' are referred to in this book as Article 1 EC, etc. Articles of the 'old' EEC Treaty are designated Article 2 EEC, etc. Most of the discussion in this book will be concerned with the provisions of the Treaties establishing and amending this 'general' Community and with legislation adopted under the enabling powers of those Treaties, in particular those governing the creation of the single market. Legally, the three Communities remain distinct, although they have common institutions, formed in 1967 by the Merger Treaty. However, the powers of the institutions differ slightly between the three Communities. The ECSC Treaty also differs from the two later Treaties in that it can be described as a *traité loi*, or 'treaty-law' which itself prescribes in detail the policies to be pursued by the Community, and leaves merely issues of policy implementation to the institutions. The EEC and Euratom Treaties were developed as *traités cadre*, or 'framework treaties', which contain only the outlines of policy objectives to which the institutions must give concrete form with legislative instruments.

The EEC Treaty was significantly amended in 1986 by the Single European Act, which established the so-called '1992' deadline, and sought to give the institutions the powers they needed to achieve the goal of completing the internal market by December 31 1992. The Single European Act also introduced a form of institutionalised intergovernmental cooperation between the Member States regarding foreign policy, termed 'European Political Cooperation'.

The effect of the Treaty of Maastricht, or 'Treaty on European Union', is to link the three Communities even closer together within the common structure of a European Union, a new entity built around the framework offered by the existing Communities. The Union does not as such have legal personality, and so is not a legal body in the same way as the Communities. The freestanding provisions of the Treaty of European Union are designated in this book Article A TEU etc. It is served by a single institutional framework, which is that of the Communities themselves. The Treaty of Maastricht also introduces a 'three pillar' structure, of which the existing corpus of law based around the Communities is the central pillar. The side pillars are (1) Common Foreign and Security Policy (which has evolved out of European Political Cooperation, and (2) cooperation in the fields of Justice and Home Affairs (see Fig 1.1). The Treaty of Maastricht was finalised in December 1991 following two intergovernmental conferences lasting one year on the subjects of economic and monetary union and political union, and was signed in February 1992. It was due to come into force on January 1 1993, but difficulties in the ratification process involving an initial rejection in a referendum in Denmark, ratification by only a small majority in a referendum in France and considerable opposition in the UK parliament delayed the coming into force of the Treaty. However, all Member States throughout retained a political and legal commitment to ratify. This book proceeds on the assumption that the Member States would complete the ratification process for the Treaty of Maastricht in the course of 1993, although the position at the time of writing was still unclear. Changes to the EC Treaties contained in that Treaty are clearly highlighted in the text, enabling easy cross-referencing with the unamended version of the Treaties. A failure to ratify the Treaty would mean, for example, that the objectives of the Community would continue to be those contained in the EEC Treaty, as amended by the Single European Act (see 1.3).

As a body based on international agreements between sovereign states, the European Community is in many senses a creature of international

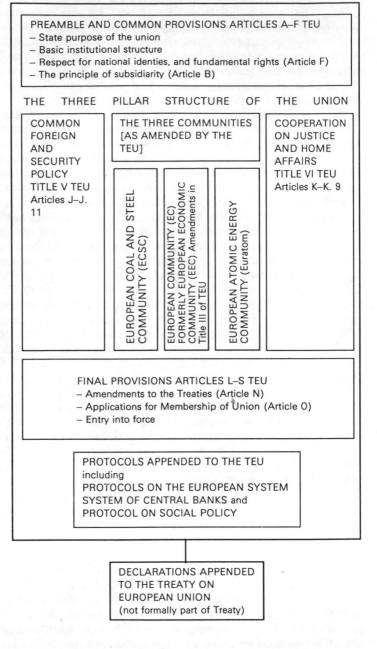

Figure 1.1 The Constitutional Structure of European Union

law; however the Member States have endowed its institutions with uniquely far-reaching powers for the achievement of the objectives contained in the Treaties.

The Community has a distinctive institutional structure. The main legislative role has so far been fulfilled by the Council of Ministers which is composed of representatives of the Member States at ministerial level. The Member States are also represented in the European Council, a summit conference of Heads of State and Government who meet twice yearly to give overall policy direction to the Community. The European Parliament, while it is now directly elected by universal franchise and is therefore representative of the people, has few powers in the legislative field, and its role is mainly confined to the consultative. Under the Treaty of Maastricht it becomes a co-legislator in some fields of Community competence. The Commission's role within the Community is sometimes exaggerated by Member States hostile to extensions of the Community's competence; in fact, the Commission's role is limited to initiating policy, implementing measures adopted by the Council and ensuring that Member States fulfil their obligations under the Treaties. It is in a sense the Community's civil service, but in many respects it is dependent upon national administrations for the actual day to day implementation of Community policies.

The fourth institution is the Court of Justice which has the task under Article 164 EC of ensuring that the law is observed. It has been assisted since 1989 by a Court of First Instance, creation of which was provided for in the Single European Act. The Court has been responsible for developing the Community's legal system in ways that were doubtless not imagined by the founders of the Treaty. Much of Parts II and III of this book will be concerned with explaining in detail those features which distinguish the European Community from an 'ordinary' international organisation, and which make the Community's legal system more akin to that of a federal state. This point will be sketched out initially in the overview of Community law contained in 1.5. The Court has also been active in ensuring that within the Community itself the rule of law is applied. Part IV examines the system of judicial control of the legality of legislative and administrative acts within the Community. This is one area in which the Community can rightly claim to have successfully emulated the characteristics of the highly evolved legal systems of its Member States.

The institutions and structures of the European Community and the European Union are not to be confused with those of the Council of Europe, an intergovernmental body fostering cooperation between European states, and in particular with its must significant Treaty-based emanation, the European Convention on Human Rights and Funda-mental Freedoms. The institutions operating under the Convention, to which all the Member States are signatories, are the Commission and Court of Human Rights, and these are based in Strasbourg. The Court of Justice of the European Communities is based in Luxembourg.

1.3   The Mission of the European Community

It is customary to find broad statements of the aims of the European Community and the more recently created European Union in the Preambles and introductory sections of the basic Treaties. Article A TEU recalls the long standing commitment in the Preamble to the EEC Treaty to the creation of an ever closer union among the peoples of Europe, and identifies the creation of the Union as a new stage in this process. A reference to the federal mission of the Union was eradicated from the final version at the insistence of the UK delegation. The Union has the following objectives (Article B TEU):

'–   to promote economic and social progress which is balanced and sustainable, in particular through the creation of an area without internal frontiers, through the strengthening of economic and social cohesion and through the establishment of economic and monetary union, ultimately including a single currency in accordance with the provisions of this Treaty;
–   to assert its identity on the international scene, in particular through the implementation of a common foreign and security policy including the eventual framing of a common defence policy, which might in time lead to a common defence;
–   to strengthen the protection of the rights and interests of the nationals of its Member States through the introduction of a citizenship of the Union;
–   to develop close cooperation on justice and home affairs;
–   to maintain in full the *acquis communautaire* and build on it with a view to considering, through the procedure referred to in Article N(2), to what extent the policies and forms of cooperation introduced by this Treaty may need to be revised with the aim of ensuring the effectiveness of the mechanisms and the institutions of the Treaty.'

The specifically economic aspects of these aims, with which we will be primarily concerned in this book, are elaborated in Articles 2, 3, 3A and 3B EC, as amended. These identify the task of the Community as being the promotion of harmonious and balanced economic development, of sustainable and non-inflationary growth respecting the environment, of a high degree of convergence of economic performance, of high levels of employment and social protection, of the raising of the standard of living and quality of life of citizens, and of economic and social cohesion and solidarity among Member States. The twin means for attaining this task are the creation of a common market and an economic and monetary union, and these are themselves to be achieved through the pursuit of the activities set out in Articles 3 (common market and common policies) and 3A (monetary union and single currency). So far, the law of the European Community has been, above all, the law of the common market which has been developing steadily since 1958. For present purposes, we can take the common market referred to in Article 2 as practically identical to the 'internal market' defined in Article 7A EC, the achievement of which has been the official central objective of the European Community since 1986. This provides that:

> 'The internal market shall comprise an area without internal frontiers in which the free movement of goods, persons, services and capital is ensured in accordance with the provisions of this Treaty.'

[Note: It should be noted that the Treaty of Maastricht renumbered Articles 8, 8A and 8B EEC as Articles 7, 7A and 7B EC. Consequently, earlier literature should be read with this in mind.]

The goal is therefore a free market ideal that, as far as possible, the territory of the twelve Member States should resemble a single national market, where there is a level competitive playing field for all economic actors and where distortions of competition based on artificial legal barriers such as differences in consumer protection or environmental regulation will be eliminated.

Article 3 EC in turn gives more details on the activities of the Community which are to be pursued with a view to attaining this goal. These include the creation of a customs union, involving the abolition of internal customs duties on trade in goods and the erection of a common external tariff and a complementary common policy on external trade, the abolition of other obstacles to trade in goods, and the free movement of services, persons and capital between the Member States. These are essentially negative measures, in that they promote integration by removing existing barriers. Positive integration measures include the the the establishment of common policies, in fields such as agriculture and transport; the creation of these policies also reveals a certain *dirigiste* element in the thinking of the founders of the Treaty, alongside the commitment to the free market principles of the four freedoms. The commitment to a policy on the harmonisation of national legislation also demonstrates a recognition that deregulated markets alone will not bring about the creation of a single market which respects the interests of consumers and the environment, to name but two interests which may be sacrificed in unfettered free market competition. In addition, although subsequent amendments to the original Treaty have brought regional policy goals of social and economic cohesion and solidarity within the remit of the Community's prescribed activities, there is no clear commitment in Article 3 to a general social policy, as a complement to the economic policies described above. Parts V and VI of this book will examine some of the policies pursued by the European Community, and assess the level of success it has so far enjoyed.

The greatest substantive contribution of the Treaty of Maastricht to the attainment of European integration lies in its provisions on economic and monetary union, and its introduction of the aim of creating a single currency. The law on these aspects of the Community's activities is not as well developed as the law of the common or single market, and it will not be given close attention in this book.

1.4 Key Terms

It will already be apparent from the preceding paragraphs that there is a distinctive language of European integration. This section aims to demystify certain key concepts, some of which have already been mentioned in passing such as **integration** and **federalism**.

The terms **federation** or **federal union** are commonly used to describe a sovereign state where power is divided between a central authority and a number of regional authorities. The basis for the division of power is generally to be found in a Constitution. Federal states are well known in the modern world: they include the United States, Canada and the Federal Republic of Germany. Sometimes federal states break up; this has happened recently in case of the Soviet Union and Yugoslavia. Within the European Community, **federalism** is propounded as one of a number of different methods for achieving the goal of an integrated Europe. Commonly **federalists** are seen as the 'radicals' advocating the rapid transition to a sovereign United States of Europe, with the relinquishing of sovereignty on the part of the Member States. A single central body would swiftly assume responsibility for the core activities typically pursued by a federal authority: foreign policy, defence and security, external trade and representation in international organisations, management of the currency, macro-economic policy, and matters concerned with citizenship. Such a federal authority would incorporate the key features of the modern democratic state, including in particular a legislature elected on the basis of universal suffrage. A judicial authority would mediate conflicts within the federal authority and between the federal authority and the constituent states on the scope of their respective spheres of power, basing its resolution of disputes on a constitutional document.

A more pragmatic position is taken by the so-called **neo-functionalists** who advocate a more incremental and piecemeal approach to European integration. **Neo-functionalism** underlay the decision of the founding fathers of the Community such as **Jean Monnet** and **Robert Schuman** to abandon grand federalist projects and to promote instead the adoption of the ECSC Treaty which concentrated simply on putting two strategically important commodities – coal and steel – into the hands of a central authority outside national control. Subsequently they supported the EEC Treaty which, in particular in its original form, had a remit limited to economic integration. The Treaty also gave a powerful role in the determination of policy to the representatives of the Member States in the Council of Ministers. The idea behind neo-functionalism is that sovereign states may be persuaded in the interests of economic welfare to relinquish control over certain areas of policy where it can easily be proven that benefits are likely to flow from a common approach to problem solving. Power is transferred to a central authority which exists at a level above the nation state, and which exercises its powers independently of the Member States – a **supranational** body. However, that transfer of powers is viewed as just part of a continuing process. One level of integration will lead on to the next; a sectoral Treaty dealing with coal and steel leads on to a general Treaty covering all economic sectors; a **customs union** incorporating the removal of internal customs tariffs and the erection of a uniform external tariff leads on to a **common** or **single market**, with comprehensive free movement for all commodities and factors of production. This in turn creates demands for some mechanism to eradicate the costs and obstacles to trade which result from shifts in the value of money between the different regions of the single market, involving either irrevocably fixed exchange rates, or even a single currency managed by a single central bank (a **monetary union**). Without serious damage to the weaker economies of the union, however, this cannot be effected without a convergence of economic policies, achieved either voluntarily, or through the transfer of macro-economic powers to a central authority (an **economic union**), and without incorporating elements of a **regional policy** to ensure an equitable geographical distribution of resources (**economic and social cohesion**).

This process is termed 'spill-over' by neo-functionalists, and during its evolution, the European Community has passed through a number of the stages described above, involving progressive transfers of power from the Member States to the Community. Spill-over has also operated in the extension of the powers of the Community out of the purely 'economic' field into other related areas such as environmental and social policy. It has also fuelled the debate about **political union** in the Community. Two aspects of this concept can be identified, one substantive and the other procedural. According to the substantive notion of political union, the Community should exercise political powers which are commensurate with its economic powers. For example, external trade competence should be linked to the introduction of foreign policy cooperation. In its procedural meaning, political union demands that the methods by which the transferred economic competence is exercised do not lead to a net decrease in democratic and popular participation in and control of decision-making processes. In the Community, this is associated with calls for the Parliament to be given greater powers.

If the functionalist logic is followed to its conclusion the supranational authority will, at a certain point, merge into a federal authority as more and more powers are transferred, and as the mechanisms for exercising these powers become increasingly separated from the nation state level. In this scenario the sovereign powers of the nation state are shared between the centre and its component parts, and power is exercised at the federal level not by the Member States, but by the autonomous organs of the federation. This means, in practice, if the traditions of Western liberal democracy are to be maintained, by a democratically elected legislature and a government which derives its legitimacy from the electoral process.

Within the Community, the European Parliament is in fact now a democratically elected body, but its legislative powers are minimal. Power in truth is exercised by the representatives of the governments of the Member States, meeting as the Council of Ministers. Pressure to alter this situation in order to remedy a **democratic deficit** within the Community is understandable and logical from a functionalist perspective.

To summarise, the essence of supranationalism is found in a gradual transfer of competences to the higher level, and in the evolution of a distinctive form of decision-making at the higher level where increasingly decisions are taken on a majoritarian basis, rather than by consensus. This form of supranationalism has been termed 'decisional supranationalism' by Weiler (1981), and has generally been an area in which the Community has been quite weak, at least until the changes in the decision-making process introduced by the Single European Act and more recently the Treaty of Maastricht. It can be distinguished from a specifically legal facet to the supranational nature of the Community, which Weiler has termed 'normative supranationalism'. This concerns the authority of the Court of Justice to give binding and authoritative rulings on the nature and effects of Community law, and to fashion a legal system in which Community law takes precedence over national law. In that respect, the Community has evolved more rapidly, and it is argued by some that the work of the Court of Justice has upset the delicate balance between the supranational and **intergovernmental** elements of the Treaties.

By **intergovernmentalism** is meant the argument that the Community should restrict itself to the types of activities more commonly undertaken by international organisations founded on Treaties, which are characterised by cooperation between states rather than by the independent action of an autonomous body. There have been conflicts throughout the history of the Community between the proponents of these two basic positions on how the Community should evolve. The policies of Margaret Thatcher and Charles de Gaulle towards the European Community fall into the category of intergovernmentalism, although they were each propounding rather different forms of **nationalism**. The battle lines are drawn over the concept of **national sovereignty**, with intergovernmentalists arguing in favour of a Community of states, or at most a **confederal union of states**, in which state sovereignty is preserved, not a 'union of peoples' as the Preamble to the EEC Treaty puts it. Intergovernmentalists will obviously oppose any extension of the supranational powers of the Community, involving either an increased range of Community competence (e.g. social policy) or an enhanced supranational element in the decision-making process through the strengthening of the powers of the Parliament and the extension of majority voting in the Council of Ministers.

Conflict is now centring upon the concept of **subsidiarity**, introduced into the EEC Treaty by the Treaty of Maastricht in order to provide a guideline for the vertical division of powers between the Community and the Member States. Article 3B EC provides:

'The Community shall act within the limits of the powers conferred upon it by this Treaty and of the objectives assigned to it therein.

In areas which do not fall within its exclusive competence, the Community shall take action, in accordance with the principle of subsidiarity, only if and in so far as the objectives of the proposed action cannot be sufficiently achieved by the Member States and can therefore, by reason of the scale or effects of the proposed action, be better achieved by the Community.

Any action by the Community shall not go beyond what is necessary to achieve the objectives of this Treaty.'

Different visions of this provision inform the various perspectives which are presently taken on the Community's emerging federalism or confederalism. One view of this provision is that it reasserts national sovereignty in a different guise. Some Member States may seek always to block Community action by arguing that it is unnecessary unless it can be positively proven that national action is insufficient. The other view sees subsidiarity as part of a general impetus towards the decentralisation of decision-making, so that decisions will always be taken as close as possible to the individual, and, where possible, not by remote governmental entities. This view finds support in Article A TEU, quoted in 1.3, which refers to the Union being one in which 'decisions are taken as closely as possible to the citizen'. This protects, for example, the sphere of powers held by regional authorities in those Member States which have federalist or regionalist systems, such as Germany and Belgium.

1.5 An Overview of the Community Legal System

An overview of any legal system should start with its basic structure, generally to be found in a constitution and associated documents. This is all the more important in the case of a federal-type legal system, where the constitution contains important rules governing the balance between central or federal and regional or state authorities in the law-making sphere, and on the relationship between federal and state law. The European Community is not, of course, explicitly termed a federation, although its legal system now displays certain of the characteristics of a federal system. Nor does it have a constitution as such, but the Court of Justice now describes the founding treaties as the Community's 'constitutional charter' (Case 294/83 *Parti Ecologiste 'Les Verts' v European Parliament* [1986] ECR 1339 at p. 1365).

However, much of the 'constitutional law' of the European Community is contained not in the Treaties themselves, but in the judicial pronouncements of the Court of Justice which plays a pivotal role in the legal system, and which has a commitment to the pursuit of integration through law. It has consistently given a maximalist interpretation of the authority and effect of Community law, of the regulatory competence of the institutions and of its power to control both the institutions and the Member States to ensure that 'the law is observed' (Article 164 EC). Inevitably, therefore, the study of Community law concentrates on the work of the Court, but that study should be tempered by an awareness that a picture of Community law in which the Court is placed at centre stage tends to give the impression that the Community's system is more advanced than in fact it is.

There is little clear indication in the Treaties as to the exact relationship between Community law and national law and of the effect of Community law within the domestic legal systems of the Member States. Article 5 EC provides:

'Member States shall take all appropriate measures, whether general or particular, to ensure fulfilment of the obligations arising out of this Treaty or resulting from action taken by the institutions of the Community. They shall facilitate the achievement of the Community's tasks.

They shall abstain from any measure which could jeopardize the attainment of the objectives of this Treaty.'

This provision has been described by AG Tesauro in Case C-213/89 *R* v. *Secretary of State for Transport, ex parte Factortame Ltd* ([1990] ECR I-2433 at p. 2454) as the key to the whole system of remedies which exists for the enforcement of Community law. In terms of specific enforcement procedures, Articles 169 and 170 EC make it possible for the Commission and other Member States to bring infringing Member States before the Court of Justice, and Article 171 EC gives the Court the power to make a declaration stating that there has been an infringement and requiring the Member State to take measures to put an end to the infringement. Financial penalties for non-compliance have been introduced by the Treaty of Maastrict. These measures allow for the 'direct enforcement' of Community law. They give no hint, however, that the obligations undertaken by the Member States under the Treaties they have signed are relevant at any level other than that of international law, which is primarily a law between states with minimal applicability to individuals. Individuals do not have recourse to the provisions in Articles 169 and 170 either to enforce Community law directly against the Member States themselves, or to force the Commission or another Member State to do this on their behalf. In fact, in an exercise of remarkable judicial creativity (Mancini, 1989), the Court of Justice has consistently distanced the Community legal system from 'ordinary' international law, arguing that by accession to the Community the Member States have transferred sovereign rights to the Community, creating an autonomous legal system in which the subjects are not just states, but also individuals. The Court has given effect to this view by enunciating four key principles:

—   Community law penetrates into the national legal systems, and can and must be applied by the national courts, subject to authoritative rulings on the interpretation, effect and validity of Community law by the Court of Justice; in other words, the duty of Community loyalty provided for in Article 5 applies to courts as well as to other organs of the Member States such as the government and the legislature;

– in this context individuals may rely upon rules of Community law in national courts, as giving rise to rights which national courts are bound to protect (the principle of 'direct effect');

– in order to guarantee the effectiveness of this structure, Community law takes precedence over conflicting national law, including national constitutional provisions (the principle of 'supremacy' or 'primacy').

– the organs and constituent bodies of the Member States, including the legislative, executive and judiciary, are fully responsible for reversing the effects of violations of EC law which affect individuals. This may, for example, involve the courts ordering the government to pay damages for loss caused by breach of Community law.

The Court has given an extensive task to the national courts which are responsible for ensuring what is often termed the 'indirect enforcement' of Community law at the instance of individuals. It has stressed the binding nature of Community law, including not only the Treaties themselves, but also those acts of the institutions (Regulations, Directives and Decisions), to which binding effects are ascribed in Article 189 EC. These can where appropriate be enforced by individuals in national courts, if their provisions are justiciable (i.e. sufficiently precise and clear). It has also stressed that the Community itself is bound by norms of international law, in particular where they are contained in Treaties which the Community itself has concluded with third countries or international organisations as an international actor exercising legal personality, or where the Community has succeeded to the international Treaty obligations of the Member States. Finally, it has articulated a body of superordinate principles, 'general principles of law', which govern the activities of the Community and of the Member States acting within the sphere of Community competence, and which include not only fundamental rights, but also procedural principles such as proportionality and legal certainty. These are not as such to be found in the Treaties but are in fact further products of the remarkable judicial creativity of the Court which has developed a body of individual rights and principles of administrative legality which ensure the application of the rule of law within the Community legal system. The Treaties, the acts of the institutions, binding norms of international law and the general principles of law together constitute the body of sources of Community law.

The key to the structure of indirect enforcement lies in the organic connection between the Court of Justice and the national courts in Article 177 EC. This provides that national courts may, and in certain circumstances must, refer to the Court of Justice questions on the interpretation and validity of provisions of Community law where such questions are raised in the context of national litigation and the national court considers a reference necessary in order to enable it to give judgment. National courts must refer questions of doubt regarding the application of Community law to the Court in two situations: first, where the national court is one of last resort; second, where it is the validity of a rule of Community law which is in doubt. Only the Court of Justice has the power to invalidate a rule of Community law. The preliminary ruling procedure has limits, and it depends for its effectiveness on cooperation between national courts and the Court of Justice. It is not an appeal by the parties to the Court of Justice. The power to ask for a ruling lies solely with the national court, and the legislative and political authorities of the Member States may not interfere with the exercise of discretion. Correlatively, the Court of Justice does not have the power in the context of a preliminary ruling hearing to invalidate a provision of national law. It cannot even formally make a declaration of incompatibility with Community law, as it can in the context of Articles 169–171. It is limited to an interpretation of *Community* law. However, the manner in which the Court of Justice has often chosen to frame its rulings has given little choice to the referring court but to apply Community law in preference to national law, and in effect to invalidate provisions of national law. This duty flows from Article 5 for the national court, and it is a duty which gives rise to some difficulty in the context of the UK where the principle of parliamentary sovereignty leads judges conventionally to regard themselves as subordinate to the will of Parliament. The European Communities Act 1972 attempts, if only imperfectly, to resolve the difficulties raised by membership of the Community in conventional constitutional doctrine. In summary, therefore, the Court has constructed a system which comes close to the power conventionally held by the supreme court in a federal system, namely the power to invalidate state legislation which contravenes the federal constitution. Examples of the interaction of the various enforcement mechanisms, such as the litigation regarding the Merchant Shipping Act 1988 in the UK (*ex parte Factortame*) will be discussed in Parts II and III.

In addition to controlling the exercise of sovereign power by the Member States, the Court also acts as the judge of the proper exercise of sovereign power by the Community, and as an umpire in disputes regarding legislative authority between the institutions and between the Community's political organs and the Member States. This form of control likewise operates both directly in the Court and indirectly in litigation before the national courts. It will be seen from the above that individuals are not restricted in the national courts simply to asserting their Community law rights against the Member States. An individual may in addition question the validity of an act of a Community institution in the context of national litigation, and a national court which is minded to accept that allegation must refer a question to the Court for a ruling on validity. There are broadly two reasons why an individual might seek to challenge a rule of Community law. First, it may be unlawful because of its effects upon the complainant as an individual or part of group (e.g. a particular class of economic actors such as the producers of a particular commodity). In this context, the Court of Justice frequently makes reference to the fundamental rights of the affected group when ascertaining the legality of a Community act. Second, the complainant may argue that the act is in breach of some more general rule of legality or constitutionality: e.g. the manner in which the act was adopted was in breach of the Treaty rules, it may fall outside the competence of the institution which adopted it, or it may fall outside the competence of the Community altogether.

It is also possible to mount such a challenge directly in the Court of Justice itself, although there are strict restrictions on the standing of individuals under the provisions of Articles 173 and 175 EC which provide for the judicial review of unlawful acts and the unlawful failure to act on the part of the institutions. Member States, the Commission, the Council and, within limits, the European Parliament may also use Article 173 in order to seek the annulment of Community acts. Through its decisions on such actions the Court of Justice has been concerned to construct a body of principles which delineate the powers of the institutions *inter se*, and of the Member States and the Community respectively. This is another area in which the Treaty, aside from setting out procedural rules which govern the legislative process and outlining minimum prerequisites of validity for Community acts such as a statement of reasons, does not provide much assistance to the Court. The tendency of the Court has been to interpret the powers of the Community broadly: the institutions are given certain tasks by the Treaties, and the Court has consistently held that they must be regarded as having either express or implied powers to carry out these tasks. Thus there is no explicit reserved area of sovereign powers for the Member States. The advent of the principle of subsidiarity as a new criterion defining the relationship between the Community and the Member States, which may be justiciable before the Court, introduces a new range of challenges for the Court of Justice.

1.6   Legal Literature

The successful study of Community law requires regular consultation of the Community's founding Treaties, its secondary legislation and other official documentation, and the case law of the Court of Justice. There are a number of English language sources for all these materials. In addition to the publications by the Office of Official Publications of the European Communities, which are available through HMSO, the Treaties are available in (portable) private collections such as Blackstone's *EEC Legislation* and Rudden and Wyatt, *Basic Community Laws*. These collections also contain much of the basic secondary legislation, and where they do not, the texts are available in less portable form either in the Community's *Official Journal*, Sweet & Maxwell's *Encyclopedia of European Community Law* or (annotated) in vol. 42A of *Halsbury's*

Statutes of England (3rd edn). The latter publications also contain copies of the Treaties. The Treaty of Maastricht is available most readily in the 3rd edn (1992) of *Blackstone's EEC Legislation*.

Every student hesitates before first confronting the mass of materials contained in the European Documentation Centre ('EDC') located, if the student is fortunate, in or near the Law Library which he or she regularly uses. First in line for consultation must be the *Official Journal of the European Communities* which contains in its 'L' series the legislative acts adopted by the institutions. The 'C' series contains preparatory documents, non-binding acts such as resolutions and recommendations, reports of the activities of the European Parliament and the Economic and Social Committee and long lists of agricultural prices. Students should also get to grips with 'Com Docs', the documents issued by the Commission. Important documents such as the White Paper on removing barriers to interstate trade which forms the basis of the 1992 legislative programme are often issued as Com Docs (Com (85) 310). Also frequently to be found in the EDC is *European Access*, a bibliographical journal which is a useful research tool for preparing projects in the Community law field.

Finally, check whether the *European Court Reports* (*ECR*), which are the official Law Reports of the European Court of Justice are held in the EDC, or with the other Law Reports. With these reports may also be typescript versions of recent Court of Justice cases, but often only in French (the working language of the Court is French). Alternatively, there may be a summary publication available in either French or English entitled the *Proceedings of the European Court of Justice*. The publication delay attributable to translation difficulties which constantly undermines the prompt production of the *European Court Reports* makes consultation of English language versions of recent cases occasionally difficult. Cross-checking with Law Reports in *The Times*, The *Independent*, the *Common Market Law Reports* (*CMLR*), and, where appropriate specialist Law Reports such as the *Industrial Relations Law Reports* (*LRLR*), sometimes uncovers an unofficial English language version.

Extracts from important cases are, of course, to be found in casebooks, a number of which have appeared in the field of Community Law. The most useful and up-to-date is Weatherill (1992a) which contains also a wide-ranging and stimulating selection of secondary literature, much of which is drawn from non-legal sources.

Each chapter of this book will contain lists of further reading to which you should refer. There is also a general bibliography containing additional works. One of the main objectives of the book is to make the specialised literature more accessible. Much of the further reading will be found in the core journals in the field: the *European Law Review* (*ELRev*), the *Common Market Law Review* (*CMLRev*), the *Yearbook of European Law* (*YEL*) and *Legal Issues of European Integration* (*LIEI*). Of the general English journals, the *Modern Law Review* probably publishes the most material on Community law. Any student pursuing a research project in Community law should consult these journals and the more detailed textbooks available such as that by Kapteyn and VerLoren van Themaat (1989). Reference may also be made to the many books published in the field which provide more specialist coverage of particular aspects of Community law (Hartley, 1988; Louis, 1990; Lasok and Bridge, 1991; Brown, 1989; Collins, 1990; Green, Hartley and Usher, 1991; Ellis, 1991; Arnull, 1990a), or which provide specific insights such as the views of the European Court judiciary (MacKenzie Stuart, 1977; Slynn, 1992).

More sceptical views of the progress towards European integration are provided by Reich and Leahy (1990), who argue from a consumerist point of view, and Snyder (1990) who argues in particular from the perspective of international political economy. Those seeking EC/US comparisons of integration in a federal context can look to the massive *Integration Through Law* series published by Walter de Gruyter (Cappelletti *et al.*, 1986). This series, like a more recent series on human rights in the European Community published by Nomos (Clapham, 1991; Cassese *et al.*, 1991a, 1991b), represents the fruits of a research project based at the European University Institute, in Florence. Many of these works benefit from 'contextual' or 'critical' analyses of Community law, which incorporate into the discussion the insights of political and economic analyses of the European Community. Snyder, in particular, argues for the necessity of context in the study of Community law. The final section of this chapter introduces some of the contributions in the fields of economics, political theory and policy studies which might assist you in making the most of the study of Community law.

1.7   Making the Most of Studying Community Law

Two specialised journals – the *Journal of Common Market Studies* (*JCMS*) and the *Journal of European Integration* (*JEI*) carry much of the analyses of the politics and economics of the Community. In addition, students should consult general politics and economics journals, using a bibliographical reference tool or periodical index. There are also a great number of books which provide up-to-date perspectives on the politics and economics of the European Community. A thorough historical survey is to be found in Urwin (1991), but many general books begin with a historical survey of the emergence of the Community in the post-war transformation of Europe and of its evolution from the ECSC Treaty to the Treaty of Union, offering a discussion of some of the different theories which have been used to explain the integration process (see George, 1991; Pinder, 1991) before diverging to concentrate on different themes. Some provide a greater emphasis upon institutional aspects (Keohane and Hoffmann, 1991; Nugent, 1991); others concentrate more on the substantive policies (El-Agraa, 1990; Lintner and Mazey, 1991). The latter two works contain an explanation of customs union theory which is essential for understanding debates about the pros and cons of the Single

Market Project. A favourable analysis of this project can be found in Cecchini (1988), which includes the results of Commission sponsored research and Wistrich (1991) who offers a federalist perspective on European integration. More sceptical views can be found in Grahl and Teague (1990), Cutler *et al.* (1989) and Bieber *et al.* (1988). General analyses of current policies are also contained in Lodge (1989), Swann (1992) and Wallace (1990), and, as part of the resurgence of work in the USA on the European Community, in Sbragia (1992) and Hurwitz and Lesquesne (1991).

Summary

This chapter introduces the study of Community law by providing the basic facts and introducing the key tools of analysis which students require. The mission of the Community is to promote integration in Europe, and both the legal and political systems of the Community should be understood in the context of this mission. The legal system of the Community is *sui generis* and has evolved in the hands of the Court of Justice into a supranational and quasi-federal system where Community consistently 'trumps' national law.

Questions

1 What is the 'European Community'? Why is this term misleading?
2 Using the Preamble and introductory sections of the Treaties of Paris and Rome, as well as the SEA and the Treaty of Maastricht, identify whether and how the basic aims of the Community have evolved since the beginning. What additional methods for promoting integration have been given to the Community? To what extent is the integration function now taken over by the European Union? (The objective of this question is to involve you in a search for the relevant documentation in the available literature and in the EDC and the Library.)
3 What are the key features of the Community legal order?

Further Reading

Full publication details for works such as Snyder (1990) will be found in the Bibliography.

Koopmans (1991a) 'European Public Law: Reality and Prospects', Publication 53.
Koopmans (1991b) 'The Birth of European Law At the Crossroads of Legal Tradition', 39 *American Journal of Comparative Law*. 493.
Mancini (1989) 'The Making of a Constitution for Europe', 26 *Common Market Law Review*, 595; also published as Ch. 6 in Keohane and Hoffmann (1991).
Slynn (1992), Ch. 1, 'Establishing a Court'.
Snyder (1990), Ch. 1, 'New Directions'.
Temple Lang (1991) 'The Development of European Community Constitutional Law', 25 *International Lawyer*, 455.

2 The Evolving Community

2.1 Introduction

This chapter uses the title 'the evolving Community' rather than the more customary phrase 'the evolution of the Community' in order to emphasise the dynamic and changing nature of the Community, and to highlight the fact that it has not yet reached a final stage of evolution. A basic knowledge of the history of the Community offers a number of benefits to the student:

- it gives a context to contemporary events, demonstrating that the current debates on the integration process have a long pedigree, and that ideas such as monetary union are not simply novelties dreamt up by Jacques Delors in the late 1980s;
- it puts the Community firmly in the context of other developments within and outside Europe, recognising the significance for the European Community of events such as the end of the Cold War and the unification of Germany;
- it highlights the ebbs and flows of the Community, which have coincided quite closely with the low and high points of the European economy since the Second World War;
- finally, the stop–start progress of political and economic integration emphasises the unparalleled contribution made by the Court at crucial points. Yet although the Court has been characterised as the 'engine of integration', when the events discussed in this chapter are reviewed subsequently in the context of developments in the Community's legal system which form the main focus of this book, it will be seen that the work of the Court of Justice has not always run parallel to the political and economic evolution of the Treaty. In particular, there often appears to be a lag of some years between the point when work begins towards a new goal in the sphere of politics and correspondingly significant progress in the construction of the Community's legal framework.

2.2 The Roots of European Integration

Although it would be wrong to characterise current developments in European integration as the direct descendants of earlier ideas and proposals, it is nonetheless of interest that the idea of a unified Europe is by no means new. The model of a Europe brought together not by military conquest, but in common pursuit of higher goals of peace, prosperity and stability has attracted the attention of thinkers since the Middle Ages. An institutional form of federal unity in Europe was argued for by prominent intellectuals of the Enlightenment such as Bentham, Rousseau, and, later, Saint-Simon. More concrete progress was made in the field of economic integration. The early period of capitalist organisation saw not only the transformation of the means of production and the shift to industrialisation, but also the integration of national markets, often achieved in parallel with national political unity. The next step was the liberalisation of trade between sovereign states, where Britain took a leading role with its commitment to free trade in the middle of the nineteenth century. However, none of the proposals for increased cooperation between states in the economic field such as a Central European customs union between the Hapsburg empire and the German states in the 1840s achieved real success, and there was a resurgence of nationalism and protectionism in the late nineteenth century which eventually culminated in the First World War.

The inter-war years saw continued discussion of the ideal of European integration as a better way forward for Europe than destructive interstate rivalry, most notably within the forum of the Pan-European Union founded in 1923 by the Austrian Count Richard Coudenhove-Kalergi. It is perhaps significant that amongst the pre-war membership of the Union were a number of politicians who played key roles in post-war Europe, including Konrad Adenauer, later Chancellor of the Federal Republic of Germany, and Georges Pompidou, later President of France. However, the influence of the Union did not succeed in saving the only initiative towards European integration of the inter-war years put forward at the governmental level, the Briand Plan of 1929–30, a proposal by the French Foreign Minister for a confederal bond linking the peoples of Europe. The logic behind French foreign policy and the Briand Plan was that of achieving security for France against Germany by tying the latter firmly into a European structure of cooperation. The theme of the 'Europeanisation' of Germany has been an enduring one which has enjoyed a renaissance since unification in 1990. Despite the modest nature of the proposals, the Briand Plan was never taken further because of scepticism and hostility in Britain, Italy and Germany.

2.3   The Postwar Climate of Change

At the end of and just after the Second World War quite different attitudes to the prospects for European unity were apparent. Even before the end of the war, voices calling for a form of unity which prevented future wars could be heard in the Resistance movements of the occupied countries of continental Europe. Prominent figures in the Resistance movements such as Altiero Spinelli, who re-emerged much later as a champion of European federalism in the European Parliament in the late 1970s and early 1980s, argued for a federal Europe with a written constitution, state institutions such as a government and a Parliament, a judicial system and a common army. Resolutions supporting these propositions were passed at a conference of Resistance representatives held in Geneva in July 1944. It was believed at the time that support for European federalism would also come from Britain, in particular from Winston Churchill, who was popular in federalist circles following his dramatic offer to the French of the creation of a Franco–British union in 1940.

However, Churchill's loss of the British premiership with the victory of the Labour Party in the 1945 General Election, and the re-emergence of pre-war political leaders in many European countries at the expense of Resistance leaders, were two factors which contributed to the failure to translate the ideals of federalism into a concrete agenda for action. The immediate imperatives of national economic rebuilding took precedence over the proposal that postwar reconstruction should occur within an entirely new political framework. The danger was present, therefore, that as before the war the ideas of unity would not take root within the institutions of the state, and that rallying calls such as Churchill's famous speech in Zurich in 1946 and the resolutions of numerous federalist groups gathered at the Congress of Europe at The Hague in 1948 would remain simply extragovernmental expressions of a desirable, but unattainable goal of integration within Europe. However, this view discounts a number of features which distinguish the two situations. These included the increasing closeness of certain federalists such as Jean Monnet to centres of political power (Monnet had become head of the French Economic Planning Commission), the willingness of federal idealists to countenance incremental strategies for achieving integration (the ideas of functionalism outlined in Chapter 1) and a greater global commitment to free trade and economic cooperation, evidenced by the adoption of the General Agreement on Tariffs and Trade (GATT) and the creation of the International Monetary Fund. Last but not least there was the need of the USA for stability in Western Europe in the context of the Cold War which followed hard on the heels of the Second World War and its consequent interest in and partial sponsorship of ideas of Western European integration.

In 1947 the USA committed itself to the so-called 'Truman Doctrine' which was a pledge of US support for 'free peoples who are resisting subjugation by armed minorities or by outside pressures'. The Americans had an interest in preventing a destabilising power vacuum in Europe. One outcome of this doctrine was the Marshall Plan to provide economic aid for reconstruction to countries in Europe committed to ideas supported by the USA, aid which, because of the underlying political motivation of the provider, was shunned by the Soviet Union and its allies in central and eastern Europe. The allocation, administration and delivery of American aid became the initial preoccupation of the first international organisation in the economic sphere set up in postwar Europe – the Organisation for European Economic Cooperation (OEEC) set up in 1948. The OEEC was a strictly intergovernmental organisation which never succeeded in achieving any of its grander ideals of economic cooperation, but nonetheless it had a wide membership within Europe and North America (sixteen founder members) which grew much larger when it gave way in 1961 to the Organisation for Economic Cooperation and Development which encompasses other Western style economies such as Australia and Japan.

The broad attractions of a loose intergovernmental form of cooperation were also evident at an early stage in the political field where the grandly styled but rather ineffective Council of Europe was established in 1949. The proposals for the Council of Europe grew out of the resolutions of the Hague Congress. Although the nature of the Council of Europe has always been bland (Urwin, 1991: 39), and it has consistently avoided controversial issues such as defence and security, it benefits from its symbolic role within Europe, including its role as a forum for discussion, and from the particular association it has acquired with political democracy and human rights. The most significant international instrument to come into being under the aegis of the Council of Europe is the European Convention on Human Rights and Fundamental Freedoms which came into force in 1953. Membership of the Council and signature of the Convention, while not demanding in the sense of requiring the signatory to relinquish a significant portion of state autonomy of action, have come to be benchmarks of acceptability amongst Western-style liberal democracies, achieved by countries emerging from dictatorship such as Spain and Portugal in the 1970s and more recently by the new democracies of central and eastern Europe. As membership of the European Community has come to appear increasingly attractive to a range of European countries, the Council of Europe has become a convenient stepping stone in the process of achieving membership. However, at no time has the Council departed from the intergovernmental consensus-based approach to international cooperation.

Finally, in the military field, cooperation took a distinctly Atlanticist turn with the conclusion in April 1949 of the North Atlantic Treaty tying together the North American states with the European parties to the 1948 Treaty of Brussels – France, the UK and the Benelux countries. Germany was later brought into the Western European Union after the failure of the initiative for a European Defence Community in 1954. In 1955 Germany joined NATO.

2.4 From Grand Ideals to Incremental Stages

A separate chapter in the evolution of integration in Europe was opened in May 1950 with the publication of the Schuman Plan, drawn up, on behalf of the French Foreign Minister Robert Schuman, by Jean Monnet. This Plan was the precursor of the European Coal and Steel Community (ECSC). The text of the Plan neatly encapsulates the small and large visions of European integration which have marked the evolution of the

European Community. The plan itself was shaped around the proposal to place French and German coal and steel production under a common authority (a 'High Authority') outside national control and open to the participation of other European countries. However, although its immediate preoccupation was with supranational control of these two commodities alone, its wider agenda was evident. It declared this to be only the first step in the federation of Europe, and asserted that 'Europe must be organised on a federal basis'. However, 'Europe will not be made all at once or according to a single plan. It will be built through concrete achievements which first create a *de facto* solidarity'. The ECSC therefore represents a clear example of the functional approach to integration.

This French proposal, attractive to Germany because it marked the first step towards recovering sovereignty over the Saarland, still then belonging to France, while allowing the fledgling Federal Republic to regain a place in the international community, attracted also the participation of the Benelux countries and Italy. Although the UK participated briefly in the negotiations leading to the conclusion of the ECSC Treaty, the plan to transfer control away from national governments to an appointed body proved unacceptable. Only a much smaller number of countries proved ready to participate in truly supranational international cooperation than in the looser arrangements of the Council of Europe.

The ECSC Treaty was concluded in Paris in April 1951, and contained an institutional structure rather different to that envisaged by the Schuman Plan itself, in particular with less strong elements of supranationalism. The actions of the High Authority at the centre of the institutional structure of the ECSC were to be tempered by a Council of Ministers, composed of representatives of the Member States, to give a greater intergovernmentalist input into the Community and to act as a political counterweight to the High Authority. Its task was to give its opinion to the High Authority which was charged with the principal decision-making power. The triad of political institutions was completed by a Common Assembly composed in the early years of representatives chosen by the national parliaments, and endowed only with consultative powers and a minimal role in ensuring the accountability of the High Authority. Some aspects of the institutional and decision-making structures were strongly supranational: decisions were to be taken and then implemented by the High Authority independently and action did not require a consensus of the Contracting Parties; furthermore, decisions of the High Authority were binding upon the Contracting Parties. However, the potential for independent decision on the part of the High Authority was restricted by the nature of the ECSC Treaty as a *traité loi*. The four-pronged institutional pattern, which was later adopted as a model for the European Economic Community (EEC) in 1957, was completed by a Court of Justice, charged with ensuring observance of the law.

The ECSC Treaty created a common market for coal and scrap (Article 4). This comprises the abolition of internal customs duties and quantitative restrictions on imports and exports, measures and practices which discriminate between producers, purchaser or consumers, government aids and subsidies and restrictive practices tending towards the sharing or exploiting of markets. These essentially free market principles were fetters upon the possible *dirigiste* tendencies of the High Authority which might have resulted from the influence of its first President, Monnet, who was known to favour a strong element of central planning in the economy. Interestingly, unlike the later EEC Treaty, the ECSC Treaty does not provide for a complete customs union for coal and steel as it does not create a common external tariff for imports from third countries. In practice, the Member States have created a system of uniform external protection to avoid anomalies between coal and steel products and other products.

The ratification of the ECSC Treaty by the national parliaments and the entry into force of the Treaty did not inexorably lead towards closer integration. The success of the ECSC Treaty was followed closely by a serious failure – the Treaty establishing a European Defence Community (EDC) and the draft Statute for a European Political Community. This initiative was also based on a French proposal aimed at managing the re-emergence of Germany on the international stage. The Pleven Plan put forward by the French Minister of Defence proposed to apply the methods of the Schuman Plan to the field of defence, allowing German rearmament, then being vigorously urged by the USA, within the context of a European Army. The Treaty establishing the EDC was concluded by the Six in May 1952 (the UK participated in early negotiations but then withdrew from the plan, despite Winston Churchill's championship of the concept of a European army in 1950), but then encountered serious difficulties at the ratification stage. However, even before ratification, the Parliamentary Assembly envisaged for the EDC was meeting and drafting, as required by Article 38 EDC, proposals for institutional reform to guarantee the democratic character of the Community in the form of a draft Statute for a European Political Community. Both plans collapsed when the EDC Treaty did not achieve ratification by the French parliament in August 1954. Some semblance of purely European cooperation in the defence field was rescued at the initiative of the UK, with the creation in 1954 of the Western European Union bringing Germany into the security framework of the West. After years of obscurity, the Western European Union has enjoyed a strange renaissance since the mid-1980s offering a distinctive Western European voice in defence issues and as the potential basis for an expansion of European integration in the defence field.

Despite these setbacks further concrete progress towards European integration was made in the 1950s. This time the initiative for a *'relance européenne'* came from the Benelux countries, already tied together in tighter economic cooperation than the other members of the ECSC. The key to the new initiative was that economic integration should precede political integration, but that new instruments were needed to go beyond both the ineffectual OEEC and the sectorally-based ECSC. This broadening and deepening of the emphasis of economic integration is often said to be a classic example of the principles of 'spillover' outlined in 1.4. The proposal was for a general common market, and for specific measures in the emerging field of nuclear energy. Out of a discussion at Messina in June 1955 between the Foreign Ministers of the Six came the decision to convene a committee to elaborate one or more treaties to give effect to these proposals. The report of the committee, named after its Chairman Paul-Henri Spaak, a Belgian, was submitted and approved by the Foreign Ministers of the Six by May 1956.

The Spaak report called for the creation of a common market, which it defined as the result of the fusion of national markets to create a larger unit of production. This, it argued, would make for greater economic growth and an accelerated increase in the standard of living. The Report foresaw three main strands to the development of this common market: the achievement of a customs union and free movement of commodities and factors of production; the creation of a policy for the common market to ensure fair competition; and the adoption of measures to facilitate the transformation and modernisation of economies and enterprises, for example through investment aid and retraining of workers. What the Report did not propose were common educational or social policies, which were not regarded as necessary for the achievement of the common market. The institutional structure was based on that of the ECSC, with a Court, a Common Assembly, a Council of Ministers, and a central supranational authority, in this case termed the Commission. Once again the Commission was to be the pivotal political institution, but endowed with rather fewer powers than the High Authority under the ECSC Treaty. The Spaak Committee accepted that the many activities to be undertaken by the institutions for the achievement of these goals could not be regulated in detail in a Treaty, and that what was needed was not a *traité loi*, but a *traité cadre*, itself giving extensive law-making powers to the institutions, in particular to the Council of Minsters. This Treaty was elaborated on the basis of the Spaak Report and signed in Rome in March 1957, along with a Treaty establishing a European Atomic Energy Community (Euratom). The process of parliamentary ratification proceeded smoothly and the Treaties entered into force on January 1 1958.

The EEC represented a reversion to the vision of a Europe created by stages, with the common market as a stepping stone towards political union. As such, it is a remarkable triumph of common interest over diversity. The Six had very different motivations and goals in seeking the creation of the Community. France had long been pursuing a policy of preventing German domination of the continent of Europe. Germany saw supranational cooperation as the means to regain self-respect and standing in the international community. The Benelux countries sought to overcome the disadvantage of smallness in an increasingly global economy. Italy was looking for a new start and respectability. All the countries saw the potential for economic benefit: in particular, the Germans sought outlets for their manufactured products, and France insisted on an agricultural policy which protected its large agricultural sector. Italy fought for the inclusion of the free movement of workers in order to capitalise on one of its greatest assets – its labour. At an institutional level, too, the document represents a compromise between federalists and intergovernmentalists, and like any document which is the result of compromise, the EEC Treaty contains inconsistencies which articulate the delicate balance between giving independence of action to the supranational institutions and retaining Member State control over the direction of the Community.

2.5   The Non-Participants in Supranational Europe

The UK excluded itself from participation in the supranational project of the European Community from the outset of the negotiations for the ECSC Treaty. Soon after the ratification of the EEC Treaty, the UK spearheaded negotiations looking at the possibility of instituting some form of free trade arrangement between the Six and the other OEEC countries, but without a common external tariff or arrangements for the harmonisation of laws to prevent distortions of competition. A number of Member States were anxious about the dangers of watering down their achievements; opposition was strongest from the French, and the negotiations came to an abrupt end when they were vetoed by General de Gaulle, then President of France. As a result of this rebuff a number of OEEC countries formed a separate, but looser arrangement for economic cooperation, the European Free Trade Association (EFTA), concluded by the Treaty of Stockholm in January 1960. The founder members of EFTA comprised the UK, Denmark, Sweden, Norway, Austria, Switzerland and Portugal. They were subsequently joined by Finland and Iceland, but numbers were reduced by the departure of Denmark, the UK and later Portugal to join the European Community. EFTA has often sought closer economic relations with the EC, and in the 1992 these culminated in the signature of the Treaty creating the European Economic Area (EEA) which largely assimilates the relations between European Community and EFTA countries to internal European Community relations, and applies the basic principles of the internal European Community common market to those relations. This treaty, too, encountered difficulties in the ratification process when it was rejected by a referendum in Switzerland. However, the failure of one state to ratify this Treaty does not preclude it coming into force. Almost all the members of EFTA are also applicants for membership of the EC.

A change of attitude in the UK towards the European Community in the early 1960s resulted in two requests for membership in 1961 and 1967, which were vetoed or stalled by de Gaulle's opposition to British membership. Only after the departure of de Gaulle was the path opened to the enlargement of the Community.

2.6 The Early Years

The years of the late 1950s and the early 1960s were years of economic boom with unprecedented growth which made the tasks of the nascent Community rather less daunting. The Treaty provided for a transitional period of twelve years, divided into three stages each of four years, ending on January 1 1970. At the end of this period, the common market should have been in place (Article 8(7) EEC). Common economic interest dictated that during the first two stages progress was smooth involving the dismantling of tariffs and quota restrictions, the erection of a common external tariff, the liberalisation of the free movement of workers and the creation of a system protecting the social security interests of migrant workers, the adoption of the initial regulations for the implementation of the Community's competition policy, and the introduction of a system of common farm prices and common organisations of the market which form the basis of the Common Agricultural Policy (CAP). Up to this point the Member States moved forward by consensus, since during the first two stages the Treaty provided for decisions to be taken by the Council of Ministers acting unanimously. The Commission under Walter Hallstein, its first President, played a key role in these achievements, initiating policy and brokering agreements between the states, and there seemed little opposition at that time to its full exploitation of the supranational potential of the tasks which it had been assigned under the EEC Treaty. The Court of Justice too was busy carving out a distinctive role for itself within the Community's system. In the ground breaking cases of *Van Gend en Loos* in 1963 (Case 26/62 [1963] ECR 1) and *Costa* v. *ENEL* in 1964 (Case 6/64 [1964] ECR 585) the Court sought to distance the Community's legal system from the conventional structure of international law by identifying the importance of the relationship between Community law and individual citizens of the Member States, and by asserting the superiority of Community law over the laws of the Member States. The Court argued that there had been a transfer of sovereign powers by the Member States to the Community.

Meanwhile, however, the warning signs for the Community had been present since 1958 when General de Gaulle came to power as the first President of the Fifth French Republic on a fiercely nationalistic platform. His view that cooperation within Europe should take place within a confederal structure in which the Member States retained full sovereignty was put forward in the Fouchet Plan of 1961, an attempt to divert the process of political union to his own ends. This proposal for a 'union of states' based on strictly intergovernmental precepts came to naught after encountering opposition in particular amongst the smaller states. Nonetheless it was clear that the favourable political circumstances in which the Community had flourished would not last for ever. The crisis point came when De Gaulle was faced with the prospect of the Community entering the third stage of the transitional period at the beginning of 1966 when many important decisions would be taken by a qualified majority in the Council of Ministers (see Table 3.1, p. 61).

2.7 De Gaulle and the Luxembourg Accords

De Gaulle objected to qualified majority voting under the EEC Treaty as he felt that it would endanger French interests within the Community. Yet majority voting was due to apply to agricultural pricing decisions – one of the issues of keenest interest for France – from 1966. De Gaulle chose to make his stand, and to precipitate the most serious crisis in the history of the Community, not over majority voting as such but over a series of linked proposals put forward by the Commission in March 1965. These concerned the financing of the CAP through a system of own resources belonging to the Community rather than through contributions by the Member States, as well as increased Parliamentary input into the making of the budget. The Commission rightly saw these matters as linked: the CAP represents the main expenditure by the Community; 'own resources' coming from the revenue of the Common Customs Tariff (CCT), agricultural levies at the external borders and a percentage of the new common turnover tax levied by all Member States – Value Added Tax (VAT) – were to give the Community financial autonomy; and greater control by the European Parliament was a necessary democratic counter-weight as control over the budget increasingly escaped the scrutiny of national Parliaments. France was not in favour of a greater role for the European Parliament, and used the lack of agreement on the package as a whole (i.e. the unwillingness of the other Member States to follow its line) to justify withdrawing from the work of the Council of Ministers from June 1965 to January 1966. This period is sometimes called the period of *'la politique de la chaise vide'* (empty chair politics), and the deadlock was broken only by an agreement between the Six known as the Luxembourg Accords.

It was agreed, in the case of decisions which are to be adopted by a qualified majority, but where very important interests of one or more Member States are at issue, that the members of the Council would attempt, within a reasonable period of time, to reach solutions capable of adoption by unanimity. The French delegation added that in its view such discussion should continue indefinitely until a unanimous decision was reached. The delegations accepted that there was no identity of view on what should be done if unanimity could not be achieved, but agreed at that stage that this disagreement should not prevent the normal work of the Community being taken up once more. The result, in practice, of the Luxembourg Accords was that there was no voting in the Council. Just as the Member States arrived at the stage where majority voting would be introduced, they baulked at the last hurdle. Thus De Gaulle had achieved his central objective of weakening certain supranational elements of the Community. The intergovernmental mode of decision-making based on consensus building prevailed over a federalist majoritarian approach as more and more of the Member States saw the attraction of maintaining the practice of unanimity. After the accession of the UK, for example the Accords allowed British politicians to maintain what they have been fond of calling the 'veto' over decisions of the Community which the UK does not like. This lies at the heart of repeated Government statements to the Westminster Parliament that British interests can always be protected by the use of the veto.

Although the Luxembourg Accords are essentially in the nature of informal understandings between sovereign states, and as such have no formal status within the Community legal system, they have proved remarkably enduring. No legal challenge can be mounted by any individual, institution or Member State to a refusal on the part of the Council of Ministers to proceed to a vote. Even the Commission which makes the proposals on the basis of which the Council acts is impotent in such a case. The Accords were responsible for nearly twenty years of legislative stagnation within the Community where negotiations lasting up to ten years might be needed before agreement was reached on the simplest pieces of legislation. There is only one recorded instance of the Council of Ministers riding roughshod over one Member State's assertion of a vital national interest in order to block qualified majority voting, and this was in May 1982 when the UK was seeking to oppose the adoption of agricultural prices. Furthermore, as the European Council became increasingly important within the Community's political structure, the practice emerged of passing on decisions which could not be taken in the Council of Ministers to the European Council where their substance would be reduced to the lowest common denominator in the best traditions of political compromise. Commitments in the European Council to break the legislative deadlock by agreeing to relinquish the practice of decision-making by unanimity proved to be empty rhetoric. Since provisions of the Treaty already provided for qualified majority voting in certain instances but these were being ignored, what was needed to revitalise the Community was not merely an increase in the range of decisions which could be adopted by a majority, but also a new willingness actually to vote on the part of the Council of Ministers. Not until the adoption of the Internal Market Programme in 1985 and the entry into force of the Single European Act on July 1 1987 were these two conditions satisfied. After that, remarkably rapid progress was made in many fields in the adoption of legislation required for the achievement of the single internal market.

The failure of the functionalist theory of European integration to take full account of the effects of resurgent nationalism as demonstrated by De Gaulle is one example of the deficiencies of the theory which led to its widespread rejection as a tool of analysis of the Community in the 1970s. However, it would be wrong to lay too much responsibility at the door of de Gaulle. The saga of the Luxembourg Accords and subsequent voting practice in the Council of Ministers is symptomatic of how the Community has evolved, at least until the adoption of the Single European Act. The pressures of a global economy in recession, the impact of the oil crisis, the loss of confidence and prestige on the part of the Commission after the departure of President Hallstein and the effects of enlargement to incorporate countries with ever more diverse interests were all factors which contributed to the years of stagnation.

2.8 The Years of Stagnation

The years following the 1965 crisis were marked not only by a protracted legislative stalemate, but also by a general loss of momentum on the part of the Community. The politics of incremental steps to European union would normally have demanded a significant reappraisal of the direction of the Community at the conclusion of the transitional period by which time the European Community was to be one, common market. Yet creating the common market proved to be much more complicated than simply legislating for a common external tariff and prohibiting internal barriers to trade and factor movement. In fact, the hidden barriers composed of the multiplicity of national rules which govern the trading environments in each of the Member States proved resistant to removal, and, as the European economy moved into recession in the mid-1970s, underwent a revival as the Member States shifted increasingly towards national protectionism. Consequently, to say that the common market was complete at the conclusion of the transitional period would be merely an empty rhetorical statement. Attempts to move on to the logical next step – the achievement of full economic and monetary union – were entirely fruitless. The Report of the Werner Committee in 1971 setting out a timetable for the achievement of monetary union by 1980 contained unrealistic goals. Currency instabilities in the 1970s destroyed a number of attempts to peg exchange rates during that decade. The Community was too vulnerable to wider economic changes to be capable of translating any amount of goodwill into concrete progress.

Moreover, commitments such as that made at the Paris Summit in October 1972 to convert the (economic) Community into a (political) European Union proved equally worthless, as the Member States were incapable of translating words into actions. The Tindemans Report of 1975 drawn up at the instance of the European Council was left on the table by the Member States. Much the same fate was suffered by the draft 'European Act' drawn up by Genscher and Colombo, the German and Italian Foreign Ministers, which resulted only in a Solemn Declaration on European Union adopted by the European Council at Stuttgart in June 1983.

The most significant source of progress towards political union between 1970 and 1985 was the gradual increase in the intensity of intergovernmental cooperation in the foreign policy field and its subsequent institutionalisation as European Political Cooperation (EPC) in Part III of the Single European Act. Wherever possible, the Community has sought to present a common face to the outside world. However political cooperation of this nature has always been entirely voluntary on the part of the Member States and tends to break down in the face of serious challenges to foreign policy cohesion such as the Argentinian invasion of the Falkland Islands in 1982 and the subsequent war between the UK and Argentina.

One proposal during this period does deserve greater attention and that is the Draft Treaty establishing a European Union (DTEU) adopted in 1984 by the European Parliament, as a counterweight to the initiatives of the diplomats and national politicians. In the climate of the time, when European Union was not high on the agenda of the Member States, the sponsorship of the DTEU by the Parliament could have been seen as a vain and impotent gesture on the part of an ineffective assembly. On the contrary, the DTEU played an important if indirect part in setting the agenda of closer integration for the second half of the 1980s.

The DTEU aimed not to sweep away the Community patrimony or *acquis communautaire*, but to build on existing achievements, albeit in an entirely new Treaty. The Treaty aimed to create a federal entity displaying the features of democratic accountability of its institutions, democracy in its decision-making processes, legitimacy through its respect for fundamental rights, and political decentralisation. The DTEU is notable for being the first semi-official Community document in which the concept of subsidiarity appeared. Article 12(2) regulates the case of concurrent competence held by the Member States and the Union:

> 'The Union shall only act to carry out those tasks which may be undertaken more effectively in common than by the Member States acting separately, in particular those whose execution requires action by the union because their dimension or effects extend beyond national frontiers.'

There are remarkable similarities between this formulation and that ultimately inserted in the Treaty of Maastricht.

In keeping with the tradition of European integration, the DTEU envisaged a combination of 'common action' (i.e. supranational action by the institutions of the Union) and 'cooperation' (i.e. intergovernmental decisions taken by the Member States and implemented by them). The aim of the DTEU was to create a bicameral legislature with the European Parliament – elected according to a uniform electoral system – holding equal powers with the Council of the Union. The Commission was to retain the right of initiative and the right to put forward amendments. The Draft proposed the institutionalisation of the European Council. The general policy aims of the Community would have remained broadly the same, although social policies would have been strengthened.

The fate of the DTEU is discussed in 2.10 on the relaunch of the Community.

2.9   Widening and Deepening

It should not be thought that the DTEU was the only bright spot of the post-transitional period era. On the contrary, during the 1970s and early 1980s the Community went through a significant process of widening and deepening. It was widened through the process of enlargement from Six to Twelve by 1986. This would not have occurred if the candidate countries had not seen the Community as a positive force creating increased economic and political cohesion in Europe. The Community was also deepened in two dimensions – the substantive and the constitutional.

In the domain of substantive competences, despite difficulties which can be attributed at least in part to the Luxembourg Accords, the Commission was able to persuade the Council to embark upon new legislative programmes which were not envisaged in the Treaty itself. The Community developed policies on the environment and in the field of research and development without actually holding specific powers in these areas. Creative use was made in these fields of Article 235 EEC which provides a residual general law-making power for the purposes of the achievement of the objectives of the Community where specific powers are not granted elsewhere in the Treaty. It was not difficult to argue that the environment with its obvious cross-border dimension, and research and development where cross-border cooperation can significantly increase the level and effectiveness of investment, should thus be brought within the ambit of Community policy-making, although countries such as Denmark were not wholly happy about such extensions of Community competence.

Less successful was the argument for the launch of a Community social policy. The roots of a more activist policy lay in the declaration of the Paris Summit in 1972 that the Member States attributed the same importance to energetic proceedings in the field of social policy as to the realisation of economic and monetary union, thereby seeking to give the Community a more human face. A Social Action Programme was elaborated by the Commission and accepted by the Council of Ministers in 1974, but it resulted in few significant legislative measures.

In the process of the constitutionalisation of the Community Treaties, the 1970s saw a number of significant developments. The Court of Justice confirmed the supremacy of Community law, holding that national legislation may be 'disapplied' where it is contrary to Community law (Case 106/77 *Amministrazione delle Finanze dello Stato* v. *Simmenthal* (*Simmenthal II*) [1978] ECR 629). It also extended the concept of direct effect to directives, allowing individuals to rely upon directives in national courts in order to claim their Community rights (Case 41/74 *Van Duyn* v. *Home Office* [1974] ECR 1337). In the field of external relations, the Court developed a theory of implied powers in Case 22/70 *Commission* v. *Council* (*ERTA*) ([1971] ECR 263) which considerably extended the scope of the Community's competence to conclude international agreements in place of the Member States. Finally, in the context of interinstitutional relations, it was established that legislation adopted by the Council would be annulled if the Council had failed to consult the European Parliament had where it was required to do so (Case 138/79 *Roquette Frères* v. *Council* [1980] ECR 3333). These are just four examples of many which illustrate that while the Community's political system partly stagnated, the Court of Justice vigorously pushed forward the development of the Community's legal system, considerably strengthening the hands of individuals claiming grievances against Member States alleged not to have observed Community law and of the supranational institutions within the Community structure, so that when the Community finally emerged into a period of positive growth in the political arena it was with a vastly changed legal system.

2.10 The Relaunch of the Community

The strong support for European Union coming from the European Parliament in the form of the DTEU was just one of the factors which lay behind the achievement of an interstate bargain needed to relaunch Europe. Indeed, the immediate impact of the DTEU should not be overestimated, since when the Draft came before the European Council at Fontainebleau in June 1984 it was not accepted, but shifted off for discussion to an Ad Hoc Committee on Institutional Affairs, commonly named after its Chairman, James Dooge of Ireland. One of the first acts of the Dooge Committee was in fact to reject the DTEU as being too radical and open-ended, and proposing unacceptable levels of institutional reform.

On the other hand, the Dooge Committee was generally in favour of some reforms of the EEC Treaty, proposing, by a majority of its members (the UK opposing) the convening of an intergovernmental conference to prepare a draft European Union Treaty. The Committee also pointed out that certain very basic things could be done to further the objectives of the Community, and these included the completion of the unfulfilled tasks under the EEC Treaty. This Report alone, however, would not have persuaded the UK and the other Member States sceptical of deeper integration to agree to significant reforms of the Treaty. Pressure came additionally from a number of different sources.

By 1984 François Mitterrand, President of France, had become a firm proponent of taking the European Community project further. In general he was supported by Helmut Kohl, the German Chancellor and the other half of the firm Franco–German alliance which has existed at the heart of the European Community since the conclusion of a Treaty of Friendship between the two states in 1963. In the first half of 1984, France assumed the Presidency of the Community, and Mitterrand was determined to leave his mark. He kept up pressure on the UK by making constant reference to the possibility of creating a two tier Europe, with those Member States prepared to go further forging ahead in the creation of a European Union, leaving others such as the UK behind. This was opposed by the UK which did not want to risk falling behind as had happened once before in the 1950s. Mitterrand also engineered a resolution of the long-running dispute between the UK and the Community concerning the so-called British budget rebate, which recognised that the UK was a net over-contributor to the Community budget. Between the European Councils at Brussels in March and Fontainebleau in June 1984 the European Community hovered on the brink of breakdown. Eventually, at Fontainebleau, Margaret Thatcher accepted a compromise deal very similar to one she had rejected at Brussels, and she did not oppose the creation of either the Dooge Committee or a second Ad Hoc Committee on a People's Europe, chaired by Adonnino.

At the same time, a new President of the Commission was appointed, the French socialist Jacques Delors, who resolved to mark his occupation of the post by succeeding where previous Commission Presidents had failed in revitalising the Community and re-establishing the prestige of the Commission. In choosing the programme to complete the internal market as his flagship he went back to the economic and incrementalist roots of the Community to be found in the Schuman Plan and the Spaak Report, and found a proposal which offered something to everyone – Euro-sceptics, federalists, European business leaders – in its promise to bring growth to the European economy. In his task, Delors was assisted by the nomination to the Commission by Margaret Thatcher of Lord Arthur Cockfield, a committed free market liberal. Cockfield, appointed Commissioner responsible for the Internal Market, put together at the request of the European Council the so-called 'White Paper' setting out a total of nearly three hundred measures which would need to be adopted to remove the physical, technical and fiscal barriers to trade in the Community. Already in January 1985 Delors started making speeches proposing the achievement of these objectives by the end of 1992 (two terms of office for the Commission) and when the White Paper came before the European Council at Milan in June 1985 it was unanimously accepted. Where some Member States differed from the others was with regard to the necessity for institutional reform to make the White Paper a reality. The UK argued that it was possible to complete the internal market simply through informal improvements in the decision-making processes of the Council. However, anxious to bring some concrete achievement out of the Italian Presidency, the Italian Prime Minister called for a vote on the convening of an intergovernmental conference to discuss amendments to the Treaty necessary to implement the goals of the White Paper, and, uniquely within the history of the Community, the proposal for a conference was carried by a majority vote, with the UK, Denmark and Greece opposing.

Reluctantly the UK participated in the conference, arguing for institutional reforms including majority voting and the strengthening of the European Parliament to be limited to those measures necessary to complete the internal market. Majority voting was successfully excluded by the minimalists from the contentious areas of fiscal harmonisation, the free movement of workers and social policy. Progress towards monetary union was kept out of the main body of the Treaty, with merely a reference being made to it in the Preamble. European Political Cooperation was included in the Treaty, but although it was given an institutional framework, it was maintained on a strictly intergovernmental basis excluding the operation of the Community rules themselves. Negotiation of what became the Single European Act proceeded exceedingly quickly, and was concluded at the European Council in December 1985 in Luxembourg, ready for signature in February 1986.

At the time, the UK believed that it had scored a significant victory in removing the impetus for a two tier Europe, in persuading the rest of the Community of the benefits of the free market, and in minimising the impact of institutional reforms. Criticisms of the Single European Act came from the European Parliament which felt cheated of any role in the negotiations and objected to the outright dismissal of its initiative, and from pro-European commentators who feared that the SEA, being more intergovernmentalist in nature, might lead to a significant watering down of the supranational content of the Community. Subsequent events have, however, proved such pessimistic prognoses to be wrong, and now require a broad reassessment of the significance of the SEA.

2.11 The Single European Act

The provisions of the Single European Act can be divided into five categories. First, and foremost, there are provisions amending the EEC Treaty, with a view to the achievement of the goals of the White Paper. These comprise principally:

- Article 8A EEC (now Article 7A EC), containing a definition of the internal market and setting the deadline of December 31 1992;
- a new law-making power to be exercised by the Council acting by a qualified majority in cooperation with the European Parliament, giving the Council the necessary means to achieve the objective in Article 8A (Article 100A EEC);
- Article 149(2) EEC, which sets out the details of the cooperation procedure, involving in essence a Parliamentary second reading of proposed legislation, after the Council has adopted a 'common position' by a qualified majority and the Commission has reviewed the amendments proposed by the Parliament on its first reading.

Further amendments to the EEC Treaty are introduced by the second category of provisions which consolidate *de jure* some of the extensions of competence which had occurred *de facto* since the early 1970s. An example is the amendment to Article 7(2) EEC (now Article 6(2) EC) which recognised the increased importance assumed within the Treaty framework of the principle of non-discrimination against Community nationals on grounds of nationality. The EEC Treaty was amended by the SEA to allow the Council by a qualified majority in cooperation with the European Parliament to introduce rules designed to prohibit such discrimination. Specific competences were also introduced in relation to regional development (Articles 130A–130E EEC), research and technological development (Articles 130F–130Q EEC) and the environment (Articles 130R–130T EEC). Finally, in this context, there were minor amendments to Title III of the EEC Treaty which is concerned with Social Policy.

In the third category comes an important addition to the institutional structure of the Community. Article 168A EEC provided for a Court of First Instance to be attached to the European Court of Justice. This court was set up by Council Decision and commenced work in 1989.

The last two categories of provisions do not amend the EEC Treaty itself. In other words, they do not form part of the supranational corpus of Community law, but operate in the conventional realm of international law. Title I of the Single European Act consolidates and institutionalises the activities of the European Council, until then merely an ad hoc and informal gathering of the Heads of State or Government of the Member States. It is now required to meet at least twice a year (Article 2) and the leaders are assisted by their Foreign Ministers and a Member of the Commission (conventionally the President).

Finally, Title III of the Single European Act put the practice of European Political Cooperation (EPC) on a much firmer footing. Throughout this Title, the Member States are referred to as the High Contracting Parties, thereby stressing the intergovernmental nature of EPC; however, there are linkages with the Community's institutional structure in so far as the Ministers of Foreign Affairs meeting within the context of EPC are chaired by the representative of whichever Member State holds the Presidency of the Council of Ministers. The Commission is 'fully associated' with the work of EPC (Article 30(3)(b) SEA) and the Presidency is responsible for informing the European Parliament of the foreign policy issues currently at issue within EPC. The voluntarist nature of EPC is stressed by Article 30(1) which merely binds the High Contracting Parties to 'endeavour jointly to formulate and implement a European foreign policy'.

Before leaving the text of the Single European Act itself to consider its aftermath, reference should also be made to the Preamble which highlights certain important broader goals of the Community, for which, however, the political consensus was not strong enough for them to be brought within the body of the Single European Act itself. These include the ultimate achievement of Economic and Monetary Union (EMU), as well as the protection of fundamental rights, an important aspect of the legitimacy of a Community which claims to exercise sovereign rights transferred from the Member States.

2.12 After the Single European Act

The immediate prognosis for the Single European Act was not good. It encountered harsh criticism on account of the vagueness of its wording, the many derogations which it allowed Member States, and its assertion that completing the internal market was somehow a new goal for a Community which since 1958 has always been committed to creating a common market (Pescatore, 1987). These criticisms, however, fail to take into account that progress for the Community must always take the form of delicate interstate bargains, which themselves may be transformed into more positive achievements by subsequent political events and by the willingness of the institutions and the Member States to implement the provisions in good faith. By 1985 the Community was suffering a serious crisis of legitimacy. It was seen by many to be a lame duck since it could never deliver on its grandiose aims, and the much vaunted common market was quite clearly a chimera. The Community lurched from one crisis to another, beset by budgetary indiscipline, agricultural spending spiralling out of control, and the lack of an obvious contribution which it could make to the pursuit of macro-economic growth in Europe. In the event, the Single European Act has revitalised the fortunes of the Community, as the Member States have become involved in a project for which all have enthusiasm. The 'Christmas Tree' (i.e. overoptimistic) economic analysis (up to 5 million new jobs; an increase in 5–7 per cent of GDP) of the team of economists charged by the Commission with the task of estimating the macro-economic benefits of the single market or, to put it another way, the 'costs of non-Europe', have generally prevailed over more sober judgments of the negative effects of uncontrolled industrial restructuring on more vulnerable regions (Cecchini, 1988; Cutler *et al.*, 1989).

From most perspectives, the progress made by the institutions towards the completion of the 1992 programme was impressive. The Commission rapidly put forward proposals for the bulk of the three hundred or so measures envisaged by the White Paper. The Council of Ministers streamlined its decision-making machinery, adopting an amendment to its working procedures to allow any one member of the Council, or the representative of the Commission who attends without a vote, to call for a vote on a measure. This, coupled with a new willingness not to seek to rely upon the Luxembourg Accords, has led to a remarkable acceleration in the legislative process. However, very many important and contentious measures still needed to be adopted unanimously, and in this context the old practice of building 'packages' which offer something for everyone in return for compromises has continued. That was evident in July 1992 when the important fiscal harmonisation measures were agreed by the Council of Ministers with the UK conceding the power of the Community to set VAT rates in return for concessions on a favourable taxation level for Scotch whisky, an important UK export.

The European Parliament meanwhile has continued to make full use of the limited powers which have been conceded to it, maintaining its fruitful alliance with the Commission in order to exercise maximum influence over the legislative procedure at both first reading and second reading. It has sought to protect the use of the cooperation procedure by preventing the Council of Ministers from using legal bases within the Treaty for measures which require a lower level of Parliamentary input. It supported the

Commission when it successfully brought an action before the Court of Justice arguing that Article 100A EEC should have been used as the legal basis for a harmonisation measure in the field of the environment, rather than the specific environmental legal basis of Article 130S EEC which requires only consultation of the Parliament (Case C-300/89 *Commission* v. *Council (Titanium Dioxide)* (11.6.1991). The Parliament also took action on its own account challenging a Council Directive of 1990 which gave the right of residence in other Member States to students, but which the Council based on Article 235 EEC which requires only consultation of the Parliament rather than what was then Article 7(2) EEC, which requires the use of the cooperation procedure. The Court of Justice accepted the Parliament's argument that failure to use Article 6(2) undermined the imperatives of the cooperation procedure (Case C-295/90 *Parliament* v. *Council* [1992] 3 CMLR 281).

The progress under the Single European Act has epitomised a new style of minimalist regulation on the part of the European Community. In case law which will be reviewed in detail in Part V, the Court of Justice had already made an important contribution to the goals of the internal market by holding that where a product is lawfully put on the market and sold in one Member State, it cannot normally be excluded from the market in the other Member States. Products must be allowed to benefit from production in one trading environment and sale in another, unless the Member State seeking to impede import or marketing can successfully argue that the rules which it is applying to the imported product (and to identical national products) are necessary for the protection of certain mandatory interests such as consumer protection, health and safety or the protection of the environment. The Commission has since altered its policy on the harmonisation of national laws in order to incorporate this principle of mutual recognition. Measures now put forward for adoption set only basic minimum standards for products which, if complied with, guarantee the right to free movement. This approach has obvious attractions for states such as the UK which have been pursuing a vigorous deregulatory approach at national level, and have argued for the adoption of this approach at Community level. The argument is that with this approach the stage is set for products to compete freely in a wider market, with consumers effectively choosing the type of trading environment in which they would like products to be produced. Consumer lawyers have countered by pointing out the risk that hard won gains at national level in the field of consumer protection may be destroyed by a Community-wide deregulatory approach.

2.13   The Social Dimension of the Internal Market

The victory of free market economics within the internal market did not wholly remain unnoticed by social policy-makers, trade unions and politicians on the political left. For example, while sponsoring the political and economic relaunch of the Community through the internal market programme, President Mitterrand constantly made clear his interest in creating a 'Social Europe'. However, his proposal for a 'European social space' in which basic principles for the protection of workers were to be introduced at a mandatory Community level languished at the bottom of the agenda until it was picked by the Belgian Presidency in 1987 with the proposal for a 'plinth of social rights'. Soon thereafter, in February 1988, some of the problems of the anticipated differential regional effects of the internal market – one of the other central 'social' concerns of the Community – were resolved at the Community level by an agreement in the European Council to restructure the European Regional Development Fund and the European Social Fund in order to channel more Community resources into regional development measures and away from the apparently bottomless pit of the CAP.

This was followed by the adoption by eleven of the twelve Member States (the UK dissenting) of a Community Charter of Fundamental Social Rights Workers at Strasbourg in December 1989. It contains a declaration on the part of the signatories that the implementation of the Single European Act must 'take full account of the social dimension of the Community', and a statement of basic social rights of workers including freedom of movement, the right to fair remuneration, the importance of the improvement of living and working conditions, and the right to adequate social protection. This purely declaratory measure, to which the Commission attached an Action Programme containing a resumé of the measures which it intended to propose, was supposed to revitalise the social policy of the Community, just like the Social Action Programme of the 1970s. The results of the initiative have been just as disappointing, since the political will amongst the Member States has proved lacking, and the EC Treaty remained weak on the social policy front, requiring in all cases except health and safety at work a unanimous vote for the adoption of social policy measures. The Social Charter is not binding and it introduces no new law-making powers into the Treaty. It also declares – with explicit reference to the principle of subsidiarity – that implementation of many of the rights is the responsibility of the Member States not the Community itself. This accords with the view of some Member States such as the UK, that the Community should be minimally concerned with social policy, which it alleges is irrelevant to the achievement of the internal market and a matter for resolution at national level. Social policy has become, therefore, almost a symbol of the reservation by Member States of a certain measure of national sovereignty. Despite these limitations upon its scope, Margaret Thatcher felt unable to sign the Social Charter on behalf of the UK.

2.14   Towards a Treaty of European Union

Despite the failure of the Single European Act significantly to extend the ambit of the Community's activities, Jacques Delors did succeed after 1986 in keeping economic and monetary union and institutional reform on the diplomatic agenda. A positive note was maintained by the February 1988 agreement on budgetary discipline and reform of the structural funds. Soon afterwards in June 1988 the Hanover European Council reaffirmed the Community's commitment to the progressive realisation of EMU, and charged a committee chaired by Delors himself with the task of identifying the concrete stages needed to realise that aim.

The Delors Committee reported in April 1989. Its report identified the three basic attributes of monetary union: full currency convertibility, complete integration of financial markets and irrevocable locking of exchange rates. The Treaties already provided for the first two attributes to be achieved. The Report therefore concentrated on the third attribute, focusing on the need not only for exchange rates to be locked, but on the further step of the adoption of a single currency which would demonstrate the irreversibility of monetary union and remove the transaction costs of converting national currencies. However, without a convergence of economic conditions in the Member States and the adoption of certain common macro-economic policies, even the locking of exchange rates cannot be successfully achieved. The Report therefore identified a crucial second stage in the achievement of monetary union in which budget deficits would be limited and European level institutions would be introduced which would gradually assume responsibility for monetary policy and exchange rate and reserve management. This would follow an initial stage (which began in July 1990) in which all the European Community currencies would be brought within the exchange rate mechanism ('ERM') of the European Monetary System (EMS) which controls exchange rate fluctuations, and in which fiscal coordination is gradually intensified. The final third stage would begin with the irrevocable locking of exchange rates and a European Central Bank taking over the role of national central banks.

The Report did not receive unanimous acceptance from the Member States; in particular, disagreement existed on when the various stages should begin, on whether transition from Stage Two to Stage Three would be automatic and fixed in advance, on whether all currencies would be replaced by the new currency and on whether the new Community banking institutions should be independent of control by politicians as they are in Germany. The UK favoured not a single currency, but a 'common currency' in which a hard, convertible ECU would be created which would compete with national currencies and might gradually supersede them. Against the opposition of the UK, the other eleven governments agreed at the Rome European Council in October 1990 that Stage Two would begin in January 1994, and this date is now provided for by Article 109E(1) EC, as amended by the Treaty of Maastricht. The UK did agree, however, to the convening of an intergovernmental conference on Economic and Monetary Union and this started work in December 1990.

Some Member States were unwilling to allow the Community to continue along the path towards EMU without significant moves towards Political Union involving the extension of the competence of the Community, and the enhancement of the democratic accountability of its institutions. Chancellor Kohl, for example, knew that a Treaty under which the Member States transferred significant competence in economic and monetary policy-making to the Community would not be acceptable either to the German Parliament, the *Bundestag*, or to the *Länder*, unless the loss of democratic input into policy-making at national level were at least in part matched by an increase in democratic input at the Community level. President Mitterrand also supported further moves to Political Union. Consequently, a parallel intergovernmental conference on Political Union was convened to consider the competences of the Union, in particular competences in foreign affairs, defence and collective security, and the institutions necessary to make the Union operational.

The outcome of diplomatic hard bargaining was the Treaty of Maastricht, agreed by the Heads of State or Government in December 1991 and signed in February 1992. The Treaty formed the results of two separate bargaining processes, brought together only at the final stage. There was little interaction between the two conferences. After the departure of Margaret Thatcher and the arrival of John Major as British Prime Minister in late 1990, the UK was able to sign up to a Treaty laying down the stages for the achievement of EMU, while retaining the right as laid down in a Protocol not to proceed to participate in the third stage of monetary union (a similar Protocol is provided for Denmark, which might require a referendum before participation). However, in contrast to the positive progress on EMU the results of the debates on Political Union were much more modest changes. Foreign policy remained outside the structures of the Community proper, and was joined there in the two parallel pillars of intergovernmentalism which stand with the pillar of supranationalism of the Community itself in the new three pillar structure of European Union, by cooperation in the fields of home affairs, immigration, asylum and the administration of justice.

2.15   The Treaty of Maastricht

European integration is now based on a European Union created by Article A TEU which represents

> 'a new stage in the process of creating an ever closer union among the peoples of Europe, in which decisions are taken as closely as possible to the citizen.'

This latter point is a reference to the principle of subsidiarity, defined in Article 3B EC (see 1.4). At the insistence of the UK a reference to the 'federal vocation' of the Union was removed and in Article F(1) TEU an explicit commitment is made to the Union respecting the national identities of the constituent states. Article A also sets out the structure of the Union, which is based on the European Community, with its strongly supranational institutional systems, 'supplemented by the forms of cooperation established by this Treaty'. These, as noted above (see also Fig 1.1), are the two pillars of foreign policy – Common Foreign and Security Policy (CFSP) – and Justice and Home Affairs. The unity of these separate pillars is, however, protected by Article C TEU which provides that the Union shall be served by a 'single institutional framework' which builds on the existing Community institutional framework. The EEC Treaty is renamed the European Community Treaty.

Titles V and VI of the Treaty of Union set out the provisions on CFSP and Justice and Home Affairs. The CFSP provisions build on Part III of the Single European Act, but with significant extensions. An element of defence and security policy is introduced within the scope of CFSP. The prospect of an eventual common defence policy and a common defence is foreseen by Article J4 TEU, which also calls upon the WEU, enjoying its late revival in importance, to implement actions of the Union which have defence implications. This has been agreed by the Member States notwithstanding that some Member States have a policy of neutrality, and not all are members of the WEU. The second innovation is in Article J3 which provides for joint action to be agreed upon where appropriate by a qualified majority. This significantly strengthens the supranational character of CFSP at the expense of intergovernmentalism. The provisions on Justice and Home Affairs are concerned principally with issues of immigration and asylum policy. Interstate cooperation in this context will typically involve the conclusion of international agreements between the Member States.

The provisions on EMU (Articles 3A, 4A, 102A – 109M EC and additional Protocols) lay down the timetable for the achievement of monetary union and the convergence conditions for the national economies which will be needed to be satisfied if the shift to irrevocably fixed exchange rates is not to be accompanied by damage to some of the Community economies. Stage Two begins on January 1 1994, and Stage Three on January 1 1997 or, if delayed by the Council of Ministers, January 1 1999. The number of participating currencies will depend upon the achievement of the convergence criteria, and the decisions of the UK and Denmark under their respective 'opt-out' Protocols. The Treaty provides for a European Monetary Institute which will take monetary policy forward to the third stage when it will be superseded by a European Central Bank (ECB), operating within a European System of Central Banks. Decisions are to be taken by majority votes in many instances.

Other amendments to the European Community Treaty itself come within the context of Political Union. These include a new form of 'codecision' which further extends the already cumbersome legislative procedure by establishing a *third reading* in which conflicts between the Council and the Parliament are to be resolved within a conciliation process. However, the legislative status of the Parliament is enhanced, since such measures will be signed jointly by the Presidents of the Council and the Parliament. This procedure is to be applied in a significant number of cases, although existing procedures are also retained. The duration and mandate of the European Commission is to be synchronised with that of the European Parliament, and the membership of the Commission is now to be approved by the Parliament. This increases the accountability of the Commission, although there are no changes to the accountability of the unelected and secretive Council of Ministers. The Treaty also enshrines the right of citizens to petition the European Parliament, and empowers the Parliament to set up Committees of Inquiry to investigate allegations of maladministration by the Community institutions. One final important institutional innovation is the creation of a Committee of the Regions to represent the particular interests of the Regions.

The substantive changes to the European Community Treaty outside the field of EMU are relatively modest. A concept of Union citizenship is to be introduced, but the attributes of citizenship will be relatively insignificant in comparison to the attributes of national citizenship. They will comprise principally the right of free movement and the right to stand and vote in municipal elections and elections to the European Parliament anywhere in the Union (new Articles 8 – 8E EC). Social policy within the Treaty itself underwent certain minor amendments, with the more significant amendments proposed by the Dutch Presidency being relegated to a Protocol and Agreement giving the UK its so-called social policy opt-out (see 16.6). This seeks to delegate to the eleven Member States other than the UK, by agreement of all twelve Member States, the power to adopt social policy measures using the procedures and institutions of the European Community. Vocational training is now regulated in more detail by the Treaty itself, and it is joined by general provisions on education, culture, health policy, consumer protection, industrial policy and development aid policy. Legislative measures in policy areas such as these, where the Community does not hold an exclusive and preemptive power to regulate, will be subject to the principle of subsidiarity enshrined in Article 3B EC.

In the final provisions to the Treaty of Union, changes to the procedures for revising the Treaties are introduced, and the automatic convening of a conference of government representatives in 1996 to review progress towards political union is provided for. While the Commission considered the progress towards Political Union contained in the Maastricht Treaty to be modest, it considered it to be a worthwhile victory to persuade the Member States to commit themselves in advance to review progress.

2.16 The Challenges of the Future

The European Community now stands at a crossroads in its development, facing challenges which make the possibility of 'two speed' or differentiated integration an increasingly likely option. On the one hand, the Member States have agreed upon a new Treaty which, while it contains, like the Single European Act many contradictory elements, nonetheless represents progress from the perspective of the federalists. However, significant difficulties have been experienced during the ratification process. While there are a number of countries with solid pro-Union majorities (Greece, Italy, Ireland, Spain, Portugal, Luxembourg, Spain, Netherlands and Belgium), in three key large countries (France, Germany and the UK), and one small country (Denmark), hostility to closer European Union became increasingly apparent during the course of 1992. A referendum in Denmark produced a small majority 'No' vote, and was followed by a referendum in France in which the Treaty was approved – again by a small majority. In September 1992, the Member States conceded that it would not be possible to complete the ratification process in order for the Treaty to come into force as planned on January 1 1993. At the European Council in Edinburgh in December 1992, the leaders of the Twelve sought to revive the ratification process by agreeing a package of deals to enable Denmark to hold a second referendum in May 1993, by putting pressure on the UK to complete the ratification process in Parliament by about the same time, and by formulating a more precise definition of the principle of subsidiarity. Yet there is no one single motive behind the opposition that has emerged: for some, the Treaty goes too far; for others, not far enough, in particular in the fields of Political Union and democratisation. It was therefore difficult to see how the various interests could be easily reconciled into a Treaty capable of being ratified by all twelve Member States.

At the same time, it is thought by some to be anomalous for the Community to be accelerating the process of deepening when its main concern should be for widening. One view is that a looser association of many more European states including the EFTA countries and the new democracies of central and eastern Europe will be much more productive of stability and prosperity in Europe than the increasingly unattainable goal of closer union. Difficulties in formulating a coherent and effective approach to the civil war in former Yugoslavia has been used to illustrate the impossibility of reconciling the disparate interests of sovereign states. However, since late 1992 negotiations have been proceeding on the accession of certain EFTA countries such as Austria which have long made known their desire to accede.

The possibility of wholesale accession of the EFTA countries leaves, however, a separate initiative to widen economic integration within Europe somewhat in limbo. The Agreement to create a European Economic Area (EEA) negotiated between the Community and the EFTA countries involved the EFTA countries accepting the application of many of the existing rules of the Community in return for free access to the Community's internal market. After long negotiations, including major difficulties injected by the Court of Justice regarding the validity and effect of the judicial mechanism proposed to ensure the enforcement of the agreement, the EEA Agreement was signed at Oporto in May 1992.

Finally, the European Community remains under considerable pressures in the economic field. The unification of Germany and the collapse of the communist domination of eastern Europe presented the Community with internal and external challenges regarding the nature and extent of the assistance which it is prepared to provide to facilitate (and fund) industrial and political transformation. As regards the evolution of world free trade, the picture also remains uncertain, with the long delay in the conclusion of the GATT Uruguay round of trade liberalisation talks which for a long time were hampered by a bitter disagreement between the USA and France.

Summary

1 The unification of the nation states of Europe has been a consistent theme in political thinking for many centuries. Only since the Second World War has significant progress been made towards realising the ideals of a unified Europe.

2 In post-war Europe, a number of intergovernmental organisations were set up, attracting a wide membership. These included the Council of Europe, the OEEC and the WEU. Tighter supranational forms of integration attracted fewer members; the original ECSC, EEC and Euratom were composed of just six members.

3 The ECSC emerged out of a French proposal to put key strategic commodities under international control. It was followed by the unsuccessful initiative for a European Defence Community, and then the relaunch of economic integration in the form of the EEC and Euratom. The thinking behind these proposals was guided by functionalism.

4 The early years of the European Community were years of economic boom and great progress was made towards completing the customs union within the agreed timetable. Less progress was made towards the completion of the common market. In 1965–66, the Community encountered a serious crisis when France withdrew from participation in protest at the move to qualified majority voting.

5 The Luxembourg Accords which brought this crisis to an end effectively committed the Community to consensus-based decision-making, a pattern which was broken only after the adoption of the Single European Act in 1986.

6 Thereafter came years of stagnation, with a legislative blockage in the Council of Ministers. This was exacerbated by a period of deep economic recession in Europe, and an increase rather than a decrease in protectionist measures erected by Member States. No proposals for advancing the structures of integration, for example through monetary union, had a serious chance of success.

7 Meanwhile, the Community had enlarged, and was consolidating its activities in certain areas, such as the CAP. Integration was largely led by the Court of Justice, which developed a strongly supranational case law.

8 The relaunch of the Community came in 1985–86, with a conjunction of factors, including the arrival of a new dynamic President of the Commission (Delors), the commitment of key political leaders such as Mitterrand and Kohl to further integration, and the realisation that the Community must revitalise itself in order to survive.

9 The adoption of the 1992 Single Market Programme and the amendments to the Treaty of Rome through the Single European Act 1986 have proved catalysts for a recovery of prestige and effectiveness of the Community.

10 While progress continued on the completion of the single or internal market, economic and monetary union and political union returned to the agenda. A committee chaired by Delors put forward a step-by-step proposal for the achievement of monetary union.

11 Twin intergovernmental conferences were convened in 1990 on EMU and Political Union and were concluded at Maastricht in December 1991. The Treaty of Maastricht suffered serious problems, however, during the ratification process, encountering significant opposition in France and Denmark, as well as the UK.

Questions

1 In what ways does the early history of the Community illustrate the strengths and weaknesses of the ideas about European integration discussed in Chapter 1?

2 How did the crisis of 'empty chair politics' affect the subsequent evolution of the Community?

3 Is it fair to describe the UK as an 'awkward partner in Europe' (George, 1990)?

4 Is the deepening of the European Community through the Treaty of Union the correct response to the pressures currently affecting the process of European integration?

Further Reading

Allen (1992) 'European Union, the Single European Act and the 1992 programme', in Swann (1992).

Artis (1992) 'The Maastricht Road to Monetary Union', 30 *Journal of Common Market Studies*, 299.

Cass (1992) 'The Word that Saves Maastricht? The Principle of Subsidiarity and the Division of Powers within the European Community', 29 *Common Market Law Review*, 1107.

Corbett (1992) 'The Intergovernmental Conference on Political Union', 30 *Journal of Common Market Studies*, 271.

Everling (1992) 'Reflections on the Structure of the European Union', 29 *Common Market Law Review*, 1053.

Nicoll (1984) 'The Luxembourg Compromise', 23 *Journal of Common Market Studies*, 35.

Nugent (1992) 'The Deepening and Widening of the European Community: Recent Evolution, Maastricht and Beyond', 30 *Journal of Common Market Studies*, 311.

Pescatore (1987) 'Some Critical Remarks on the Single European Act', 24 *Common Market Law Review*, 9.

Schoutheete (1990) 'The European Community and its sub-systems', in Wallace (1990).

Swann (1992) 'The single market and beyond – an overview', in Swann (1992).

Urwin (1991) *The Community of Europe. A History of European Integration since 1945*, Longman.

Part II

The Community at Work

3 The Institutions of the European Community

3.1 Introduction

This chapter examines the composition and basic powers and functions of the Community institutions. Discussion of the institutions at work is reserved for consideration in Chapter 4.

The institutional structure of the European Community established by Article 4 EC is *sui generis*. It ressembles neither the typical governing structure of an international organisation, in that its institutions exercise sovereign powers transferred by the Member States, nor (yet) the institutional framework of a modern parliamentary democracy. It is, for example, not possible to identify a clear separation of powers between the legislative and the executive functions (Lenaerts, 1991a). The legislative function is presently divided between the Council of Ministers and the Parliament, with inputs from the Commission and other subsidiary bodies. The executive function is largely held by the Commission, but often under delegated powers from the Council which retains control through a committee structure, and such powers can only properly be exercised with the active cooperation of the Member States. There is no single legislative or executive procedure which can be described in simple terms. Reference must always be made to the Treaties to ensure that the institutions are acting within their powers as required by Article 4 EC. Within these limits, however, the institutions have broad autonomy of action, and may establish their own Rules of Procedure, which once created must be observed. The Court of Justice exercises a supervisory control over the division of powers between the institutions, as it does over the division of powers between the Community and the Member States.

The four cornered structure – Commission, Council of Ministers, Parliament and Court of Justice, assisted by the Economic and Social Committee – envisaged by the original Treaties of Paris and Rome was described briefly in Chapter 1. The institutions of the three founding Treaties have been merged since 1967, although the powers conferred by each Treaty upon the various institutions continue to differ. The discussion of the powers of the institutions in this chapter is focused on the powers granted by the EC Treaty. With the Treaty of Maastricht this structure has now expanded; the Court of Auditors, which ensures financial discipline and prudentiality within the Community, has been given the status of an institution, and a Committee of the Regions has been established to make an additional advisory input into the legislative process (Article 4 EC). New institutions of EMU have also been established.

Since the inception of the Community, although the basic outline of the political institutions has remained largely the same, the details of the structure have altered considerably. Changes have been the product both of the enlargement of the Community which has necessitated the enlargement of the institutions and changes in their working patterns, and of the evolution of the functions and powers of the Community. The pattern of development has frequently been one of the *de facto* development of new activities and interinstitutional relationships, followed by subsequent *de jure* recognition of the changes in an amendment to the constitutive Treaties. At no point does a study of the Treaties alone give a complete picture of the institutions at work.

The new bodies which have emerged inside and outside the existing framework, while making the pattern of policy-making at the Community level ever more complex, have not always brought improvements in the efficiency, transparency or accountability of the activities of the Community. The balance of power between the institutions has altered in significant ways. For example, the intergovernmental element in the decision-making process, represented by the Council of Ministers, has exercised a more dominant role than envisaged in the founding treaties, and has tended to prevail over the supranational element, represented by the Commission and the Parliament. This is not just because the Council has largely retained the core legislative power, but because its influence has been strengthened by the following key developments:

- the evolution of the European Council;
- the emergence of the distinctive role of the Presidency;
- the establishment of the intergovernmental structures of political cooperation, and cooperation in home affairs matters;
- the work of the Committee of Permanent Representatives (COREPER); and
- the evolution of a structure of committees of national representatives which advise, assist and sometimes control the Commission ('comitology').

In sum, the Council has expanded 'upstream' in such a way as to influence the initiation of policy, and 'downstream' so as to exercise more control over the implementation of policy. The expansion of its roles has been largely at the expense of the Commission.

The European Parliament, while unable to overcome the dominance of the Council, has gradually emerged as a more significant political actor. It has worked to maximise its most important powers through:

- its increasing input into the legislative and budgetary processes, which ensures an element of democratic legitimacy for the Community;

- its powers of supervision and control over the other political institutions which promote executive accountability.

Despite the evolution of the other institutions and the proliferation of other bodies, however, the Commission still retains a pivotal role within the institutional structure. Consequently, a discussion of the political institutions needs to begin by considering the composition, duties and tasks of the Commission.

3.2 The Commission: Composition and Basic Character

The Commission was originally intended as the 'bonding element' within the supranational institutional structure of the Community (Urwin, 1991: 81). It would drive forward the motor of integration, recommending policies for action, administering the Treaties and acting as a guardian and watchdog of the Community interest. It grew out of the High Authority, created by the ECSC Treaty, which has greater powers of decision under the more detailed provisions of that Treaty. The Commission is based in Brussels, although it has an important outpost in Luxembourg.

In legal terms, the Commission is a college of seventeen Commissioners – at least one from each Member State – chaired by a President. By convention, two Commissioners are drawn from each of the five larger Member States (France, Germany, Italy, Spain and the UK), and one from each of the seven smaller states. The Commissioners are appointed by common accord of the Member States (Article 158 EC), although in practice governments rarely oppose each other's nominations. By convention also, the UK's two Commissioners come from the two main parties – Conservative and Labour. In theory, the President was in fact supposed to be appointed from amongst the Members of the Commission. In practice, the name of the President emerged before that of the other Commissioners, and this practice has now been given legal force in Article 158 EC as amended by the Treaty of Maastricht. The Member States will now nominate the President, after consulting the European Parliament, and the nominated person will be consulted in the process of nominating the rest of the Commissioners. The new Commission is then subject to a vote of approval as a body by the European Parliament, and only after this will the President and Commissioners be appointed by common accord of the Member States. This is one of the features of the Treaty of Maastricht which renders the Commission a more politicised and less purely bureaucratic and administrative body. It may be seen increasingly as a prototype European government.

The term of office of the Commission has also been extended from four to five years by the Treaty of Maastricht, and by transitional arrangements in Article 158(3) intended to synchronise the mandates of the European Parliament and the Commission, the Commissioners who came into office in 1993 will have to be replaced or reappointed from January 1995.

According to the Treaty, the qualities of the Commissioners are their general competence and an independence which is beyond doubt (Article 157(1) EC). Although appointed by the Member States, the Commissioners are not national representatives. Their independence is guaranteed by Article 157(2) which prohibits them from taking instructions from any government or other body, from taking any action incompatible with their duties, and from engaging in other occupations, and which enjoins them to act during and after their term of office with integrity and discretion. They give a solemn undertaking at the beginning of their term to respect the obligations of office. In return, they are protected from dismissal except for failure to fulfil the conditions required for the performance of their duties or serious misconduct, in which case the Court of Justice may compulsorily retire an errant Commissioner (Article 160 EC). In practice, the controls are greater, since the possibility of non-renewal in post at the expiry of a term of office may be sufficient occasionally to remind a Commissioner that ultimately he or she owes the appointment to the exercise of national discretion. Margaret Thatcher's well publicised refusal to renominate Lord Cockfield, the architect of the Commission's White Paper, for the second Commission under Jacques Delors is a good example of the use of the renewal of the mandate as an instrument of discipline.

At the beginning of the term of office, the President allocates policy portfolios to the other sixteen Commissioners. The President's nominally free hand in this task is fettered by the need to balance national interests, which jealously demand the allocation of important and prestigious portfolios to *their* Commissioner(s), and by the general competence and reputation of the nominees. Not all the policy portfolios carry the same workload, or degree of policy coherence. Each Commissioner is assisted by a *cabinet*, composed of officials personally appointed by the Commissioner existing outside the formal bureaucracy of the Commission. The *cabinets* are headed by the *Chefs de cabinet*, who meet on a regular basis to prepare the work of the Commission itself. These meetings fulfil something of the same role in relation to the Commission as the Committee of Permanent Representatives (COREPER) in relation to the Council of Ministers (3.10).

Most of the day to day work of the Commission is done by a body of European civil servants who are employees of the Community. Those 'Eurocrats' concerned with policy and executive functions number around 10,000, and contrary to popular demonology, this represents a small bureaucracy both in comparison to the tasks which it is required to undertake and in relation to the size of the national civil services. Eurocrats are normally appointed on the basis of entry examinations, and while officially there are no national quotas, in practice a balance must be maintained, particularly in the more senior posts. The Commission is divided into twenty-three departments or Directorates-General ('DGs'), plus a number of special units and services such as the Secretariat General, the Legal Service, the Statistical Office and the Translation and

Interpretation Services. Amongst the most important DGs are DG III (Internal Market and Industrial Affairs), DG IV (Competition), DG V (Employment and Social Affairs), and DG VI (Agriculture). Others, such as DG XXIII (Enterprises' Policy, Distributive Trades, Tourism and Social Economy) have a less clearly defined and coherent policy remit. The size of the DGs varies, as does their degree of influence and input into the policy-making process. There is no clear match between the DGs and the policy portfolios of the Commissioners. Some find themselves reporting to two or more Commissioners in respect of the various aspects of their work. Some Commissioners must liaise with two, three or more DGs. This mismatch, which can make for difficult relationships between the DGs and the Commissioners and their *cabinets*, coupled with the rigid organisational structure and the lack of overall policy oversight within the Commission, means that policy-making is in general fragmented and lacking in coherence.

As a college, decisions must be taken collectively by the Commissioners, who meet every week in private session. The Commission takes decisions by a simple majority vote. The Commission's own internal Rules of Procedures allow for a 'written procedure', whereby copies of draft decisions are circulated in advance to the Commissioners, and are adopted without discussion if there is no opposition. The Commission may also delegate the power to take management and administrative decisions to individual commissioners and senior members of the Commission staff (Article 27 of the Rules of Procedure).

A recent judgment of the Court of First Instance has confirmed that there are strict limits upon the valid delegation of power, and reasserted that the text of Decisions must actually be adopted by the Commission itself. In Cases T-79/89, etc. *BASF AG et al.* v. *Commission* [1992] 4 CMLR 357 the Court held that a Decision of the Commission imposing heavy fines on a number of chemical companies in respect of an alleged cartel in the market for PVC was so vitiated by defects of form and procedure as to be 'non-existent' (see 9.4). The Court held that it was not permissible for the administrative services of the Commission to change (other than to correct grammatical, orthographical or typographical errors) the text of a Decision once adopted by the Commission. The judgment also imposes tight restrictions on the adoption of Decisions which are addressed to more than one person or Member State and thus involve more than one official language. Altogether five official languages were involved in the PVC proceedings, but only the German, French and English draft Decisions went before the Commission itself. After the substance of these Decisions had been agreed, the Commissioner responsible for competition was given a delegated power to adopt the authentic Dutch and Italian versions, as well as the Danish, Greek, Portuguese and Spanish versions, which were only required for purposes of the publication of the Decision in the Official Journal. The Court of First Instance held that the Commission itself must adopt each of the language versions which are actually addressed to a person or Member

State (i.e. it should have adopted the Dutch and Italian versions). The adoption of translated Decisions on the basis of an authenticated original is not a management or administrative measure which can validly be delegated to a single Commissioner. This judgment has been appealed by the Commission to the Court of Justice.

The independence of the Commission makes it uniquely qualified to give a 'European perspective' upon the progress of European integration, although in practice it is of course never entirely separated from national or sectoral pressures and lobbies. It has developed a role as the mediator and conciliator between disparate and conflicting interests, in particular within the Council of Ministers, and has operated as the broker in the resolution of numerous intractable disputes such as those over budgetary contributions and financial discipline within the Community.

The powers and tasks of the Commission are set out in Article 155 EC:

'In order to ensure the proper functioning and development of the common market, the Commission shall:

– ensure that the provisions of this Treaty and the measures taken by the institutions pursuant thereto are applied;
– formulate recommendations or deliver opinions on matters dealt with in this Treaty, if it expressly so provides or if the Commission considers it necessary;
– have its own power of decision and participate in the shaping of measures taken by the Council and by the European Parliament in the manner provided for in this Treaty;
– exercise the powers conferred on it by the Council for the implementation of the rules laid down by the latter.'

In practice, the role of the Commission is best described by dividing it into the four basic functions described in the following paragraphs:

– the formulation of policy;
– the execution and administration of policy;
– the representation of the interests of the Community;
– the guardianship of the Treaties.

3.3 The Policy-making Function

There are three main mechanisms whereby the Commission develops the policy of the Community. It makes proposals for action; it drafts the budget which determines the allocation of resources (see 4.8); and it takes policy decisions within the limited powers it is granted by the Treaties.

Proposals for action take either a 'small' or a 'large' form. 'Small' initiatives are draft legislative acts prepared by the Commission for adoption by the Council of Ministers under the law-making powers of the Treaties. Almost all the provisions of the Treaty which grant a law-making power to the Council of Ministers begin 'on a proposal from the Commission . . .'. The Commission has a broad discretion in putting forward policy proposals, although some limits are imposed by the Treaty itself. For example, when making proposals for the adoption of measures in relation to the completion of the internal market, the Commission is required by Article 7C to take into account the difficulties faced by weaker economies as they prepare for the internal market. Article 100A(3) EC further requires all proposals made for measures concerned with the completion of the internal market under that provision which concern health, safety, environmental protection and consumer protection to take as a base a high level of protection.

'Large' initiatives are Commission's proposals for Community action within a broad field. Perhaps the best known is the Commission's White Paper *Completing the Internal Market*, but others include the *Social Action Programme* issued as the basis for action to implement the Community Social Charter, and more recently the so-called *Delors II* plan, on the restructuring of the Community's finances for the achievement of European Union (see 4.8).

The Commission has a limited power of decision under the Treaty. One example is Article 118 EC which gives the Commission the task of promoting close cooperation between the Member States in various fields of social policy including employment, labour relations, working conditions, vocational training and social security. In Cases 281/85, etc. *Germany et al.* v. *Commission (Migration Policy)* ([1987] ECR 3203) the Court of Justice held that where the Commission is granted a specific task under the Treaty, it must be regarded, implicitly, as having the power to take steps to achieve this task, including the power to adopt binding measures such as decisions. The Commission is also responsible for developing the Community's competition policy, which involves not only the enforcement of the prohibitions in Articles 85 and 86 EC on anticompetitive and monopolistic conduct against individual undertakings (a function better characterised as enforcement rather than policy implementation: 3.6), but also the development of general policy initiatives aimed at dismantling rigidities in public sector markets such as telecommunications. To this end it has a power of decision under Article 90(3) EC.

In the development of policy, the Commission's internal bureaucracy is assisted by internal working groups and Advisory Committees composed of national experts, or civil servants representing national interests, by networks of experts, and by 'Euroquangos' such as CEDEFOP, the Community's centre for the promotion of vocational training. The Commission – like the other political institutions – is also subject to intense lobbying by national and Community-based interest groups (Harlow, 1992).

3.4   The Executive and Administrative Function

Since the Community's bureaucracy is extremely small, and largely centrally-based, it relies for the most part for the implementation of policies upon the administrations of the Member States. The examples of 'direct implementation' of Community policy by the Commission are few, and can more accurately be characterised as activities of the Commission aimed at protecting the legal fabric of the Community such as the enforcement of the competition rules and the rules on state aids (see 3.6). The Commission's role in the 'indirect implementation' of the major policy areas such as external trade, customs, agriculture and social security for migrant workers is likewise supervisory, and consists in large part in the making of rules which the national administrations must observe and then ensuring that they are observed. The duty of loyalty to the Community contained in Article 5 EC requires national administrations to cooperate in the implementation of Community policies.

In laying down the rules for national administrations to follow, the Commission is commonly exercising a power delegated by the Council of Ministers under Article 145 EC. As amended by the Single European Act, this provision envisaged the creation by the Council of a clearer structure for the long-standing practice of delegating powers to Commission subject to the supervision of committees of national representatives chaired by a representative of the Commission. This structure is known as 'comitology', and is one mechanism whereby the Member States have extended their input into Community activities beyond the legislative role of the Council itself (see 4.7).

In its executive role, the Commission manages the Community's finances, and supervises both revenue collection and expenditure. More than half of the Community's funds go to the European Agricultural Guidance and Guarantee Fund, the Guarantee Section of which is charged with implementing the Community's agricultural price support system. The Commission also administers the Community's structural funds aimed at ensuring economic and social cohesion, namely the European Social Fund, the European Regional Development Fund and must now take on the task of managing the new Cohesion Fund. The management of smaller incentive funds, such as, for example, the programme of grants available under the ERASMUS scheme to encourage student mobility, is now frequently contracted out to outside bodies which are responsible to the Commission for the proper management of the funds.

3.5   The Representative Function

The supranational composition and role of the Commission make it uniquely qualified to fulfil the function of representing the interests of the European Community on the wider global stage. The Commission President is recognised as an important international statesman, attending international conferences, acting within international organisations and speaking on behalf of the Community, often in conjunction with the leader of the Member State which holds the Presidency of the Council of

Ministers. As third countries increasingly choose to deal with the Community rather than individual Member States, the Commission's role in establishing Community diplomatic missions in third countries and accrediting diplomatic missions from those countries is becoming more important.

The Commission also has the task of recommending the opening of negotiations with third states and of conducting negotiations leading to the conclusion of international agreements on behalf of the Community under the procedures in Article 228 EC.

3.6 Guardian of the Treaties

The Commission is the guardian of the legal framework of the Treaty, a role explicitly conferred by Article 155 EC. The Commission has a general power under Article 169 EC to refer to the Court of Justice alleged violations by the Member States of the Treaties and of the rules adopted thereunder (see Chapter 6). It has additional specific enforcement powers, for example in relation to state aids (Article 93 EC) and the control of the anti-competitive activities of public undertakings and undertakings entrusted with the performance of public services (Article 90 EC). It may in some circumstances authorise Member States to depart from the strict rules of Treaty; for example, it may authorise the Member States to restrict imports of third country products in free circulation in other Member States under Article 115 EC (12.12). It also supervises the right of the Member States to apply national measures to protect environmental and health and safety policies under Article 100A(4) EC, even where the Community has adopted harmonising measures (6.11 and 14.16).

Under Council Regulation 17 adopted in 1962, the Commission was granted numerous enforcement powers in relation to Articles 85 and 86 EC, which proscribe anti-competitive and monopolistic conduct on the part of undertakings within the Community. In exercising these powers, the Commission is subject to the control of the Court of Justice over the legality of its procedures.

3.7 The Council of Ministers: Composition and Basic Character

The Council of Ministers is composed of representatives of the Member States, at ministerial level 'authorised to commit' their government (Article 146 EC, as amended). The Council represents the intergovernmental element within the Community institutional structure. It meets, generally, in Brussels, where its Secretariat is based. The Presidency of the Council circulates on a six monthly rotation between the Member States. The President sits in the chair at Council meetings (see also 3.11). The Council meets when convened by the President, or at the request of one of its members or the Commission. As this implies, a member of the Commission with appropriate responsibilities normally attends Council meetings, although without a vote. The membership of the Council is not static. Although there is a body conventionally designated the 'General Council' composed of the Foreign Ministers of the Member States, which discusses issues of general concern to the Community, much of the practical work of the Community is undertaken by the sectoral, specialised Councils such as the 'Internal Market Council', composed of trade and industry ministers with special responsibility for the completion of the internal market and the 'Agriculture Council', composed of Agriculture ministers who oversee the development and implementation of the CAP. The fragmentation of the Council weakens its effectiveness, as there is insufficient general policy coherence within the legislative activities of the Community, although this function is fulfilled in part by the Commission, the European Council and the Presidency.

The tasks of the Council are set out in Article 145 EC. They are to ensure the coordination of the general economic policies of the Member States, to take decisions and to delegate implementing powers to the Commission. There is a tension between the first two tasks, in that they illustrate the sometimes irreconcilable dual role of the Council: to act as the forum for the representatives of the Member States, and to act as the Community's decision-making body. The Council also has the power under Article 152 EC to request the Commission to undertake any studies the Council considers desirable for the attainment of the objectives of the Community, and to submit to it any appropriate proposals. Used extensively this power could significantly limit the policy-making function of the Commission.

It is not possible to know exactly what happens within the Council. It deliberates in secret and no record of its business is published. Press Releases and briefings by national ministers are the only sources of information, apart from the published record in the Official Journal of legislative acts which the Council passes, or resolutions which it adopts. The members of the Council of Ministers are not politically accountable to any Community institution for their acts. The Parliament can and does ask questions of the Council, but the answers given are not always full or helpful. However, a convention is developing that the Presidency presents its programme of action for the next six months for debate in the Parliament. The level of accountability at the national level varies between the Member States. The Danish Parliament – the *Folketing* – exercises the tightest control, with the Danish representatives on the Council of Ministers being frequently required to delay Community decision-making processes in order to consult at a parliamentary level. Scrutiny within the UK Parliament is not as strict. The Council of Ministers is subject, like all the institutions, to the rule of law. This largely leaves its legislative discretion unfettered, although there are a number of overriding principles which legislative acts may not violate (see 5.4–5.7). This can lead to the annulment of legislative acts adopted by the

Council, or to actions for damages (see Part IV). Within narrow limits the Council is also responsible for a failure to act in the legislative field. In Case 13/83 *Parliament* v. *Council* ([1985] ECR 1513) the Parliament successfully challenged the failure of the Council to create a common transport policy using Article 175 EC. Although the Court of Justice would not substitute itself for the legislature and lay down what form such a policy should take, the case was widely interpreted as a rap on the knuckles for the Council for dilatory exercise of its legislative function.

Article 148 EC provides for simple majority voting, unless the Treaty provides otherwise. In practice, the Treaty almost always does so provide, and most legislative measures require the achievement of unanimity or a so-called qualified majority. Qualified majority voting means that under Article 148(2) EC, the votes of the Member States are weighted as in Table 3.1.

A qualified majority requires there to be at least 54 votes cast in favour of a measure. The weighting of votes in this manner departs in part from the theory of the equality of all states in international law, although the weighting does not fully reflect population differentials. The voting power of Germany has not been strengthened after unification although it is now much the biggest Member State. The weighting of the voting and the requirement of a minimum of 54 votes has the effect of allowing what would normally be at least three dissenting Member States to block a measure to be adopted under qualified majority voting. The reluctance of the Council of Ministers actually to commit itself to qualified majority-voting has been one of the consistent themes of institutional development in the Community. The Council has its own bureaucracy or Secretariat which, while smaller than the Commission's, fulfils a similar policy-making function. It is assisted by its own Legal Service.

Table 3.1 Qualified Majority Voting

Belgium	5
Denmark	3
Germany	10
Greece	5
Spain	8
France	10
Ireland	3
Italy	10
Luxembourg	2
Netherlands	5
Portugal	5
United Kingdom	10
Total	76

3.8   The Council of Ministers Acting as an Intergovernmental Body

On certain occasions, in particular where the subject-matter of the meeting falls outside the scope of Community competence, the representatives of the Member States will meet on an intergovernmental basis. The best known and most formalised instance of this is European Political Cooperation governed by Part III of the Single European Act and described in Chapter 2. This is now to be replaced by the Common Foreign and Security Policy (CFSP) under the Treaty of Maastricht, which is rather wider in scope and more supranational in nature with the possibility of qualified majority decision-making provided for. Intergovernmental cooperation between the Member States also grew up to coordinate policies on immigration, asylum, police cooperation and other home affairs matters. The Trevi Group and the Ad Hoc Group on Immigration in which the Member States met to discuss these matters are now to be replaced by the more formalised arrangements of Justice and Home Affairs in Title VI TEU.

The Community structures have also provided a framework for intergovernmental cooperation in certain areas lying at the margins of Community competence such as policy on culture, education and health. Measures adopted in this field have commonly been designated 'Decision of the Representatives of the Governments of the Member States, meeting in the Council'. An example is the Resolution of the Ministers for Culture Meeting within the Council of June 7 1991, on the development of the theatre in Europe (OJ 1991 C188/3). After the Treaty of Maastricht, such a resolution could be adopted within the context of the Community's own limited new competence in relation to culture (Article 128 EC). Most of these measures are not intended to be legally binding and are merely political declarations. This is acceptable provided the subject-matter of such acts does not trespass upon areas of Community competence. The Treaty of Maastricht should reduce the number of occasions on which resort is had to this formula. With the expansion of Community competence into areas such as culture, education and health, where the Community is given powers to encourage the coordination of national policies and to contribute to national policies (as opposed to powers to implement a common Community policy), it is to be anticipated that the legal form of the Council Recommendation will be used instead.

3.9   The European Council

The most prominent and most powerful form of intergovernmental cooperation within the Community is the European Council. The practice of summit meetings between the leaders of the Member States has long existed. Regular meetings have occurred since 1974, and the European Council was finally formalised in Article 2 of the SEA. This provided that the European Council should meet at least twice a year and that it should be attended not only by the Heads of State or Government, assisted by their Foreign Ministers, but also by the President of the Commission and one other Commissioner. Since, however, Article 2 SEA did not amend the constitutive Treaties of the Community itself, the European Council remained formally outside the structures of the Community, not subject to the control of the Court of Justice, but conversely with no legal power to act in pursuance of the Community's objectives. Of course, there would be nothing to prevent the Heads of State or Government meeting as the Council of Ministers; however, one of the strengths of the European Council, which has increasingly come to fulfil a troubleshooting role in pushing forward the process of European integration and resolving the conflicts between the Member States at the highest level, lies precisely in its informality. Article D TEU now designates the European Council as having a specific status within the European Union (as opposed to the narrower legal conception of the European Community). Its role is to 'provide the Union with the necessary impetus for its development' and to 'define the general political guidelines' for the Union.

A European Community without the European Council has now become unimaginable, although such a crucial role for the Member States in policy formulation was not envisaged by the founders of the Treaty. In practice, the European Council is not simply an opportunity, as it is sometimes portrayed in the British media, for the leaders of Member States reluctant to press further with European integration to halt the entire process. For example, Margaret Thatcher found the regular meetings of the European Council to be occasions when she could not always resist pressure for conformity, as with the agreement over the British budget rebate at the Fontainebleau summit in June 1984 (see 2.10). Furthermore, a Commission President such as Jacques Delors is able to exploit alliances with pro-integrationist leaders such as President Mitterrand of France in order to carry forward the objectives of the Community. An example of this is the budgetary discipline settlement agreed at the special meeting in Brussels in 1988. The essence of the European Council's function, more than any other Community body, is compromise. Leaders, whose domestic fate in elections will be judged largely according to their economic success, need to find a balance between promoting the 'good' elements of integration, whilst hindering the 'bad' ones. That means choosing between those Community proposals which are perceived, from the perspective of the domestic agenda, as excessively intrusive or insufficiently beneficial, and those which are not.

3.10 The Committee of Permanent Representatives (COREPER)

In addition to the help it gets from 'above' in the form of the resolution of serious conflicts at the level of the European Council, the Council of

Ministers also receives assistance from 'below' in the form of the preparatory work of the Committee of Permanent Representatives (COREPER). The Permanent Representatives are in effect the Ambassadors of the Member States to the Community, who are based in Brussels and who provide a continuity of presence which political representatives cannot. COREPER meets at two levels: COREPER I (deputy Permanent Representatives) whose remit covers more technical matters and COREPER II (Permanent Representatives themselves) who discuss the more controversial political matters, identifying the differences of view which the Council itself must settle at a political level. The workings of COREPER and the Council are further facilitated by working groups and committees which meet on a regular or ad hoc basis to discuss Community policy proposals at an early stage.

Formally, COREPER facilitates Council deliberations by permitting the division of the Council agenda into two parts. Part A contains items on which a unanimous view has been obtained within COREPER. These points can be agreed without discussion. Part B contains the points on which a decision cannot be reached without further discussion and probably compromise within the Council itself. These matters are regulated by the Council's own Rules of Procedure, which themselves represent, however, a fetter on the extent to which the Council can delegate effective authority to COREPER (see Case 68/86 *United Kingdom* v. *Council (Hormones)* ([1988] ECR 855) where the Court declared a Directive to be void, as the Council was in breach of its own Rules of Procedure in adopting a Directive by a written vote when two Member States (the UK and Denmark) were known to be against it).

3.11 The Presidency

The Presidency of the Council of Ministers circulates at six monthly intervals between the Member States, normally arranged alphabetically according to the title of the country in the national language (Belgique, Danmark, Deutschland, Eire, Ellas (Greece), etc.). In the present round of Presidencies, which began in January 1993, the Member States are reversed in pairs, to ensure that they alternate between the January–June slot and the July–December slot (i.e. Denmark, Belgium, Ireland, Germany etc.). In the first half of the year, the Community's everyday work is dominated by the CAP; in the second half of the year, it is the budget which normally occupies the agenda.

On paper the task of the Presidency of the Council of Ministers is a modest one. It is to convene and chair meetings of the Council, and to sign, on behalf of the Council, legislative and other acts adopted by the Council, or by the representatives of the Member States meeting within the Council. The Presidency acts as the Chair within all the fora convened within the Community structures, in the largest sense. This includes not only the General Council, the Sectoral Councils, the European Council and COREPER I and II, but also other fora of intergovernmental cooperation such as CFSP/EPC and Justice and Home Affairs. In practice, however, the Presidency has become a great deal more significant, usurping in part many of the policy-making and mediation functions of the Commission. The country holding the Presidency usually sees it as an opportunity to leave a distinctive mark upon the Community scene, and to be seen by the outside world as synonymous with the Community itself. It prepares and presents a programme of action for the Presidency and prioritises particular measures which it would like to see passed in the Council of Ministers. This it can achieve by controlling the agenda of the Council of Ministers, in conjunction with the Council's own Secretariat. The Dutch Presidency of the second half of 1991 was given the onerous responsibility of brokering the outcome of the intergovernmental conferences on Economic and Monetary Union and Political Union, and the agreement within the European Council on the text of the Treaty of Maastricht. The uneven progress of the ratification process in late 1992 was influenced by the somewhat ambivalent attitude of the UK Presidency. Not all Presidencies contain such important events in the calendar of integration, but Member States do vie with each other to have the most 'productive' term of office, although not all share the same idea of what this means. It is not clear to what extent the Community has benefited from the tendency of the Presidency to match the Commission's functions as mediator and broker of compromise deals, as initiator of policies, and as representative of the Community towards the outside world. The effect of the latter function is to emphasise the nature of the Community as a union of states, rather than a supranational entity.

3.12 The European Parliament: Composition, Basic Character and Powers

The European Parliament is composed of 518 directly elected representatives of the peoples of the States brought to together in the Community. The number of MEPs elected in each Member State is set out in Table 3.2 (Article 138(2) EC).

The Members of the European Parliament are elected in a five yearly cycle, with elections in 1979, 1984, 1989, 1994, etc. Since 1989, there has been a centre-left majority in the Parliament for the first time, with the Socialists as the largest single grouping. However, given the powers of the Parliament there is no governing party political coalition in the conventional sense. There is at present no uniform electoral procedure, and the UK is out of step with the other Member States in so far as it continues to elect the representatives for mainland Britain (Scotland, Wales and England) on the basis of single-member constituencies with a first-past-the-post system. Proportional representation is used in Northern Ireland. It is the task of the European Parliament to draw up proposals for a uniform electoral procedure, and, since the Treaty of Maastricht, to give

Table 3.2 Membership of the European Parliament

Belgium	24
Denmark	16
Germany	81
Greece	24
Spain	60
France	81
Ireland	15
Italy	81
Luxembourg	6
Netherlands	25
Portugal	24
United Kingdom	81

its assent to any provisions adopted for this purpose by the Council of Ministers, which must act unanimously. However, any changes to the existing system will need to be ratified by the Member States according to the national constitutional requirements, and so far the UK has remained trenchantly opposed to adopting a system of proportional representation based on multi-member constituencies.

The Treaty of Maastricht did not deal with the controversial problem of expanding the European Parliament to include more representatives from a unified Germany which is now much larger in population terms than the other Member States which also currently have 81 MEPs. However, a declaration attached to the Treaty committed the Member States to examine the problem with a view to settling, before the 1994 elections, the number of MEPs At the Edinburgh Summit in December 1992, the Member States agreed to increase the number of MEPs to 567, giving Germany 99 MEPs compared to 87 for France, Italy and the UK (see now Council Decision 93/81 OJ 1993 L33/15).

The origins of the European Parliament are extremely modest. Designated the 'Assembly' in the original Treaties, the Parliament was composed simply of delegates nominated by the national Parliaments and endowed with a narrow range of consultative and supervisory powers. Until the changes introduced by the Single European Act, the only input into the legislative process which was given to the Parliament (a name which it gave itself from 1962 onwards, and which was formally recognised in the Single European Act), was to be consulted by the Council on proposals made by the Commission. It has had mild supervisory powers over the Commission, including the right to put questions to the Commission (Article 140 EC) and the right to discuss the annual general report submitted by the Commission (Article 143 EC). It has also held from the beginning a draconian power of censure over the Commission, namely the power, by a two-thirds majority vote, to require the Commission to resign as a body. However, although threatened, this power has never been used, and in any event there would be nothing to prevent the Member States reappointing the same Commissioners.

Since then, the Parliament has grown in size as consequence of enlargement, changed its character through direct elections and acquired an important range of new powers. Clearly, there has always been a strong case for developing the role of the Parliament within the Community system, both in terms of its input into the decision-making process, and in terms of its control and supervisory power over the other institutions. The Community suffers from a serious 'democratic deficit', in so far as it exercises sovereign powers transferred by the Member States, but without the same degree of legislative input by an assembly of representatives elected by universal suffrage, and without the executive accountability of the Commission or the Council to such a body. Ironically, so long as the Parliament remained a non-elected body with 'dual mandate' members (national Parliament and European Parliament), the case for more powers could be defeated, by pointing to the low calibre and the low level of commitment of its members, who were generally more committed to their role as members of national Parliaments. Even now, some critics point to the absence of a coherent transnational party structure, the relatively low level of popular interest in the Parliament, and its alleged tendency to adopt positions on European integration which are out of step with popular feeling as reasons for continuing to limit the powers of the Parliament. The real reason may have more to do with the jealous protection of national sovereignty. The institution of a proper, effective European Parliament endowed with the full range of legislative and supervisory powers associated with Parliaments in liberal democracies would mean acknowledging that the Community had in truth reached the stage of a federation. At present, however, democracy is suffering, since power has been effectively taken out of the hands of national Parliaments, and given to Ministers who are not collectively responsible to any representative body. A step towards the enhancement of a 'European' party system comes in a new Article 138A EC which asserts the importance of political parties at the European level as a factor promoting integration, since they contribute to forming a European awareness and to expressing the political will of the citizens of the Union.

The Parliament has the power to organise its own work by adopting Rules of Procedure (Article 142 EC). It has maximised the effectiveness of its input by creating a committee structure in which the range of political views within the Parliament are represented, with individual Committees responsible for preparing draft amendments to legislative proposals. To maximise the effectiveness of its scrutiny of proposed legislation, since 1988 the Parliament has been able to agree an annual legislative programme with the Commission in order to enable it to manage its workload. The Parliament also acts on its own initiative in certain policy areas. The best known example is the setting up of a Committee concerned with institutional reform after the first elections in 1979 which drew up the DTEU. The business of the Parliament is managed by its President and

Vice-Presidents, who are elected from amongst the MEPs (Article 140 EC), and by the so-called Enlarged Bureau, on which the President and Vice-Presidents are joined by the Chairs of the Committees. The final say is held by the Plenary session of the Parliament, which meets eleven times a year. The current work of the Parliament is hampered by its geographical fragmentation: in accordance with established agreements between the Member States, plenary sessions are held in Strasbourg and occasionally in Luxembourg, but most of the Parliament's bureaucracy and support staff are located in Luxembourg, and Committee meetings are held in Brussels. There is longstanding conflict between the Parliament and certain Member States, since the Parliament would prefer to be relocated in a single city, but that desire was again frustrated by the European Council meeting in Edinburgh in December 1992 which largely preserved the status quo.

At present the European Parliament holds the following powers under the EC Treaty, in addition to those with which it was endowed under the original Treaties and described above. By Budgetary Treaties of 1970 and 1975 amending Articles 203–4 EC, the Parliament was given the status as co-budgetary authority with the Council of Ministers, although its power, in practice, to affect how the Community's resources are spent is very limited (see 4.9). The Commission is responsible to the Parliament in respect of accounting for expenditure. The Single European Act significantly increased the powers of the Parliament by giving it the power of assent (and therefore of veto) over the accession of new members (now Article O TEU) and the conclusion of association agreements with third states (now Article 228(3) EC). The Single European Act also introduced the cooperation procedure which allows the Parliament to give a second reading, and to propose further amendments, to certain legislative acts (4.4). Finally, the Single European Act extended the range of provisions where an opinion of the Parliament is required. These include the new competences – environment, economic and social cohesion, research and technological development – and a number of provisions of an institutional nature.

The Treaty of Maastricht takes Parliamentary involvement in the legislative procedure one step further. The assent provisions are expanded to include the adoption of a uniform electoral procedure (Article 138 EC), aspects of Community citizenship (Article 8A EC), reorganisation of the structural funds (Article 130D EC), certain aspects of the supervision of the ECB (Article 105(6) EC and the amendment of the Statute of the ECB (Article 106(5) EC). It gives the Parliament a power which parallels that given to the Council by Article 152 EC to request the Commission to submit proposals to it on matters which it considers Community legislation to be necessary (Article 138B EC). In addition to widening the instances in which the cooperation procedure is to be applied (e.g. environment, vocational training), the Treaty also introduces co-decision (see 4.5). Many provisions where the cooperation procedure previously applied have now been 'upgraded' to co-decision.

The Treaty of Maastricht also significantly enhances the position of the European Parliament as the guardian of the interests of Community citizens. Article 138C EC empowers the Parliament to set up temporary Committees of Inquiry to investigate alleged instances of maladministration on the part of the other institutions or bodies established under the Treaties, Article 138D EC formalises a right on the part of citizens of the Union to petition the Parliament on any matters coming within the Community's field of activity which affect them directly, and Article 138E EC provides for the appointment of an Ombudsman by the Parliament to receive and investigate complaints of maladministration by the Community institutions.

The range of powers held by the Parliament in relation to the intergovernmental activities of the Community in the sphere of foreign policy is very limited (Bieber, 1990). Article 30(4) Single European Act merely required the Parliament to be kept informed concerning European Political Cooperation, although in practice there was a greater level of contact, channelled through the Presidency, which has reported to the Parliament regularly and held meetings with the Committee on Political Affairs. The level of involvement is not significantly changed by the introduction of the new provisions on Common Foreign and Security Policy by the Treaty of Maastricht (Article J7 TEU) or the new pillar of Justice and Home Affairs (Article K6 TEU).

It still not possible, even after Maastricht, to characterise the Parliament as a fully operational democratic legislature; it has, for example, not received increased powers in the context of either the ECSC or Euratom Treaties. It is, however, important to stress its symbolic role within the Community political system. It has become the platform on which statesmen and women from inside and outside the Community choose to address their thoughts on European integration. The address given by Queen Elizabeth II to the European Parliament in May 1992 constituted an historic event from the perspective of both the UK and the Parliament itself in its search for greater international recognition.

3.13 The Economic and Social Committee (ECOSOC) and the Committee of the Regions

The idea of the ECOSOC, and now, after the Treaty of Maastricht, the Committee of the Regions, is to provide for the formal representation, within the Community structure, of disparate economic, social, and now regional interests. The ECOSOC originated in a similar body – the Consultative Committee of the European Coal and Steel Community (Article 18 ECSC). Under Article 193 EC the ECOSOC is given advisory status, and this in practice means being consulted by the Council and Commission where the Treaty so provides (e.g. Article 100A), or where those institutions consider it appropriate (Article 198 EC). In practice, it also issues 'own initiative' opinions, and this practice is formalised by Article 198 EC, as amended.

The 189 members of the ECOSOC are allocated between the Member States as set out in Table 3.3.

Table 3.3 Membership of the ECOSOC

Belgium	12
Denmark	9
Germany	24
Greece	12
Spain	21
France	24
Ireland	9
Italy	24
Luxembourg	6
Netherlands	12
Portugal	12
United Kingdom	24

They are appointed by the Council of Ministers, on the nomination of the Member States, for four years, with appointments renewable. The members are appointed in their personal capacity and must not be bound by any mandatory instructions. This is strengthened by Article 194 EC, as amended, which insists that the members of the ECOSOC must be 'completely independent in the performance of their duties, in the general interest of the Community'.

The interests to be represented are listed, on a non-exhaustive basis, in Article 193 EC. They include representatives of producers, framers, carriers, workers, dealers, craftsmen and professional occupations and representatives of the general public. In practice, members are divided into three categories: I – employers; II – workers; III – others, including agricultural interests, professional associations and consumers. The ECOSOC is organised in specialised sections (e.g. agriculture, transport, etc.) which prepare draft reports on legislation for consideration in plenary session.

The Treaty of Maastricht established a Committee of the Regions, composed of representatives of regional and local bodies (Articles 198A–C EC). Like the ECOSOC, the Committee has 189 members, divided on the same basis amongst the Member States. The provisions on the appointment of members by the Council and the organisation of the work of the Committee largely parallel those governing the ECOSOC. It is to be consulted where the Treaty so provides, and where the Council and Commission so decide. It may also issue own initiative opinions, and is to be advised of instances where the ECOSOC is to be consulted, but it is not, with the possibility that it might then decide to submit an opinion, believing there to be significant regional interests affected (Article 198C EC). The new provisions on a Community policy in the field of culture

(Article 128 EC, as amended), as well as the revised provisions on Economic and Social Cohesion (regional policy) (Articles 130A–E EC, as amended) provide for the consultation of the Committee of the Regions but the amended provisions on environmental policy do not, despite the obvious links with regional policy (Articles 130R–T EC).

3.14   The Court of Auditors

Under the Treaty of Maastricht, the Court of Auditors acquires the status of an institution. Accordingly, the provisions governing the establishment, composition, tasks and duties of the Court of Auditors (Articles 188A–C EC) have been shifted into the Chapter on the institutions. It has been in existence since 1977, and consists of twelve members – one for each Member State – who are persons qualified to serve on a body which has the task of carrying out the Community audit, and whose independence is beyond doubt. They are appointed for six year terms by the Council of Ministers. The European Parliament, which has particular budgetary responsibilities, is consulted on the appointments. The protected legal status of the members of the Court of Auditors during their term of office resembles that of the members of the Court of Justice, although they can be deprived of their office by the Court of Justice (Article 188B(7) EC).

The auditing task of the Court of Auditors extends not only to the revenue and expenditure of the Community itself, but also to all bodies set up by the Community, unless other arrangements have been made. By providing a statement of assurance regarding the reliability of the accounts and the underlying financial transactions conducted by the Community, the Court of Auditors assists the Parliament in giving the Commission a discharge in respect of the implementation of the budget.

3.15   The European Investment Bank (EIB)

The European Investment Bank has separate legal personality, although it is governed by the provisions of the EC Treaty – now Articles 198D–E). It was established by the original Treaty of Rome, and it has a particular function to provide investment loans to assist the funding of projects aimed at promoting regional development within the Community, and projects of particular interest to two or more Member States. Its revenue is derived from money subscribed by the Member States and money which it raises on the international capital markets. The management of the Bank is entrusted to a Board of Governors, a Board of Directors and a Committee of Management.

3.16   The Institutions of Economic and Monetary Union

The institutions of Economic and Monetary Union, which are established by Article 4A and Title VI of the EC Treaty, as amended by the Treaty of

Maastricht, replace the earlier institutions such as the European Monetary Cooperation Fund. The most important bodies are the European System of Central Banks (ESCB), composed of the European Central Bank (ECB), which is established with separate legal personality, and the national central banks (Article 106 EC). Details are contained in the Treaty and in the associated Protocols and Declarations. Eventually, the European Central Bank will have the exclusive right to authorise the issue of banknotes within the Community (Article 105A EC). The seat of the Bank is as yet unresolved. Preparation for the work of the ESCB and the ECB will be undertaken by the European Monetary Institute (EMI) established under the transitional provisions of Article 109F EC, which takes over from the existing Committee of Governors of Central Banks. The transition to monetary union, and the associated coordination of national policies, will also be assisted by a temporary Monetary Committee with advisory status (Article 109C(1) EC) which will be dissolved and replaced on transition to the third stage of monetary union by an Economic and Financial Committee (Article 109C(2) EC).

3.17   The Court of Justice and the Court of First Instance

Since 1988 there have been two courts at the Community level sitting in Luxembourg: the Court of Justice, and, attached to it, and empowered to hear only certain categories of case, the Court of First Instance (Article 168A EC and Council Decision 88/591 OJ 1988 L319/1). Appeal lies on points of law from the Court of First Instance to the Court of Justice itself. The Court of Justice has thirteen judges (one for each Member State, plus an additional judge to make an odd number for plenary sessions) and the Court of First Instance has twelve judges. The Court of Justice is assisted by six Advocates General, who submit opinions on each of the cases heard by the Court. The Court of Justice is often influenced by the views of the Advocate General. Advocates General have the same status and privileges as judges. The Court of First Instance does not have Advocates General, but a member of the Court may adopt that role where the Court considers it necessary. The Judges and Advocates General of the Court of Justice are chosen from persons 'whose independence is beyond doubt and who possess the qualifications required for appointment to the highest judicial office in their respective countries or who are jurisconsults of recognised competence' (Article 167 EC). The qualification to be a judge of the Court of First Instance is likewise independence, and 'the ability required for appointment to judicial office' (Article 168A(3) EC).

The members of both courts are appointed by common accord of the Member States for six years, with partial replacement every three years (Articles 167 and 168A EC). Each court elects a President. Further provisions governing the operation of the Court of Justice and the Court of First Instance are contained in the Statute of the Court of Justice appended to the founding Treaties, the Court of Justice's own Rules of Procedure which are approved by the Council, and the Council Decision establishing the Court of First Instance referred to above.

The Court of Justice sits in plenary session, or in chambers of five or three judges. In order to make the work of the Court more effective, and to limit the role of the plenary session to that of deciding the most important cases, it now sits in plenary session only in cases to which an institution or a Member State is party, where a request is made by one party. Most preliminary rulings are also heard by chambers. The Court of First Instance normally sits only in chambers of three or five judges.

The basic task of the Court of Justice is simple: it is to ensure that the law is observed (Article 164 EC; see also Article 31 ECSC). Articles 169–186 and 215 EC govern the most important types of action which can be brought before the Court and the types of rulings which it may give. Reference should be made to 1.5 for an outline of the basic work of the Court. The jurisdiction of the Court of First Instance is restricted; it hears only staff cases brought under Article 179 EC, certain actions under the ECSC Treaty between the Commission and undertakings, and appeals brought by undertakings against decisions of the Commission in relation to the competition rules in Articles 85–90 EC. Although it was originally created in order to lessen the excessively heavy workload on the Court of Justice and to reduce time delays in hearing cases, the Court of First Instance has tended to be underemployed since its inception. The possibility exists for an additional transfer of jurisdiction, most obviously of cases brought by undertakings aggrieved by the imposition or refusal to impose countervailing anti-dumping duties on goods alleged to be imported into the Community from third countries at subsidised prices; however, the Member States are not willing and have so far stalled the proposals of the Court. Since the right of appeal on points of law continues to exist, and since that right is likely to be taken up by most undertakings in competition cases who fail at first instance, it is not clear that the new judicial structure will be any better than the old one, or that delays will be substantially reduced. One alternative so far rejected by the Member States has been substantially to increase the number of judges within the Court of Justice itself thus creating many more chambers. The proposal by Jacqué and Weiler (1990) for a new judicial architecture with four regionally-based Community Courts and a European High Court of Justice has also not found favour.

The Treaty of Maastricht has brought a number of important changes to the jurisdiction of the Court of Justice. Amendments are made to include the new institutions of Economic and Monetary Union, in particular the European Central Bank, within the system of judicial review. Judicial review is extended to cover the acts of the European Investment Bank and the Parliament which have legal effects. Provision is also made for financial penalties to be imposed on Member States which fail to comply with judgments of the Court of Justice establishing an infringement of the Treaties or rules adopted thereunder.

At first glance, the role of the Court of Justice, like the other institutions, is limited by the principle of 'attributed powers'. As a creature of Treaty, the Court of Justice can only hear actions and give remedies where provided for in the constitutive Treaties; however, it is arguable that with the evolution of the institutional structure and the range of competences and activities of the Community the overriding duty of the Court to ensure the rule of law should be regarded as more important than the strict limitations of the Treaties. In fact, the Court of Justice has made a number of innovations within the jurisdictional structure of the Treaties, allowing acts of the European Parliament to be subject to judicial review and giving it a limited power to bring actions against the acts of the other institutions. These are *de facto* developments now formally recognised by the Treaty of Maastricht. Arnull (1990b) has gone further and has argued that in fact the Court of Justice has an inherent jurisdiction which requires it where appropriate to fill in gaps in the system of legal remedies under the Treaties. In his view, in extending its jurisdictional scope, the Court is acting no differently to the other institutions which have *de facto* extended their powers in response to political imperatives.

Summary

1 The role and tasks of the institutions are not exhaustively stated in the Treaties. Regard must also be had to constantly changing interinstitutional dynamics.

2 The Commission is the pivotal political institution. It has policy-making, executive, enforcement and representative functions.

3 The Council of Ministers has the primary legislative function. It is also the body which represents the national interest, and tends towards intergovernmentalist methods, relying on the achievement of consensus. It has seen an increase in its influence, in particular through related bodies and structures: the European Council, COREPER, comitology etc. The Presidency of the Council of Ministers has also evolved into an important motor of the Community integration process.

4 The Parliament is gradually evolving into a legislature, ensuring democracy and accountability within the Community.

5 The interests of employers, unions, consumers and other corporatist interests are protected by the Economic and Social Committee (ECOSOC). Regional interests are protected by the Committee of the Regions introduced by the Treaty of Maastricht.

6 The Court of Justice and the Court of First Instance ensure the rule of law in the Community. They have acquired a central role in maintaining the momentum of integration.

Questions

1 Identify the mechanisms whereby national interests are recognised and represented within the institutional structures of the Community. To what

extent does the influence of national interests extend outside the Council of Ministers, which is intended to represent national interests?

2 Would you agree with the suggestion that the Community does not possess an institutional structure which easily facilitates overall coherence of policy formulation and policy implementation?

3 To what extent has the Council usurped the roles of the other institutions?

4 Which institution would you consider to have changed most since the establishment of the Community, and in what ways?

Workshop

Formulate a set of proposals for the reform of the Community institutions which make them:

(a) more democratic and accountable in composition and working methods; and

(b) more effective in accomplishing their tasks under the Treaty.

Further Reading

Harlow (1992) 'A Community of Interests? Making the Most of European Law', 55 *Modern Law Review*, 331.

Jacobs and Corbett, (1991) The European Parliament, Longman.

Lodge (1989) 'EC Policymaking: institutional considerations', in Lodge (1989).

Ludlow (1991) 'The European Commission', in Keohane and Hoffmann (1991).

Pinder (1991) Ch. 2, 'Institutions or Constitution'.

Williams (1991) 'Sovereignty and Accountability in the European Community', in Keohane and Hoffmann (1991).

4 The Community and its Institutions at Work

4.1 Introduction

This chapter introduces the work of the Community, focusing on its ability to make binding legal acts, to raise and to spend its own revenue, and on the key mechanisms which have evolved to make these activities more effective and to extend the role of the Community. The Chapter concludes with a discussion of interinstitutional disputes.

4.2 Community Legal Acts

There are certain basic conditions which a valid legal act of the Community institutions must satisfy. These are in part contained in the Treaty, and can in part be derived from the case law of the Court of Justice. Article 190 EC requires Regulations, Directives and Decisions adopted by the Council, by the Commission or by the Council and Parliament jointly to refer to any proposals and opinions required to be obtained under the Treaty, and to contain a statement of reasons. A statement of reasons facilitates the process of judicial review, allowing any interested parties, and the Court where appropriate, to discover at a glance the circumstances which enjoined the adopting institution to act (see Case 24/62 *Commission* v. *Germany (Brennwein)* [1963] ECR 63). The intensity of the duty to give reasons depends upon the type of act adopted (a general legislative act requires less specific reasons than an individual act, such as one which imposes a pecuniary sanction on an undertaking for breach of the competition rules) and the circumstances in which an act is adopted. Where the institution must act urgently, a cursory statement of reasons may be sufficient (Case 16/65 *Firma Schwarze* v. *Einfuhr- und Vorratstelle für Getreide und Futtermittel* [1965] ECR 877). Article 191 EC further makes provision for the entry into force of binding acts of the institutions, and for their publication in the *Official Journal* and notification to addressees as appropriate.

Every legal act requires a legal basis, and reference must normally be made in the recitals to the concrete enabling power, generally to be found in the Treaty itself, but in the case of delegated legislation, located in an enabling legislative act. Under the Treaty system, because of the specific organisation of the powers of the institutions which may mean that the choice of legal basis affects the degree of input of a particular institution, the choice of legal basis is an important element in the legislative process. According to the Court of Justice it is a matter of law:

'the choice of the legal basis for a measure may not depend simply on an institution's conviction as to the objective pursued but must be based on objective factors which are amenable to judicial review' (Case 45/86 *Commission* v. *Council (Generalised Tariff Preferences)* [1987] ECR1493 at p. 1520).

An incorrect reference or a general reference to the Treaty as a whole is insufficient. Although an explicit reference is not absolutely necessary, the absence of such a reference will render a measure subject to challenge if the parties concerned and the Court of Justice are left uncertain as to the precise legal basis in fact used (Case 45/86 *Commission* v. *Council (Generalised Tariff Preferences)*). The problem of incorrect legal bases, and the litigation to which this has given rise in the context of interinstitutional disputes, is considered in 4.12.

There is no single law-making process for the Community. A complete picture of the law-making process can only be derived from a detailed study of the Treaties. There are, however, three basic patterns to which the majority of provisions in the EC Treaty which grant a law-making power to the Council of Ministers conform. The simplest procedure involves the Council acting, either by a qualified majority, or unanimously, on a proposal from the Commission, and after consulting, where required, the Parliament and/or the Economic and Social Committee (ECOSOC). This model dates from the original Treaty of Rome, but is still used for certain provisions, and has been introduced in new areas of competence where the Member States have sought to minimise parliamentary input. It is termed here the 'old procedure', and is discussed in 4.3. It could also be termed the single reading procedure. The Single European Act introduced the co-operation procedure and this is examined in 4.4. Most recently, the Treaty of Maastricht introduced co-decision, a form of joint legislative action by the Council and the Parliament. This is discussed in 4.5. Both these two models also require the Commission to initiate legislation.

The right of proposal is important. The Commission maintains control over the proposal until its adoption or rejection by the Council. This is confirmed by Article 189A EC, as amended by the Treaty of Maastricht. The Commission may amend its proposal at any point during the law-making process, and the Council requires unanimity in order to amend a Commission proposal, regardless of whether the law-making power under which it acts requires only a qualified majority for the adoption of an act (formerly Article 149(1) EEC). In Case 355/87 *Commission* v. *Council (Italo–Algerian Maritime Transport)* ([1989] ECR 1517) the Commission objected to what it saw as the abuse of the Council's right of amendment. It argued that the Council had reversed the effect of its proposal. The Court found for the Council by holding on the facts that both the measure adopted and the proposal were designed to achieve the same objective, without ruling on the greatly differing submissions made by the two institutions on the scope of the right of amendment. The Commission can, of course, prevent the Council from adopting an amended version of its proposal to which it objects by withdrawing it from consideration.

A minority of law-making powers under the Treaty differ significantly from this pattern. An example is Article 168A(2) EC which makes provision for the transfer of additional categories of cases to the Court of First Instance. That provision requires the Council to act, on the request of the Court of Justice, and after consulting the European Parliament and the Commission. Here the Commission's role is merely consultative.

4.3   The Old Procedure

The simplest form of the old procedure involves a Commission proposal and a Council decision. This is illustrated by Article 51 EC which provides for adoption of measures by the Council aimed at securing the social security rights of migrant workers. More frequently, consultation with the ECOSOC, and/or the European Parliament is mandated. Article 128 EEC on vocational training was one of the few examples of ECOSOC consultation without Parliament consultation, but this anomalous provision has now been replaced by Article 126 EC. The old style procedure retains its attraction for the Member States as evidenced by Article 100C(1) EC, a new power granted to the Council to determine, unanimously, on a proposal from the Commission, and after consulting the European Parliament, the categories of third countries nationals who require a visa in order to enter the Community. A number of variants on the old style are included in the EC Treaty, as amended; an example is Article 8A(2) which provides for the adoption of measures to give effect to the general right of residence for Community citizens set out in Article 8A(1) EC by the Council acting unanimously, on a proposal by the Commission, and after obtaining the *assent* of the European Parliament.

The old style is used for two of the Treaty's important general law-making powers which will be discussed below in 4.10, namely Articles 100 and 235 EC, which both require a unanimous decision of the Council. A few instances remain in the Treaty where the old style procedure is used in conjunction with a qualified majority (Article 43 EC – agricultural policy; Article 113 EC – external trade policy), but in most instances law-making powers requiring only a qualified majority in the Council were altered by the SEA to increase parliamentary input from consultation to cooperation.

Consultation of the ECOSOC and the Parliament means just that; there is no obligation on the part of the Council to follow the opinion. However, the Council must actually receive the opinion, not simply ask for it (Case 138/79 *Roquette Frères* v. *Council* [1980] ECR 3333). A measure adopted by the Council before it receives the Parliament's opinion can be annulled for breach of an essential procedural requirement. The Parliament must be given sufficient time to adopt its opinion; this can take some time, since the draft opinion is first worked on within the Parliament's committee structure, before it comes to the plenary session for adoption. However, failure by the Parliament to issue an opinion within a reasonable time limit would probably not prevent the Council from validly adopting an act without the opinion.

Effective consultation always depends on the goodwill of the parties. Relations between the Council and the Parliament are not perfect. Despite the *Roquette* case, the Parliament regularly documents instances where the Council takes at least a preliminary decision before receiving the Parliament's opinion, although it has yet to take action before the Court on this matter. On the other hand, the Council has a practice, when applying Article 113 which does not require consultation of the Parliament, to consult it voluntarily in any event. The Council also reconsults the Parliament in cases where it proposes to change the legal basis of a measure, in particular where this changes the procedure under which it is adopted. An example is provided by the Titanium Dioxide Directive which gave rise to litigation discussed in 4.12, where the legal basis was changed from Article 100A EC (internal market – cooperation procedure) to Article 130S EC (environment – simple consultation). Reconsultation should likewise occur where the Council departs markedly from the text on which the Parliament has given its opinion. This point was tested recently in Case C-65/90 *Parliament* v. *Council (Cabotage Regulation)* (16.7.1992) where the Court held that where there was a lapse of three years between the Parliamentary Opinion and the adoption of the Regulation, and the Council had adopted a substantially different proposal, reconsultation was required.

4.4 The Cooperation Procedure

The introduction of the cooperation procedure essentially appends a second reading of proposed legislation in the European Parliament onto the existing consultation procedure. It usually operates in combination with ECOSOC consultation. This not only gives the Parliament a 'second bite at the cherry' in the process of formulating Community legislation, but it also involves it in a more complex interactive process with the Council. The details of the cooperation procedure, originally introduced by Articles 6 and 7 SEA and now to be found in Article 189C EC (as amended by the Treaty of Maastricht), are set out in Fig 4.1. The principal law-making powers in the EEC Treaty covered by the cooperation procedure after the adoption of the Single European Act included Article 100A (measures for the completion of the internal market) Articles 49, 54(2), 56(2) and 57 (measures for the achievement of free movement of workers, providers of services and the self-employed), and Article 118A

Figure 4.1   The Cooperation Procedure – Article 189C EC

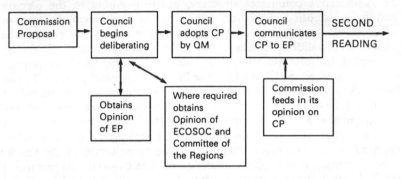

FIRST READING

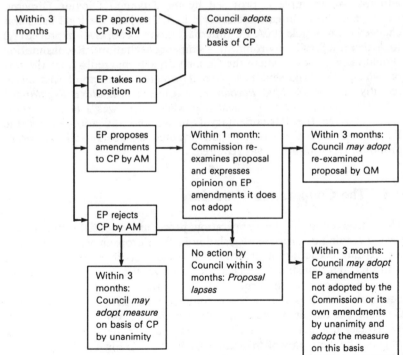

SECOND READING

ABBREVIATIONS

CP = Common Position   SM = Simple Majority of MEPs voting
AM = Absolute majority of   QM = Qualified Majority
     MEPs = 518/2 + 1 = 260   EP = European Parliament

(health and safety of workers). With the exception of Article 118A, each of these law-making powers is now, after the Treaty of Maastricht, 'upgraded' to Council–Parliament co-decision.

Table 4.1 sets out the most significant Treaty provisions in which Article 189C EC is now to be used following the amendments introduced by the Treaty of Maastricht.

The cooperation procedure is also to be used in the context of the Social Policy Protocol agreed by all the Member States with the exception of the United Kingdom.

The introduction of the cooperation procedure was important because it revealed the first signs of Council accountability to the Parliament. The Council has the obligation under Article 189C(b)(1) EC to inform the Parliament of the reasons which led it to adopt its common position. The Parliament has objected on numerous occasions that the Council has adopted a cavalier attitude towards this vitally important aspect of the cooperation procedure. Rarely does the Parliament obtain what it ideally wants, namely a specific reaction to each of the amendments it proposed on first reading. In order to prevent the second reading becoming cumbersome, the Parliament has, in its Rules of Procedure, restricted the range of amendments which can be considered on second reading in general terms to a return to its position on first reading or changes to the original draft contained in the Council's common position. Formally, if the common position amounts to a significant change from the original

Table 4.1 The cooperation procedure under Article 189C EC

EC Treaty Article	Nature of power
75	Common transport policy
103	Multilateral surveillance of economic policies to ensure closer coordination
104A and 104B	Equal access to financial institutions
105A(2)	Issuing of coins
118A	Health and safety of workers
125	Implementing decisions on the work of the European Social Fund
127	Vocational training policy
129	Incentive measures in the public health field
129D	Trans-European networks
130E	Implementing decisions in relation to the European Regional Development Fund
130S(1)	Environment
130W	Development cooperation

draft put before the Parliament, reconsultation (i.e. a new first reading) should be required. Occasionally there has been dispute between the Parliament and the Council as to whether it is reconsultation or a second reading when the measure comes back to the Parliament, although the latter body has been prepared to back down in order to avoid blocking the passage of measures which it is in favour of. The Parliament has been vigilant in protecting its prerogatives under the cooperation procedure through legal basis litigation (see 4.12).

4.5   Council-Parliament Co-decision

Article 189B EC introduces the new legislative procedure, termed 'co-decision' by the commentators, but not by the Member States themselves, who shied away from using the term in the Treaty of Maastricht. Measures adopted under the new procedures are signed by the Presidents of both the Parliament and the Council, and consequent amendments have been introduced into the judicial review procedures of the Treaty to recognise the co-responsibility of the two institutions. Essentially, the co-decision procedure, as set out in Fig 4.2 constitutes a more complex attempt to achieve Parliament and Council consensus on a common legislative text. In addition to the second reading procedure, which is materially identical to that used in the context of the cooperation procedure, a Conciliation Committee and a possible third reading are grafted on. In the context of a failure to agree within the Conciliation Committee, the Council retains a positive final say, in that it can seek to adopt a text based on its common position; the Parliament has only a negative final say, in that it can block the adoption of the Council's preferred text. This may create a destabilising element in the whole procedure, and the Parliament will come under great pressure not to cause a legislative blockage.

The Conciliation Committee is composed of the members of the Council and an equal number of representatives of the Parliament. Within the Committee, agreement can be reached only where a qualified majority of the members of the Council and a simple majority of the representatives of the Parliament are in favour. The Rules of Procedure of the Parliament determine the delegation of members of the Parliament to the Committee, and their responsibility to the Parliament as a whole. The task of the Commission in the final phase of the co-decision procedure is to participate in the work of the Conciliation Committee and to promote the achievement of agreement between the Parliament and the Council. The Commission's legislative role is reduced in the context of the co-decision procedure.

Table 4.2 sets out those fields in which Article 189B co-decision applies under the EC Treaty as amended.

Figure 4.2 Council/European Parliament Co-decision: Article 189B EC

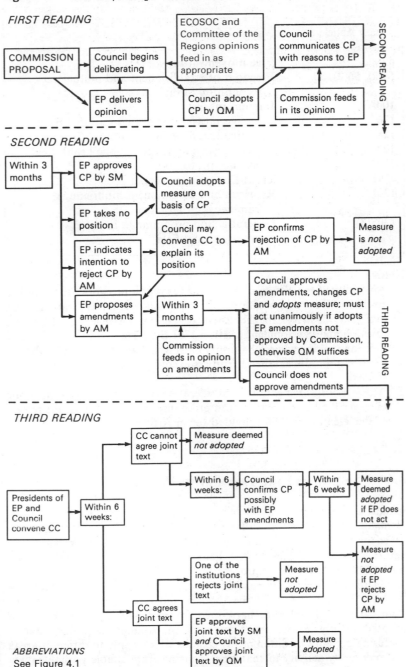

Table 4.2   Co-decision under Article 189B EC

Treaty Article	Nature of power
49	Free movement of workers
54(2), 56(2), 57	Freedom of establishment and mutual recognition of diplomas
100A	Internal market
126	Incentive measures in the educational field
128	Incentive measures in the cultural field
129	Incentive measures in the public health field
129A	Consumer protection
129D	Trans-European networks
130I	Research and development multi-annual framework programme
130S(3)	General action programmes in the environmental field

Notes:

1. An oddity of the Treaty of Maastricht is that it provides for the use of co-decision in combination with Council *unanimity* (rather than qualified majority) in the areas of culture (Article 128 EC) and research and development (Article 130I EC). The rigidities of Council decision-making where unanimity must be achieved may render the co-decision procedure rather a fruitless exercise for the Parliament in that context.
2. Article 189B(8) EC calls for consideration of the widening of the scope of application of the co-decision procedure in the context of the review of the Treaties in 1996 provided for in Article N(2) TEU.

4.6   The State of the Legislative Process

It must be concluded that while the legislative process of the European Community is now vastly different and more complex than that established in the original Treaties, it is still strongly intergovernmental in nature. This contributes to the generally high level of secrecy which surrounds the law-making process, and to the absence of transparency. The increase in complexity has not overcome the lack of accountability on the part of the Council for the manner and type of decisions it takes. Community legal acts are bargained for and negotiated, rather than debated openly. Some areas such as environmental policy have a confusing plethora of different procedures which apply to different areas of Community activity in that field, ranging from simple parliamentary consultation to co-decision. Significant areas of Community competence are also still excluded from the new procedures, including agricultural policy, indirect taxation and the system of Community own resources, as well as the general legislative powers in Articles 100 and 235 EC. The general lack of agreement between the institutions on essential elements of the law-making process has resulted in a proliferation of disputes being submitted to the Court of Justice for resolution in the legal sphere, in particular in the matter of legal basis (4.12).

The democratic deficit is only very partially offset by alternative mechanisms whereby different interests can ensure input into the legislative process. Although the intensity and effectiveness of lobbying in the Community has increased dramatically since the early 1980s, it remains only a partial substitute for a 'genuinely' democratic and legitimate legislative process (Harlow, 1992).

The legislative process should not be examined in isolation from the extensive structures of 'comitology' which largely determine the manner in which powers under primary legislative instruments are exercised in practice.

4.7 Comitology

The term 'comitology' refers to the practice within the Council of delegating implementing powers by primary legislation to the Commission, to be exercised in conjunction with committees of national civil servants which wield varying degrees of influence over the executive process. Whether one regards the practice of comitology as an enhancement of the effectiveness of the Community's institutional structure, or as a bureaucratic mechanism which rids Community decision-making of its last vestiges of democratic accountability is a moot point. Certainly, the creation of the supervisory committee system whereby delegations by the Council of Ministers to the Commission under the third indent of Article 145 EC are subject to the control of national representatives has been described as 'possibly one of the most significant organic developments in the Community's institutional structure' (Bradley, 1992: 720).

As set out in Council Decision 87/373 (OJ 1987 L197/33), comitology now takes three basic forms, with a number of variants. The least intrusive Committee is the Advisory Committee (Procedure I), to which the Commission submits a draft of the measures it proposes to adopt. The Commission must take 'the utmost account' of the opinion delivered by the Committee, but is not prevented by a negative opinion from adopting the measure. Under Procedure II, the draft is considered by a Management Committee, which has the power, by a qualified majority, to delay the adoption of the measure by the Commission, during which time the Council itself can adopt a different decision by a qualified majority. The most restrictive type of Committee is the Regulatory Committee (Procedure III), where the support of a qualified majority of the committee is required for the Commission draft. If there is not sufficient support, the power of decision reverts to the Council, but if this institution does not act within three months, the Commission may adopt the act. The three procedures themselves incorporate a number of variants, and the delegating power granted by the Council will specify which procedure and variant applies in each case.

Comitology in this form is not supported by the Commission, which feels its discretion is excessively limited by Member State interference; this argument has strength in the sense that the intention of the third indent of Article 145 was surely to intensify the separation of powers within the Community by consolidating the executive function within the Commission, not to intensify the powers of the Member States. The Parliament too is opposed since it fears that its prerogatives under the legislative process are restricted by forms of delegation of powers to the Commission under which the Council and the Member States retain control, but which bypass the consultative role of the Parliament. The Parliament unsuccessfully attempted to challenge the Council's Decision formalising the structures of comitology (Case 302/87 *Parliament* v. *Council (Comitology)* [1988] ECR 5615), but its attempt failed on the procedural question of its standing to bring annulment actions under Article 173 EC before the Court of Justice, rather than an examination of the merits of its arguments. To protect the Parliament's interests, the Commission has agreed that draft measures going before the Committees will be forwarded to the Parliament for information.

4.8 Community Finances

The budgetary regime envisaged by the original Treaties of national contributions – the traditional method of funding international organisations – is now entirely supplanted by the 1970 and 1975 Budgetary Treaties, the 1984 agreement on the UK budget rebate, the 1988 agreement between the Member States on the restructuring of the budget and the reallocation of revenues (the so-called Delors I package – see 2.13), and the 1988 interinstitutional agreement which has significantly reduced the potential for conflict within the budgetary process. Major budgetary proposals are now on the table before the Council of Ministers. This is a proposal termed the 'Delors II package' which is intended to update the financial structure and resourcing of the Community in order to make it possible to achieve the goals of Maastricht (*From the Single Act to Maastricht and Beyond: the Means to match our Ambitions* Com (92) 2000). The Community's budget, standing in 1992 at the level of 66.5 billion ECU, amounts to just over 1% of the Community GDP, and under 4% of the national budgets of the Member States. The Delors II package proposed a budget of 87.5 ECU for 1997 (at 1992 prices), a rise from 1.15% to 1.37% of Community GNP. At the Edinburgh European Council in December 1992, a compromise was reached on the basis of a Community budget of 1.2% of GNP in 1993, rising to 1.27% by 1999.

The European Community is now, in principle, financed by a system of 'own resources', that is revenue to which it is entitled as of right, rather than national contributions. Contributions can, of course, be withheld; own resources cannot. This should mean that the money accrues to the Community automatically, irrespective of the relative wealth or poverty of the Member States. The Community's revenue has four components:

– customs duties charged on goods at the Community's external frontiers;
– levies charged on agricultural products at the external frontiers;
– a proportion of the VAT levied by the Member States up to a ceiling of 1.4%;
– since the 1988 budget agreement between the Member States, a fourth resource calculated according to national GNP, which makes up the shortfall between the three 'traditional' own resources and the Community's necessary expenditure.

The fourth resource represents a return towards the notion of national contributions. However, the concern has grown, as the Community has enlarged to include Member States at greatly differing levels of economic development and prosperity, that the effect of the traditional own resources was increasingly regressive. That is, it was penalising the poorer Member States at the expense of the richer ones. This is because the proportion of customs duties and levies within the total Community revenues has been dropping as customs duties have gradually been reduced in the move towards global free trade, and as the Community has become increasingly self-sufficient in agricultural resources, and the VAT element, which the Member States were under pressure to increase because of the need for increased Community revenues, was weighing heavily on the poorer Member States with high tax rates and a greater level of consumption in relation to production. This led to the reintroduction of a contributory element, related to ability to pay. In 1992, VAT still accounted for over 50% of Community revenue. The Delors II package proposed reducing reliance on VAT by reducing the maximum call-in rate from 1.4% to 1%, to be offset by an increase in the fourth resource. This was agreed at Edinburgh. Of course, the Community does not raise revenue like a state by direct or indirect taxation. Proposals have, however, been made but not yet agreed to fund the Community's activities at least partially on the basis of an energy tax.

The legal basis for an alteration to the basis of the Community's revenues is Article 201 EC. It is for the Council to lay down provisions on revenue, acting unanimously on a proposal from the Commission and after consulting the European Parliament; however, such provisions are merely themselves recommendations to the Member States which must then be ratified or accepted by them according to their respective constitutional requirements.

In addition to the Common Agricultural Policy (CAP) and the structural funds, the Community spends its revenue on the buildings, staff and other administrative costs of the Community institutions and other policies including development aid, research and development support, educational and vocational training support programmes. The 1988 overhaul affected expenditure as well as revenue. It brought a major shift in emphasis from the CAP towards the structural funds, a shift mandated both by the increasingly widespread acceptance that the level of support going to the CAP was now too great, and by the commitment in the Single European Act to the development of regional policies.

Developments in Community expenditure have continued since then. With the changes in and after 1989 in central and eastern Europe and the ex-USSR, the Community has been faced with the challenge of spearheading an international effort to facilitate the transformation of the planned economies of these countries into market economies. A similar challenge, although this time in the internal arena, is posed by the unification of Germany and the incorporation of what was the German Democratic Republic into the Community. Spending in the external field has become a significant budget head since 1989. The Delors II package proposed reducing the proportion of CAP spending from its present 55–60% share of the Community budget in 1992, to 45–50% by 1997, but no changes were agreed at Edinburgh.

4.9   The Budgetary Process

It is one of the constant complaints of the Parliament that there is no institutional parallelism between the revenue and expenditure sides of the Community finances. Revenue raising remains in the hands of the Council and the Member States, with Parliamentary input limited to consultation (Article 201 EC); expenditure falls under the joint control of the Parliament and the Council. The budgetary process is governed by Article 203 EC, as amended by the Budgetary Treaties of 1970 and 1975. The present provisions need to be read in the light of the 1988 interinstitutional agreement which introduced an element of medium-term financial planning into the budgetary process and thereby significantly reduced the potential for conflict between the institutions in the context of agreeing each annual budget. In the agreement the basic outlines of the next four budgets ('financial perspective') were agreed in advance, and any revisions required the cooperation of the Commission and the consent of the Council and the Parliament.

Under the provisions of Article 203 the Commission draws up a preliminary draft budget for the next calendar year on the basis of expenditure estimates made by each of the institutions. This is then sent to the Council for amendment and approval, on a qualified majority, before October 5. The Parliament then has 45 days to consider the draft budget as established by the Council.

For these purposes, a distinction must be made between compulsory and non-compulsory expenditure within the budget. Compulsory expenditure (CE) is that which results necessarily from obligations under the

Treaty or acts adopted thereunder – for example spending on the CAP. Non-compulsory (NCE) is other, discretionary, expenditure. In considering the budget, the Parliament has more restricted powers over CE than over NCE. It can, by a majority of members, propose amendments to NCE. These amendments will stand if they are not rejected or modified by the Council, acting by a qualified majority, within 15 days. In the latter event, when the budget returns to the Parliament for second reading, it can, within 15 days, in effect reinstate its amendments by a majority of its members and a three fifths majority of the votes. In the case of CE, the Parliament can merely propose modifications, acting by a majority of votes. Where these increase the total expenditure of an institution, the modifications will be included in the budget only if they are positively accepted by the Council within 15 days. Modifications which do not increase the total expenditure of any institution must be positively rejected by the Council within 15 days; otherwise they are included in the budget. It will be apparent, therefore, that the Parliament's real control over the content of the budget is not so great as might appear from its designation as joint budgetary authority.

In the event of great dissatisfaction with the draft budget, the Parliament does have the power to reject it as a whole for 'important reasons', provided it acts by a majority of its members and two-thirds of the votes cast. It has done this twice – in 1979 and 1984. In this event, a new draft budget must be prepared by the Commission. The President of the Parliament also has the final power to declare the budget adopted at the conclusion of the budgetary process. This can in turn lead to disputes, since in 1985 the Parliament adopted a budget for 1986 containing what the Council considered to be proposed expenditure in excess of the 'maximum rate' set each year by the Commission, and used as a rule to restrict expenditure growth. The act of the Parliament was successfully challenged by the Council before the Court of Justice, the budget annulled, and the 1986 budgetary process reopened in the middle of the year (Case 34/86 *Council* v. *Parliament* [1986] ECR 2155). Provision is made in the budgetary process for the spending to continue on a pro rata basis in the event of the non-adoption of the budget before the beginning of the year. In fact, the immediate effect of the 1988 budgetary arrangements was that the budget for 1989 – unlike a number of previous budgets in the 1980s – was agreed in December 1988 largely without difficulty. Difficulties have arisen, however, as the unexpected changes within Europe highlighted in the last paragraph began to affect the Community's expenditure priorities. Conflicts between the institutions on budgetary matters are once again increasing.

4.10   The Range of Community Powers

At first glance, the activities of the Community are closely circumscribed by the law-making powers which are ascribed to the institutions, many of which have been alluded to in this chapter, which must be exercised for the specific purpose of achieving a particular policy goal. In practice, the work of the Community has evolved in a more dynamic fashion as a result of two main legal factors, which have operated in conjunction with the constant pressure from the Commission and the Parliament upon the Council to extend the range of the Community's activities. These factors are:

– the development by the Court of Justice of a theory of implied powers in both the internal and external spheres (see 4.11);
– the creative use by the institutions of the more general law-making powers available within the EC Treaty, namely Articles 6(2), 100, 100A and 235 EC, which will be examined in this section.

Article 100 EC provides a general power for the adoption of directives aimed at harmonising national laws which 'directly affect the establishment or functioning of the common market'. Article 100 requires unanimity on the part of the Council of Ministers, and the consultation of the Parliament and the ECOSOC. It was used, for example, as the legal basis for a 1975 Directive harmonising national laws relating to the protection given to workers in the event of collective redundancies (Council Directive 75/129 OJ 1975 L48/29). The motivation for the Directive was that the differences in standards of protection between the Member States affected the functioning of the common market, allowing companies operating in Member States with lower standards a competitive advantage over those in states with high standards of protection. Much the same justification can be used for a measure adopted under Article 100A.

Article 100A EC differs in that it requires only a qualified majority in the Council and involves, after Maastricht, the Parliament–Council co-decision procedure. However, the scope of Article 100A is limited in that it cannot be used to adopt tax harmonisation measures, or measures in the fields of free movement of persons or rights and interests of employed persons (Article 100A(2)). The legislative policy of the Community in the adoption of measures under Article 100A for the achievement of the internal market will be examined in more detail in Part V. The restriction on the use of Article 100A(2) in relation to the free movement of workers is partly offset by Article 6(2) which provides a general power for the Council to adopt measures which eradicate discrimination based on grounds of nationality. The relationship between this provision and Article 235 is considered briefly below.

Article 235 EC is the most general legislative power in the Treaty. It is not limited in scope, for example, to harmonisation measures. It provides:

'If action by the Community should prove necessary to attain, in the course of the operation of the common market, one of the objectives of the Community and this Treaty has not provided the necessary powers, the Council shall, acting unanimously on a proposal from the

Commission and after consulting the Assembly, take the appropriate measures.'

An example of the use of Article 235 in order to extend the range of Community activities is Council Regulation 2137/85 of July 25 1985 establishing the European Economic Interest Grouping (EEIG) (OJ 1985 L199/1). The EEIG provides a specifically 'European' vehicle for companies, professional partnerships and other types of business association to cooperate with each other at a transnational level unrestricted by the limitations of any one national law.

To facilitate law-making activities under Article 235, the Court of Justice has given the individual elements of this Article a consistently broad interpretation. For example, in *Commission* v. *Council (ERASMUS)* (Case 242/87 [1989] ECR 1425) the Court held that the pursuit of a 'People's Europe' was one of the objectives of the Community. Nowhere was such a goal explicitly to be found in the Treaties then in force but the Court read it into the system of the Treaty. Moreover, it is implicit in the Court's case law that it will not seek to restrict *de facto* extensions of competence into the areas covered tangentially rather than explicitly by the Community (see Case 8/73 *Hauptzollamt Bremerhaven* v. *Massey-Ferguson* [1973] ECR 897). This is legitimate since that no measure would have been adopted under Article 235 if all the Member States had not been in favour.

To restrict overenthusiastic reliance upon Article 235, and to encourage the Council to make full use of other law-making powers, the Court has also confirmed the genuinely residual nature of this legal basis. The Council may have resort to Article 235 EC only when a more specific power elsewhere in the Treaty is lacking (Case 45/86 *Commission* v. *Council (Generalised Tariff Preferences)*). The Council cannot, for example, have recourse to Article 235 in order to avoid using a legal basis requiring only a simple majority of votes (see Case 242/87 *Commission* v. *Council (ERASMUS)* which concerns the relationship between Article 128 EEC (vocational training) and Article 235) or one which provides for the use of the cooperation procedure (see Case C-295/90 *Parliament* v. *Council* [1992] 3 CMLR 281 which concerns the relationship between what was then Article 7(2) EEC [now Article 6(2) EC] and Article 235). In other words, it is notable that the Court has paid greater attention to delineating the distinction between Article 235 and the other more specific powers under the Treaty, in order to limit recourse to this relatively restrictive legal basis, than it has to restricting the incremental growth of Community competence through the gradual adoption of novel measures such as the EEIG Regulation, or the early environmental measures based on this Article. Specific powers have now been given under the Treaty allowing for the adoption of many of the measures for which, in the early days, recourse to Article 235 was required (e.g. Articles 130R–T EC, as amended). It may be that in light of these specific powers, and of the introduction of the principle of subsidiarity as a fetter on legislative activities, that recourse to Article 235 will be less common in the years immediately following the Treaty of Maastricht.

4.10   Implied Powers in Community law

The concept of implied powers, as applied in Community law, aids the effectiveness of the work of the institutions. It allows the Community to take decisions where no specific power is given, but where an obvious duty or task exists under the Treaty. Article 235 is, of course, a specific expression of the concept of implied powers. The Court of Justice has also applied a general doctrine of implied powers both internally and externally, to facilitate the evolution of Community competence.

In the internal sphere, the concept of implied powers has been applied in particular to extend the scope of the Commission's power of decision. In *Germany et al.* v. *Commission (Migration Policy)* (Case 281, etc./85 [1987] ECR 3203) the Court was required to interpret the meaning of Article 118 EC. This gives the Commission the task of 'promoting close cooperation between the Member States in the social field'. On the basis of this provision, the Commission adopted a decision requiring Member States to communicate information regarding their policies on migrant workers from third states. A number of Member States challenged the competence of the Commission to adopt such a decision, arguing that such a measure should have been adopted by the Council of Ministers on the basis of Article 235, if it fell within the competence of the Community at all. The Court held that:

> 'where an article of the EEC Treaty – in this case Article 118 – confers a specific task on the Commission it must be accepted, if that provision is not to be rendered wholly ineffective, that it confers on the Commission necessarily and *per se* the powers which are indispensable in order to carry out that task.'

Accordingly, the Court found for the Commission as regards its power to adopt a binding decision.

The Court has also applied the doctrine of implied powers in order to extend the Community's external powers and to create a parallelism between internal and external competence. In *Commission* v. *Council (ERTA)* (Case 22/70 [1971] ECR 263), the dispute concerned whether the Community as such should be participating in the negotiation and conclusion of the European Road Transport Agreement, an international multilateral treaty. The effect of the Court's judgment was to confirm that wherever the Community has an internal competence which it has exercised, it possesses also a parallel external competence, and the Member States may no longer act independently of the Community. Indeed, the power of the Community actually pre-empts the power of the Member States, so that they may no longer validly act. An example of the

Community's use of its implied powers in the external sphere is offered by Council Regulation 1360/90 establishing the European Training Foundation (OJ 1990 L131/1). The aims of the Foundation are to act as a vehicle for the delivery of aid in the form of assistance for vocational training from the Member States of the European Community (and certain other third countries) to the new democracies of central and eastern Europe. The political justification for the Member States acting together in this way, rather than separately, is that it enhances the effectiveness of the aid. The legal justification is that the Community has an external competence in relation to vocational training which matches its internal competence (Article 128 EEC; Articles 126 and 127 EC). An important mechanism exists within the Treaty, which the Commission in particular has used in order to give the Court the opportunity to expound upon the scope of the Community's treaty-making powers. Article 228(6) EC, as amended by the Treaty of Maastricht, provides:

'The Council, the Commission or a Member State may obtain the opinion of the Court of Justice as to whether an agreement envisaged is compatible with the provisions of this Treaty. Where the opinion of the Court of Justice is adverse, the agreement may enter into force only in accordance with Article N of the Treaty on European Union' [which provides for amendments to the Treaty].

A specific example of the Community's express treaty-making powers in operation, namely its power under Article 113 EC to formulate a Common Commercial Policy, will be discussed in Chapter 12.

4.12 Disputes between Institutions

In an evolving Community, disputes between the institutions are as inevitable as disputes between the Community and its Member States. Comitology, as described above, is just one example of an evolving institutional structure which continues to 'set institution against institution' (Bradley, 1992: 721). In so far as disputes exist between the Community's more and less supranational institutions (e.g. between the Commission and the Council), disputes between the institutions may also conceal an element of dispute between the interests of the Member States and those of the Community. A number of corrective mechanisms have emerged within the Community's political and legal systems whereby disputes may be resolved. These exist in addition to the normal channels of compromise and negotiation which mark the activities of any complex political organisation.

Most drastically, there is litigation before the Court of Justice, a mechanism which has already formed a consistent theme within the early chapters of this book. Amongst the examples already seen have been those alleging an incorrect legal basis for a Community act, the lack of competence of the enacting institution, the failure to adopt measures implementing common policies and the use of incorrect procedures (4.2). In order to extend the scope of judicial protection, the Court of Justice was required to recognise the standing of the Parliament to bring an annulment action based on Article 173 (see 9.5). Although this point is now of largely academic interest following the alteration of this Article by the Treaty of Maastricht to extend *locus standi* to the Parliament, it is worth reconsidering briefly the two contradictory cases in which the Court first denied and then accepted the principle that the Parliament has the right to pursue an action before the Court, at least in order to protect its prerogatives. It should be noted that neither the Court, through its judicial legislation, nor the Member States in their amendments to the Treaty, have recognised a generalised right of action on the part of the Parliament in order to protect the general interest such as is accorded by Article 173(1) to the Council, the Commission and the Member States.

In Case 302/87 *Parliament* v. *Council (Comitology)*, the Court dismissed the Parliament's action as inadmissible, refusing to draw parallels between Article 173 (where it was not accorded an explicit right of action) and Article 175 (where it is, in order to bring actions for failure to act), or between the right of others to bring the Parliament before the Court in respect of allegedly unlawful acts (e.g. Case 294/83 *Parti Ecologiste 'Les Verts'* v. *Parliament* [1986] ECR 1339) and the right of the Parliament itself to bring an action. The Court's decision was heavily criticised by commentators (Weiler, 1989; Bradley, 1988). Just over a year later the Court reversed its position (Case C-70/88 *Parliament* v. *Council (Chernobyl)* [1990] ECR I-2041), allowing the Parliament to bring an action, this time to challenge the legal basis used by the Council to adopt a measure regarding the marketing of foodstuffs affected by radiation. The Parliament successfully argued here that the measure should have been adopted on the basis of Article 100A EC rather than Article 31 Euratom. The Court acknowledged its right to bring an action in order to protect its prerogatives (e.g. involvement in the cooperation procedure, or the right to be consulted). In *Chernobyl* it was the right to be involved in the cooperation procedure which was at issue (Article 31 Euratom requires merely consultation of the Parliament) and it must have been significant for the Court's judgment that in this case the Commission did not support the Parliament's views and therefore had no incentive to protect the rights of the Parliament, although this was the mechanism which the Court had suggested in *Comitology* was the means by which the interests of the Parliament should be protected.

The effect of the *Chernobyl* judgment was to recognise more fully the specific identity of each of the institutions, and to acknowledge the need for a legal mechanism to be available to each institution in order to ensure that its prerogatives are not harmed in the dynamic process of integration. In this way, the intensely political issue of the choice of a legal basis can be reduced to the scenario of a legal dispute between institutions, where procedural rules rather than substantive political choices appear to predominate. The most dramatic example of this scenario is offered by Case C-300/89 *Commission* v. *Council (Titanium Dioxide)* (11.6.1991) in which the Commission (with the support of the Parliament) challenged the decision of the Council to use Article 130S EC as the legal basis for Directive 89/428/EEC approximating national programmes for the reduction and eventual elimination of pollution caused by waste in the production of titanium dioxide. The Directive had an admittedly dual function, namely to protect the environment (Article 130S) and to harmonise national measures which had an impact upon the completion of the internal market. From the latter perspective the measure would fall within the remit of Article 100A, thus requiring only a qualified majority vote in the Council and the use of the cooperation procedure. In contrast, Article 130S is an 'old style' legislative power, requiring unanimity in the Council and involving only the consultation of the Parliament. The Court ruled out a dual reference to both articles, since this would in practice defeat the very purpose of the cooperation procedure, which is to expand the influence of the Parliament, and held that such a measure must be based on Article 100A alone (see Weatherill, 1992b: 311 *et seq.*). The effect of this decision is very significantly to limit the scope of application of Article 130S, and to assert the dominance of the procedural imperatives of the cooperation procedure over the substantive resolution of the appropriate content of an environmental protection measure. The Court has since repeated its arguments on the protection of the cooperation procedure, when discussing the relationship between Article 6(2) EC and Article 235 EC in Case C-295/90 *Parliament* v. *Council*.

The institutions have not always found it necessary, or possible, to go to court in order to settle their differences. There is a tradition of interinstitutional arrangements which have the effect of reducing tension in difficult areas such as the budget. The 1988 interinstitutional agreement on the budget is one example. Another is the Conciliation Procedure, created by a 1975 agreement to facilitate agreement between the Council and the Parliament on legislative measures with significant financial implications (OJ 1975 C89/1). This Procedure also illustrates the final mechanism available for resolving interinstitutional disputes and for shifting the institutional balance. This is the introduction of amendments to the Treaty, in order to give concrete form to evolving mechanisms for preserving the interinstitutional balance, or in order to bring the Community into line with existing changed practice. The Treaty of Maastricht contains a number of examples of such changes. For example, Article 173 now gives *locus standi* to the Parliament, acknowledging the earlier judicial recognition of standing. It also illustrates how the process of Treaty amendment can benefit from past experiences. The new co-decision procedure in Article 189B in some respects builds on the experiment of the conciliation procedure referred to above, with its provisions for the setting of a Conciliation Committee to resolve Council–Parliament disagreements on the substance of legislation.

Summary

1 The basic conditions of legality for Community legal acts are a statement of reasons and a legal basis. The question of the correct legal basis for an act is a question of law, resolvable on the basis of objectively ascertainable facts. There is no single law-making process under the Treaties, but in general a power of proposal is given to the Commission.

2 The old procedure, in particular as envisaged under the original treaties, is based around the basic pattern of Commission proposal, Parliament consultation, and Council unanimous decision, although with variants. This old style retains its attraction for new law-making powers attributed to the Community under the Treaty of Maastricht.

3 The cooperation procedure is an advance in terms of Parliamentary input, providing for a second reading. It enhances the accountability of the Council.

4 The introduction of co-decision for a limited range of law-making powers under the Treaty of Maastricht raises the Parliament to the status of co-legislature. Co-decision provides for a third reading, and the possibility of convening a Conciliation Committee.

5 The Community derives its revenue – termed 'own resources' – from customs duties, agricultural levies, a proportion of VAT collected by the Member States, and a fourth resource based on Member State GNPs.

6 The budgetary process sees the Council and Parliament as joint budgetary authorities. The budgetary process is governed by Article 201 EC and has been the subject of a number of disputes before the Court. The 1988 interinstitutional agreement on financial perspectives is intended to reduce the level of budgetary dispute.

7 The range of Community activities is greatly increased by the availability of general law-making powers in Articles 6(2) 100, 100A and 235 EC. The latter is a genuinely residual law-making power which can be used only where another more specific power does not give the means necessary for the attainment of an objective of the Community. Article 235 provides an example of the doctrine of implied powers operating in Community law, a doctrine which the Court has developed in general terms in order to expand the role of the institutions and of the Community.

8 Comitology may also make a contribution to the effectiveness of Community policy-making, although in its current form it is perceived by the Commission and the Parliament as bringing about excessive levels of Member State supervision.

9 Disputes between institutions are inevitable in an evolving Community. Litigation, interinstitutional agreements and changes to the Treaties are the mechanisms, apart from negotiation and compromise, most commonly used for the settlement of interinstitutional disputes.

Questions

1 What impact does the lack of a single law-making process for the European Community have upon the effectiveness of the institutions?

2 Does the Parliament have sufficient control over the collection of Community revenues and the allocation of expenditure?

3 How does Comitology work, and who is opposed to it and why?

4 Explain the operation of the doctrine of implied powers in the Community context.

5 How are disputes between the institutions normally resolved in the Community?

Further Reading

Bieber (1984) 'The settlement of institutional conflicts on the basis of Article 4 of the EEC Treaty,' 21 *Common Market Law Review*, 505.

Bradley (1991) 'Sense and Sensibility: *Parliament* v. *Council*, continued', 16 *European Law Review*, 245.

Bradley (1992) 'Comitology and the Law: Through a Glass, Darkly', 29 Common *Market Law Review*, 693.

Corbett (1989) 'Testing the New Procedures: The European Parliament's First Experiences with its new 'Single Act' Powers', 27 *Journal of Common Market Studies*, 359.

Lodge (1989) 'The European Parliament – from 'assembly' to co-legislature: changing the institutional dynamics', in Lodge (1989).

Weiler (1989) 'Pride and Prejudice – *Parliament* v. *Council*', 14 *European Law Review*, 334.

5   The Sources of Community Law

5.1 Introduction

We are concerned in this chapter with identifying the body of legal rules which comprise the sources of Community law and, where this is not already clear from earlier discussion, the origins and authors of these rules. Sources of law are often divided into different categories; for example, there are external sources (international agreements) and internal sources (the founding treaties, Community legislation), as well as primary sources (treaties, general principles of law) and secondary sources (Community legislation). All these categories of sources of law will be considered in this chapter, which also outlines certain basic features of each type of legal rule (e.g. nature and extent of binding force). Discussion in detail of the relationship between Community law and national law is reserved for consideration in Chapter 8.

5.2 The Founding Treaties

The Court of Justice has on a number of occasions referred to the founding or constitutive treaties as the Community's constitution (see 1.5). The structure of this constitution is now extremely complex. In addition to the three pillar structure introduced by the Treaty of Maastricht which was described in Chapter 1, incorporating within the Union the ECSC, Euratom and EC Treaties and the Single European Act, the founding treaties also comprise the various Acts of Accession, the Merger Treaty, and the Budgetary Treaties. All of these treaties have required conclusion and ratification by the Member States according to their respective constitutional requirements before entry into force. Once these procedures have been completed, the Member States are bound to comply with their obligations; certain of these obligations are also enforceable at the instance of individuals in national courts. The Community institutions are also bound by the contents of the Community constitution. As with any legal system, the Community's constitutional documents represent the supreme internal source of law.

5.3 Other International Agreements

A second primary source of Community law comprises the other international agreements by which the Community is bound. These include agreements with one or more third states or other international organisations concluded by the Community itself in exercise of its external relations powers, of both a bilateral nature (e.g. an association or cooperation agreement with a third state) and a multilateral nature (e.g. a trading arrangement regarding a particular commodity, such as the Multi-fibre Agreement). This category also contains agreements predating the foundation of the Community under which it has succeeded to the rights and obligations of the Member States. An important example is the General Agreement on Tariffs and Trade (GATT), which represents the basic framework for the evolution of global free trade. The Court of Justice will enforce the Community's international legal obligations within the Community legal system. In certain circumstances, individuals may also be able to rely on provisions of international agreements by which the Community is bound as creating rights which they may invoke in national courts.

5.4 General Principles of Law

The final category of primary sources are the general principles of law, a body of superordinate rules of law, for the most part unwritten and derived by the Court of Justice by reference to its general duty to ensure that the law is observed (Article 164 EC). These principles bind the Community, its institutions, and, within the sphere of Community competence, the Member States and individuals. 'General principles of law' are a familiar source of law within those Member States with 'civil law' systems based on the traditions of Roman Law. They offer a background statement of values and basic standards which courts can use to inform their interpretation of rules of written law and to fill gaps in the written law. General principles comprise rules which are sufficiently general, such as 'the right to equality' or 'the principle of legal certainty', to be widely accepted. It is the application of such principles to specific fact situations which is more likely to cause controversy than the principles themselves.

The International Court of Justice is explicitly called upon to apply general principles of law in its case law. Article 38(c) of its Statute provides:

'The Court . . . shall apply . . . the general principles of law recognised by civilised nations.'

In contrast, the Community treaties provide no equivalent statement, although general support for the practice of the Court in using general principles can be derived from the treaties. In addition to Article 164 EC, referred to above, Article 173 EC gives as one of the grounds for review of the legality of Community acts:

'infringement of this Treaty or *any rule of law relating to its application*' (emphasis added).

More explicit reference to general principles, albeit within a more limited remit, is to be found in Article 215(2) EC which governs the tortious liability of the Community for wrongful acts. The Court is to decide disputes:

> 'in accordance with the general principles common to the laws of the Member States.'

The reference to what is 'common' to the laws of the Member States highlights the comparative method which has frequently marked the Court's search for general principles. This comparative method appears most clearly in the Opinions of the Advocates-General rather than the judgments of the Court itself (see for example A-G Warner in Case 17/74 *Transocean Marine Paint* v. *Commission* [1974] ECR 1063 – the right to a fair hearing in competition proceedings, and the excursus given by Usher, 1976: 370). For a principle to be 'common' does not necessarily mean that it must be recognised in all the Member States in precisely the same form. It is sufficient that a general trend can be discerned amongst the Member States. As an alternative to comparative methodology, the Court may find inspiration for a Community general principle in international instruments such as the European Convention of Human Rights and Fundamental Freedoms and the International Covenant of Civil and Political Rights. However, whatever the source of inspiration, the Court invariably stresses the 'Community' nature of the principle once expressed. The general principles of law are Community principles, elaborated in the specific context of the Community with its particular mission and subject to the authoritative interpretation of the Court of Justice alone.

Three main groups of general principles can be identified although a number of important general principles such as 'equality' straddle all three categories. These are:

- certain rules and standards which operate as restrictions upon the exercise of Community administrative and legislative powers either by the Community itself or by the Member States where they are required to implement Community measures;
- the economic freedoms contained in the Treaty, which the Court has consistently elevated to the status of 'general principles', and which act principally as fetters upon the Member States. For example, in Case 240/83 *Procureur de la République* v. *Association de défense des brûleurs d'huiles usagées* ([1985] ECR 520) the Court stated (at p. 531):

  'It should be borne in mind that the principles of free movement of goods and freedom of competition, together with freedom of trade as a fundamental right, are general principles of Community law of which the Court ensures observance;'

- a somewhat ill-defined body of fundamental rights. It could be said that fundamental rights are the most deeply entrenched and morally important value statements of a given social grouping, and as such can be encompassed within the first two categories of the general principles. In view of the general importance of fundamental rights and of the specific history of the protection of those rights within the Community it is, however, useful to analyse them as a third separate category.

The general principles of law represent a product of judicial activism and creativity which is typical of the Court. The proactive role which has been taken by the Court in this regard has been used as one basis for the claim that the Court has exceeded its judicial role and trespassed into the realm of politics (Rasmussen, 1986).

5.5   Principles of Administrative and Legislative Legality

The comparative methodology referred to above has been particularly useful for the Court in the context of the development of those general principles which can be characterised as principles of administrative and legislative legality. A number of pointers to the development of this group of principles are to be found in the Treaty itself. For example, Article 173 EC cites 'lack of competence' and 'infringement of an essential procedural requirement' as well as infringement of the Treaty and 'any rule of law' as grounds for review. Article 190 EC also requires all Regulations, Directives and Decisions to be accompanied by a statement of reasons. However, there are also many unwritten principles of administrative and legislative legality, and these have evolved through the case law of the Court which has drawn much of its inspiration in this field from the national administrative systems of the Member States. The most important are the principles of legal certainty and proportionality, and the rights to non-discrimination and procedural fairness.

Procedural fairness is particularly important in those areas of Community law where the Community institutions must enforce the law directly against individuals, such as competition law and anti-dumping law. The *Transocean Marine Paint Case* provides an example of the development of the right to a hearing in the competition law field for those whose trading activities come under the scrutiny of the Commission on the grounds of alleged anti-competitive or monopolistic effects; Case C-49/88 *Al-Jubail Fertiliser* v. *Council* ([1991] 3 CMLR 377) extends this principle to companies which are required to pay anti-dumping duties imposed on allegedly subsidised imports into the Community. A rather different principle of procedural fairness was developed in Case 155/79 *A.M. & S.* v. *Commission* ([1982] ECR 1575) where the Court of Justice recognised the confidentiality of communications between lawyer and client in the context of Commission competition investigations. This right of legal professional privilege extends only to independent lawyers established within the Community; it does not apply to communications with lawyers outside the Community, or with in-house lawyers. *A.M. & S.* provides the first significant instance of the Court drawing more heavily upon the common law heritage offered by English and Irish law.

Other procedural rights have been developed by the Court as fetters upon the investigatory activities of the Commission which are more akin to fundamental rights, such as the right to be protected against arbitrary administrative action; this will be considered below.

The principle of legal certainty has been cited by the Court in a number of diverse contexts. For example in Case 43/75 *Defrenne* v. *SABENA* ([1976] ECR 455) legal certainty was used as a justification for imposing a temporal limitation upon the effects of a preliminary ruling under Article 177 EC. In that case, the Court concluded that Article 119 EC could have direct effect; in other words, individual women and men could bring equal pay claims in national courts on the basis of Article 119 itself. The Court held that this applied only for the future, so that with the exception of claims already submitted at the date of the ruling, back pay could not be claimed in respect of periods of service at an unequal rate of pay prior to that time. The Court has made it clear that the limitation of the temporal effects of a ruling is a wholly exceptional measure imposed on grounds of legal certainty because of the seriously disruptive effects of the ruling; such reticence is desirable since the imposition of such a limitation on a Court ruling represents one of the most blatant examples of judicial legislation within the Community legal system, and wholly abandons the pretence that the Court is merely interpreting, as opposed to making, the law.

Legal certainty may also take the form of the protection of 'legitimate expectations'. Since the Community is actively involved in the customs and agricultural fields in the management of the market by intervening to set prices, levies and duties, it must take care not to violate the legitimate expectations of those concerned which it might previously have aroused. This is illustrated by Case 74/74 *CNTA* v. *Commission* ([1975] ECR 533). Here it was held that the Commission was not permitted to abolish without warning so-called 'monetary compensatory amounts' ('MCAs') granted to exporters of agricultural products to compensate them for fluctations in exchange rates since:

'a trader may legitimately expect that for transactions irrevocably undertaken by him because he has obtained, subject to a deposit, export licences fixing the amount of the refund in advance, no unforeseeable alteration will occur which could have the effect of causing him inevitable loss, by re-exposing him to the exchange risk' (p. 550).

Finally, legal certainty operates in the guise of the principle of non-retroactivity. Legislation is presumed not to take effect retrospectively unless this is expressly stated, and retroactivity will not be permitted unless it is essential for the purpose of the measure to be achieved and the legitimate expectations of the persons affected have been protected. In Case 108/81 *Amylum* v. *Council* ([1982] ECR 3107) the conditions for retroactivity were met. This concerned a Council Regulation imposing a system of quotas and levies on the production of isoglucose (a sugar substitute) intended to equalise the production conditions of the two products. Since an earlier Regulation to the same effect had been annulled on procedural grounds (failure to consult the Parliament: see 4.2), it was permissible to pass a second Regulation imposing the same system with retrospective effect. The objective of equality could not otherwise be achieved, and the isoglucose producers were presumed to be put on notice about the scheme by the earlier abortive Regulation.

Equality and non-discrimination themselves operate as important general principles governing the legality of Community action. This is expressed most clearly in Article 40(3) EC which demands that the common organisations of the market set up under the Common Agricultural Policy (CAP) must 'exclude any discrimination between producers or consumers within the Community', and there are many cases in which this principle of equality has been successfully invoked to challenge Community legislation in the agricultural field (see for example the *Skimmed Milk Powder* Case – Case 114/76 *Bela Mühle Josef Bergman* v. *Grows-Farm* [1977] ECR 1211). The principle also has a wider impact as the principle that the Community legislature may not treat similar situations differently unless differentiation is objectively justified. In Case 41/84 *Pinna* v. *Caisse d'allocations familiales de la Savoie* ([1986] ECR 1) the Court held that the Council was not permitted, when legislating to determine the conditions under which migrant workers enjoy family benefits, to differentiate between those who were subject to French legislation and those who were not (a differentiation created on the insistence of France which has a particularly generous system of family benefits). This legislative intervention by the Council had the effect of accentuating the existing disparities between the national systems and was not permitted.

Proportionality is a concept which has entered Community law primarily out of German law, where it is given constitutional status. Essentially it requires a measure to be no more burdensome than is necessary to achieve its objective. Once the objective of a measure is identified, a threefold test can be applied: is the measure capable of achieving the objective, is the measure necessary for the achievement of the objective, and is there a reasonable relationship between the measure and the objective? An example is offered by Case 181/84 *R* v. *Intervention Board for Agricultural Produce, ex parte Man (Sugar) Ltd* ([1985] ECR 2889) where the Court held that it was disproportionate for a Community Regulation to require the forfeiture of the entire security deposited by a company, where the security is intended to ensure that goods for which an export licence is to be obtained will actually be exported (the primary obligation), for failure to satisfy a secondary obligation, namely the duty to submit the licence application within a certain time period. The sanction was particularly harsh since the applicant was only four hours late in submitting the application.

Proportionality has become an extremely important principle in the economic law of the European Community. Not only is it used to assess the legality of the measures of Community law and implementing measures of the Member States in the context of customs and agricultural law but, like the principle of equality, it has also become a vital component in assessing interferences by the Member States in the economic freedoms guaranteed under the Treaty which have been elevated to the status of general principles.

5.6   The Pillars of Economic Integration as General Principles of Community Law

The Court of Justice has consistently repeated its view that the four basic economic freedoms under the Treaty (free movement of goods, persons, services and capital), along with the general right to non-discrimination on grounds of nationality contained in Article 6 EC are protected not just as written rules within the Treaty system, but also as general principles of Community law. The breadth of protection now offered by Community law is illustrated by Case 186/87 *Cowan* v. *Le Trésor public* [1989] (ECR 195). The Court held that a British tourist attacked, robbed and injured while on holiday in Paris was entitled to make a criminal injuries compensation claim under French law under the same conditions as a French national. As a recipient of services (tourism), Cowan fell within the scope of the application of the Treaty, and he was therefore entitled to the protection of what was then Article 7 EEC. The Court stated (at p. 222) that:

> '[national] legislative provisions may not discriminate against persons to whom Community law gives the right to equal treatment or restrict the fundamental freedoms guaranteed by Community law.'

The Court also makes extensive use of the concept of proportionality in order to assess the legitimacy of interferences by the Member States in these freedoms. This point will be examined further in Chapter 14 below.

Finally, in a number of cases the Court has stressed the importance of associated procedural rights to due process without which the exercise of the fundamental freedoms is meaningless. For example, where a public authority takes a decision which impinges upon an individual's Community rights, he or she has the right to be given reasons, to make it possible to challenge this decision in court. In Case 222/86 *UNCTEF* v. *Heylens* ([1987] ECR 4097), Heylens' application for the recognition in France of his Belgian diploma as a football trainer was rejected on the basis of an adverse opinion given by a special committee which gave no reasons for its decision. Without that recognition Heylens could not work in France. The Court held that reasons must be given for such a decision to enable effective judicial review, since the adverse opinion affected a fundamental right conferred by the Treaty on Community workers, namely the right of free access to employment.

Community legislation has been held to confer a right to judicial review on beneficiaries of Community rights. In the field of sex discrimination, the Court held in Case 222/84 *Johnston* v. *Chief Constable of the Royal Ulster Constabulary* ([1986] ECR 1651) that an alleged victim of sex discrimination bringing a claim for equal treatment guaranteed by the Equal Treatment Directive (76/207) could not be denied access to a judicial remedy by a ministerial order.

These cases are expressions of a general principle that individuals must be given effective remedies against the Member States, which allow them to protect or assert their rights under Community law. In Cases 6 and 9/90 *Francovich* v. *Italian State* ([1992] IRLR 84) the Court held that it is for national courts to ensure the full effect of the provisions of Community law, and to protect the rights which Community law confers on individuals.

5.7 Fundamental Rights

The emergence of a specific category of general principles termed 'fundamental rights' is attributable to the need on the part of the Court of Justice to assert the supremacy of the Community legal order, even in the face of national constitutions, such as that of the Federal Republic of Germany, which enshrine the protection of fundamental human rights. In effect, the Court has read into the Community legal order an unwritten Bill of Rights, drawing on both national constitutional expressions of fundamental rights and international human rights instruments as the sources of inspiration for Community fundamental rights. The articulation of a specific category of rights termed 'fundamental' was in part forced upon the Court by the reluctance of certain national courts, notably German and Italian courts, to acknowledge the full supremacy of Community law. In particular, these courts were reluctant to accept that the superior nature of Community law precluded them from testing provisions of Community legislation against *national* constitutional guarantees of fundamental rights. The German Federal Constitutional Court held in the case of *Internationale Handelsgesellschaft* ([1974] 2 CMLR 549) that so long as an adequate standard of fundamental rights protection was not offered under Community law itself, it would not regard itself as precluded from scrutinising measures of Community law for conformity with *German* fundamental rights, and where necessary, invalidating or disapplying such measures within Germany. Recognising the progress made by the Court of Justice, however, the Federal Constitutional Court decisively shifted its position in the case of *Wunsche Handelsgesellschaft* ([1987] 3 CMLR 225) indicating that an effective level of protection was now generally ensured and scrutiny by the national court was no longer required.

The position previously taken by the German court, and still maintained by the Italian Constitutional Court (Gaja, 1990; Schermers, 1990), is in fact inconsistent with the position taken by the Court of Justice on the supremacy of Community law (8.11). However, in practice, the Court of Justice felt constrained to defend its position by developing a line of case law beginning with Case 29/69 *Stauder* v. *City of Ulm* ([1969] ECR 419) in which it has proclaimed the existence of fundamental rights enshrined within the Community legal order which are protected as general principles of law. To reassure the national courts, it was stressed in *Internationale Handelsgesellschaft* (Case 11/70 [1970] ECR 1125), that Community human rights are inspired by the constitutional traditions common to the Member States. That source of inspiration was extended in Case 4/73 *Nold* v. *Commission* ([1974] ECR 503) to include 'international treaties for the protection of human rights on which the Member States have collaborated or of which they are signatories'. In Case 44/79 *Hauer* v. *Land Rheinland Pfalz* ([1979] ECR 3740) the Court made an extensive examination of the right to property as protected in a number of the national constitutions, as well as Article 1 of the First Protocol to the ECHR, before concluding that there had been no human rights violation by the Community when it adopted an agricultural regulation which prohibited the planting of new vines for three years. In 1989 the Court referred for the first time to the International Covenant of Civil and Political Rights as a potential source of Community fundamental rights (Case 374/87 *Orkem* v. *Commission* ([1989] ECR 3283). However, whatever the sources of inspiration for its case law, the Court has always stressed that Community fundamental rights, like the other general principles of law, become specifically Community rights, subject to interpretation 'within the framework of the structure and the objectives of the Community' (Case 11/70 *Internationale Handelsgesellschaft*).

This frank admission of the influence of the objectives of the Community upon the interpretation of fundamental rights, when viewed in the light of specific purpose of the Court when it first introduced the doctrine of Community fundamental rights protection, has led some commentators to doubt the real effectiveness of Community human rights protection (Coppel and O'Neill, 1992). This claim can be supported by reference to the paucity of cases in which the Court has in fact held that there has been a human rights violation by the Community institutions. Successful claims are largely confined to the realm of competition law. In Case 46/87 *Hoechst* v. *Commission* ([1989] ECR 2859) the Court held that undertakings which are under investigation by the Commission for alleged infringements of the competition rules have the right to be protected against arbitrary or disproportionate interventions on the part of public authorities in their sphere of activities. This means in practice that before conducting surprise searches of the premises of undertakings under investigation the Commission is obliged to observe whatever procedural formalities apply within the

Member State where the undertaking is established, such as the duty to obtain a search warrant before a judge.

Although it was thought in the early stages of the evolution of fundamental rights doctrine in the Community that the Court would apply this analysis only as a means of testing the validity of measures adopted by the Community institutions themselves, in more recent cases it has logically extended the scope of protection to the full ambit of Community competence, whether measures are adopted by the institutions or by the Member States. The Court has frequently made reference to fundamental rights in its case law in order to enhance, in general terms, the foundations on which the Community is constructed (e.g. the reference to the fundamental right of access to employment in *Heylens*; the reference to the fundamental right of sex equality as one of the general principle of Community law in Case 149/77 *Defrenne* v. *SABENA* [1978] ECR 1365). Frequent reference to fundamental rights reinforces the legitimacy which the Community can claim as a body subject to the rule of law, as the Court asserted in Case 294/83 *Parti Ecologiste 'Les Verts'* v. *Parliament* ([1986] ECR 1339).

More significant than these generalised assertions has been the principle developed by the Court since Case 5/88 *Wachauf* v. *Federal Republic of Germany* ([1989] ECR 2609), whereby Member States, when implementing Community measures, are bound to respect the fundamental rights guaranteed under Community law. This principle operates in fields of Community competence, such as the CAP, which have been exhaustively regulated by the Community, and where the role of the Member State is limited to implementing Community law. It also applies in areas where the Community has not regulated, but where the Member States are precluded from taking measures which hinder the achievement of the Community's objectives, such as freedom of movement. For example, in Case C-260/89 *Elliniki Radiophonia Tileorasi (ERT)* v. *Dimotiki Etairia Pliroforissis* (16.6.1991) the Court considered the admissibility of national public policy derogations from the principle of free movement of services under Articles 56 and 66 EC. It held that the prohibition in Greece on the broadcasting of television programmes by all undertakings apart from the State Television Company, which Greece sought to justify by reference to important public policy interests protected by Articles 56 and 66 had to be assessed in the light of general principles of law, notably fundamental rights. In particular, the principle of freedom of expression, enshrined in Article 10 ECHR, could be invoked before the national court called upon the assess the validity of the purported exception from the principles of Community law.

The logical corollary of this point is that Community fundamental rights protection does *not* extend to areas which fall within the jurisdiction of the Member States, rather than the Community (see Cases 60-1/84 *Cinéthèque* v. *Fédération nationale des cinémas français* [1985] ECR 2605). This pattern is in marked contrast to the scope of human rights protection afforded by the Supreme Court of the USA under the US Constitution, where creative judicial interpretation of the Fourteenth Amendment which guarantees the right to due process has allowed extensive federal judicial oversight over how the states manage their residual legislative and administrative competences (see Lenaerts, 1991b).

The case of *Society for the Protection of Unborn Children (Ireland) Ltd (SPUC)* v. *Grogan* (Case C-159/90 [1991] 3 CMLR 689) illustrates the difficulties which now surround the piecemeal judicial protection of fundamental rights in the Community. In that case, the applicants, SPUC, had relied upon Article 40.3.3 of the Irish Constitution which guarantees the right to life of the unborn, in order to obtain an injunction prohibiting the distribution of information about abortion clinics in the UK. The students union which was responsible for distributing the details argued that Article 59 EC precluded the application of the Irish Constitution in such a way as to hinder the free movement of services; Community law required the free availability of the information required by Irish women if they were to take advantage, as recipients of services, of abortions lawfully available in other Member States. On a reference by the Irish High Court concerning these points the Court held that abortion – at least where it is provided for remuneration – is a service for the purposes of Article 59. It should follow that any measures taken by Ireland which hinder the free movement of such services and of the recipients of such services should be capable of scrutiny under Community law, including Community fundamental rights, in this case freedom of expression protected by Article 10 ECHR. However, the Court avoided the need to consider the issue by holding that the distribution of abortion information by the students union fell outside the ambit of the Treaty. Since there was no economic link between the provider of the service (the UK clinics) and the advertiser of the service (the students union), the situation fell outside the scope of Article 59. No charge was made to the UK clinics in respect of the advertisements contained in the handbooks.

This distinction is, of course, a tenuous one, and could easily be circumvented in a future instance by the imposition of even a small charge for the advertisements. The Court would then have to confront the issue of the availability of information about abortion in a Member State where abortion itself is unlawful and, consequently, the possible conflicts between the freedom of information of the service recipients and providers and the right to life of the unborn which underlies the prohibition on abortion in Ireland. For having classed abortion as a service, the Court will logically be faced with the question of whether national variations in the conditions under which abortion is available, including a constitutional prohibition, represent restrictions on the free movement of services, in the same way that variations in product standards are categorised as potentially restrictive of the free movement of goods (see the *Cassis de Dijon* case law discussed in Chapter 14). This could lead to the undermining of what is an important constitutional value in one Member State, and tends in general to indicate that those Member States which assert constitutional values which are not shared by the others may find them under attack from the imperatives of the internal market which requires the sweeping away of restrictions on trade. At the very least it requires Ireland to justify the operation of its prohibition on abortion, at least in so far as that has effects outside the Irish jurisdiction (Phelan, 1992).

It is not possible, therefore, for the Court of Justice entirely to sidestep the problems of conflicts between differing constitutional values. At present, through its decision in *Grogan*, the Court may have avoided addressing these delicate issues of national sovereignty by making a distinction between the 'economic' and 'non-economic' provision of information and thus by giving a relatively restricted interpretation of the scope of Community competence. However, as the subsequent attempt in the Irish courts by the Attorney-General to prevent a pregnant fourteen year old victim of an alleged rape from travelling to the UK for an abortion showed, the issue of the interrelationship between Community rights and national constitutional traditions is likely to be an enduring theme (see *Attorney General* v. *X* [1992] 2 CMLR 277, Irish Supreme Court).

5.8   Fundamental Rights outside the European Court

This discussion has demonstrated that there may be cause for doubt regarding both the effectiveness and the coherence of the fundamental rights protection provided by the Court. However, that institution has at least gone much further than the political institutions towards developing a framework which ensures that existing national systems of protection are not undermined by the transfer of sovereign powers to the Community. Outside the field of the Community itself, the Member States already operate a dual system of fundamental rights protection. In addition to more or less comprehensive and effective systems of protection within the domestic order, all the Member States are signatories of the ECHR and recognise the right of individual petition to the institutions of the ECHR which may pronounce upon alleged fundamental rights violations within those states. While it seems probable that those institutions would not hesitate to hold each of the twelve Member States responsible for fundamental rights violations within their territories which stemmed from the exercise of sovereign powers transferred to the Community, it would be more desirable if the Community itself were subject to a written catalogue of fundamental rights which *directly* guaranteed the observance of basic standards, in order to avoid a possible conflict of jurisdiction or substance between the ECHR institutions and the Court of Justice. This task would be by no means simple, since there are substantial differences between the catalogues of fundamental rights currently subscribed to by the various Member States. In any case, such a catalogue has yet to be provided by the Community's political institutions, notwithstanding pressure from the European Parliament, which has adopted a number of resolutions on this matter, and from the Commission which has considered the possibility of the Community acceding, as if it were a state, to the ECHR. This would have the effect of subordinating the jurisdiction of the Court of Justice to that of the European Court of Human Rights in respect of fundamental rights issues.

So far only 'soft law' (see 5.14) measures have been agreed between the institutions, comprising in particular a Joint Declaration on Fundamental Rights, adopted by the three political institutions in 1977 (OJ 1977 C103/1). Further progress was made in 1993, since the newly established European Union is committed to respecting fundamental rights, as guaranteed by the ECHR and 'as they result from the constitutional traditions common to the Member States, as general principles of Community law' (Article F TEU). This exactly replicates the formula generally used by the Court of Justice. Regrettably, however, Article F is one of the 'Common Provisions' of the Treaty of Maastricht which is not justiciable before the Court of Justice. There remains, therefore, neither a definite Treaty basis for the protection of fundamental rights, nor a clear written catalogue laying down the rights which must be observed, and the permissible derogations from those rights. This failure, together with the continuing democratic deficit within the legislative process, highlights the extent to which the Community continues to differ in structure and nature from the liberal democratic state.

5.9 Acts of the Institutions – Community Legislation

The acts of the institutions are classified and described in brief terms in Article 189 EC which provides:

'In order to carry out their task and in accordance with the provisions of this Treaty, the European Parliament acting jointly with the Council, the Council and the Commission shall make regulations and issue directives, take decisions, make recommendations or deliver opinions.

A regulation shall have general application. It shall be binding in its entirety and directly applicable in all Member States.

A directive shall be binding, as to the result to be achieved, upon each Member State to which it is addressed, but shall leave to the national authorities the choice of form and methods.

A decision shall be binding in its entirety upon those to whom it is addressed.

Recommendations and opinions shall have no binding force.'

The legislative process whereby Community measures may be adopted and the basic requirements for the lawful adoption, entry into force and publication of such measures including the duty to give reasons, and the requirement of a legal basis were considered in Chapter 4. It remains here to describe in brief terms the basic nature of each form of Community act, leaving for Chapter 8 the detailed consideration of the effects of such acts within the domestic legal systems of the Member States. As a preliminary point it should be noted that although there is a crude hierarchy of Community acts, with Regulations ranking as the strongest form and non-binding recommendations and opinions as the weakest, there is no very clear logic as to where the Treaty will mandate, in a particular provision, the adoption of one or more specific forms of legislation, or where it leaves it open to the adopting institution to adopt any necessary 'measures'. Furthermore, the Court has consistently held that it is the content of a measure which is decisive as to its nature, not the form which it is given by the adopting institution. In Cases 41–44/70 *International Fruit Company* v. *Commission* ([1971] ECR 411) the Court held that a measure labelled a Regulation was in truth a bundle of individual Decisions. This finding was crucial as it affected the ability of the applicant company to bring a challenge to the measure in question under the Community's administrative law provisions (see Chapter 9). It is therefore necessary to scrutinise in all cases both the concrete enabling provision (legal basis) to ensure that the relevant institution has acted within its power and the substance of the act adopted to ensure that it is what it purports to be.

Finally, the system used in Article 189 EC, although replicated in Article 161 Euratom, did not adopt that already used in the ECSC Treaty. Under the ECSC Treaty only three types of measure are envisaged; these are Decisions, Recommendations and Opinions. An ECSC Decision is broadly equivalent to either an EC Regulation or an EC Decision, depending upon whether it is general or individual in nature. An ECSC Recommendation can be equated to an EC Directive, and ECSC Opinions, like their EC counterparts, have no binding force. The analysis throughout this book follows the EC schema.

5.10   Regulations

Regulations are like Community 'Acts of Parliament'. Regulations have 'general application', are binding in all respects and 'directly applicable'. Thus they are general, non-individualised legislative measures which take effect directly in the national legal order, without need for national implementing measures. Indeed national re-enactment is not permitted, unless it is required by the terms of the Regulation (Case 34/73 *Variola* v. *Italian Finance Administration* [1973] ECR 981). The Court held (at p. 990):

> 'the direct application of a Regulation means that its entry into force, and its application in favour of or against those subject to it are independent of any measure of reception into national law . . . Member States are under a duty not to obstruct the direct applicability inherent in Regulations. Strict compliance with this obligation is an

indispensable condition of the simultaneous and uniform application of Community Regulations throughout the Community.'

Examples can be given of Regulations which are explicitly stated to be dependent upon national implementation. The Tachograph Regulation (Council Regulation 1463/70 OJ 1970 (Sp. Ed.) p. 482) provides:

'Member States shall, in good time and after consulting the Commission, adopt such laws, regulations and administrative provisions as may be necessary for the implementation of this Regulation.'

In crude terms, the existence of a Regulation in a particular field adopted by the Community normally acts as a 'keep out' sign to the national legislature (Usher, 1981: 17). The pre-emptive effect of Community legislation will be examined further in the context of the discussion of supremacy in 8.12.

5.11 Directives

The specific character of Directives lies in the type of obligation which they impose upon addressees. Directives amount only to obligations of result, not obligations of conduct. However, the implementation of Directives is a positive obligation for the Member States, and the effective implementation of Directives is one of the keys to the realisation of the Community's objectives in the internal market sphere. Under new arrangements put in place by the Commission, enforcement proceedings under Article 169 EC are begun automatically in the event of failure by a Member State to implement a Directive by the time limit which it is set in each measure (usually between one and three years).

The Member States have a discretion as to how they implement Directives. This normally involves either adopting or changing legislation, but exceptionally nothing need be done if existing legislation is sufficient. They may also be given alternatives within the Directive itself. In practice, the mis-implementation of Directives is as serious a problem as the failure to implement, and the Court of Justice is frequently faced with preliminary references regarding the interpretation of particular Directives where national courts are required to decide upon the adequacy of national implementing measures. Specific examples of this and related problems will be discussed in 8.8 *et seq.*, where the important question is often whether the provisions of Directives can themselves be invoked in national courts as giving rise to rights for individuals and, if this is not possible, the scope of the duty upon the national court to achieve a harmonious resolution of apparently conflicting provisions in the Directive and the national implementing measures. A new element of enforceability of Directives emerged in the case of Cases C-6 and 9/90

Francovich v. *Italian State* where the Court held that a Member State
could be liable for the damage which results from its failure to implement
a Directive.

5.12   Decisions

These are measures of an individual nature which may be addressed either
to individuals or undertakings, or to Member States. Article 115 EC, for
example, gives a power to the Commission to adopt Decisions addressed
to the Member States authorising them to restrict imports of third country
products from other Member States, in derogation from the normal
principle that third country products, once they have entered the
Community, may circulate freely. Decisions adopted by the Commission
under Regulation 17 in application of Articles 85 and 86 EC (the
competition rules) offer an example of Decisions addressed to individuals
or undertakings. Decisions are not normally normative, in the sense of
creating generally applicable Community law; this is certainly the case
with competition Decisions which do not create general rules of conduct
for undertakings, but merely bind those to whom they are addressed. On
the other hand, Decisions adopted by the Commission in pursuance of a
policy objective laid down by the Treaty such as that of coordinating
cooperation between the Member States in a field of social policy (Article
118 EC) are more akin to a general normative act (see Cases 281, etc./85
Germany et al v. *Commission* [1987] ECR 3203).

5.13   *Sui Generis* Acts

Not all binding legal acts of the institutions are readily capable of
inclusion within the categories set out in Article 189 EC. The Court has
recognised a further category of so-called *sui generis* acts. These include in
particular internal management measures of the Community institutions,
such as measures establishing committees, or allocating funds for
European Parliament elections (see Case 294/83 *'Les Verts'*). This
category also includes certain measures which might be thought, at first
sight, to fall within the 'soft law' category of non-binding acts such as
recommendations and opinions. An example of this is the 'resolution'
adopted by the Council determining the format for Community participation in the negotiation of the European Road Transport Agreement. In
Case 22/70 *Commission* v. *Council (ERTA)* ([1971] ECR 263), the
Commission successfully established that such a measure could be
challenged under Article 173 EC which provides that the 'Court of
Justice shall review the legality of *acts . . . other than recommendations
or opinions*' (emphasis added). The important point in such a case is the
binding nature of the act, which must in some way change the legal
position of those affected by it. Challenges to resolutions of the

Parliament have also been declared admissible: in Case 230/81 *Luxembourg* v. *Parliament* ([1983] ECR 255) Luxembourg brought the first of a number of cases in which it has challenged resolutions concerned with the geographical relocation of the Parliament.

5.14 'Soft Law'

The fact that recommendations and opinions (and the other forms of Community 'soft law' such as 'conclusions', 'declarations', 'action programmes' and '*communiqués*') do not have binding legal force within the Community legal order does not mean that they are entirely legally irrelevant. On the contrary, the content of such provisions may be used as persuasive guides to interpretation of other measures adopted by the Community or the Member States, and may influence the conduct of those parties (Wellens and Borchardt, 1989). We shall see in 8.15 that the Court has held that Community soft law measures may need to be used by national courts for the purposes of interpreting national legislation (see Case C-322/88 *Grimaldi* v. *Fonds des Maladies Professionnelles* [1989] ECR 4407). Where a policy field lies at the margins of Community competence, the evolution of a common Community policy may well shift from the soft to the hard over a period of time, with non-binding measures such as those cited above forming a useful prelude to the adoption of more rigorous measures. Such a development has taken place in the field of vocational training. Less positively, soft law can also be the refuge of the Council of Ministers when it is unable to agree upon binding measures. This has occurred in particular in the social policy field, where some of the proposals put forward by the Commission under the Social Action Programme agreed in 1974 (see 2.9) were watered down from Directives to Recommendations.

5.15 The Case Law of the Court of Justice

Although the task of the Court of Justice is to interpret and not to make the law, and although the Court itself is not bound by its own previous decisions, it is nonetheless true that in a practical sense the case law of the Court is an important source of law within the Community jurisdiction. We have seen already the unwritten general principles which the Court has distilled from national and international traditions as being 'inherent' in the Community system. We have referred also to the Court's occasional practice of limiting the retrospective effect of its preliminary rulings. This case law is, of course, binding upon national courts; nowhere is this clearer than in the UK where sec. 3(1) of the European Communities Act 1972 states:

'any question as to the meaning or effect of any of the Treaties, or as to the validity, meaning or effect of any Community instrument, shall be treated as a question of law (and, if not referred to the European Court, be for determination as such in accordance with the principles laid down by and any relevant decision of the European Court or any court attached thereto).'

Following the case law of the Court of Justice is made easier by the fact that the Court is generally consistent in its judgments, and, since 1973, has frequently referred to its earlier judgments as one, or even the sole line of argument in a subsequent judgment. The various phrases used by the Court to indicate that a case is located within an established line of case law reveal on occasion an element of impatience that a particular point is not in fact seen as established law. Thus it sometimes states '. . . as the Court has repeatedly held. . .' (Koopmans, 1991b: 504). An example of a line of case law becoming in effect a 'rule of law' is to be found in 13.3, where the concept of a charge having equivalent effect to a customs duty on trade between the Member States is defined. The element of *stare decisis* in Community law has now become so strong that when the Court occasionally changes its mind it makes it clear that it is doing so (e.g. Case C-70/88 *Parliament* v. *Council (Chernobyl)* [1990] ECR I-2041 in which the Court reversed its finding in Case 302/87 *Parliament* v. *Council (Comitology)* [1988] ECR 5615 that the Parliament did not have standing under Article 173 to challenge the acts of other institutions).

Summary

1 The following are the main sources of Community law:
   - the constitutive treaties and other international instruments binding the Community;
   - general principles of law;
   - the acts of the institutions, including where relevant, non-binding measures (soft law);
   - the case law of the Court of Justice.
2 The important body of general principles of law can in turn be subdivided into three groups:
   - principles of administrative legality, and due process;
   - the economic pillars of the internal market;
   - fundamental rights.
3 General principles bind the Community and, in so far as their activities fall within the scope of Community competence, the Member States.
4 At present fundamental rights protection in the Community remains at an uncertain stage of development with a lack of clarity as to the scope of protection, the range of rights protected, and the interaction between important constitutional values subscribed to by the Member States and the economic pillars of the internal market.

5 The main features of the acts of the institutions are described in Article 189 EC; however, the legal nature and effects of these acts have been the subject of creative interpretation by the Court of Justice.

6 The case law of the Court of Justice has been an important source of law within the Community since its inception, and is now more firmly based within an evolving system of *stare decisis*.

Questions

1 Why and how has the protection of fundamental rights within the Community evolved? What are the challenges which the Community currently faces in achieving a satisfactory resolution of the conflicts caused by the differences in fundamental rights protection within the Member States?

2 What are the important features which distinguish Regulations, Directives and Decisions?

3 Using the material discussed in this and earlier Chapters identify some examples of creative 'law-making' by the Court of Justice? Would you agree with the argument that the Court oversteps the limits of acceptable judicial intervention-ism?

Further Reading

Clapham (1990) 'A Human Rights Policy for the European Community', 10 *Yearbook of European Law*, 309.

Grief (1991) 'The Domestic Impact of the European Convention on Human Rights as Mediated through Community Law', *Publication*, 555.

Lenaerts (1991b) 'Fundamental Rights to be included in a Community Catalogue', 16 *European Law Review*, 367.

Phelan (1992) 'Right to Life of the Unborn v. Promotion of Trade in Services: The European Court of Justice and the Normative Shaping of the European Union', 55 *Modern Law Review*, 670.

Schermers (1990) 'The Scales in Balance: *National Constitutional Court* v. *Court of Justice*', 27 Common Market Law Review, 97.

Schwarze (1991) 'Tendencies towards a Common Administrative Law in Europe', 16 *European Law Review*, 3.

Usher (1976) 'The Influence of National Concepts on Decisions of the European Court', 1 *European Law Review*, 359.

Weiler (1986) 'Eurocracy and Distrust: Some Questions concerning the Role of the European Court of Justice in the Protection of Fundamental Human Rights within the Legal Order of the European Communities', 61 *Washington Law Review*, 1103.

Wellens and Borchardt (1989) 'Soft Law in European Community Law', 14 *European Law Review*, 267.

6 The Implementation and Enforcement of Community Law

6.1 Introduction

Two of the most important factors which distinguish the Community legal order from that of other international legal orders are the complexity of the regulatory structure and associated implementation mechanisms and the relative effectiveness of the enforcement mechanisms available. It is crucial that the binding legislative measures envisaged by the Treaty should not only be passed, but also implemented and enforced. However, the Community largely lacks the means and personnel whereby it can itself implement Community law. It cannot, for example, police and enforce the external borders and collect customs duties and agricultural levies, or carry out the detailed implementation of the Common Agricultural Policy (CAP). Only exceptionally is direct implementation by the Community envisaged, although where it is, it is the Commission which is the institution charged with this task (see 3.4). The Community is therefore in large measure dependent upon the effective implementation of Community law by the national administrations, in accordance with detailed procedures laid down in individual Community measures and the general duty of Community loyalty incumbent upon the Member States by virtue of Article 5 EC. This is termed 'indirect implementation'. Here the Commission's role will principally be that of supervising the Member States in order to ensure the effective enforcement of Community law (see 3.6). To this end, the Treaty provides a mechanism in Article 169 EC which permits the Commission to bring alleged Treaty violations by the Member States before the Court of Justice for a declaratory judgment. A similar procedure is also available to Member States in Article 170 EC, which can themselves pursue the interests of the Community by taking defaulting states before the Court of Justice.

This Chapter examines the effective implementation and enforcement of Community law by reference, in particular, to Articles 5 and 169–171 EC.

6.2 The Role of Article 5 EC in the Implementation and Enforcement of Community Law

Article 5 EC reads as follows:

'Member States shall take all appropriate measures, whether general or particular, to ensure fulfilment of the obligations arising out of this

Treaty or resulting from action taken by the institutions of the Community. They shall facilitate the achievement of the Community's tasks.

They shall abstain from any measure which could jeopardize the attainment of the objectives of this Treaty.'

The role of Article 5 in the system of the Treaty has grown over the years. It is a general statement of the duties of Member States in relation to the achievement of the tasks of the Community which are in any case implicit in the binding force of the Treaties, and in the obligation under international law upon the Contracting Parties not to hinder the operation of the Treaties. Until recently it was thought that Article 5 took effect only when read in conjunction with the objectives of the Treaty, and other provisions of Community law which set out the Community's policies (Temple Lang, 1990). However, in recent years, the Court of Justice has shown a markedly increased tendency to refer to Article 5 as a separate source of Member State obligations within the Treaty system (e.g. Case C-374/89 *Commission* v. *Belgium* (19.2.1991)). It is therefore appropriate to analyse it as a distinct feature of the Community's constitutional structure, emphasising here its particular importance in the context of implementation (see Chapter 8 for the role of Article 5 in the context of the relationship between Community law and national law).

In Cases 205–215/82 *Deutsche Milchkontor GmbH* v. *Germany* ([1983] ECR 2633 at p. 2665) the Court stated:

'According to the general principles on which the institutional system of the Community is based and which govern the relations between the Community and the Member States, it is for the Member States, by virtue of Article 5 of the Treaty, to ensure that Community regulations, in particular those concerning the common agricultural policy, are implemented within their territory.'

Thus Article 5 imposes the obligation on the Member States to adapt their national provisions and practices to the requirements of Community law. The Court has held that the obligations under Community law fall upon all organs of the state, including the legislature, executive and judiciary, and apply at all levels of authority. It amplified this point in Case C-8/88 *Germany* v. *Commission* ([1992] 1 CMLR 409) when stressing that, while all state authorities must ensure observance of the rules of Community law within their sphere of competence, the Commission was not empowered to rule upon the division of competences made by national rules (e.g. between federal and regional levels), but could merely verify whether internal supervisory and inspection procedures were effective to ensure the Community law is applied. The duty of national courts is to ensure the effective application of Community law (Case 14/83 *Von Colson and Kamann* v. *Land Nordrhein Westfalen* [1984] ECR 1891). This point will be addressed in Chapter 8.

Article 5 also contains a duty of cooperation; the Member States have the duty to facilitate the achievement of the Commission's tasks under Article 155, and this includes, where necessary, providing information which is requested. The Commission has a general right to obtain information from the Member States about their implementation of Community law, quite apart from any specific reporting requirement contained in Community legislation (Case C-33/90 *Commission* v. *Italy* [1992] 2 CMLR 353). The duty of loyalty is mutual, and applies also to the Community institutions. In Case C-2/88 Imm *Zwartveld* ([1990] ECR I-3365) the Court used Article 5 as the basis for a duty on the Commission to respond to a request for mutual assistance made by a Dutch examining magistrate in which he asked for information regarding fisheries inspections carried by Commission inspectors, which he required to pursue an investigation into alleged violations of Community fish marketing regulations. It has since applied these principles in the context of Article 85 EC; it held in Case C-234/89 *Delimitis* v. *Henninger Bräu AG* ([1991] ECR I-935) that the Commission must, where requested, assist the national courts in their task of applying Community competition law. It must not only supply information about the state of any relevant proceedings before the Commission itself, but also make available any information of a legal and economic nature which might assist the national court in resolving the case before it.

6.3 Enforcement Proceedings under Articles 169–171 EC

It is in pursuit of the Commission's obligation under Article 155 EC to 'ensure that the provisions of this Treaty and the measures taken by the institutions pursuant thereto are applied' that the primary obligation of direct enforcement of Member State obligations falls upon that institution. The principal instrument of enforcement is Article 169 which provides:

> 'If the Commission considers that a Member State has failed to fulfil an obligation under this Treaty, it shall deliver a reasoned opinion on the matter after giving the State concerned the opportunity to submit its observations.
>
> If the State concerned does not comply with the opinion within the period laid down by the Commission, the latter may bring the matter before the Court of Justice.'

Article 170 EC gives a similarly framed power to the Member States which they may use against each other. It has been rarely used. The successful challenge by France to the UK's unilateral fishery conservation measures (Case 141/78 *France* v. *United Kingdom* [1979] ECR 2923) is one of the few examples of the invocation of this procedure. The use of the Article 170 procedure will always increase the tension and conflict between two states which are in dispute. The Member States prefer to leave the enforcement role primarily to the Commission; although in appropriate cases they are prepared to intervene in support of the Commission before the Court.

Remedies under the enforcement procedures of Articles 169 and 170 are set out in Article 171 EC. Prior to the Treaty of Maastricht, the Court of Justice was limited to a 'finding' of breach of the Treaty and the obligation which fell upon the Member State in breach was merely to take the necessary measures to comply with the judgment of the Court. However, although failure to comply with Court judgments has never been as serious a problem as non-compliance in general, a new paragraph was inserted in Article 171 by the Treaty of Maastricht which provides as follows:

'If the Commission considers that the Member State concerned has not taken such measures [i.e. to comply with a judgment of the Court] it shall, after giving that State the opportunity to submit its observations, issue a reasoned opinion specifying the points on which the Member State concerned has not complied with the judgment of the Court of Justice.

If the Member State concerned fails to take the necessary measures to comply with the Court's judgment within the time-limit laid down by the Commission, the latter may bring the case before the Court of Justice. In so doing it shall specify the amount of the lump sum or penalty payment to be paid by the Member State concerned which it considers appropriate in the circumstances.

If the Court of Justice finds that the Member State concerned has not complied with its judgment it may impose a lump sum or penalty payment on it.'

A number of preliminary points can be made about the enforcement procedures of Articles 169–171. First, Articles 169 and 170 both divide the enforcement process into an administrative and a judicial phase. Opportunities for settlement exist throughout the administrative phase, but once the Commission has brought the matter before the Court at the conclusion of the period for compliance laid down in the reasoned opinion, it may continue with the proceedings, notwithstanding compliance by the Member State during the course of the proceedings (Case 240/86 *Commission* v. *Greece* [1988] ECR 1835), for the purposes of obtaining a clarification of the law by the Court. The Court indicated that such a declaratory judgment would still be useful, since it would clarify the possible liability of the Member State at national level for breach of the Treaty, and make it unnecessary for a national court to make a subsequent reference under Article 177 EC. This point may be increasingly important in view of the decision of the Court in Cases C-6 and 9/90 *Francovich* v. *Italian State* ([1992] IRLR. 84) regarding the award of damages against Member States for loss stemming from the failure to implement a Directive.

Secondly, the Commission cannot take binding measures under Article 169 to *order* the compliance of the Member State, or to state the nature of the infringement. In this context, Article 169 should be contrasted with the enforcement of the competition rules against individuals under Articles 85 and 86 EC and Regulation 17. In that context, the Commission may issue binding Decisions which are enforceable against individuals unless successfully challenged in the Court. The Commission also has similar powers under Article 90(3) EC which enables it to address Decisions or Directives to the Member States in order to enforce the provisions of Article 90 on the application of the competition rules to public undertakings. General enforcement proceedings under Article 88 ECSC also consist of a Decision taken by the High Authority, which may be challenged before the Court.

The basic elements of a successful action by the Commission are the following:

(a) The Commission takes the view that a Member State is in breach of its obligations; the relevant obligations include those flowing from the constitutive treaties and any other international instruments which impose obligations upon the Member States, and from secondary acts of a binding nature. Failure to apply a general principle of law in the interpretation of provisions of Community law would probably also engage Member State responsibility under Article 5 and give rise to an Article 169 action, although the Court has not stated this explicitly (Temple Lang, 1990: 655).

(b) The Commission informs the State of its view and gives it an opportunity to answer the allegation or to end the offending practice or to repeal the offending law.

(c) The Commision delivers a reasoned opinion demonstrating the existence of the infringement.

(d) The State fails to comply with its Treaty obligation within the time limit laid down by the Commission. [*End of the administrative phase.*]

(e) [*Beginning of the judicial phase.*] The Commission brings the matter before the Court.

(f) The Court finds a violation.

6.4 The Range of National Conduct Capable of Engaging State Responsibility

The defendant in an enforcement action is the State, not the government, although it is conventionally the government which conducts the defence on behalf of the State. It is 'state conduct' which engages state responsibility, and the Court has defined this category broadly. It includes the following:

- acts or omissions on the part of the legislature, including the maintenance in force of an infringing statute, even if it is not applied (Case 167/73 *Commission* v. *France (French Merchant Seamen)* [1974] ECR 359);
- acts or omissions on the part of the executive, including the maintenance in force of an infringing administrative measure, even if it is not applied;
- actions of constitutionally independent public authorities, such as local or regional authorities (Case 1/86 *Commission* v. *Belgium (Water Pollution)* [1987] ECR 2797) or the constituent states within a federation (Case 9/74 *Casagrande* v. *Landeshauptstadt München* [1974] ECR 773);
- decisions of national courts, which are subject to the duty of Community loyalty under Article 5. It was suggested by AG Warner in Case 30/77 *R. v. Bouchereau* ([1977] ECR 1999) that mere judicial error should not engage state responsibility, but only the deliberate flouting of Community law by a national court. In fact, the Commission has been extremely hesitant to take proceedings in respect of judicial conduct citing 'the universal principle of the independence of the judiciary' as the reason (*Sixth Annual Report by the Commission to the European Parliament on the Monitoring of the Application of Community Law 1988*, Com (89) 411, p. 95). Such proceedings have been started by the Commission, but have never actually been brought before the Court.

More contentiously, the Court has extended state responsibility to cover the acts of a private party under the control of the State. In Case 249/81 *Commission* v. *Ireland (Buy Irish)* ([1982] ECR 4005), Ireland was held responsible for the actions of the Irish Goods Council, a private limited company funded by the government, with a management appointed by and policies determined by the government, which was charged with the running of a 'buy Irish' campaign which contravened Community rules on the free movement of goods.

6.5 The Administrative Phase

The administrative phase is itself subdivided into an informal and a formal phase. In the informal phase, the Commission investigates the possibility of a breach, and attempts to settle matters informally. In the formal phase, the Commission requests the Member State to submit its observations, stating the alleged infringement and laying down a time limit for the submission of observations (the formal letter of notice); if it is not satisfied by the replies it receives it may deliver a reasoned opinion. Article 169 EC incorporates the principle of *audi alteram partem* (the right to a fair hearing). Consequently, it is incumbent upon the Commission to ensure that the Member State is told in clear terms exactly what constitutes the alleged violation in order that it may submit its observations (Case 211/81 *Commission* v. *Denmark* [1982] ECR 4547).

The alleged violations must be defined by the reasoned opinion; the Commission cannot subsequently raise matters before the Court which were not contained in the reasoned opinion (Case 31/69 *Commission* v. *Italy (Export Rebates)* [1970] ECR 25). It gives a time limit for the Member State to comply with Community law, which must be reasonable. This may vary according to the circumstances of the case. In Case 85/85 *Commission* v. *Belgium* ([1986] ECR 1149), the Commission required Belgium to remove a property tax imposed on Community officials resident in Belgium within two weeks of the reasoned opinion. The Court held that the time limit was reasonable because the Belgian Government knew of (and had not contested) the Commission's position long before the Article 169 procedure was initiated. However, in Case 293/85 *Commission* v. *Belgium* ([1988] ECR 305) two weeks was considered an unreasonably short time limit for Belgium to remove discriminatory fees imposed on foreign nationals studying within the Belgian higher education system. In Case 74/82 *Commission* v. *Ireland (Imports of poultry)* ([1984] ECR 317) the Court even accepted a five day time limit.

The reasoned opinion cannot be challenged by an aggrieved private party (or a Member State) by way of Article 173 EC annulment proceedings, as it is not an act which produces legal effects; it is merely a step in the proceedings (Case 48/65 *Lütticke* v. *Commission* [1966] ECR 19) (see 9.4). However, a Member State which is subject to proceedings will have an opportunity in the context of the judicial phase to raise irregularities in the reasoned opinion, such as the failure to state reasons, as it can any other procedural irregularities which have occurred during the course of the administrative phase. No party can force the Commission to take enforcement proceedings; failure to act is not actionable under Article 175 EC (Case 247/87 *Star Fruit* v. *Commission* [1989] ECR 291). The Commission's discretion is likewise unfettered as to when it may wish to bring enforcement proceedings. In Case 7/71 *Commission* v. *France (Euratom Supply Agency)* ([1971] ECR 1003 – an action brought under the materially identical Article 141 Euratom) – the Court held:

'The action for a declaration that a State has failed to fulfil an obligation ... does not have to be brought within a predetermined period, since, by reason of its nature and purpose, this procedure involves a power on the part of the Commission to consider the most appropriate means and time-limits for the purposes of putting an end to any contraventions of the Treaty.'

Of course, Member States can have recourse to Article 170 if they are dissatisfied with the conduct of the Commission, but an aggrieved private party can only seek to bring proceedings in the national court which have the effect of enforcing Community law against the national authorities.

The Commission's discretion is also not restricted by any form of 'estoppel' whereby it is deemed to have consented by previous informal or even formal approval of the Member State's conduct. It may at any point revise its view and take infringement proceedings (Case 288/83 *Commission* v. *Ireland (Potatoes)* [1985] ECR 1761).

6.6 The Judicial Phase

In the judicial phase, the Court will examine both the procedural propriety of the action as so far conducted by the Commission, as an issue of the admissibility of the action, and the substance of the alleged violations. The following paragraphs set out the arguments put forward by the Member States which have consistently been judged by the Court to be ineffective defences to enforcement actions.

6.7 Questions of National Law in General

No matter pertaining to the status of the national measure in question can hinder a finding of infringement by the Court. In Case 48/71 *Commission* v. *Italy (Art Treasures II)* ([1972] ECR 527) Italy cited as a defence the difficulties of parliamentary procedure it had experienced in abolishing a tax on the export of artistic and historical treasures to other Member States, owing to the need to observe the relevant constitutional requirements. Attributing the obligation to comply to the supremacy of Community law, the Court stated that:

'the attainment of the objectives of the Community requires that the rules of Community law established by the Treaty itself or arising from procedures which it has instituted are fully applicable at the same time and with identical effects over the whole territory of the Community without the Member States being able to place any obstacles in the way. The grant made by Member States to the Community of rights and powers in accordance with the provisions of the Treaty involves a definitive limitation on their sovereign rights and no provisions whatsoever of national law may be invoked to override this limitation.'

6.8 Legislative Paralysis and Change of Government

The ineffectiveness, permanent or temporary, of the national political system cannot be used as a defence. There is no element of fault contained in a finding of infringement of the Treaty under Article 169; the finding is a simple objective statement of fact concerning the failure of the Member State to fulfil its obligations, and it is irrelevant whether the failure stems from inertia or opposition (see Case 322/82 *Commission* v. *France* [1983]

ECR 3705, per AG Rozès). In Case 77/69 *Commission* v. *Belgium (Pressed Wood)* ([1970] ECR 237) the Belgian government was unable to secure the passage through the legislature of a bill revising a law which imposed a discriminatory tax upon imported pressed wood. The constitutional separation between the legislature and the executive did not preclude the responsibility of Belgium for infringement. In Italy, frequent changes of government have often hampered the effective implementation of Community Directives, but this has not been accepted as a defence by the Court (e.g. Case 136/81 *Commission* v. *Italy* [1982] ECR 3547 – failure to implement Directive harmonising provisions of company law).

6.9 Defences Related to the Nature of the Relevant Provision of Community Law

The obligation upon Member States under Article 5 and more specific provisions of the Treaty is to implement Community law in full and proper form. Thus it is insufficient and no defence to adopt a circular binding only upon the administration but with an uncertain effect *vis-à-vis* third parties in order to implement a Directive on atmospheric pollution (Cases C-261/88 and C-56/89 *Commission* v. *Germany* (30.5.1991)). Similarly the Member State may not rely upon the direct effect of a Directive as a substitute for implementation. It was held to be no defence in proceedings against the Netherlands for failure to implement a Council Directive on the quality of drinking water that regional and local authorities were in any case directly bound by the Directive, provisions of which were justiciable before national courts, and that the authorities had in fact implemented the Directive in the practical management of water quality (Case 96/81 *Commission* v. *Netherlands* [1982] ECR 1791).

It is not clear whether the alleged unlawfulness of the Community measure with which non-compliance is alleged is an effective defence. Case 156/77 *Commission* v. *Belgium* [1978] ECR 1881 and Case 3/59 *Germany* v. *High Authority* [1960] ECR 53 are usually cited as demonstrating that if a Member State has failed to challenge a Community measure directly under the relevant provisions of the European Community or ECSC Treaties, it cannot raise the unlawfulness of the measure in Article 169 enforcement proceedings. However, there may be an exception for measures which contain such serious and manifest defects that they can be regarded as 'non-existent' (Case 226/87 *Commission* v. *Greece* [1989] 3 CMLR 569; [1988] ECR 3611) (see 9.4).

6.10 The Principle of Reciprocity

The Community legal order differs sharply from the general public international legal order in that there is no defence of reciprocity. A Member State cannot escape a finding of infringement by claiming that another Member State is also failing to comply (Case 232/78 *Commission* v. *France (Lamb Wars)* [1979] ECR 2729). The same principle applies to the claim that the Community institutions are in breach of their obligations. In Cases 90 and 91/63 *Commission* v. *Luxembourg and Belgium (Dairy Products)* ([1964] ECR 625) the Court declared:

'except where otherwise expressly provided, the basic concept of the Treaty requires that the Member States shall not take the law into their own hands. Therefore the fact that the Council failed to carry out its obligations cannot relieve the defendants from carrying out theirs.'

6.11   Expedited Proceedings

Expedited proceedings, which allow the Commission to bring an alleged infringement before the Court without observing the procedural requirements laid down in Article 169, are provided for *inter alia* in Articles 93 and 100A(4) EC. Articles 92 and 93 charge the Commission with the task of reviewing state aids, and where necessary, with issuing Decisions requiring Member States to abolish, to alter or not to bring into force aids which are incompatible with the Common Market. A Member State which fails to comply with such a Decision may be brought directly before the Court by the Commission, without prejudice to Articles 169 and 170. Article 100A(4) gives a similar power to the Commission to police the use by Member States of the right which they are given under Article 100A to derogate from Community harmonising measures in the field of the internal market and to continue to apply stricter national measures which protect important public policy interests (e.g. in order to protect the public health or the environment).

6.12   Interim Measures

Article 186 EC states:

'The Court of Justice may in any cases before it prescribe any necessary interim measures.'

This possibility applies both to Article 169 proceedings (e.g. Case 61/77R *Commission* v. *Ireland (Fisheries)* [1977] ECR 937) and to expedited proceedings under Article 93 (e.g. Cases 31 and 53/77R *Commission* v. *United Kingdom (Pig Producers)* [1977] ECR 921). An application for interim relief may be made at any time once the administrative stage has been completed. Applications for interim measures are heard generally by the President sitting alone, without the assistance of an Advocate General. Interim measures may be awarded if two conditions are satisfied; the Commission must show:

- a *prima facie* case (i.e. the case must not be manifestly ill-founded);
- urgency, which is assessed in relation to the necessity for interim measures in order to prevent serious and irreparable damage to the interests of the Community.

At first sight it might appear that the powers of the Court are greater in interim proceedings than they are in the main proceedings. This is because the Court's judgments are framed in more trenchant terms (e.g. the order to suspend the application of the Merchant Shipping Act 1988 in Case C-246/89R *Commission* v. *United Kingdom* [1989] ECR 3125); however, the judgment remains declaratory in effect.

6.13 Sanctions

The declaratory nature of the Court's judgment under Article 169 means that the Court does not have the power to declare national measures void. On the other hand, it would be inconsistent with the principle of the supremacy of Community law for a national court which was aware of such a finding on the part of the Court to apply an infringing national rule; national law is thus in effect rendered 'inapplicable' (Case 106/77 *Amministrazione delle Finanze dello Stato* v. *Simmenthal (Simmenthal II)* [1978] ECR 629; see 9.19).

The declaratory judgment is binding, and thus failure to comply with a Court judgment is itself a Treaty obligation and can therefore be the subject of further enforcement proceedings. For a number of years, the Commission argued that there was a need for more effective sanctions, and it put before the Intergovernmental Conference (IGC) on Political Union convened in 1990 proposals for the imposition of financial penalties for failure to give effect to a judgment. These proposals attracted the support in particular of the UK, and consequently, amendments to Article 171 were introduced by the Treaty of Maastricht. The initial proposal to impose a penalty comes from the Commission, but the discretion to fine lies with the Court. Members of the Court of Justice were known to be reluctant to be given the entire responsibility for fining Member States. The question remains open whether fines will need to be high to bring about compliance and to deter recidivism, or whether the simple fact of the imposition of a fine, however small, and the associated political opprobrium, will be sufficient.

There were other proposals to enhance the sanctions system put before the IGC, including the suggestion that the Court should be given the power to strike down infringing (i.e. unconstitutional) national legislation, a power held by the constitutional courts of many federal states. An alternative suggestion was that the Court should have the power to award compensation to the victims of an infringement in the context of enforcement proceedings, but the Court has come closer to giving effect to this suggestion by articulating the responsibility of Member States for damage caused by failure to implement a Directive in *Francovich*.

Under Article 93(2) the Commission has a policy of requiring Member States to reclaim monies paid to the beneficiaries of state aids which are found to be incompatible with the Common Market (OJ 1983 C318/3). However, the Commission has to take care to observe the procedural rights of the interested parties. This is illustrated by the Rover/British Aerospace 'sweetener'. In 1988 the Commission issued a Decision authorising certain capital aids by the UK to Rover in connection with its acquisition by British Aerospace. It later came to the conclusion that certain financial concessions had been made which were not authorised by the Decision, and it issued a further Decision ordering the UK to reclaim the payments. This was successfully challenged by British Aerospace and Rover (Case C-292/90 *British Aerospace and Rover Group Holdings plc* v. *Commission* ([1992] 1 CMLR 853). The Court held that if the Commission objected to the granting of a new aid, it was obliged to follow the procedures laid down in Article 93 once more in order to respect the rights of the defence of interested parties, in particular the right to be heard. It could not short-circuit these procedures by simply requiring the aid to be reclaimed.

6.14   The Problem of Non-compliance

Enforcement of the law is taken very seriously within the Community legal order. The pursuit and prosecution of violations of the Treaty is viewed as one aspect of the application of the rule of law. Non-compliance is therefore a challenge to the fabric of the legal order, as well as a failure to give effect to the intentions of the drafters of the Treaty and of the framers of legislation. The Commission has responded to this challenge by monitoring national compliance and it submits *Annual Reports* on the Application of Community Law to the Parliament (see most recently the *Ninth Annual Report for 1991* Com (92) 136). It has adopted measures to improve the effectiveness of the enforcement procedures. For example, it has created two categories of enforcement proceedings: actions for failure to implement Directives and actions in respect of other breaches of the Treaty. Proceedings for failure to implement Directives – a serious concern given the degree to which the success of the Internal Market Programme rests upon the adoption and implementation of Directives – are now begun routinely and mechanically whenever Member States fail to notify the Commission of the measures taken to notify a particular Directive. The latest figures indicate much higher implementation rates: of the Directives due to be transposed by December 31 1991, implementation rates at the end of 1991 varied between 76.5% (Italy) and 97% (Denmark). Difficulties in one of the main trouble spots, Italy, have been alleviated by the adoption of a new procedure in 1988 whereby an annual

Community law is passed implementing en bloc all applicable Community legislation. Each year the Commission opens between 800–1,000 new proceedings by issuing formal letters of notice. Its new procedures in relation to Directives have led to a sharp rise in the number of reasoned opinions delivered (up from 251 in 1990 to 412 in 1991). However, there is no corresponding increase in the number of actions actually reaching the Court, and indeed a small decline (from 77 in 1990 to 64 in 1991) suggests that earlier compliance is becoming the norm now that it is clear just how restricted a range of excuses the Court is prepared to accept. However, apart from monitoring the implementation of Directives, the Commission is very greatly indebted to the vigilance of the public to enable it to uncover infringements of the Treaty. It receives more than 1000 complaints per year from private parties, and has now produced a standard complaint form (OJ 1989 C26/7; [1989] 1 CMLR 617) to facilitate the process of making a complaint.

There are a multitude of reasons for non-compliance; only rarely is it outright opposition to a particular measure or the protection of national sovereignty which lies behind a failure to comply. Of course, being outvoted in the adoption process is one reason why a Member State might very well drag its heels over the implementation process, but it may equally be the fact that a Community measure is badly drafted and subject to misinterpretation or that representatives of the Member States were not fully and properly involved in preliminary negotiations within the Commission. Reasons which are internal to the Member States themselves are often significant; legislative paralysis has been a particular problem where there are coalition governments or frequent changes of government. Executive inefficiency with no clear line of authority determining who is responsible for ensuring the implementation of Community law, and the particularities of the national division of power within each state can also be contributing factors. The alleged infringement may also result from a measure which previously the Commission has shown no particular inclination to enforce, but for which compliance is now required following a change in policy.

The enhancement of sanctions for non-compliance with a Court judgment is just one mechanism aimed at solving a more general problem. It may be that in addition to its perennial need for more resources, the Commission also needs a clear order of priority for the pursuit of cases of non-compliance. Perhaps, for example, complaints brought by entire sectors of industry should be given a higher status. Finally, it has often been suggested that the task of bringing about compliance should be hived off to a separate service, thus separating the enforcement role from the policy-making role.

The enforcement proceedings contained in the Treaty need to be viewed in the context of the alternative mechanisms available for the enforcement of Community law against the authorities of the Member States in the form of proceedings brought before the national courts. Direct and indirect enforcement need to be seen as two aspects of one overall structure; indeed, frequently they will run side by side, with the same issue coming before the Court for decision in the context of different proceedings. This occurred with the litigation surrounding the restrictions on non-national fishing boats introduced by the Merchant Shipping Act 1988. In Case C-246/89R *Commission* v. *United Kingdom*, the Court awarded interim measures against the UK at the behest of the Commission, who had received complaints from Spanish fishing boat owners based in the UK; just a few months later, in Case C-213/89 *R.* v. *Secretary of State for Transport, ex parte Factortame* ([1990] ECR I-2433) the Court gave a judgment making it clear that the House of Lords should give an interim remedy in the national proceedings concerned with the same dispute.

Private enforcement is efficient in the sense that it does not use Community administrative resources. It also emphasises the relationship between the Community citizen and the Community legal system. The disadvantage is that such an approach depends upon the vagaries of individual decisions to litigate and upon the varying attitudes of national courts to Community law. Part III will examine the grounds for bringing actions based on Community law in national courts, addressing the status of Community law within the national legal order and the range of sanctions for non-compliance which courts must make available for failure to observe the Treaty. First, however, the organic connection in the form of Article 177 EC between the national courts and the Court of Justice will be examined.

Summary

1 Community law is principally implemented by the Member States, rather than by the Commission. Article 5 EC imposes a duty of loyalty upon the Member States in the implementation of Community law, breach of which may give rise to an enforcement action under Article 169 EC by the Commission.

2 Enforcement proceedings may be brought by the Commission or by a Member State under Articles 169 and 170 EC. They comprise an administrative and judicial phase.

3 Failure to comply with any obligation arising under Community law, by any organ of the state, may engage the responsibility of the Member State.

4 The Court of Justice will not accept defences to enforcement proceedings based on national law.

5 The sanctions available under Article 171 EC prior to the adoption of the Treaty of Maastricht were solely declaratory. Article 171 has now been amended to provide for the possibility of financial penalties being imposed upon Member States which fail to comply with a declaratory judgment of the Court which states that they are in breach of their Community obligations.

6 The availability of stiffer sanctions is one means by which the problem of non-compliance with Community law can be dealt with. The procedures for enforcement can also be made more effective.

Questions

1 What obligations does Article 5 EC impose upon Member States in relation to the implementation and enforcement of Community law?

2 How could the system of enforcement mechanisms available under the European Community Treaty be made more effective?

Workshop

In June 1991 the Council adopted a Directive which required, on grounds of the protection of the consumer, that all milk sold in the European Community should be packaged in cylindrical 1.5 litre cartons. Measures were to be brought into force by the Member States to give effect to the Directive before December 31 1991. The measure was adopted by a qualified majority with the States of Ajax and Zeno voting against. The Parliament, when consulted, had been unhappy about the measure, but the Council ignored its objections. In June 1991, the Parliament brought an action for annulment against the meaure arguing that the Directive should be declared void because it was adopted using the wrong legal basis; Article 100A should have been used instead of Article 43. This action is still pending. Zeno agrees with the proceedings brought by the Parliament, but has neither joined the Parliament as a co-applicant, nor intervened in the case.

In Zeno, instead of implementing the Directive, the Minister of Agriculture and Consumer Protection issued an instruction to all Trading Standards Officers ordering them not to enforce the Directive. Cowcrop, a company which already sells its milk in cylindrical cartons, challenges the validity of these instructions in the Zeno administrative courts, arguing that they give a competitive advantage to companies which are not adopting the European Community standard and are in breach of Community law. The matter proceeds quickly to the Zeno Supreme Administrative Court, which refuses to refer the matter to the Court of Justice on the grounds that Directives cannot give rise to rights which individuals may enforce.

Cowcrop has also complained to the Commission. After a period of informal consultation in which Zeno has shown itself unwilling to compromise or accept the Commission's objections, the Commission issued a reasoned opinion on February 4 1992, stating as the basis of Zeno's violation the instructions issued to Trading Standards Officers. It gave Zeno fourteen days in which to bring its conduct into line with the Treaty, and then on February 19, brought the matter before the Court, citing as an additional ground of objection the refusal of the Zeno Supreme Administrative Court to refer the matter to the Court of Justice. It is now seeking the award of interim measures by the Court.

Zeno objects that Ajax is also not enforcing the Directive, and that the Commission has not brought proceedings against Ajax. In addition it points out that another Member State (Kenjo) has unilaterally stopped all imports of milk from Ajax and Zeno on the grounds that the latter two Member States are in flagrant breach of Community law. Zeno argues that while there is a clearly a political issue which needs to be settled in the Council of Ministers, this is not an appropriate matter for the Court of Justice.

Discuss

[**Note**: It would be useful to review again this Workshop after you have completed work on Chapters 7 and 8]

Further Reading

Dashwood and White (1989) 'Enforcement Actions and Article 169 and 170', 14 *European Law Review*, 388.

Everling (1984) 'The Member States of the European Community before their Court of Justice,' 9 *European Law Review*, 315.

Temple Lang (1990) 'Community Constitutional Law: Article 5 EEC Treaty', 27 *Common Market Law Review*, 645.

Weiler (1988) 'The White Paper and the Application of Community Law', in Bieber *et al.* (1988).

Community Law
and National Law

7 Article 177 EEC – The Organic Connection Between National Courts and the European Court of Justice

7.1 Introduction

Article 177 EC makes provision for national courts to ascertain from the Court of Justice its views on the status and meaning of Community law. After amendment by the Treaty of Maastricht to incorporate the institutions of EMU, it now provides:

'The Court of Justice shall have jurisdiction to give preliminary rulings concerning:

(a) the interpretation of this Treaty;
(b) the validity and interpretation of acts of the institutions of the Community and of the ECB;
(c) the interpretation of the statutes of bodies established by an act of the Council, where those statutes so provide.

Where such a question is raised before any court or tribunal of a Member State, that court or tribunal may, if it considers that a decision on the question is necessary to enable it to give judgment, request the Court of Justice to give a ruling thereon.

Where any such question is raised in a case pending before a court or tribunal of a Member State, against whose decisions there is no judicial remedy under national law, that court or tribunal shall bring the matter before the Court of Justice.'

The grand objectives of the Community legal order, which include the intermeshing of Community law and national law, could not be achieved without some organic mechanism for ensuring the uniform application of Community law, in which the Court of Justice can give authoritative rulings on the meaning of Community law. The Court of Justice frequently reminds us that it is the purpose of Article 177 to provide such a mechanism:

'Article 177 is essential for the preservation of the Community character of the law established by the Treaty and has the object of ensuring that in all circumstances the law is the same in all States of the Community' (Case 166/73 *Rheinmühlen-Düsseldorf* v. *Einfuhr- und Vorratstelle für Getreide und Futtermittel* [1974] ECR 33 at p. 43).

With this purpose in mind, the Court has been able to use Article 177 preliminary rulings as the centrepieces for the construction of a legal edifice in which Community law can be uniformly interpreted and enforced within the national courts of the Member States in the same terms as it is within the Court of Justice itself. To this end, of course, Article 177 references have given the Court the opportunity to articulate the principles on which it is possible for individuals to enforce Community law against infringing Member States and, where this is permitted under Community law, against infringing individuals. In addition, however, Article 177 is a key element of the administrative law of the Community, and its role in this context will be reconsidered in Part IV. For Article 177 provides a mechanism for indirect challenges to the validity of Community legal acts in national courts, using the medium of direct challenges to national implementing acts based on an allegedly invalid 'parent' Community acts.

As Article 177 provides a 'reference procedure' in the hands of the referring court and not an 'appeals procedure' in the hands of parties who consider their rights under Community law to be infringed or feel themselves to be the victims of an invalid Community act, its success has always rested on the willingness of national courts to collaborate by making references and by accepting the subsequent judgments of the Court. The Court has based its approach on a philosophy of the separate functions of national court and Community court, a philosophy which can be derived from the views of AG Lagrange in the first case submitted under Article 177. In Case 13/61 *Bosch* v. *de Geus* ([1962] ECR 45 at p. 56) he asserted that:

'applied judiciously – one is tempted to say loyally – the provisions of Article 177 lead to a real and fruitful collaboration between the municipal courts and the Court of Justice of the Communities with mutual regard for their respective jurisdictions. It is in this spirit that each side must solve the sometimes delicate problems which may arise in all systems of preliminary procedure, and which are necessarily made more difficult in this case by the differences in the legal systems of the Member States as regards this type of procedure.'

A similar view emerges from the ruling of the Court itself in Case 16/65 *Firma Schwarze* v. *Einfuhr- und Vorratstelle für Getreide und Futtermittel* ([1965] ECR 877 at p. 886):

'[Article 177 establishes] a special field of judicial cooperation which requires the national court and the Court of Justice, both keeping within their respective jurisdiction, and with the aim of ensuring that

Community law is applied in a unified manner, to make direct and complementary contributions to the working out of a decision.'

The 'separate functions' conception gives the national court a broad discretion to formulate the questions which it believes to be appropriate. However, as the Court put it in the early case of *Costa* v. *ENEL* (Case 6/ 64 [1964] ECR 585), the fact that a question is 'imperfectly formulated' does not deprive the Court of the power to extract from that question those matters which are relevant to the interpretation of the Treaty. It will pull in provisions of Community law which it considers pertinent, even though these were not raised by the national court (see Case 78/70 *Deutsche Grammophon* v. *Metro-SB-Grossmärkte* [1971] ECR 487). In fact, the Court rarely hesitates to rephrase questions posed by national courts. On the other hand, it has frequently used the separation of functions argument in order to evade the argument that it is overstretching its remit as the Community's court, stressing that it has no jurisdiction to interfere with the discretion of the national court as to what to refer, or indeed when to refer. When challenged about the nature of its case law, the Court insists on the fine line between the interpretation and application of Community law, maintaining it is restricted in the Article 177 context only to the former. It frequently insists on the right of the national court to judge the relevance of the questions which it poses to the litigation before it (e.g. Case C-186/90 *Durighello* v. *INPS* (28.11.1991)). The only requirements which the Court places upon the questions which it receives are that they arise out of a 'genuine dispute' before the national court and that they are not purely hypothetical questions.

7.2 The Requirement of a Genuine Dispute

In the two *Foglia* v. *Novello* cases, the Court articulated and applied the requirement of a genuine dispute. In Case 104/79 *Foglia* v. *Novello (No. 1)* ([1980] ECR 745) the Court was asked by the Italian court before which the case had come to assess the compatibility with Community law of a French tax imposed on imported wine. It appeared that the parties were in agreement that the tax was in breach of Community law, and that they had artificially constructed the litigation before the Italian courts, involving an action by Foglia (a dealer) to force Novello (an importer) to pay the French tax, knowing that an Italian court was more likely than a French court to expose the tax to the scrutiny of the Court of Justice by making a reference. The Court unexpectedly refused to answer the questions, sending the case back to the Italian court in the following terms (at p.759):

'It thus appears that the parties to the main action are concerned to obtain a ruling that the French tax system is invalid for liqueur wines by the expedient of proceedings before an Italian court between two private individuals who are in agreement as to the result to be attained and who have inserted a clause in their contract in order to induce the Italian court to give a ruling on the point . . .

The duty of the Court of Justice under Article 177 of the EEC Treaty is to supply all courts in the Community with the information on the interpretation of Community law which is necessary to enable them to settle genuine disputes which are brought before them. A situation in which the Court was obliged by the expedient of arrangements like those described above to give rulings would jeopardise the whole system of legal remedies available to private individuals to enable them to protect themselves against tax provisions which are contrary to the Treaty.'

Quite why the Court chose to argue that such allegedly apocalyptic consequences would result from the 'misuse' of the Article 177 reference procedure in these circumstances is not clear. The expedient of friendly litigation is practised and tolerated in many countries including the UK. What is more, judges in many of the Member States find themselves subject to a prohibition on refusing to give judgment. In keeping with the view that the judge's role is to interpret the law, not to judge the appropriateness of litigation or to interfere in the political sphere, the so-called *déni de justice* (refusal to judge) is a violation of the judge's duty and a criminal offence in France (Article 4 of the *Code civil*). On the other hand, the Court's position is not the same as the conventional national judge. It has claimed a unique and highly political position within the Community legal order, and it is arguable that fictitious litigation (as opposed to friendly litigation, if a distinction can be drawn) is damaging to the gradual evolution of the supranational system in that it may unnecessarily bring into conflict the courts and governments of different states. In that case, it may be legitimate to argue that the rights of the defence of states which find their laws impugned before the courts of other Member States will be undermined. The Court may well have been concerned to avoid handing down a decision which the French Government would be unwilling to execute, and thereby to endanger the system of enforcement of Community law. The decision in Case 104/79, and its follow-up in Case 244/80 *Foglia* v. *Novello (No. 2)* ([1981] ECR 3045) where the Court reproduced the substance of its views when re-questioned by the Italian court and reinforced the point that it is not subject to a duty to give advisory opinions at the request of national courts, have divided academic commentators and the arguments for and against can be found in Barav (1980) Wyatt (1982) Bebr (1982).

However, while the *Foglia* v. *Novello* case law has never been overruled by the Court of Justice, it has not in practice shown a great readiness to apply it. For example, it has accepted implicit challenges to the validity of legislation in the court of another Member State, such as the challenge to an Italian law in the German courts in Case C-150/88 *Eau de Cologne* v. *Provide* ([1989] ECR 3891). In that case it stated that there was a genuine dispute and that the Court is under a duty to provide the national court with the answers to questions of interpretation which it needs to settle the dispute.

It made it clear that it did not by any means intend to exclude the possibility that the courts of one Member State may determine the compatibility of the laws of another Member State with Community law, and that it will participate by providing any necessary interpretations of Community law.

The Court of justice recently extended its case law in this field by refusing to answer certain questions regarding the interpretation of the Second Company Law Directive, and the compatibility with this Directive of certain German case law in Case C-83/91 *Meilicke* v. *ADV/ORGA* (16.7.1992). The Court characterised the questions referred by the German court as 'hypothetical', and, with a passing reference to *Foglia* v. *Novello* and other cases on the cooperative structure of the Article 177 procedure, reached the conclusion that it could not answer the questions as it would be exceeding its proper function under Article 177 if it did so. One of the difficulties which the Court faced when assessing the relationship between the litigation in the German court and the questions referred to it by that court, was that if the Court of Justice had given the interpretation of Community law which the plaintiff sought, he would in fact have lost his case in the national court. He would, however, have succeeded in his ulterior goal, which was to establish the incompatibility of the German case law which he had challenged in the domestic litigation with Community law. Unlike the Court itself, AG Teasuro did not decline to answer the rather convoluted questions referred by the national court, but rather found a way to reformulate them so they could be answered.

7.3   Provisions of Community Law which may be Referred

Article 177 itself defines those provisions which may be referred. These are provisions of the Treaty, acts of Community institutions and the statutes of bodies established by an act of the Council (for an example of the latter category see Case 44/84 *Hurd* v. *Jones* [1986] ECR 29). Acts of the Community institutions which can be referred include non-binding acts such as Recommendations and opinions; in Case C-322/88 *Grimaldi* v. *Fonds des Maladies Professionelle* ([1989] ECR I-4407) the provisions referred were contained in Commission Recommendations on the adoption of a European schedule of occupational diseases, and on the conditions for the granting of compensation to those suffering from such diseases. The fact that agreements with third countries are concluded by the Council has provided a convenient justification for the acceptance of references on the interpretation of such agreements (e.g. Case 12/86 *Demirel* v. *Stadt Schwäbisch Gmund* [1987] ECR 3719 – a reference on the Association Agreement between the Community and Turkey). More tenuous is the decision of the Court to accept references on international agreements to which the Community has never formally adhered, but where it has succeeded to the rights and obligations of the Member States, such as the GATT (Cases 267–269/81 *SPI* [1983] ECR 801). The best justification for this practice is the fact that such agreements are binding upon the Community, and the Court regards the provisions of these agreements as penetrating the Community legal order and as giving rise, where appropriate to rights upon which individuals may rely in national courts.

General principles of law alone do not appear to be capable of forming the basis of a reference, although in practice a national court may request a ruling from the Court of Justice on how *other* provisions of Community law should be interpreted in the light of Community general principles of law (Case 44/79 *Hauer* v. *Land Rheinland Pfalz* [1979] ECR 3740).

7.4   Court and Tribunals of the Member States Capable of Making a Reference

References may be made by the whole range of bodies which embody the judicial power of the state, regardless of what title they are given. For example, in Case 61/65 *Vaassen* ([1966] ECR 261) the Court accepted a reference from a Dutch arbitral tribunal or *Scheidsgericht*, pointing to those features which it displayed which brought it within the ambit of Article 177. It was a permanent body instituted by the law, with members appointed by a Minister; it was given compulsory jurisdiction over the cases assigned to it by law, used a form of adversarial procedure, and applied the law in its decisions. A Dutch general practitioners' registration appeal committee was also held to fall within Article 177 in Case 246/80 *Broeckmeulen* ([1981] ECR 2311). The Court stated that (at p. 2328).

'in the absence, in practice, of any right of appeal to the ordinary courts, the Appeals Committee, which operates with the consent of the public authorities and with their cooperation, and which, after an adversarial procedure, delivers decisions which are in fact recognized as final, must, in a matter involving the application of Community law, be considered as a court or tribunal of a Member State within the meaning of Article 177 of the Treaty.'

A judicial body exercising investigatory functions within an inquisitorial system of criminal law is likewise capable of making a reference, even at a preliminary stage of the investigations where the potential defendants have not yet been identified. In Case 14/86 *Pretore di Salò* v. *X.* ([1987] ECR 2545) the Court accepted a reference from the Italian pretore or examining magistrate, which requested an interpretation of Community pollution legislation precisely with a view to identifying the potential defendants in criminal pollution proceedings.

. Commercial arbitration is excluded from the scope of Article 177. This was decided by the Court in Case 102/81 *Nordsee* v. *Reederei Mond* ([1982] ECR 1095). Although the decision of an arbitrator has force of law between the parties, and although the arbitrator must apply the law, it is more significant that the jurisdiction is contractual and therefore not compulsory and that, as a private arrangement, does not involve the public authorities. The Court therefore concluded that the link between the arbitration procedure and the organisation of legal remedies through the court structure was insufficiently close for the arbitrator to be deemed a 'court or tribunal'. The importance in practice of avoiding incorrect applications of Community law in national arbitration proceedings is emphasised by the indication given by the English Court of Appeal in *Bulk Oil* v. *Sun International* ([1984] 1 WLR 147) that the existence of a point of Community law for decision before an arbitrator should become a ground for giving leave to appeal to the court against the decision of an arbitrator.

7.5 The Discretion to Refer: Article 177(2)

Article 177 is concerned with two separate constellations of fact. The first is the discretion to refer, which is held by all courts faced with questions of Community law. The second is the obligation to refer, imposed only on courts of last resort.

The discretion to refer given to lower courts is entirely unfettered. References are not precluded by, for example, the existence of a prior ruling by the Court of Justice on a similar question (Cases 28-30/62 *Da Costa en Schaake NV* [1963] ECR 31). Nor may internal rules governing the hierarchy of the court structure limit the discretion of inferior courts. An inferior court which regards itself as *internally* bound by a rule of law stated by a superior court either in the same case or in an earlier case (e.g. the common law system of binding judicial precedent) is not prevented from making a reference to the Court of Justice if it believes applying the internal rule would lead it to a violation of Community law (Case 166/73 *Rheinmühlen*).

In the light of this conclusion in *Rheinmühlen*, it was therefore some-what surprising that in the same case the Court went on to hold that as a matter of Community law nothing precluded an *internal* appeal against the decision of an inferior court to refer, and that such appeals were to be regulated by national rules on procedure. However, where a reference has been made but is under appeal, the Court will proceed to the hearing of the reference which will be regarded as valid and effective until such time as it has actually been revoked. In this decision the Court went against the view of AG Warner who argued that orders to refer should not be available as a matter of *Community law*, and this is the view which has been espoused by the Irish Supreme Court in *Campus Oil* v. *Ministry for Industry and Energy* ([1984] 1 CMLR 479) which held that appeals against orders to refer are precluded within Ireland by the terms of Article 177 which it held to be part of Irish law.

The discretion to refer also extends to a discretion as to when to refer. We have noted already the early reference made by an Italian *pretore* (Case 14/86), and the Court will not reject a reference on the grounds that it is too 'early'. However, the Court has suggested that it might be convenient for the national court to decide the facts and issues of purely national law before making the reference, in order to enable the Court itself to take fuller cognisance of the relevant circumstances of the case (Cases 36 and 71/80 *Irish Creamery Milk Suppliers Association* v. *Ireland* [1981] ECR 735). This is presumably in order to increase the effectiveness of the reference procedure from the perspective of the Court of Justice.

Finally, although the question of Community law must be necessary in the sense of being relevant to the resolution of the dispute, the Court has not placed any restrictions on the meaning of such a question. In Cases C-297/88 and C-197/89 *Dzodzi* v. *Belgium* ([1990] ECR I-3763) the Court asserted the primary importance of the uniform interpretation and application of Community law when it held that it had jurisdiction to give a ruling on a preliminary reference made by a national court which is required to interpret purely national law (relating to a matter falling outside Community competence) where the national law made reference to the content of Community law. The overwhelming need to ensure uniformity required the Court to be able to interpret Community law for the purposes of the interpretation of national law.

Although the English inferior courts remain free to exercise their discretion to refer, subject to appeals (under *Rules of the Supreme Court*, Order 114, r.6 in the case of the High Court and above), in fact Lord Denning MR purported in the early stages of UK membership of the Community to give some guidance on the question of references. In *Bulmer* v. *Bollinger* ([1974] Ch. 401; [1974] 2 All ER 1226) he argued that before a reference is made the judge must be certain that the point is conclusive of the case and that there is no previous ruling of the Court of Justice or no grounds for applying the doctrine of *acte clair* (see below 7.6, although this point is not strictly relevant to the exercise of the *discretion* to refer). Finally, he or she should decide the facts first, and should bear in mind the delay caused by a reference and the workload of the Court of Justice. These guidelines have been criticised as encouraging courts too strongly not to refer (Arnull, 1990c: 382).

A much more positive attitude towards the Court is displayed by Bingham J in *Commissioners of Customs and Excise* v. *Samex ApS* ([1983] 3 CMLR 194) who pointed out that the Court of Justice is much better equipped than an English court to decide matters of Community law, as a consequence of the linguistic advantages it enjoys in the scrutiny of the various different language texts, the oversight it has over the whole field of Community law, and its particular understanding of the highly purposive methods of interpretation which it is necessary to apply to Community law.

7.6 The Obligation to Refer: Article 177(3)

The obligation to refer falls upon a court against whose decisions there is no judicial remedy under national law. This formulation has led to the development of two different theories of the scope of the obligation. First there is the abstract or organic theory whereby the court of last resort within the judicial hierarchy against which there is never a judicial appeal carries the obligation to refer. This would cover the House of Lords, the Irish Supreme Court and other comparable courts. Support for this theory can be obtained from the wording of Article 177(3) which refers in plural to the 'decisions' of such courts. The opposing theory is the concrete or specific case theory which considers the case in question, not the court in abstract. This would obviously, in appropriate cases, cover the English Court of Appeal, or even inferior courts where the right of appeal is restricted by the nature of the case. Support for this view comes from Case 6/64 *Costa* v. *ENEL* ([1964] ECR 585) which involved a reference from an Italian *guidice conciliatore*, a magistrate who is the judicial authority of last resort for certain minor cases; the Court stated (at p. 592) that:

'by the terms of [Article 177], however, national courts against whose decisions, as *in the present case*, there is no judicial remedy, must refer the matter to the Court of Justice' (emphasis added).

The adoption of this position, however, still leaves the English Court of Appeal in a rather ambiguous position, since it is not clear until the end of any particular case – i.e. after the decision not to refer to the Court has been taken – whether the case may in fact be appealed to the House of Lords. In *R.* v. *Henn and Darby* ([1978] 3 All ER 1190 (CA); [1980] 2 All ER 166 (HL)) the question was not discussed in the Court of Appeal, which refused to refer and refused leave to appeal. The House of Lords granted leave to appeal, and made a reference to the Court of Justice. The matter has still not been settled authoritatively.

There are three sets of circumstances in which there is no obligation to refer on a court of last resort (although, of course, there remains a *discretion* to refer). First, there is no duty to refer a question of *interpretation* in interlocutory proceedings providing that the findings of law are subject to review in main proceedings. In Case 107/76 *Hoffmann-La-Roche* v. *Centrafarm* ([1977] ECR 957 at p. 973) the Court held that Article 177(3)

'must be interpreted as meaning that a national court or tribunal is not required to refer to the Court a question of interpretation . . . mentioned in that Article when the question is raised in interlocutory proceedings for an interim order, even where no judicial remedy is available against the decision to be taken in the context of those proceedings, provided that each of the parties is entitled to institute proceedings or to require proceedings to be instituted on the substance of the case and that during such proceedings the question provisionally decided in the summary proceedings may be re-examined and may be the subject of a reference to the Court under Article 177.'

Interlocutory proceedings involving challenges to the validity of Community legislation are discussed in 7.7.

The second category of cases in which the obligation to refer lapses is where the Court has previously answered a materially identical question. This point emerges from Cases 28-30/62 *Da Costa en Schaake* where the Court referred to the authority of a previous ruling which it had given on a materially identical question as in effect depriving a subsequent preliminary reference of its *raison d'être*. A similar situation arises where the Court has already declared an act of one of the Community institutions void; this is sufficient reason for a court in another Member State to treat that act as void and to be exonerated from the duty to refer (Case 66/80 *International Chemical Corporation* v. *Amministrazione delle Finanze dello Stato* [1981] ECR 1191).

Finally, it is argued that the doctrine of *acte clair* can override the obligation to refer. This doctrine, espoused in particular by certain French courts in the early stages of development of the Community legal order, holds that a sufficiently clear legal provision does not require interpretation, but only application. Since application falls within the remit of the national court under the principle of the separation of functions, it should follow that there is no question of interpretation to be referred. This doctrine was eventually accepted by the Court in Case 283/81 *CILFIT* ([1982] ECR 3415), but in such a qualified and watered-down form that it is questionable whether the Court was not also seeking simultaneously to destroy its substance. In its judgment the Court referred to *Da Costa*, and indicated that further circumstances in which references might be meaningless included those where the previous rulings of the Court effectively decided a point of law even though the questions at issue where not materially identical, and where the correct application of Community law is so obvious as to leave no scope for any reasonable doubt as to how the question raised is to be resolved.

However, the Court went on to say (at p. 3430) that

> 'before it comes to the conclusion that such is the case, the national court or tribunal must be convinced that the matter is equally obvious to the courts of the other Member States and to the Court of Justice. Only if those conditions are satisfied may the national court or tribunal refrain from submitting the question to the Court of Justice and take upon itself the responsibility for resolving it.'

The Court then indicated the factors to be taken into account by the national court in deciding this point. These include the characteristic features of Community law, and the particular difficulties to which its interpretation gives rise, the fact that Community law is drafted in several languages and that the different language versions are all equally authentic; the existence of difficulties relating to terminology and legal concepts, the meanings of which may vary significantly between Member States and between national and Community law; and finally the fact that Community law must be interpreted in its context, having regard to its purpose and object. It would be rare that a provision of Community law would satisfy these requirements of simplicity and clarity, or indeed that a national court would feel itself equipped with the resources for the comparative analysis which ought to underlie a faithful application of the *CILFIT* criteria. Notwithstanding this ruling, there have been subsequent instances of the application of *acte clair* by national courts, including examples from case law in the UK (see *SA Magnavision NV* v. *General Optical Council* [1987] 1 CMLR 887 and [1987] 2 CMLR 262 (Div. Court). Even more worrying, perhaps, is the decision of the House of Lords in *R.* v. *London Boroughs' Transport Committee, ex parte Freight Transport Association* ([1991] 3 All ER 915) in which it declined to make a reference in circumstances of uncertainty over the precise interpretation of certain Community directives (which the Court of Appeal and the House of Lords interpreted quite differently), without referring to what other judges have called the 'cautionary comments' of the Court of Justice in *CILFIT* (see for a contrast *R.* v. *Secretary of State for Transport, ex parte Factortame* [1989] 2 CMLR 353) (see generally, Weatherill, 1992b). However, the complexities of faithfully applying the *CILFIT* criteria may be such that the ruling must be regarded as 'unrealistic and unworkable in practice' (Bebr, 1988:355).

Failure by a court of last resort to make a preliminary reference where unresolved issues of Community law remain crucial to the resolution of a case is, of course, a breach of a Treaty obligation by the judicial arm of the state which could potentially form the subject matter of an action under Article 169 EC. There is no individual redress available against the failure to refer.

7.7 Rulings on Validity

Only the Court of Justice has the power to declare a Community act invalid. In Case 314/85 *Firma Foto-Frost* v. *Hauptzollamt Lübeck* ([1987] ECR 4199) the Court acknowledged that this point was not definitively settled by the Treaty itself, but concluded that while national courts have the power to decide that there are no serious grounds for impugning the validity of Community legislation without recourse to the Court of Justice, it would be contrary to the objective of ensuring the uniform application of Community by national courts, which underlies Article 177, to allow them to decide on the invalidity of a Community act. In this context, divergences in national interpretation would be intolerable from the perspective of the unity of the Community legal order, the cohesion of the system of remedies under the Treaty and the imperatives of legal certainty. It follows from this decision that there is in effect an *obligation* on all courts to refer issues of validity to the Court of Justice.

In *Foto-Frost* the Court explicitly left open the question of how national courts should deal with the problem of the alleged invalidity of a Community act in the context of interim proceedings, where the urgency of matters would tend to render a reference to the Court meaningless. In Cases C-143/88 and C-92/89 *Zuckerfabrik Süderithmarschen & Zucker-fabrik Soest* [1991] ECR I-415, the Court was confronted directly with this issue, but again it refused to allow the national court the power to declare Community measures invalid. Instead it stated that the national court should, in interim proceedings, invalidate the national implementing measures which are based on the impugned Community act, if there are factual and legal matters brought by the applicants before the national court which suggest that there are serious doubts about the validity of the Community Regulation. There must also be evidence that the matter is urgent and that the applicant is threatened by grave and irreparable harm if no action is taken by the national court, and the national court must not act before it has taken into account the interests of the Community. With respect to the latter point, the Court indicated that some form of guarantee could be required from the applicant against loss which might be suffered by the Community if the national measure is suspended in these circumstances.

We shall review the role of Article 177 in the system of judicial review of Community acts in Chapter 9.

7.8   The Authority and Effects of Rulings of the Court of Justice

No provision in the Treaties prescribes the effects or authority of rulings of the Court of Justice within the national legal orders. However, the Court has evolved an extensive case law on the effects of Article 177 rulings *vis-à-vis* the parties to the case, third parties and national courts.

A ruling of the Court of Justice in proceedings in which a reference has been made is binding on the national court, at least in so far as it chooses to resolve the case on the basis of Community law (Case 29/68 *Milch-Fett- und Eierkontor* v. *HZA Saarbrücken*). On the other hand, a ruling on the interpretation of Community law does not have the effect of *res judicata* (decided issue) in other proceedings raising similar or identical questions (Cases 28–30/62 *Da Costa*). This means that the Court will not dismiss as inadmissible references made on points which it has already decided although, of course, the referring court may choose to withdraw the questions. The key question is whether a national court is bound to follow the rulings of the Court of Justice, or, where it disagrees with the ruling given by that Court, to ask it to reconsider its case law. This happened in Case 28/67 *Molkerei Zentrale Westfalen* v. *HZA Paderborn* ([1968] ECR 143) when the referring court asked the Court to review its interpretation of Article 95 EC in Case 57/65 *Lütticke* v. *HZA Saarlouis* ([1966] ECR 205). Although the point is not made explicitly, however, it must follow from Article 5 EC that all national courts are bound to decide cases in accordance with the case law of the Court of Justice. In the UK, sec. 3(1) of the European Communities Act 1972 removes all remaining doubts, in that it provides that questions of Community law, if not referred to the Court of Justice for a ruling, must be decided in accordance with the principles laid down by any relevant decision of the Court. In other words, the Court is inserted at the apex of the system of binding judicial precedent in the UK.

The position *vis-à-vis* other courts has been articulated more clearly by the Court in relation to the effects of rulings on invalidity. Although such a ruling is not strictly binding *erga omnes*, it is nonetheless 'sufficient reason for any other national court to regard that act as void' (Case 66/80 *International Chemical Corporation* v. *Amministrazione delle Finanze dello Stato* [1981] ECR 1191 at p. 1216). It follows from a finding of invalidity that a national court must not apply any national provisions based on the invalid Community act (Case 162/82 *Cousin* [1983] ECR 1101).

Using Article 174(2) EC as a starting point, the Court of Justice has shown itself prepared to modulate the effects of a preliminary ruling according to the circumstances. Article 174(2) provides, in the context of the annulment of acts by means of direct actions under Article 173, that:

'In the case of a regulation . . . the Court of Justice shall, if it considers this necessary, state which of the effects of the regulation which it has declared void shall be considered as definitive.'

The Court has implicitly claimed a similar power in the context of preliminary rulings, holding in Case 4/79 *Providence Agricole de la Champagne* ([1980] ECR 2823) that it may rule that an act is valid for the past but invalid for the future. It has likewise asserted the power to place a temporal limitation upon the effects of an interpretative ruling under Article 177 (Case 43/75 *Defrenne* v. *SABENA* [1976] ECR 455 – the direct effect of Article 119; see more recently Case C-262/88 *Barber* v. *Guardian Royal Exchange* [1990] ECR I-1889 – the application of Article 119 to occupational pensions). However, it is clear that only the Court itself may place a temporal limitation upon the effects of a ruling, and that it must place that restriction in the context of the actual judgment in which it rules upon the interpretation or validity of the relevant provision (Case 61/79 *Denkavit Italiana* [1980] ECR 1205).

7.9 The Assessment of the Preliminary Reference Procedure

The Article 177 reference procedure has been described as a specific expression of the duty of mutual cooperation between the Community and its Member States contained in Article 5 EC, creating a system of judicial cooperation which has worked remarkably well and in which the Court has delivered numerous judgments of constitutional significance for the Community legal order (Slynn, 1992: 9–10). This is in part attributable to the manner in which the Court has chosen to frame its interpretative role, breaking down the barrier between interpretation and application, and phrasing its judgments on some occasions in terms which leave little doubt to the national court as to how it should apply the ruling. In this book, perhaps the clearest example of this practice will be found in Chapter 14 on the interpretation of Article 30 EC which prohibits non-tariff barriers to trade in goods between the Member States. Equally important it has construed the task of giving *interpretations* of provisions of Community law as allowing it also to determine the *effect* of those provisions. This can be seen, for example, in the many rulings delivered by the Court since the groundbreaking case of Case 26/62 *Van Gend en Loos* v. *Nederlandse Administratie der Belastingen* ([1963] ECR 1) in which it has held that in certain circumstances provisions of Community law give rise to individual rights which national courts must protect.

The most important factor has, however, been the willingness of national courts to refer questions to the Court. Although 'reference rates' vary considerably between the Member States with, for example, Belgian courts showing themselves amongst the most ready to refer, and UK judges closer to the bottom of any reference 'league table', the success of Article 177 in terms of volume of cases which have been generated cannot be denied. The Court now receives nearly 200 references each year from national courts, and decides rather over 100. Although this disparity can in part be accounted for by cases dealt with other than by the rendering of a judgment (e.g. withdrawal of the reference by the national court), it inevitably means that the average length of proceedings has risen and now hovers around eighteen months for preliminary references. Thus in many ways, the Court has become a victim of its own success, since by interpreting Article 177 in such a way as to expand its jurisdiction and to encourage national courts to refer it has a created a flood of cases with which it is barely equipped to deal, even after the transfer of jurisdiction in other areas to the Court of First Instance. Yet in principle the reference procedure should be a relatively light procedure for the Court. It does not decide cases, but merely answers questions. It does not decide the facts, or take a position (at least in principle) on matters of national law.

Extensive work has been done on proposals to reform Article 177, both structurally and procedurally (Schermers *et al.*, 1987; Watson, 1986). Procedural proposals to reduce delays have included making the Article 177 procedure entirely written, with no oral argument. Structural reforms have concentrated on considering the reconciliation of two objectives: that the Court of Justice should continue to hear and to decide the important cases which develop the law and that national courts should increasingly decide the less important cases without recourse to the Court itself. Of course, judicial education is widely recognised as a vital component in such a strategy, but measures falling within the control of the Court which have been suggested are 'docket control' (the Court chooses the cases it wishes to take) and a simplified procedure under which the Court can give a 'green light' to an interpretation proposed by the national court. None of these proposals has yet been adopted.

Summary

1 Article 177 EC provides an organic connection between national courts and the Court of Justice, enabling national courts to obtain authoritative rulings on the interpretation and validity of provisions of Community law.

2 The preliminary reference procedure is based on a separation of functions between the national court and the Court of Justice, and its effectiveness depends upon the cooperative application of this distinction by all courts.

3 In general the Court of Justice does not interfere with the discretion of the national court in referring questions. However, it will not answer abstract or hypothetical questions, and has imposed the requirement that there be a genuine dispute in the national court.

4 Article 177 provides for references on questions of the interpretation (and, implicitly, the effect) of:

- provisions of the Treaty and other international agreements binding the Community;
- provisions of Community legislation, including non-binding acts.

References on validity can be made in respect of binding legal acts of the Community.

5 The concept of a 'court or tribunal' of a Member State is interpreted broadly as any body representing the judicial power of the state.

6 Inferior courts have a discretion to refer; orders for references may be appealed within the national juridical structure. The obligation to refer is imposed on courts of last resort, and is qualified in only three cases:

- in interlocutory proceedings, where the issues of Community law can be reconsidered at trial;
- where the Court has already answered materially identical questions;
- where the limited doctrine of *acte clair* as laid down by the Court in *CILFIT* applies.

7 Only the Court of Justice may rule upon the validity of Community acts. The Court has indicated that in cases of urgency a national court should invalidate the national measures implementing a Community act which is allegedly invalid, making a reference on the validity of the latter.

8 The authority of rulings of the Court of Justice is such that in general no national court should depart from a position taken by the Court of Justice. The Court has asserted the power in limited circumstances to restrict the temporal effects of its rulings.

9 The preliminary rulings procedure has been effective in generating a flow of cases to the Court of Justice in which it has laid down many of the central constitutional precepts of the Community legal order. In some ways, Article

177 has proved too successful, with increasingly long delays before the Court is now able to give judgment on preliminary references.

Questions

1 What purposes does Article 177 serve within the Community legal order?

2 What is meant by the 'separation of functions' in the context of Article 177?

3 Which bodies may refer questions to the Court of Justice?

4 Why did the Court refuse to answer the questions posed by the Italian court in *Foglia* v. *Novello*?

5 In what circumstances is a national court obliged to make a preliminary reference to the Court of Justice?

6 Why does the Court maintain that it has sole authority to declare invalid provisions of Community law?

Workshop

'In providing for references on questions of the interpretation and validity of Community law from national courts to the Court of Justice, the authors of the Treaty settled on a compromise solution to the problem of developing á uniform application of EEC law within the Community under the control of a single supranational court.'

Discuss in the light of the detailed provisions and conditions which govern the operation of Article 177.

Further Reading

Arnull (1990c) 'References to the European Court', 15 *European Law Review*, 375.

Barav (1980) 'Preliminary Censorship? The Judgment of the European Court in *Foglia* v. *Novello*', 5 *European Law Review*, 443.

Bebr (1982) 'The possible implications of *Foglia* v. *Novello II*', 9 *Common Market Law Review*, 421.

Bebr (1988) 'The Reinforcement of the Constitutional Review of Community Acts under Article 177 EEC', 25 *Common Market Law Review*, 684.

Dashwood and Arnull (1984) 'English Courts and Article 177 of the EEC Treaty', 4 *Yearbook of European Law*, 255.

Schermers *et al.* (eds.) (1987), esp. Bebr, 'The Preliminary Proceedings of Article 177 EEC – Problems and Suggestions for Improvement', p.345.

Watson (1986) 'Asser Institute Colloquium on European Law 1985: Experience and Problems in applying Article 177 EEC', 23 *Common Market Law Review*, 207.

8 Community Law and the Legal Systems of the Member States

8.1 The Nature of the Community Legal Order

The problem we shall consider in this chapter is how the evolving Community legal order has established itself as a superior legal order operating within, but nonetheless independent of the national legal systems. It demonstrates how the Court of Justice has used the organic connection offered by Article 177 EC both to assert its own ability to give authoritative interpretations of the meaning and effect of Community law, and to emphasise that where Community law applies, national courts themselves must act as 'Community courts', interpreting and applying Community law subject to the authority of the Court.

The edifice of rules and principles set out in this chapter has been built out of relatively unpromising material. The constitutive treaties themselves contain little indication of the precise nature of the relationship between Community law and national law or of the extent to which, if at all, the legal order created by the Treaties of Paris and Rome should be regarded as differing from the system of international law in general. Reference can be made, of course, to Article 5 EC (the duty of Community loyalty applying to Member States and institutions alike) and Article 164 EC (the duty of the Court of Justice to ensure that 'the law is observed'). With the exception of these provisions, the principles of a unique supranational legal order have evolved entirely judicially.

This chapter will describe the essential features of an effective supranational legal order, in which the law and the institutions entrusted with the tasks of enforcing and applying the law have claimed a central role as motors of the integration project. The key features have commonly been termed the direct effect and supremacy of Community law, and these have been referred to already in earlier chapters. They will be considered in greater detail here, and will be located within the broader notion of the 'effectiveness' or '*effet utile*' of Community law. In a classic exposition of the doctrine of direct effect, Pescatore (1983) argued that it is fundamental to any legal system that the institutions responsible for its stewardship should seek always to render the law operative. In keeping with this pragmatic philosophy the approach taken here is not simply that of describing the important legal concepts and principles, but rather of identifying the practical mechanisms evolved by the Court of Justice in order to make the Community legal order fully and uniformly effective throughout the Member States.

In two early statements of principle, the Court laid down the markers for establishing the parameters of the Community legal order. In Case 26/62 *Van Gend en Loos* v. *Nederlandse Administratie der Belastingen* ([1963] ECR 1 at p.12) it asserted that:

> 'the Community constitutes a new legal order of international law, for the benefit of which states have limited their sovereign rights, albeit within limited fields, and the subjects of which comprise not only member states but also their nationals.'

It continued in similar vein the following year in Case 6/64 *Costa* v. *ENEL* ([1964] ECR 585 at p. 593):

> 'By contrast with ordinary international treaties, the EEC Treaty has created its own legal system which, on the entry into force of the Treaty, became an integral part of the legal system of the member states and which their courts are bound to apply.'

These oft-quoted statements require brief comment. In the first place, rather than being mere descriptions of what the Community legal order then was, they constituted at the time normative assertions by the Court about what it wished that order to resemble. It is remarkable not only that the Court expressed itself in those terms in the early 1960s in cases of first impression on the relationship between Community law and the national legal orders, but also that it has experienced astonishing success in fashioning a legal order after the model put forward in those cases. Secondly, the two statements contain all the important elements required fully to describe the Community law/national law interface;

(a) the Community legal order is a separate and autonomous system distinct from the general order of public international law; the Court has therefore been able to claim a free hand in evolving the substance of that legal order;

(b) Community law is part of national law, which means that national courts can and must apply it in accordance with the authoritative rulings of the Court of Justice;

(c) the Community legal order is based on a transfer of sovereign powers by the Member States to the Community; Member States can no longer exercise those powers which have been transferred to the Community, and must abstain from any acts which hinder the Community in its exercise of these powers;

(d) Member States and Community citizens are the subjects of Community law, and as subjects have rights and obligations flowing from and under the Treaties.

The rest of the chapter will illustrate how the Court has given concete form to these points, which have provided the key to ensuring the effectiveness of the Community legal order. In order to test empirically the progress which has been made by the Court in ensuring the acceptance of the ideas it propounds, discussion in the final paragraphs will concentrate on national reactions to the demands of the Community legal order, with a particular focus on the UK.

8.2 The Penetration of Community Law into the Domestic Legal Order

The first prerequisite of the effectiveness of Community law is that it must become part of the national legal order. From the perspective of the Court, this follows simply from the nature of Community law combined with the fact of accession. The strict logic of the transfer of sovereign powers thesis is that the Treaties themselves and any legal acts adopted by the Community institutions within the scope of their competence take their place within the domestic legal order and form part of the sources of law which the national judge must apply. Within the sphere of Community competence, Community law must take precedence. Moreover, as the Court emphasised in Opinion 1/92 *Re the Draft Agreement on a European Economic Area* ([1992] 2 CMLR 217), the transfer of competence has occurred 'in ever wider fields' (para. 21 of the judgment).

The structure is akin to a federal legal system, with the federal and state authorities acting within their respective spheres of competence, and with courts adjudicating over the boundaries between those spheres. In this chapter we shall refer to this quality of Community law as its 'direct applicability'. For the avoidance of terminological confusion, two points of explanation must be made.

First, the use of 'direct applicability' in this sense accords well with the terminological usage of the Court, which has referred to this concept as meaning

'that the rules of Community law must be fully and uniformly applied in all the Member States from the date of their entry into force and for so long as they continue in force' (Case 106/77 *Amministrazione delle Finanze dello Stato* v. *Simmenthal SpA* (*Simmenthal II*) [1978] ECR 629 at 643).

It is to be distinguished in this context from the justiciability of provisions of Community law or, to explain this concept, from the question of whether a particular provision is capable of giving rise to rights and obligations enforceable by a court of law. This is the concept of 'direct effect'.

Second, confusion need not arise from the fact that Article 189 EC refers to Regulations, and apparently only Regulations, as being 'directly applicable in all the Member States'. The Court has made it plain on numerous occaions that it is not only Regulations which are directly applicable in the sense of being part of the national legal system. Directives are undoubtedly also part of the national legal system. However, this does not detract from the fact that Regulations do have certain special qualities, amounting in the view of Usher (1981) to a 'stop sign' to national legislatures which make them particularly useful instruments for the Community law-maker in fields where absolute uniformity of the rules applied is of paramount importance (e.g. customs, agriculture, social security of migrant workers) (see also 5.10). Direct applicability in this sense is a matter of legislative technique. In this chapter we use a broader notion which includes but also transcends the 'stop sign' argument, and extends to cover also the wider 'pre-emptive' qualities of Community rules of law generally (see 8.12).

8.3 National Constitutions and the Reception of Community Law

The attraction of basing the penetration of Community law within the domestic legal systems upon its own inherent qualities, rather than upon some constitutional mechanism for giving effect to Community law is that it prevents the effectiveness of Community law being contingent upon the vagaries of national constitutional and judicial attitudes to incorporating the provisions of a 'foreign' legal system. In other words, it should enhance the uniform application of Community law. In reality, of course, as the Treaty itself recognises in its references to national mechanisms for ratification of international instruments (e.g. Article N TEU which provides for amendments to the Treaties to enter into force after ratification), the incorporation of Community law into the domestic legal system usually depends upon the creation of the appropriate 'gateway'. In the UK, where courts will refuse to take account of Treaties until they have been translated into domestic law by Act of Parliament, that gateway is to be found in the European Communities Act 1972, in particular secs. 2 and 3. This will be examined in 8.5.

The written constitutions of some of the other Member States create models for the transfer or delegation of sovereign powers to international organisations which are more or less perfectly in accordance with the simplicity of the Court's own transfer thesis. For example, Article 92 of the Dutch constitution, Article 25*bis* of the Belgian constitution and Article 24 of the German constitution all provide for the possibility of the transfer or attribution of sovereign powers to international organisa-tions. Article 28(3) of the Greek constitution is rather more detailed. It provides that

'Greece may freely proceed, by virtue of an Act passed by the votes of the absolute majority of the total number of members of Parliament, to limitations on the exercise of national sovereignty, provided that this is dictated by an important national interest, does not affect human rights and the foundations of democratic government and is effected in conformity with the principles of equality, and on condition of reciprocity.'

As we shall see, it is not possible for the domestic constitution to place riders such as these upon its transfer of powers to the European Community, although in practice national judges may be unwilling for a variety of reasons to recognise the full force of Community law in the domestic system. Such provisions may also be important in a wider political context, in so far as they may express particular national aspirations in relation to the Community, or may reflect the experiences of a country recently emerged from dictatorship.

8.4 Conceptions of International Law in the Member States

The second factor conditioning the reception of Community law is the conception of the relationship between public international law and national law. Classically, there are two conceptions: monism and dualism (Jackson, 1992). Under monism, international law and municipal law are conceived of as part of one single legal system, with international law taking precedence. A dualist conception views international law and municipal law as two separate systems, each supreme within its own sphere. For example, since Parliament in the UK is sovereign, a dualist position on international law must necessarily be adopted by the UK courts which can recognise international obligations only once, and to the extent that, they have been incoprorated into national law by Parliament in the form of a statute (*British Airways* v. *Laker Airways* [1984] 3 All ER 39). No account was taken of the Economic Community Treaties after agreement by the Crown on behalf of the UK but before the passing of the European Communities Act 1972 (*Blackburn* v. *Attorney General* [1971] 1 All ER 1380). In contrast, both the Dutch constitution (Articles 91–94) and the French constitution (Article 55) provide that duly ratified international obligations take precedence over municipal law. The Belgian courts have also achieved the same constitutional position in the absence of an explicit provision by proclaiming that international obligations have an effect superior to domestic law in the Belgian legal system (*Fromagerie Le Ski* [1972] CMLR 330).

Ostensibly since the ratification such as that referred to in the Dutch and French constitutions will often require some form of parliamentary approval, there is little difference between the monist and dualist positions in terms of the formalities required before international law can be recognised domestically. Where a difference does remain is in judicial attitudes subsequent to incorporation. The UK judges consistently betray their dualist heritage, either because they treat the application and enforcement of Community law principally as a matter of construction of the European Communities Act 1972 (see, for example, *Duke* v. *GEC*

Reliance [1988] 1 All ER 626 discussed below at 8.20), or because they treat the rules of Community law which they do apply as if they were statutes, interpreting them accordingly (see for example the interpretation of breach of Articles 85 and 86 EC as if it were a breach of statutory duty in *Garden Cottage Foods* v. *Milk Marketing Board* [1984] AC 130). In contrast, even the French Conseil d'Etat (Supreme Administrative Court) – long resistant to the claims of Community law – has now begun to refer to the basis for the authority of Community law in France as being the transfer of sovereign powers (*Boisdet* [1991] 1 CMLR 3).

8.5   Community Law and the Sovereignty of Parliament

There remain substantial obstacles to the successful reconciliation of the implications of membership of the European Community with the classic Diceyian thesis of the sovereignty of Parliament. The sovereignty of Parliament is to be distinguished from the sovereignty of the UK as a nation state. The sovereignty of all the Member States is limited, or perhaps better 'pooled' or 'shared' by accession to the Community. However, the existence of a set of rules governing the conduct of the UK courts in relation to Parliament, under which the latter is recognised as the supreme law-making body, does present particular difficulties for the reception of Community law in the UK. Of most significance are the rule that Parliament may do anything except bind its successors and the universally accepted principle that courts may not call into question the validity of Acts of Parliament. From the first principle, it would appear that future Parliaments could not be restrained from legislating expressly in a manner which is inconsistent with the UK's Community obligations. If this principle is coupled with the doctrine of the implied repeal of Acts of Parliament, it is arguable that the European Communities Act 1972 would be vulnerable to change as a result of subsequent inconsistent enactments, regardless of whether a repudiation was intended or not. Upholding the sovereignty of Parliament thus comes into conflict with the loss of national sovereignty inherent in accession to the Community. This is expressed most clearly by the Court of Justice in Case 6/64 *Costa* v. *ENEL* (at p.594):

> 'The transfer by the States from their domestic legal systems to the Community legal system of the rights and obligations arising under the Treaty carries with it a permanent limitation of their sovereign rights, against which a subsequent unilateral act incompatible with the concept of the Community cannot prevail.'

The transfer of sovereign powers thesis denies the effectiveness of unilateral repudiations of Community obligations. Such repudiations would be seen merely as violations of the Treaty system. In the absence of a negotiated return of the powers originally transferred, a state will not be released from its obligations under the Treaties. Such a position is also in conformity with the international law principle of *pacta sunt servanda*.

At the time of the accession of the UK to the Community, a position emerged on the sovereignty of Parliament which contrasted somewhat with Diceyian absolutism. Authors such as Mitchell (Mitchell, Kuipers and Gall, 1972; Mitchell, 1979) argued that British constitutional history has always demonstrated a capacity for constitutional change, in recognition of changes in political circumstances. It is precisely out of political circumstances that a convention of Parliamentary sovereignty has arisen. Now that the UK has acceded to a political entity within which absolute Parliamentary sovereignty is no longer tenable, it must be regarded as abrogated, with legislative and judicial sovereignty passing to the European Community, within its spheres of competence. However, the majority of British constitutional lawyers still adhere to the orthodox position that the binding effect of Community law in the UK flows only from the European Communities Act 1972, an Act which Parliament remains as free to repeal as any other Act, although for the time being it chooses not to (e.g. Munro, 1987).

Not surprisingly, the courts have for the most part declined to pass comment on theoretical conflicts between Parliamentary sovereignty and Community obligations. The essential problem is, of course, whether the UK judges now owe their allegiance to the Community authorities in respect of matters falling within the competence of those authorities, just as they undoubtedly owe allegiance to the Westminster Parliament in respect of matters falling within the jurisdiction of that body. According to Lord Denning MR in *Macarthys* v. *Smith* ([1979] 3 All ER 325 at p.329):

'If the time should come when Parliament deliberately passes an Act with the intention of repudiating the Treaty or any provision of it or intentionally of acting inconsistently with it and says so in express terms then I should have thought it would be the duty of our courts to follow the statute of our Parliament. I do not envisage any such situation . . . Unless there is such an intentional and express repudiation of the Treaty, it is our duty to give priority to the Treaty.'

For the most part, however, the judges have contented themselves with resolving, in generally satisfactory terms, the specific practical problems thrown up by the penetration of Community law into the UK legal system. These problems will be examined, using examples, in 8.20.

8.6 The Justiciability of Community Law in National Courts

The principle that provisions of Community law may be justiciable in national courts provided they satisfy certain conditions has been recognised since the landmark case of *Van Gend en Loos*. In that case, the Court held that an importer could rely upon the standstill clause in Article 12 EC prohibiting any increases in customs duties between the Member States after the coming into force of the Treaty in order to challenge such an increase by the Dutch authorities in the Dutch courts. The self-executing nature of Treaty provision is a phenomenon not entirely unknown in international law generally (Jackson, 1992; Wyatt, 1982) and flows from the principle of direct applicability as enunciated in this chapter. The most powerful justification for the doctrine of direct effect, as it is known, is that it enhances the effectiveness or *'effet utile'* of binding norms of Community law. As a doctrine which principally protects the individual, and often gives individuals rights which they can rely upon as against Member States, it sets up a mechanism for the individual or indirect enforcement of Community law. In practical terms, this relies upon the operation of the preliminary rulings procedure examined in Chapter 7. The existence of a centralised enforcement procedure in the hands of the Commission under Article 169 EC has never been considered an argument for preventing the decentralised enforcement of Community law.

However, the doctrine of direct effect is not simply limited to the Member State/Community citizen interface. Although the principle that states should not be able to rely upon their own failure or inefficiency in implementing Community law in order to deny to individuals the rights which flow from Community provisions – the so-called 'estoppel argument' (Curtin, 1990b) – is a powerful argument for direct effect, it is not the only one. The need to ensure the effectiveness of Community law in some circumstances applies to relations between private parties. In appropriate cases, Community law is also justiciable in disputes between individuals. In other words, certain provisions of Community law may be horizontally as well as vertically directly effective.

8.7   Prerequisites of Direct Effect

To be directly effective, a provision of Community law must constitute a complete legal obligation capable of enforcement as such by a court. This means that it must be sufficiently precise and unconditional (Cases C-6 and 9/90 *Francovich* v. *Italian Republic* [1992] IRLR 84). In its early case law the Court appeared to limit direct effect to negative obligations, such as that contained in Article 12 EC, which prohibited Member States from raising their customs duties or introducing any new customs duties after the coming into force of the Treaty. It was held in *Van Gend en Loos* (at p.13) that

'the wording of Article 12 contains a clear and unconditional prohibition which is not a positive but a negative obligation. This obligation, moreover, is not qualified by any reservation on the part of States which would make its implementation conditional upon a positive measure enacted under national law. The very nature of this prohibition makes it ideally adapted to produce direct effects in the legal relationship between Member States and their subjects.'

That limitation has since been dropped, and the Court has subsequently held that numerous provisions of the Economic Community Treaty are capable of judicial enforcement, including Article 30 (prohibiting non-tariff barriers to interstate trade in goods erected by Member States), Article 48 (guaranteeing free movement of workers), Articles 52 and 59 (guaranteeing freedom of establishment and freedom to provide services), Articles 85 and 86 (prohibiting anti-competitive conduct by undertakings) and Article 95 (prohibiting taxation by the Member States which discriminates against imported products) (for a summary of the directly effective Treaty provisions, see Collins, 1990: 122 *et seq.*). Articles 85 and 86 provide a perfect example of Treaty provisions which are horizontally directly effective. The prohibitions on anti-competitive agreements and the abuse of a dominant position enacted in these provisions are by their very nature aimed at economically active individuals, defined as 'undertakings'. The obligations inherent in the provisions can be enforced against infringing undertakings, at the instance of other individuals injured by anti-competitive conduct, in national courts. Some provisions, such as Article 6 EC (the general prohibition on discrimination on grounds of nationality) are judicially enforceable in combination with another provision of the Treaty. For example, Article 128 EEC, as it was drafted prior to the Treaty of Maastricht, established an outline competence of the Community in relation to the creation of a Community vocational training policy. Article 128 read in conjunction with what was then EEC Article 7 created a right to non-discrimination on grounds of nationality for vocational training students who move to study in another Member State, at least as regards matters of educational access (Case 293/83 *Gravier* v. *City of Liège* [1985] ECR 593 – e.g. they cannot be charged fees when domestic students are not).

Those Treaty provisions which have been held not to be capable of judicial enforcement are those which are worded in conditional or contingent terms. For example, Article 71 EC provides that

'Member States shall endeavour to avoid introducing within the Community any new exchange restrictions on the movement of capital and current payments connected with such movements, and shall endeavour not to make existing rules more restrictive.'

In Case 203/80 *Casati* ([1981] ECR 2595 at p.2616 the Court noted that

'by using the term "shall endeavour", the wording of that provision departs noticeably from the more imperative forms of wording employed in other similiar provisions concerning restrictions on the free movement of goods, persons and services. It is apparent from the wording that, in any event, the first paragraph of Article 71 does not impose on the Member States an unconditional obligation capable of being relied upon by individuals.'

Similarly there are certain provisions which grant a discretion to Member States which make it impossible to identify a particular obligation to which they are subject. An example is Article 97 EC which states that:

'Member States which levy a turnover tax calculated on a cumulative multi-stage tax system may, in the case of internal taxation imposed by them on imported products or of repayments allowed by them on exported products, establish average rates for products or groups of products' (see Case 28/67 *Molkerei Zentrale Westfalen* v. *HZA Paderborn* [1968] ECR 143).

8.8   Provisions of Community Law Capable of Judicial Enforcement

All provisions of Community law containing a binding obligation of conduct or of result are capable of direct judicial enforcement, providing they are sufficiently precise and unconditional. No category of legal acts is *a priori* excluded. Thus in addition to Treaty provisions, the Court has held that provisions of Regulations (Case 43/71 *Politi* v. *Italian Minister of Finance* [1971] ECR 1039), Directives (Case 41/74 *Van Duyn* v. *Home Office* [1974] ECR 1337), Decisions (Case 9/70 *Grad* [1970] ECR 825) and agreements with third countries (Case 104/81 *Kupferberg* [1982] ECR 3641) are all capable of giving rise to rights which individuals can enforce in national courts.

In the case of Regulations there was little doubt that they should be capable of enforcement in national courts, since they are epxressed to be 'directly applicable', which according to the Court in *Politi* (at p. 1048) means that

'by reason of their nature and their function in the system of the sources of Community law, regulations have direct effect and are as such capable of creating individual rights which national courts must protect.'

Occasionally, however, Regulations will not be capable of judicial enforcement, because of the nature of the obligations which they contain (e.g. they are too vague, or are contingent upon action by a third party). This point was recognised by AG Warner in Case 131/79 *R.* v. *Secretary of State for Home Affairs, ex parte Santillo* ([1980] ECR 1585). An analogy can be drawn with Acts of Parliament in the UK, not all provisions of which are enforceable by the courts. For example, sec. 23 of the British Telecommunications Act 1981 expressly provides that no action in tort shall lie against British Telecom in respect of failure to provide or delay in providing a telecommunications services. If this line of argument is pursued it is clearly possible to maintain a conceptual distinction between direct applicability and direct effect, as suggested by Winter (1972) and as argued in this chapter, even though the terminology used by the Court has had a tendency to confuse the two concepts.

An extended controversy surrounding the direct effect of Directives was finally resolved by the Court in *Van Duyn*. It had been argued that since Directives contain obligations of result, and not of conduct (see 5.11), and since only Regulations are expressed to be 'directly applicable' in Article 189 EC, they could not be capable of judicial enforcement. The Court refuted these arguments in the following terms (at p.1348):

'If . . . by virtue of the provisions of Article 189 regulations are directly applicable and, consequently, may by their very nature have direct effects, it does not follow from this that other categories of acts mentioned in that article can never have similar effects. It would be incompatible with the binding effect attributed to a directive by Article 189 to exclude, in principle, the possibility that the obligation which it imposes may be invoked by those concerned.'

The Court showed itself prepared, therefore, to overlook the fact that the binding obligation in a Directive is principally an obligation to implement, not a substantive obligation; while that may originally have represented a slender foundation for arguing the direct effect of Directives, it cannot be denied that subsequent developments have rendered this doctrinal shift irreversible. In *Van Duyn* the Court held that the applicant, who was threatened with exclusion from the UK on the grounds of her membership of the Church of Scientology – an organisation which attracted official disapproval in the UK, but was not actually proscribed – could rely upon the provisions of Directive 64/221 in order to claim certain procedural rights which limited the exercise of the UK's discretion to exclude Member State nationals on public policy grounds.

Consequently, as with other provisions of Community law, the question is one of construction. The fact that the Directive gives a choice to Member States as between alternative methods of attaining a given result does not necessarily mean that the provisions in question are not capable of judicial enforcement. The time limit given for the implementation of the Directive is, however, crucial. Before the time limit has expired, the provisions cannot be regarded as containing perfect legal obligations (Case 148/78 *Ratti* [1979] ECR 1629).

8.9   Horizontal and Vertical Direct Effect and the Consequences of the Distinction

Having held that Directives can have direct effect, the Court was then faced with a subsidiary question of scope, namely whether Directives

...rizontally directly effective. This matter was decided in Case ...*arshall* v. *Southampton and South West Hampshire AHA* ([1986] ...*R* 723). The Court held (at p. 749):

'With regard to the argument that directives may not be relied upon against an individual, it must be emphasised that according to Article 189 of the EEC Treaty the binding nature of a directive, which constitutes the basis for the possibility of relying on the directive before a national court, exists only in relation to "each Member State to which it is addressed". It follows that a directive may not of itself impose obligations on an individual and that a provision of a directive may not be relied upon as such as against such a person.'

In relation to the direct effect of Directives, therefore, it can be said that the so-called 'estoppel' justification has prevailed. The objective sought by allowing individuals to rely upon Directives is to deny to Member States the benefits which they might derive from their failure to implement Directives. This being so, it would be inconsistent to allow horizontal as well as vertical enforcement. The effect of this finding is, of course, to create an important borderline which is not based upon the nature of the provision to be enforced, but upon the actual nature of the dispute between the parties. In fields where Community law frequently takes the form of Directives, and where it is aimed ultimately at altering the conduct of individuals as well as states (e.g. environmental law, labour law and social law) the potential for injustice is clear. For example, a public sector employee may rely upon the guarantee of equal treatment as regards sex in employment matters contained in the Equal Treatment Directive (76/207) in order to challenge alleged sex discrimination on the part of his or her employer, whereas a private sector employee may not. Injustices could also emerge as between the Member States given that the numbers and types of public sector jobs do vary greatly between the different states. Three mechanisms have consequently emerged which soften the harshness of this distinction. The first is concerned with the interpretation of the scope of direct effect; the latter two go beyond the scope of direct effect, and illustrate that it is just one mechanism of several aimed at ensuring the effective enforcement of Community law.

First, the Court has developed a broad interpretation of precisely what is this 'state' which is not allowed to benefit from its own wrong in failing to implement the Directive. In *Marshall* itself the Court held that the state includes the state as employer as well as the state as public authority. In Case C-188/89 *Foster* v. *British Gas plc* ([1990] ECR I-3313) the Court provided general guidance on the concept of the 'emanation of the State', holding that the definition of this concept is a matter of Community law, not national law. It is for the national court to decide whether a given body falls within the criteria offered by the Court. *Foster* involved the question of whether certain women employees made redundant by (pre-privatisation) British Gas in circumstances in which they would not have been made redundant had they been men, could rely upon the Equal Treatment Directive as against their employer. The Court summarised the bodies previously held to be emanations of the State: tax authorities (Case 8/81 *Becker* [1982] ECR 53); local or regional authorities (Case C-221/88 *ECSC* v. *Acciaierie e ferriere Busseni* ([1990] ECR I-495; see also Case 103/88 *Fratelli Costanzo* v. *Milano* [1989] ECR 1839); the police (Case 222/84 *Johnston* v. *Royal Ulster Constabulary* ([1986] ECR 1651); and bodies responsible for State-funded health care (*Marshall*). It then went on to say (at p. 3348) that

'a body, whatever its legal form, which has been made responsible pursuant to a measure adopted by the State, for providing a public service under the control of the State and has for that purpose special powers beyond those which result from the normal rules applicable in relations between individuals is included in any event among the bodies against which the provisions of a directive capable of having direct effect may be relied upon.'

The categories of 'emanation of the state' are clearly, therefore, not yet closed. Moreover, on this interpretation it is not clear that a post-privatisation utility would necessarily be held not to be an emanation of the state if it retains sufficient special statutory powers.

The second way in which the Court has sought to alleviate the consequences of the limitation which it has placed upon the direct effect of Directives has been through its promotion of the principle of construction which requires national courts, in conformity with their duty under Article 5 EC to give full effect to Community law, to interpret all national law in the light of relevant Community law, regardless of whether it has direct effect. Although this principle of construction is sometimes called *Von Colson* effect, following the case in which it was first discussed (Case 14/83 *Von Colson and Kamann* v. *Land Nordrhein Westfalen* ([1984] ECR 1891), it has more recently been termed 'indirect effect' (Fitzpatrick, 1989), the doctrine of 'substantive effectiveness' (Mead, 1991), and, descriptively, the duty of national courts to interpret provisions of national law in accordance with Community law (Docksey and Fitzpatrick, 1991). It is considered in more detail in 8.14.

Finally, the Court has held that the failure by a Member State to implement a Directive may give rise to an action for damages against the state at the instance of an individual who suffers loss thereby, regardless of whether the Directive is capable of having direct effect, in the sense of containing a perfect legal obligation (Cases 6 and 9/90 *Francovich* v. *Italian State*) (8.19). *A fortiori* this possibility will equally pertain in circumstances where, although the Directive itself is capable of judicial enforcement, the potential defendant would be another private party who is not subject to obligations arising under the Directive.

It is possible to draw certain conclusions about the future role of direct effect from these recent developments. Together they indicate the evolving maturity of the Community legal system in terms of the range of sanctions and remedies which will be generated within the domestic legal system for breach of Community obligations. Pescatore described 'direct effect' itself as an 'infant disease' of Community law (Pescatore, 1983). The justiciability of provisions of Community law was an instrument devised at an early stage in the history of the Community legal order for maximising the effectiveness of Community law. Historically, it has proved most important in those Member States such as the Netherlands and the UK where, as a matter of national law, Community law appears capable of overriding national law only where it generates rights enforceable by individuals (see 8.20). Subsequent developments in Community law itself have demonstrated that no strict division will need to be drawn in the future between Community norms with direct effect and those without.

8.10   The Superior Nature of Community Law

Nowhere in the constitutive Treaties is it stated that Community law takes precedence over national law, although such a position can be derived from the duty of Community loyalty contained in Article 5 EC). Nonetheless, the supremacy of Community law has not seriously been challenged since the early 1960s. Possible bases for supremacy lie in stressing either the federal or the international nature of the Community legal system. For example, in legal systems which have a monist conception of international law, the latter is generally regarded as having a higher authority than municipal law and therefore as taking precedence. The better view is probably to accept that supremacy is inherent in the ideal of creating a new 'federal-type' legal order which lies at the heart of the project of economic integration in Europe, which has always had as its ultimate objective a 'union of peoples' (see the Preamble to the Treaty of Rome establishing the EEC). The process of economic integration would be much less effective if Member States were able to hinder the attainment of Community goals by denying the superiority of Community norms.

Of greater import than the theory of supremacy are its implications, which have been worked through by the Court in a series of constitutional cases, in particular those in which it has examined aspects of the duty of Member States to cooperate in the achievement of Community objectives under Article 5.

8.11   Community Law Prevails over National Constitutions

In Case 11/70 *Internationale Handelsgesellschaft* ([1970] ECR 1125), the Court held that Community law prevails over all forms of national law, including national constitutions and fundamental rights enshrined in those constitutions. Community measures derive their validity solely from Community law, and thus the validity of a Community measure or its effect within a Member State cannot be affected by objections that it runs counter to either fundamental rights as guaranteed by the constitution of that State or the principles of a national constitutional structure.

In order to counter the objection that it is not reasonable to replace the sovereignty of nation states which offer citizens constitutional guarantees of fundamental rights with a European Community which does not, and in order to head off possible rebellions by the German and Italian Constitutional Courts, the Court has evolved the Community doctrine of fundamental rights (see 5.7).

8.12   Supremacy Limits National Law-making Powers: the Pre-emptive Effect of Community Law

In Case 106/77 *Simmenthal II* the Court deduced from the principles established in Case 6/64 *Costa* v. *ENEL* that the supremacy of Community law logically must limit national law-making powers. It held ([1978] ECR 629 at at p. 643):

'Furthermore, in accordance with the principle of the precedence of Community law, the relationship between provisions of the Treaty and directly applicable measures of the institutions on the one hand and national law of the Member States on the other is such that those provisions and measures not only by their entry into force render automatically inapplicable any conflicting provision of current national law but – in so far as they are an integral part of, and take precedence in, the legal order applicable in the territory of each of the Member States – also preclude the valid adoption of new national legislative measures to the extent to which they would be incompatible with Community provisions.

Indeed any recognition that national legislative measures which encroach upon the field within which the Community exercises its legislative power or which are otherwise incompatible with the provisions of Community law had any legal effect would amount to a corresponding denial of the effectiveness of the obligations undertaken unconditionally and irrevocably by Member States pursuant to the Treaty and would thus imperil the very foundations of the Community.'

In practice, of course, these principles can be put into effect only by the domestic institutions themselves. The Court has no power to invalidate national legislation, although it may state in a preliminary ruling that national legislation of the type at issue in a given case is inconsistent with Community law, or make a declaration under Article 171 in proceedings brought under Articles 169 or 170 EC that a given provision of national law is incompatible with Community law. The pre-emptive effect of Community law is particularly apparent in those areas where Community legislature has exhaustively regulated the field, in particular using legislation in the form of Regulations. This is so, in particular, under the rules governing the Common Agricultural Policy (CAP). In Case 16/83 *Prantl* ([1984] ECR 1299 at p.1324) the Court stated that:

'once rules on the common organisation of the market [in wine] may be regarded as forming a complete system, the Member States no longer have competence in that field unless Community law expressly provides otherwise.'

8.13 Member States have a Duty to Enforce Community Law

This was discussed in Chapter 6 and is clearly stated in Cases 314/81, etc. *Procureur de la République* v. *Waterkeyn* ([1982] ECR 4337 at p.4360):

'all the institutions of the Member State concerned must . . . ensure within the fields covered by their respective powers, that judgments of the Court are complied with.'

For example, contravention of national legislation which breaches Community law may not be prosecuted by the domestic authorities as a criminal offence (Case 269/80 *R.* v. *Tymen* [1981] ECR 3079. Conversely, Member States have a duty to prosecute breaches of Community law using national criminal legislation as diligently as they would in purely domestic circumstances (Case 68/88 *Commission* v. *Greece* [1989] ECR 2965). This duty also comprises the duty on national courts to interpret national law in the light of Community law and the duties on national courts to give effective remedies in respect of breaches of Community law.

8.14 The Interpretative Duties of National Courts: Indirect Effect

The evolution of the indirect effect doctrine was referred to briefly above on the context of the limitations placed upon the direct effect of Directives. The doctrine itself flows from the direct applicability and superior nature of Community law. The duty on the national court to apply the law in such a way as to facilitate the achievement of the Community's objectives flows directly from the penetration of Community law into the national legal system, and is expressed most clearly in Article 5 EC. It is not limited to giving effect to Community rules which are judicially enforceable as such, but also extends to the development of a range of interpretative devices which derive their force from Community law. In other words, Community law does not have to be directly effective in order for it to benefit from the general doctrine of supremacy.

In *Von Colson*, where the doctrine first emerged, the Court found itself unable to hold that a particular provision of the Equal Treatment Directive was sufficiently precise and unconditional to support the implication alleged by the plaintiff. It nonetheless held that (at p. 1909):

> 'the Member States' obligation arising from a directive to achieve the result envisaged by the directive and their duty under Article 5 of the Treaty to take all appropriate measures, whether general or particular, to ensure the fulfilment of that obligation, is binding on all the authorities of Member States including, for matters within their jurisdiction, the courts. It follows that, in applying the national law specifically introduced in order to implement Directive No. 76/207, national courts are required to interpret their national law in the light of the wording and purpose of the directive in order to achieve the result referred to in the third paragraph of Article 189.'

The Court held that Article 6 of the Equal Treatment Directive, which guarantees the victims of sex discrimination in employment matters the right to a judicial remedy, is not sufficiently precise to support the implication that a particular sanction (in that case the obligation on the discriminating employer to conclude a contract of employment with the victim) must be applied by the national court. In general terms, however, it does include the right to a sufficient remedy, which constitutes an adequate deterrent against future acts of discrimination. It is in the light of this general interpretation that the national court was required to intepret the German Equal Treatment Act, passed to implement the Directive.

As Fitzpatrick (1989) pointed out, *Von Colson* left two matters undecided. First, it was not clear what categories of national law had to be interpreted in the light of Community law. *Von Colson* itself contained an ambiguity, with the Court appearing to refer at some points (such as the paragraph cited) only to national legislation specifically introduced to implement a Community obligation, but at other points to cast the net wider to include potentially all national law. A third possibility would be to include all national legislation implementing Community law, whether specifically adopted with that objective in mind, or subsequently deemed to represent a sufficient implementation of a given Community obligation. On this point of doubt, the Court repeated, but had no need to apply, the wider formula in *Johnston*. The same formula also found strong words of support from AG Van Gerven in Case C-262/88 *Barber* v. *Guardian Royal Exchange* ([1990] ECR I-1889).

The second uncertainty concerned the scope of the rule of construction: how far, precisely, were national courts required to go in order to ensure conformity between national law and Community law? Was there in truth any difference between disapplying conflicting national legislation under the *Simmenthal* doctrine, and construing it in conformity with Community law (including, if necessary, reading words into a statute or reconstructing the intention of the legislature)? If not, that would appear to reduce further the consequences of the rules on the judicial enforceability of Community law.

Both difficulties now appear to have been resolved by the Court in favour of the widest possible ambit of the indirect effect principle. In Case C-106/89 *Marleasing SA* v. *La Comercial Internacional de Alimentacion* ([1990] ECR I-4135) the Court repeated its formulation from *Von Colson* on the responsibilities of national courts, going on to say (at p. 4159) that:

'in applying national law, whether the provisions concerned pre-date or post-date the directive, the national court asked to interpret national law is bound to do so in every way possible in the light of the text and the aim of the directive to achieve the results envisaged by it and thus to comply with Article 189(3) of the Treaty.'

There seems to be no limitation in this judgment that the national provisions subject to interpretation in the light of Community should be those intended or deemed to implement Community law. Potentially, therefore, UK courts could be required to reconsider the rules of the common law in the light of Community obligations. Second, courts must do 'everything possible' to achieve a resolution of Community law and national law. Does this mean that national courts must depart from national canons of construction when performing their interpretative duties under Article 5? Must UK courts abandon their preference for the literal rule of statutory interpretation and their adherence to the convention of *stare decisis* when applying Community law? Certainly, the methods of interpretation used by national courts must match those preferred by the Court of Justice, looking for the purpose of a measure, and going beyond its literal meaning (Millett, 1989; Kutscher, 1976).

However, it is still possible to discern a difference between the approach of the Court in *Marleasing* which calls on national courts to do everything 'possible' to achieve an interpretation of national law in conformity with a non-justiciable provision of a Directive and its approach in *Simmenthal* where it requires them to do everything 'necessary' to achieve the enforcement of justiciable provisions of Community law, including the setting aside of national law. For example, in *Barber* AG Van Gerven indicated that nothing in Article 5 required national courts to interpret national legislation *contra legem*, i.e. contrary to its express words, in order to achieve conformity with Community law which is not judicially enforceable, and this view finds strong judicial echoes in the case law of the House of Lords on the application of the indirect effect principle in the UK (*Duke* v. *GEC*; see 8.20).

8.15   The Scope of the Indirect Effect Principle

The interpretative duties of national courts apply also in relation to certain non-binding measures of Community law. In Case C-322/88

Grimaldi v. *Fonds des Maladies Professionnelles* ([1989] ECR I-4407) the Court applied the indirect effect principle to the Commission Recommendations on the adoption of a European schedule of occupational diseases and on the conditions for granting compensation to persons suffering from occupational diseases. Such (non-binding) Recommendations had to be taken into consideration by a national court in order to enable it to decide disputes, in particular where they are capable of clarifying other provisions of national or Community law.

However, the application of the indirect effect principle by national courts is limited by reference to other general principles of the Community legal order, such as the prohibition on retroactivity and the principle of legal certainty. This point is made by AG Van Gerven in *Marleasing* and is illustrated by the judgment of the Court in Case 80/86 *Kolpinghuis Nijmegen* ([1987] ECR 3969) where the use of the principle of indirect effect would have come into conflict with the principle of *nulla poena sine lege*. A national judicial authority could not rely upon an unimplemented Directive in order to 'sharpen' existing domestic sanctions on the marketing of unfit goods. The Court stated (at p. 3986):

'A directive cannot, of itself and independently of a national law adopted by a Member State for its implementation, have the effect of determining or aggravating the liability of persons who act in contravention of the provisions of that directive.'

In other words, the State cannot benefit from the operation of the principle of indirect effect.

8.16 The Relationship between Direct Effect and Indirect Effect

In Case 222/84 *Johnston* v. *Chief Constable of the Royal Ulster Constabulary* the Court appeared to link the two concepts of direct effect and indirect effect together, indicating that it was the first duty of national courts to seek to interpret national law in conformity with Community law, and only if this was not possible, to enforce Community law itself in preference to national law through the doctrine of direct effect. To formulate the duty of the national court thus matches the attempts by Pescatore (1983) to de-emphasise the significance of direct effect. It is also consistent with the evolution of a wider array of mechanisms concerned with increasing the effectiveness of Community law within the domesic legal system, through a focus on sanctions for breach of Community law rather than on the precise nature of the provision which is alleged to have been breached. It has the advantage of maintaining national procedural autonomy in determining the precise form of the remedy given, without undermining the crucial uniformity of Community law.

8.17   National Remedies and Breach of Community Law

National courts are under a duty to give comprehensive remedies to individuals seeking redress against national law in conflict with Community law, or seeking to enforce Community rights (Case 811/79 *Amministrazione delle Finanze dello Stato* v. *Ariete SpA* [1980] ECR 2545). In 5.5, we stressed the importance of procedural rights such as the right to due process, the right to be given reasons and the right to a judicial remedy; these are crucial to the effective protection of Community rights, and are given the status of general principles of Community law. Rights granted to individuals by Directives or other Community provisions must be capable of protection by judicial process (Case 222/84 *Johnston* v. *Chief Constable of the Royal Ulster Constabulary*).

The nature of the remedies granted are a matter for national courts, but they must be no less favourable than those accorded by the court in respect of violations of similar rights arising under national law. However, although the procedural conditions, such as limitation periods or *locus standi* rules, which govern actions for the enforcement of Community are a matter for national law (at least until they have been harmonised by the Community legislature), national procedural rules which make it practically impossible to exercise the rights granted by Community law would themselves amount to a breach of the Treaty (Case 45/76 *Comet* v. *Produktschap* [1976] ECR 2043). In recent years, the Court has given increasingly direct instructions to national courts in its case law on national remedies. For example, in Case C-208/90 *Emmott* v. *Minister for Social Welfare* ([1991] IRLR 387; [1991] 3 CMLR 894) it held that time limits can only begin to run against an applicant bringing an action for breach of Community law against the State as from the date when the Community provision in question is transparently implemented by that state. In similar vein it has held that the rights granted by Community law may not be limited by the application of additional substantive conditions. For example, in Case C-177/88 *Dekker* v. *Stichting Vormingscentrum voor Jong Volwassenen* ([1990] ECR I-3941) the Court held that national provisions may not subject liability for sex discrimination in employment matters to the requirement that the victim show fault on the part of the employer where all that is required under the Directive is proof of the simple fact of discrimination. Finally, in Case C-377/89 *Cotter and McDermott* v. *Minister for Social Welfare* (*No. 2*) ([1991] IRLR 380; [1991] 3 CMLR 507), the Court held that the State may not defeat a claim to a social benefit based on the right to sex equality, by claiming that the applicant would be unjustly enriched by the receipt of the benefit because she has received an equivalent benefit via her husband. Unjust enrichment may not, therefore, be a valid defence to a claim based on Community rights.

In practice, the types of claims which national courts must recognise must include the power to set national legislation aside for breach of Community law and the power to award damages. In each of the important recent cases, the Court has also stressed how the duty falling on national courts is derived from Article 5 EC.

8.18 Disapplying National Legislation

Simmenthal II tells national courts that they are responsible for 'disapplying' national law which comes into conflict with Community law (Gravells, 1989; Barav, 1989). The idea of disapplying an Act of Parliament is a novel concept for a UK judge, accustomed to occupying subordinate position in relation to the legislature. However, as the Court made clear in its ruling on the reference from the House of Lords in Case C-213/89 *R. v. Secretary of State for Transport, ex parte Factortame Ltd* ([1990] ECR I-2433), it is inherent to the system of Community law that national courts must be able, in either final or interim proceedings, to issue appropriate orders to give effect to Community law. It held (at p. 2473):

'In accordance with the case law of the Court, it is for the national courts, in application of the principle of co-operation laid down in Article 5 of the EEC Treaty, to ensure the legal protection which persons derive from the direct effect of provisions of Community law . . .

The Court has also held that any provision of a national legal system and any legislative, administrative or judicial practice which might impair the effectiveness of Community law by withholding from the national court having jurisdiction to apply such law the power to do everything necessary at the moment of its application to set aside national legislative provisions which might prevent, even temporarily, Community rules from having full force and effect are incompatible with those requirements, which are the very essence of Community law . . .

It must be added that the full effectiveness of Community law would be just as much impaired if a rule of national law could prevent a court seised of a dispute governed by Community law from granting interim relief in order to ensure the full effectiveness of the judgment to be given on the existence of the rights claimed under Community law. It follows that a court which in those circumstances would grant interim relief, if it were not for a rule of national law, is obliged to set aside that rule.'

On these grounds the House of Lords was obliged to abrogate, at least as regards matters of Community competence, the rule prohibiting the granting of interim injunctions against the Crown, as it had indicated in its judgment prior to ordering a reference that it would be prepared to do if required by the Court (*R v. Secretary of State for Transport, ex parte Factortame Ltd* [1990] 2 AC 85; [1989] 3 CMLR 1; award of interim relief: [1991] 1 All ER 70; [1990] 3 CMLR 375). The Court also held that a national court must be prepared to grant such a remedy even in advance of an authoritative ruling by the Court on the existence of an infringement of Community law.

8.19   Damages for Breach of Community Law

In appropriate cases, a national court must be prepared to award damages to an individual seeking to rely upon justiciable or directly effective provisions of Community law in a national court where a remedy in damages is apt to compensate the individual for harm suffered. In Case 60/75 *Russo* v. *AIMA* ([1976] ECR 45 at p.56) the Court held that:

'if . . . damage has been caused through an infringement of Community law the state is liable to the injured party of the consequences in the context of the provisions of national law on the liability of the state.'

However, the Court has yet to make statements regarding the conditions in which damages should be the remedy for breach of directly effective Community law which match the precision with which it addressed the issue of injunctive relief in *Factortame*.

Instead it has developed its case law on damages in a different direction holding in Cases C-6 and 9/90 *Francovich* v. *Italian Republic* that there is a separate principle based on Article 5 coupled with the general principles of Community law which requires national courts to hold Member States liable for damage caused by the failure to implement a Directive. It has offered a remedy which is triggered by a separate test and operates irrespective of whether Directive is directly effective. *A fortiori* it will have a particular utility precisely where there is no direct effect. This makes Member States liable not just for their acts which breach Community law, but also for their omissions.

The claims in *Francovich* were brought by workers in Italy made redundant when their employers became insolvent, who received no compensation or redundancy payments because no funds were available from employers themselves, and because Italy had failed to implement Directive 80/987 which requires Member States to set up guarantee funds to cover the compensation claims of employees made redundant in the event of their employers' insolvency. The employees claimed that the Italian State was responsible for payment of the compensation, either by virtue of the direct effect of the Directive, or on grounds of liability for a failure to act.

In its judgment in *Francovich* the Court returned to first principles in deriving the right to damages from the specific nature of Community law, its justiciability and superior nature, going on to hold (at para. 33 of the judgment):

'It should be stated that the full effectiveness of Community provisions would be affected and the protection of the rights they recognise undermined if individuals were not able to recover damages when their rights were infringed by a breach of Community law attributable to a Member State.'

This repeats, in similar terms, the position already reached in *Russo* v. *AIMA*, and highlights the availability of damages for breach of a substantive Community obligation by a Member State. It then went on to hold (at para. 34 of the judgment):

'The possibility of obtaining damages from the State is particularly essential where, as in the present case, the full effect of Community provisions is conditional on the State taking certain action, and, in consequence, in the absence of such action being taken, individuals cannot rely on the rights accorded to them by Community law before national courts.'

Having considered the provisions of Directive 80/987, the Court reached the conclusion that those provisions concerned with the creation of a minimum guarantee were not sufficiently precise in themselves to support a claim for the lost wages against the Italian State. In particular, the failure to implement the Directive meant that the State had not chosen what form the guarantee would take, and how it would be funded. The argument that the Directive was directly effective therefore failed since the Directive gave a discretion in the implementation process to the Member States. The only remaining remedy, therefore, was a right to damages for non-implementation.

The right to damages is subject to a test based on the nature of the provisions, which is similar, but not identical, to the test applied to determine the direct effect of a provision. Three conditions must be satisfied: the result prescribed by the provision must involve the conferring of rights on individuals; the content of the rights must be capable of definition on the basis of the Directive; and there must be a causal link between the violation of the Treaty obligation by the Member States and the loss suffered by the individual. In applying these conditions the national court is bound to apply national procedural rules which are no less favourable than those governing similar actions. The provisions of Directive 80/987 would appear to satisfy these tests, since the beneficiary of the rights and the nature of the rights were defined; the Directive failed only to define the subject of the obligation, namely the precise nature of the guarantee fund.

In sum, there would now appear to be two separate actions for damages available under Community law. The right to damages for breach of a substantive Community obligation, and the right to damages for breach of the general principle in Article 5 that Member States must loyally enforce and implement Community law, in particular the obligation to implement Directives.

The difficulty with the *Francovich* action would appear to be that it drives a coach and horses through the formulations of national procedural autonomy contained in earlier cases such as *Comet*. A number of Member

States simply do not recognise actions against the State for loss caused by legislative action or inaction; it is difficult, therefore, to imagine how analogies can be drawn between the *Francovich* action and the national procedural rules governing non-existent similar actions. The national courts may be required to invent *de novo* a cause of action against the State.

In contrast, the advantages of the *Francovich* action are many. It avoids the need to make the provisions of the Directive themselves justiciable before the national courts using direct effect, or to achieve an uncomfortable resolution between irreconcilable provisions of Community law and national law through strained constructions under the doctrine of indirect effect. It also avoids the possibility that either increasingly marginal 'emanations of the state' (through the *Foster* doctrine) or even private parties (through the medium of indirect effect) will be asked to carry the principal burden of giving effect to the substantive rights for individuals contained in Directives. Instead it concentrates on what has always been the primary obligation of the Member State under a Directive, namely the obligation to implement, and attaches a rigorous sanction to failure to fulfil that obligation. It is arguable that this mechanism will be a much more effective way of securing compliance on the part of Member States in the implementation of Community law than either direct effect or indirect effect.

8.20 Domestic Responses to the Challenges of Community Law

Details were given 8.3 and 8.4 regarding the differing constitutional responses which the national legal systems have made to the demands of Community law. The final part of the chapter will now concentrate, in the spirit of the pragmatic philosophy of securing the effectiveness of Community law, on the progress made towards a complete acceptance of the approach of the Court of Justice in national courts. Ideally the Court should always seek to balance its approach between the need to promote dynamism within the Community legal order, and the need to avoid accelerating beyond the bounds of what national courts consider acceptable. It is from the reactions of the national courts that it is possible to discern whether the Court has achieved that balance.

For example, some courts such as the French *Conseil d'Etat* (Supreme Administrative Court) and the German Federal Finance Court have been unwilling to accept that Directives could give rise to rights justiciable at the instance of individuals. The views of the two courts in *Minister of the Interior* v. *Cohn-Bendit* ([1980] 1 CMLR 543) and *Kloppenburg* v. *Finanzamt Leer* ([1989] 1 CMLR 873) were founded on an analysis of Article 189 which focused on the differences between Regulations and Directives, and which has found support amongst academic commentators also (e.g. Hamson, 1976).

The *Conseil d'Etat* has also experienced difficulties accepting the full consequences of the supremacy of Community law. However, in recent cases such as *Boisdet* ([1991] 1 CMLR 3) it has accepted an interpretation of the Article 55 of the French Constitution which allows Community law to take precedence over subsequent French laws, an interpretation which accords with the position already long adopted by the highest French court in the private law field, the *Cour de Cassation* (*Café Jacques Vabre* (1975)).

In the UK debate has centered around key provisions of the European Communities Act 1972. These should ensure the effective application and enforcement of Community law in the UK.

Sec. 2(1) enshrines the concept of direct effect:

'All such rights, powers, liability, obligations and restrictions from time to time created or arising by or under the Treaties, and all such remedies and procedures from time to time provided for by or under the Treaties, as in accordance with the Treaties are without further enactment to be given legal effect or used in the United Kingdom shall be recognised and available in law, and be enforced, allowed and followed accordingly.'

The supremacy of Community law appears to be guaranteed by the rather obscurely worded sec. 2(4) which contains the text:

'any enactment passed or to be passed, other than one contained in this Part of this Act, shall be construed and have effect subject to the foregoing provisions of this section.'

The best view of sec. 2(4) is as a rule of construction for national law aimed at avoiding conflicts with Community law. According to Lord Bridge in *Factortame* ([1989] 2 All ER 692 at p.701) sec. 2(4):

'has precisely the same effect as if a section were incorporated in [Part II of the Merchant Shipping Act 1988] which in terms enacted that the provisions with regard to registration of British fishing vessels were to be without prejudice to the directly enforceable rights of nationals of any Member States of the EEC.'

At the practical level, the House of Lords in *Factortame* complied fully with the requirements of Community law as laid down by the Court, with Lord Bridge remarking on the rehearing of the case following the judgment of the Court ([1990] 3 CMLR 375) on the misconceived comments of those who regarded the requirement that the courts override national legislation in violation of Community law as a novel and dangerous invasion of the sovereignty of the UK. He regarded the approach taken by the Court as mandated by the supremacy of Community law, a concept well entrenched in the Community legal order before even the UK acceded to the Treaties.

A less positive approach has been taken by the UK courts in the context of damages actions. There is only rather oblique authority for the proposition that Articles 85 and 86 EC should give rise to an action in damages by a person injured by anti-competitive or monopolistic conduct (*Garden Cottage Foods* v. *Milk Marketing Board* 1984] AC 130) and in *Bourgoin* v. *MAFF* [1986] QB 716 the Court of Appeal gave an even more restrictive interpretation of the right to damages in respect of conduct of the State in violation of Article 30 EC.

It refused to accept the principle that breach of Article 30 of itself gave rise to a right to damages by way of civil action, arguing that the primary remedy in English law must lie by way of judicial review in the public law field. Damages could be awarded only for particularly grave conduct amounting to an abuse of power, or misfeasance in public office. This additional requirement of fault seems difficult to support in the light of the approach taken by the Court in *Dekker* to the requirement of fault in sex discrimination cases. In any event, it is generally acknowledged that *Bourgoin* is ripe for reconsideration in the post-*Francovich* era. This, for example, was the view put forward *obiter* by Lord Goff in *Kirklees BC* v. *Wickes Building Supplies Ltd* ([1992] 3 All ER 717 at p.734).

In that case, the House of Lords declined to review the *Bourgoin* case law. It also held that the possibility that a Member State may be liable in damages for breach of Article 30 because it has maintained in force an Act of Parliament (in that case, the Shops Act 1950, sec. 47 which prohibits Sunday Trading) which is in breach of Article 30 is not sufficient to require a local authority, which seeks to enforce the Act by way of a civil injunction, to give a cross-undertaking in damages against the eventuality that the Act may subsequently be held to be in breach of Community law by the Court of Justice. It founded its view on the belief that, in the event that sec. 47 of the Shops Act was found to be incompatible with Article 30, the primary obligation to make good loss suffered by traders denied the right to trade on Sunday would fall on the UK government, not on local authorities.

In one further respect English case law also requires substantial revision in the light of the evolution of Community law. The judges have generally shown themselves willing to give sympathetic interpretations of national provisions introduced with the specific purpose of implementing Community legislation. In *Pickstone* v. *Freemans plc* ([1988] 2 All ER 813) the House of Lords interpreted sec. 1(2)(c) of the Equal Pay Act 1970, which was introduced by the Equal Value Regulations 1983 in order to bring UK law into conformity with the requirements of Article 119 EC on equal pay, in order to give effect to what it saw as the purpose of Parliament. This meant that it was permissible to give an interpretation of the words in the light of the *purpose* of the equal value principle and to allow it to function effectively to deal with the 'mischief' which it was introduced to counter. In an equal value claim, one group of workers is compared against another group of workers in order to assess the respective value of the work done by each group of workers. Sec. 1(2)(c) should not be rendered inoperative by the employment of one token man amongst what is normally a disadvantaged group of female workers; it should be sufficient that the group of workers disadvantaged was predominantly female (or, exceptionally, male).

A similar approach was taken in *Litster* v. *Forth Dry Dock and Engineering Co Ltd* ([1989] 1 All ER 1134) to the Transfer of Undertakings Regulations 1981, passed to implement the Acquired Rights Directive 77/187.

However, in a case where there was at the time when the facts arose no specific implementing legislation, the House of Lords found itself unable to adopt the same approach. In *Duke* v. *GEC Reliance* ([1988] 1 All ER 626) the House was asked to interpret the provisions of the Sex Discrimination Act 1975 on retirement ages in accordance with the provisions of the Equal Treatment Directive 76/207, in order to give a remedy to a woman working in the private sector who was made redundant earlier than a man in the same position, on grounds of having reached a (discriminatory) retirement age. This would have equalised the position of private and public sector workers, since the latter had a remedy based on the direct effect of the Directive as interpreted by the Court of Justice in Case 152/84 *Marshall* v. *Southampton and South West Hampshire AHA* ([1986] ECR 723). The House of Lords used the European Communities Act 1972 in order to draw a much stronger distinction between Community law which is and is not justiciable than is probably tenable in the light of the case law of the Court of Justice on indirect effect, holding that sec. 2(4) only applies the supremacy principle to directly effective Community law, and that no other principle of Community law required it to give what it considered to be a strained interpretation of the Sex Discrimination Act in order to achieve a reconciliation with the terms of the Equal Treatment Directive. In the absence of specific implementing legislation the House regarded itself as outside the duty of sympathetic interpretation which it was fulfilling in Pickstone and *Litster*. It would now appear from the decision of the Court in *Marleasing* that the case of *Duke* is in urgent need of review.

Yet in a recent decision on pregnancy discrimination the Court of Appeal in effect applied the ruling in *Duke* and declined to apply the broad principle of indirect effect (*Webb* v. *EMO* [1992] 1 CMLR 793). It refused to use the indirect effect principle in order to reconcile the differences in the basic approach to pregnancy discrimination as a form of sex discrimination between the Sex Discrimination Act 1975 as interpreted in the UK courts and the Equal Treatment Directive as interpreted in the Court of Justice in Case C-177/88 *Dekker* v. *Stichting Vormingscentrum voor Jong Volwassenen* and Case C-179/88 *Handels- og Kontorfunktionærernes Forbund i Danmark* v. *Dansk Arbeijdsgiversverforening* ([1990] ECR I-3979). The House of Lords ([1992] 4 All ER 929) seemed a little more receptive to the arguments based on the two Court of Justice cases cited here, and referred a number of questions on the meaning of pregnancy discrimination to the Court for decision.

This line of case law reveals most clearly the difficulties which flow in the UK from the dualist inheritance under which the authority of Community law is seen as deriving its force from the European Communities Act 1972, rather than from its inherent qualities as interpreted by the Court of Justice using the theory of the transfer of sovereign powers.

Summary

1   The underlying theme of the case law of the Court of Justice on the relationship of Community law and national law is that of ensuring the effectiveness or *'effet utile'* of Community law.

2   The basic principles of justiciability and supremacy based on a transfer of sovereign powers to the European Community and a penetration of Community law into the national legal systems can be derived from the early statements of principle by the Court of Justice in cases such as *Van Gend en Loos* and *Costa* v. *ENEL*.

3   The basic approaches to Community law taken by the national legal orders are conditioned by the particular constitutional regime in force, and the general position taken on the reception of international law into the domestic legal order.

4   There are particular theoretical difficulties with reconciling membership of the Community with a strict view of the sovereignty of the Westminster Parliament, but for the most part the European Communities Act 1972 offers the UK courts the means whereby they can resolve any practical difficulties which arise.

5   The justiciability, or direct effect, of Community law in national courts is well-established, and depends on a construction of the individual provision at issue. Provisions of Community law which are sufficiently precise and unconditional may be enforced in national courts at the instance of individuals to whom they grant rights.

6   Treaty provisions and binding acts of Community secondary legislation have been held capable of having direct effect, although some have expressed doubts as to whether the provisions of Directives should be held to be directly effective. These have been held to be vertically but not horizontally directly effective.

7   The limitations placed upon the direct effect of Directives have been qualified by the evolution of a wide doctrine of the 'emanation of the state', the concept of indirect effect, and the *Francovich* principle of the liability of the state for non-implementation of Directives.

8   The doctrine of supremacy allows Community law to prevail over all national law, including national constitutions. It also limits the law-making powers of the Member States and imposes duties to enforce Community law on the authorities of the Member States, including the courts.

9   The interpretative duties of national courts in relation to Community law are extensive, and extend to interpreting all national law in the light of the text and spirit of relevant Community law, and to do everything possible to achieve a resolution of the two.

10 National courts must give comprehensive remedies for breach of Community law, and although subject to national procedural conditions, these must be at least as generous as those applicable in equivalent national actions and not such as to render the Community rights incapable of enforcement in practice.

11 Particularly important are injunctive remedies disapplying conflicting provisions of national law, and remedies in damages for breach of Community law. There appear to be two separate rights to damages: damages for breach of a substantive obligation imposed by Community law (available against the state or individuals, depending upon the nature of the obligation which may fall on individuals and/or the state), and damages for breach of the obligation on Member States to implement Community law, which can be derived from Article 5 EC.

12 The record of national legal systems in giving effect to the case law of the Court of Justice is mixed. In the UK particular difficulties centre around the right to damages, and the willingness of the courts to make use of the indirect effect principle, the latter problem resulting from the interpretation of the European Communities Act 1972, and the continued insistence of the courts upon that Act as the foundation for the enforcement in the UK of Community law, rather than its inherent qualities, as interpreted by the Court of Justice.

Questions

1 In what ways do the statements of principle by the Court of Justice in *Van Gend en Loos* and *Costa* v. *ENEL* define the fundamental relationship between Community law and national law?

2 What, if anything, is the difference between direct applicability and direct effect?

3 How can the right of individuals to rely upon provisions of Community law as giving rise to justiciable rights in national courts be justified?

4 What other mechanisms exist to give effect to the principle of the effectiveness of Community law?

5 In what ways does the *Francovich* principle add to the previous system of remedies available for breach of Community law?

6 Assess the success of the UK courts in giving effect to Community law.

7 In 2.1 it was suggested that there was often a time lag between significant developments in the political arena led by the Member States, and the achievement of comparably important legal goals. Assess this assertion, by reference to the historical survey in Chapter 2 and the pattern of Community constitutional development which emerges in this chapter.

Workshop

In July 1990, the Council of Ministers adopted (fictitious) Directive 90/8000 requiring Member States to introduce a principle of strict liability for personal injury and property damage on the part of occupiers for the escape of toxic substances from their premises. It also requires Member States to establish a guarantee fund out of which compensation is to be paid to victims of accidents resulting from the escape of toxic substances where the occupier is unable, because of inadequate insurance, to satisfy a judgment debt. The Directive does not determine the details of the operation and funding of the guarantee fund. The Directive was to be implemented by December 31 1992.

Consider the following sets of circumstances:

1 The UK has not implemented the Directive by the due date. On January 2 1993, Anna is injured by the escape of a toxic chemical from a Government Research

Institute situated near to her house. Discuss the nature of her claim for damages under Community law.

Would your answer be any different if the toxic chemical escaped from (a) a University or (b) a pharmaceutical company?

2 The UK believes that the Directive is fully implemented by the existing (fictitious) Toxic Substances (Occupiers Liability) Act 1970, under which occupiers are subject to a reversal of the burden of proof requiring them to prove that any escapes of toxic substances from their premises are not the result of any lack of reasonably care on their part. Bert claims that his garden has been contaminated by the escape of contaminated substances during a flood from the premises of Rip Off plc, a manufacturer of chemicals. Assess the likelihood that Bert will succeed with his claim.

Would your answer be any different if Rip Off plc has gone into liquidation, and it is discovered that it had no insurance to cover the loss such as that caused to Bert?

3 The UK is fundamentally opposed to the Directive, believing it to be inconsistent with the principle of subsidiarity. Parliament adopts the (fictitious) Toxic Substances (Derogation) Act 1993 under which it specifically prohibits the UK courts from giving effect to the Directive. Advise the Community Rights Group, a pressure group concerned with the proper enforcement and implementation of Community law, of the likelihood of a successful challenge to the Act in the UK courts.

In the event that you conclude that a challenge would be possible in principle, consider whether the Community Rights Group could properly be denied standing to challenge the Act on the grounds that it has suffered no damage.

Further Reading

Barav (1989) 'Enforcement of Community rights in the National Courts: the Case for a Jurisdiction to grant interim relief', 26 *Common Market Law Review*, 369.

Curtin (1990a) 'The Province of Government: Delimiting the Direct Effect of Directives in the Common Law Context', 15 *European Law Review*, 195.

Curtin (1990b) 'Directives: The Effectiveness of Judicial Protection of Individual Rights', 27 *Common Market Law Review*, 709.

De Burca (1992) 'Giving Effect to European Community Directives', 55 *Modern Law Review*, 215.

Docksey and Fitzpatrick (1991) 'The Duty of National Courts to Interpret Provisions of National Law in Accordance with Community Law', 20 *Industrial Law Journal*, 113.

Fitzpatrick (1989) 'The Significance of EEC Directives in UK sex discrimination law', 9 *Oxford Journal of Legal Studies*, 336.

Gravells (1989) 'Disapplying an Act of Parliament pending a Preliminary Ruling: Constitutional Enormity or Community Law Right?', *Public Law*, 568.

Gravells (1991) 'Effective Protection of Community Law Rights: Temporary Displication of an Act of Parliament', *Public Law*, 180.

Mead (1991) 'The obligation to apply European law: is Duke dead?', 16 *European Law Review*, 490.

Pescatore (1983) 'The Doctrine of 'Direct Effect': An Infant Disease of Community Law', 8 *European Law Review*, 155.

Prechal (1990) 'Remedies after *Marshall*', 27 *Common Market Law Review*, 451.

Ross (1993) 'Beyond *Francovich*', 56 *Modern Law Review*, 55.

Snyder (1993) 'The Effectiveness of European Community Law: Institutions, Processes, Tools and Techniques', 56 *Modern Law Review*, 19.

Szyszczak (1990a) 'Sovereignty: Crisis, Compliance, Confusion, Complacency', 15 *European Law Review*, 480.

Szyszczak (1992a) 'European Community Law: New Remedies, New Directions?', 55 *Modern Law Review*, 690.

Wyatt (1982) 'New Legal Order or Old?', 7 *European Law Review*, 147.

Part IV

The Control of the
Community Institutions

9 The Judicial Review of Community Action

9.1 Introduction

Every developed legal system needs a system of judicial control which places fetters upon the exercise of state power. In the European Community the clear mandate for such a system lies in the task of the Court under Article 164 to ensure that the law is observed. This was elaborated by the Court in Case 294/83 *Parti Ecologiste 'Les Verts'* v. *Parliament* ([1986] ECR 1339) in the following terms (at p.1365):

'It must first be emphasised in this regard that the European Economic Community is a Community based on the rule of law, in as much as neither its Member States nor its institutions can avoid a review of the question whether the measures adopted by them are in conformity with the basic constitutional charter, the Treaty. In particular, in Articles 173 and 184, on the one hand, and in Article 177, on the other, the Treaty established a complete system of legal remedies and procedures designed to permit the Court of Justice to review the legality of measures adopted by the institutions. Natural and legal persons are thus protected against the application to them of general measures which they cannot contest directly before the Court by reason of the special conditions of admissibility laid down in the second paragraph of Article 173 of the Treaty. Where the Community institutions are responsible for the administrative implementation of such measures, natural or legal persons may bring a direct action before the Court against implementing measures which are addressed to them or which are of direct and individual concern to them and, in support of such an action, plead the illegality of the general measure on which they are based. Where implementation is a matter for the national authorities, such persons may plead the invalidity of general measures before the national courts and cause the latter to request the Court of Justice for a preliminary ruling.'

This chapter will describe the structure of the system of direct and indirect judicial review, based on a combination of Articles 173, 177 and 184 EC, which is intended to ensure that 'state' authorities (i.e. Community institutions and national authorities acting under Community law) are bound by the rule of law in their enforcement of Community law *vis-à-vis* individual subjects, and to provide an appropriate balance between the requirements of administrative efficiency and protection of the individual. It also examines the complementary provisions of Article

175 EC which offer protection against wrongful failures to act on the part of the Community institutions. Liability for damage caused by the Community institutions is examined in Chapter 10.

It is not the sole objective of these provisions to protect *individuals* against unlawful *administrative* action. In the first place, protection is available in certain circumstances against unlawful *legislative* action; in this respect, judicial review is broader than in the UK, where the actions of administrative bodies in the domestic field cannot be impugned on the basis of some alleged illegality of an underlying statutory power. Community law, in contrast, provides for the constitutional review of legislative action by individuals, and the Court has paid particular attention to ensuring the creation of what it sees as the proper structures for constitutional challenges to legislation, particularly those based on alleged breaches of fundamental rights. Second, Articles 173 and 175 provide also the mechanisms whereby the Court can control the divisions of powers within the Community between the institutions, as well as the division of powers between the Community and the Member States. To this end, the Court hears many cases brought by the institutions against each other, or by the Member States against the institutions which challenge the exercise of power by the institutions. Thus these provisions have the additional objective of providing the forum within which the constitutional checks and balances of the separation of powers can be articulated.

9.2 Access to Judicial Review

It will be seen in this chapter that it is a consistent theme of the Court's case law on Articles 173, 175, 177 and 184 only to countenance direct challenges in the Court itself by individual subjects of Community law to measures which affect them as individuals. Only if an individual applicant (as opposed to an institution or a Member State) can point to a Community measure of an administrative nature by which he or she is immediately affected will a direct challenge be possible in the Court of Justice. Challenges to general legislative measures which are implemented by the Member States should be brought against the implementing measures of the national authorities in the national courts, and the challenge to the underlying Community measure effected indirectly via a reference on validity under Article 177. This structure is enforced through a restrictive interpretation of the *locus standi* rules in Article 173, and through an insistence on the obligation of national courts to make a reference for a preliminary ruling if the validity of a Community measure is in doubt (Case 314/85 *Foto-Frost* v. *HZA Lübeck Ost* [1987] ECR 4199). As the quotation from '*Les Verts*' indicates, the Court makes much of the completeness and coherence of this system.

However, increasingly as the competence of the Community extends, the Court may be called upon to adjudicate in cases concerned with associated rights of due process which are necessary to ensure the principle of administration according to law. We noted in 5.6 the importance of rights of access to judicial review for the effective protection of Community economic rights. In the fields of competition law and anti-dumping law, the Court has been challenged to ensure the observance of procedural rights where the Community institutions are responsible for the direct implementation of Community law (e.g. Case 46/87 *Hoechst* v. *Commission* [1989] ECR 2859 – rights of the defence in competition law; Case C-49/88 *Al-Jubail fertiliser* v. *Council* [1991] 3 CMLR 377 – anti-dumping law). Increasingly, also, interest and pressure groups are beginning to argue that they should have the right to be involved in cases concerned with the lawfulness of Community action.

In Cases 228 and 229/82 *Ford of Europe Inc* v. *Commission* [1984] ECR 1129, two groups – BEUC (the *Bureau Européen des Consommateurs*, an umbrella group partly funded by the Commission) and the UK Consumers' Association – were granted the right by the Court of Justice to intervene in an appeal by Ford against an unfavourable decision of the Commission under the competition rules. However, in Case C-170/89 *BEUC* v. *Commission* ([1992] 1 CMLR 820) the Court refused to take these rights any further, rejecting an attempt by BEUC to gain access to confidential documentation in an anti-dumping case concerning the importation of audio cassettes from the Far East. Significantly, the Court did not dispose of the action by holding that BEUC had no standing to challenge a Commission ruling denying the access to documentation, but dismissed the arguments on their merits, observing in its conclusions that it was for the Community legislature to consider the introduction of the types of procedural rights which BEUC was claiming.

9.3   The Key Provisions

Article 173 provides for the review of unlawful acts of the institutions:

'The Court of Justice shall review the legality of acts adopted jointly by the European Parliament and the Council, of acts of the Council, of the Commission and of the ECB, other than recommendations and opinions, and of acts of the European Parliament intended to produce legal effects *vis-à-vis* third parties.

It shall for this purpose have jurisdiction in actions brought by a Member State, the Council or the Commission on grounds of lack of competence, infringement of an essential procedural requirement, infringement of this Treaty or of any rule of law relating to its application, or misuse of powers.

The Court shall have jurisdiction under the same conditions in actions brought by the European Parliament and by the ECB for the purpose of protecting their prerogatives.

Any natural or legal person may, under the same conditions, institute proceedings against a decision addressed to that person or against a decision which, although in the form of a regulation or a decision addressed to another person, is of direct and individual concern to the former.

The proceedings provided for in this Article shall be instituted within two months of the publication of the measure, or of its notification to the plaintiff, or, in the absence thereof, of the day on which it came to the knowledge of the latter, as the case may be.'

In the event of a finding by the Court of Justice that these principles of legality have been breached, the consequence is annulment. Article 174 EC provides:

'If the action is well founded, the Court of Justice shall declare the act concerned to be void.

In the case of a regulation, however, the Court of Justice shall, if it considers this necessary, state which of the effects of the regulation which it has declared void shall be considered as definitive.'

In the event that a general measure of the Community is at issue in Article 173 proceedings, Article 184 makes provision for indirect challenge:

'Notwithstanding the expiry of the period laid down in the fifth paragraph of Article 173, any party may, in proceedings in which a regulation adopted jointly by the European Parliament and the Council, or a regulation of the Council, of the Commission, or of the ECB is at issue, plead the grounds specified in the second paragraph of Article 173, in order to invoke before the Court of Justice the inapplicability of that regulation.'

Indirect challenge in the context of national proceedings against implementing measures is covered by the provision in Article 177 for references for preliminary rulings on the validity of acts of the institutions. Articles 184 and 177 do not in themselves constitute separate 'causes of action' against unlawful administrative action, but mechanisms whereby the Court of Justice can, in the context of other proceedings, review the legality of underlying Community acts, particularly those of a general legislative nature.

Finally, Article 175 is intended to complement the provisions on challenge to unlawful *acts*, by making provision for challenges to unlawful *omissions*:

'Should the European Parliament, the Council or the Commission, in infringement of this Treaty, fail to act, the Member States and the other institutions of the Community may bring an action before the Court of Justice to have the infringement established.

The action shall be admissible only if the institution concerned has first been called upon to act. If, within two months of being so called upon, the institution concerned has not defined its position, the action may be brought within a further period of two months.

Any natural or legal person may, under the conditions laid down in the preceding paragraphs, complain to the Court of Justice that an institution of the Community has failed to address to that person any act other than a recommendation or an opinion.

The Court of Justice shall have jurisdiction, under the same conditions, in actions or proceedings brought by the ECB in the areas falling within the latter's competence and in actions or proceedings brought against the latter.'

The consequences of a successful action under Articles 173 or 175 are dealt with in Article 176 EC which provides:

'The institution (or institutions) whose act has been declared void or whose failure to act has been declared contrary to this Treaty shall be required to take the necessary measures to comply with the judgment of the Court of Justice.

This obligation shall not affect any obligation which may result from the application of the second paragraph of Article 215 [the obligation to pay compensation for wrongful acts causing loss].

This Article shall also apply to the ECB.'

A successful action to challenge an unlawful act or omission presupposes the following basic requirements:

(a) a reviewable act or omission;
(b) locus standi on the part of the applicant;
(c) illegality on the part of the defendant (i.e. the presence of the grounds for review in Article 173 or the violation of a duty to act in the context of Article 175).

9.4   Article 173: Reviewable Acts

To be reviewable by the Court of Justice in the context of Article 173, an act must be covered by the terms of that Article. The terms of Article 173, as amended by the Treaty of Maastricht, are now clear: certain acts of the . Parliament are explicitly included, along with those of the Council and the Commission, and of the Council and the Parliament acting jointly as legislator using the co-decision procedure. The exclusion in the original Treaty of acts of the Parliament did cause problems in the context of the increased role and powers of the Parliament. Judicial recognition of these changes was gradually given by the Court.

In Case 230/81 *Luxembourg* v. *Parliament* ([1983] ECR 255) the Court annulled a resolution of the Parliament concerning the moving of its seat from Luxembourg to Strasbourg and Brussels which obviously affected the Parliament's role under all three founding Treaties. However, the annulment was effected under Article 38 ECSC alone, which explicitly recognises the power to annul acts of the Parliament. The Court went one stage further in *'Les Verts'* annulling the decision of the Bureau of the Parliament allocating money to parties for campaigning in the 1984 direct elections. It stated ([1986] ECR 1339 at p.1365):

'It is true that, unlike Article 177 of the Treaty, which refers to acts of the institutions without further qualification, Article 173 refers only to acts of the Council and the Commission. However, the general scheme of the Treaty is to make a direct action available against "all measures adopted by the institutions . . . which are intended to have legal effects", as the Court has already had occasion to emphasize in [Case 22/70 *Commission* v. *Council* (*ERTA*)] . . . The European Parliament is not expressly mentioned among the institutions whose measures may be contested because, in its original version, the EEC Treaty merely granted it powers of consultation and political control rather than the power to adopt measures intended to have legal effects *vis-à-vis* third parties.'

After a comparison with the system of judicial control under the ECSC Treaty, the Court went on:

'An interpretation of Article 173 of the Treaty which excluded measures adopted by the European Parliament from those which could be contested would lead to a result contrary both to the spirit of the Treaty as expressed in Article 164 and to its system. Measures adopted by the European Parliament in the context of the EEC Treaty could encroach on the powers of the Member States or of the other institutions, or exceed the limits which have been set to the Parliament's powers, without its being possible to refer them for review by the Court. It must therefore be concluded that an action for annulment may lie against measures adopted by the European Parliament intended to have legal effects *vis-à-vis* third parties.'

In application of these principles, and in recognition of the role of the European Parliament in relation to the budget, the Court also held that the Order of the President of the Parliament adopting the 1986 budget could be annulled in Case 34/86 *Council* v. *Parliament* ([1986] ECR 2155). The inclusion of the concluding words of the Court *verbatim* in the revised third paragraph of Article 173 is testimony to the role of the Court as the originating force of many of the institutional developments contained in the Treaty of Maastricht.

The second element of a reviewable act has already been referred to in the quotations from *'Les Verts'*, and that is the requirement that it be one which produces 'legal effects'. This requirement was read into Article 173 by the Court in recognition that it has been faced with annulment proceedings concerned with acts of the institutions which do not fit neatly into the typology of legal acts offered by Article 189. An early example of such a *sui generis* act is provided by the challenge to the minutes of the Council incorporating a resolution which determined the negotiation procedures for the European Road Transport Agreement brought by the Commission in Case 22/70 *Commission* v. *Council (ERTA)* ([1971] ECR 263). The reason the Commission sought the annulment was in order to demonstrate that these negotiations were matters falling within Community rather than national competence. The Court held that it was not an obstacle to judicial review that a legal act does not formally fall within the system set up by Article 189, but that there is a category of *sui generis* legal acts. The only question is whether the act has legal effects.

There is an obvious case for the application of these principles to the many internal management measures of the institutions, such as staffing decisions (Case 15/63 *Lassalle* v. *Parliament* [1964] ECR 31), the decision of the Parliament Bureau in *'Les Verts'* concerning the allocation of electoral campaign funds, the internal Commission instructions on the management of the EAGGF successfully challenged by France in Case C-366/88 *France* v. *Commission* ([1990] ECR I-3571) and a Code of Conduct concerning the management of the structural funds issued by the Commission (Case C-303/90 *France* v. *Commission* 13.11.1991). They have also proved important in the context of the control of the legality of competition proceedings, where the Court has found it important to identify the stages at which undertakings may legitimately challenge preliminary decisions taken during the course of such proceedings, without waiting for the final decision. The Court decided in Cases 8-11/66 *Cimenteries* v. *Commission (Noordwijks Cement Accoord)* [1967] ECR 75) that a Decision under Article 15(6) of Regulation 17 whereby the Commission removes from an undertaking, after a preliminary investigation, the protection from fines accorded to them if they notify their agreement to the Commission, could be challenged under Article 173. The Court held (at p.91):

> 'this measure deprived them of the advantages of a legal situation which Article 15(5) attached to the notification of the agreement, and exposed them to a grave financial risk. Thus the said measure affected the interests of the undertakings by bringing about a distinct change in their legal position. It is unequivocally a measure which produces legal effects touching the interests of the undertakings concerned and which is binding on them. It constitutes not a mere opinion but a decision.'

The Court repeated substantially the same arguments in holding in Case 60/81 *IBM* v. *Commission* ([1981] ECR 2639) that a letter informing IBM that the Commission was of the opinion that it had abused a dominant position in breach of Article 86 and a 'statement of objections' containing the Commission's allegations were not reviewable acts. A reviewable act must be one which definitively lays down the position of the institution in question on the conclusion of a procedure, and is not merely a provisional or preparatory measure which itself could be challenged if the final decision was challenged.

In certain exceptional circumstances an act may be so vitiated by defects that it is 'non-existent', and therefore incapable of annulment by the Court. Such an act is not reviewable; neither, however, does it have legal effects. The definition of a non-existent act has not been extensively discussed in the Court, but in Cases 1 and 14/57 *Société des Usines à Tubes de la Sarre* v. *High Authority* ([1957] ECR 105) the Court held that the absence of reasons renders an act non-existent. In a more recent application of this doctrine, the Court of First Instance held a Commission Decision imposing heavy fines on a number of chemical companies in respect of an alleged cartel to be so vitiated by defects of form and procedure as to be non-existent (Cases T-79, etc./89 *BASF AG et al.* v. *Commission* [1992] 4 CMLR 357) (see 3.2).

9.5   *Locus Standi*

Applicants under Article 173 now fall into three categories. There are privileged applicants (Commission, Council and Member States) who may challenge any measures adopted by any of the institutions. They need prove no specific interest in the act challenged, but must be presumed to have a general interest to act. At the opposite end of the scale are the non-privileged applicants – any natural or legal person – who are subject to restrictive rules on standing. An intermediate category was created by judicial evolution of the standing of the Parliament, and has since been confirmed by the terms of the Treaty of Maastricht, which allows two bodies – the Parliament and the ECB – to take action against the other institutions only for the purpose of protecting their prerogatives.

This is, therefore, another example of institutional developments in the Treaty of Maastricht directly shadowing the developments promoted by the Court. However, the position now confirmed by the Treaty was not reached without a change of heart by the Court, which initially denied the standing of the Parliament in Case 302/87 *Parliament* v. *Council (Comitology)* ([1988] ECR 5615), refusing to draw parallels with either Article 175 which has always recognised the right of the Parliament to bring actions for failure to act, or with its decision in '*Les Verts*' in which it confirmed that the Parliament was capable of being a defendant in Article 173 proceedings. It asserted that the Parliament was adequately protected by Commission's general right to take action on behalf of the Community interest, working on the assumption that the Commission would always have an interest and desire to take action to protect the interests of the Parliament. The Parliament had to be contented with this and the right to intervene in Article 173 proceedings brought by other parties (Article 37 of the Statute of the Court) (see Case 138/79 *Roquette Frères* v. *Council* [1980] ECR 3333 – failure to consult the Parliament before the adoption of a Regulation).

Less than two years later the Court reviewed its position, and adopted the halfway house offered by Advocate General Darmon in *Comitology*, and since incorporated in the Treaty of Maastricht, namely that the Parliament is treated as a special case able to take action only in order to protect its own prerogatives. In so concluding it held that the Parliament's action in Case C-70/88 *Parliament* v. *Council (Chernobyl)* ([1990] ECR I-2041), which it had begun before the decision in *Comitology* and declined to withdraw in the light of that judgment, was admissible. The Court later also accepted the Parliament's arguments on the substance of the case concerning the appropriate legal basis for a Regulation on permissible levels of radioactivity in foodstuffs. The question of legal basis, which may crucially affect the nature of the procedure before the Parliament (co-decision, cooperation procedure, mere consultation, or no consultation at all), is obviously one of the most important matters in which the prerogatives of the Parliament are at issue and which it may therefore litigate in order to protect.

9.6 *Locus Standi*: Non-Privileged Applicants

The rules governing the *locus standi* of non-privileged applicants are to be found in the fourth paragraph of Article 173, and are designed to restrict access to judicial review in the Court of Justice to measures which are in essence individual rather than general, and in which the applicant has a personal interest. Consequently, the reference in Article 173 to 'decision' means a decision in the material sense of an individual measure having legal effects, regardless of its formal designation. Challenge is restricted to:

- decisions addressed to the applicant;
- decisions (a) addressed to third parties or (b) 'in the form of' Regulations which are of 'direct and individual concern' to the applicant.

In general, the provisions have been narrowly interpreted by the Court, but there have been inconsistencies in its approach such that it is not possible to identify a single line of authority. In particular, there are special rules governing standing to challenge measures adopted by the Council and the Commission which are the result of quasi-judicial procedures, such as anti-dumping Regulations, and competition and state aids Decisions. There are also a number of anomalous cases which will be highlighted in this discussion, where the result achieved by the Court has been clearly determined by policy considerations. Where judicial review is not possible within the Court itself, an alternative route can normally be taken via the national court and the indirect review of the measure in question using Article 177. There are a number of cases where the Court has rejected the standing of the applicant in an Article 173 case only to examine the validity of the offending measure in the context of an Article 177 ruling. An example is offered by the 'Berlin butter' cases: in

Case 97/85 *Union Deutsche Lebensmittelwerke* v. *Commission* ([1987] ECR 2265) an Article 173 challenge was unsuccessfully brought against a Commission scheme based for the sale of cheap butter in Berlin. The scheme was adopted in the form of a Decision addressed to Germany which the applicant had no standing to challenge. However, in Case 133-6/85 *Walter Rau* v. *BALM* ([1987] ECR 2289), in the context of a challenge in the German courts to the German implementing measures, which was based on the argument that the originating Commission measure was invalid, the Court was prepared to review the legality of the underlying Community act in the context of an Article 177 reference. It held the measure valid.

The simplest case is that of the decision addressed to the applicant. Decisions of the Commission adopted under the procedures laid down in Regulation 17 are frequently challenged by their addressees – the alleged infringers of the competition rules. In this context, the Court also has the power to review the fines imposed by the Commission (Article 172 EC).

Decisions addressed to third parties can only be challenged by those who are directly and individually concerned. These criteria must be examined separately.

9.7 Direct Concern

A measure will be of direct concern provided that there is a relationship of cause and effect between the act and its impact on the applicant. The question must be asked whether there is any intervening discretion between the decision and the applicant, for example, on the part of a Member State.

In Case 69/69 *Alcan* v. *Commission* ([1970] ECR 385) the applicant importers were held to be not directly concerned by a Commission Decision refusing a request from the Belgian government for a quota of unwrought aluminium imports at a reduced rate of duty. The Belgian government could have declined to use the quota once it had received it, or could have granted it to other importers. In contrast, the applicant in Case 62/70 *Bock* v. *Commission* ([1971] ECR 897) was held to be directly concerned. Bock had applied to the German authorities for a permit to import Chinese mushrooms and was told that the request would be refused as soon as the authorisation had been obtained from the Commission. When the Commission took a Decision addressed to the German government authorising the refusal of the application, Bock was able to challenge the Decision. The Court held that there was direct concern because the German government had already made it clear what it would do with the authorisation once received. A further example of direct concern is Case 11/82 *Piraiki-Patraiki* v. *Commission* ([1985] ECR 207), a case which is notable for its generous interpretation of the rules on individual concern, where the possibility that the French government would not take advantage of a Commission authorisation to impose restrictions on imports of cotton yarn from Greece was held to be 'purely theoretical' when the measures were challenged by Greek manufacturers.

The criterion of direct concern precludes challenges to measures adopted by the Community which grant discretionary powers to the Member States, such as the Commission Decision authorising Luxembourg to grant aids to steel firms which undertook reductions in capacity, which was unsuccessfully challenged in Case 222/83 *Municipality of Differdange* v. *Commission* ([1984] ECR 2889).

9.8 Individual Concern

In Case 25/62 *Plaumann* v. *Commission* ([1963] ECR 95), an early case which set the tone of restrictive interpretation for the entire system of direct judicial review in the Court of Justice, a German importer of clementines sought to challenge a Commission Decision addressed to Germany refusing it an authorisation to levy only 10% duty on imports of clementines into the Community from third countries, in place of the full duty of 13%. On the question of admissibility the Court held that (at p.107):

'Persons other than those to whom a decision is addressed may only claim to be individually concerned if that decision affects them by reason of certain attributes which are peculiar to them or by reason of circumstances in which they are differentiated from all other persons and by virtue of these factors distinguishes them individually just as in the case of the person addressed. In the present case the applicant is affected by the disputed decision as an importer of clementines, that is to say, by reason of a commercial activity which may at any time be practised by any person and is not therefore such as to distinguish the applicant in relation to the contested decision as in the case of the addressee.'

In practice, in the course of an extensive case law in which many cases have been declared inadmissible on the grounds of no individual concern, it has emerged that the Court requires the applicant to be part of a closed class, membership of which is fixed and ascertainable at the date of the adoption of the contested measure. An example is provided by Cases 106-107/63 *Toepfer* v. *Commission* ([1965] ECR 405) where the applicant was held to be individually concerned by a Commission Decision confirming the decision of the German government to refuse licences for imports of cereals from France, since the measure applied only to a closed class of importers who had applied for an import licence on a particular day. This test can also explain the distinction between cases such as Case 62/70 *Bock*, where the applicant was held to be individually concerned by a Commission Decision adopted in response to its request to the German government for an import licence and authorising the refusal of that licence, and Case 231/82 *Spijker Kwasten* v. *Commission* ([1983] ECR 2559), where the action failed. In Spijker Kwaasten, the applicant sought annulment of a Commission Decision addressed to the Dutch government authorising it to ban imports of Chinese brushes for six months following the applicant's submission of a request for a licence. The applicant's difficulty was that although there was some evidence that the Decision was passed specifically to deal with its position, and indeed it was the only importer of Chinese brushes into the Benelux countries at that time, the ban was imposed for a period subsequent to the application for a licence, a period during which, hypothetically, other persons could have made an application for an import licence. Consequently, the action was held inadmissible on grounds of no individual concern.

A more generous interpretation of the rules was given in Case 11/82 *Piraiki-Patraiki*. Certain Greek yarn manufacturers who had already entered into contracts to export cotton to France were held to be individually concerned by the Commission Decision permitting France to impose restrictions on imports because Article 130 of the Greek Act of Accession, which empowered the Commission to adopt such a measure, required it to take into account the interests specifically of those who were bound by contractual arrangements. It could be argued that the evidence derived from the Act of Accession distinguished the applicants from a wider group of persons who might suffer prejudice as a consequence of the measure in question.

Finally, Case 294/83 *'Les Verts'* must be taken as an exceptional application of the rules on individual concern. On the face of it, the French Green Party was affected by the decision of the Bureau of the Parliament concerning the allocation of electoral funds only as a member of an indeterminate class, namely parties which might stand in the elections and were not already represented in the Parliament. On policy grounds the Court granted standing, since the applicants had a good case on the merits, and there was no obvious alternative route whereby the applicants could enforce the principle of equality in the context of the Parliament's organisation of its own business.

9.9   Challenges to Regulations

The effect of the standing rules in Article 173 is that individuals may only challenge Regulations which are in essence decisions. It is very difficult in practice to prove that what is in form a general normative measure is in truth a bundle of individual measures although the applicants in Cases 41–44/70 *International Fruit Co* v. *Commission* ([1971] ECR 411) succeeded in precisely this task when they challenged a Commission Regulation laying down the rules for granting or refusing licences for the importation of apples from non-Member States. At that time, the national authorities received the applications for licences and passed them on to the Commission. The Court held that the Regulation establishing the rules for licences to be granted in a particular week, which was framed directly in response to the number of applications received by the Member States, was in truth a bundle of individual decisions and held the actions by the applicants who had requested licences to be admissible.

In practice, however, applicants have generally found it extremely difficult to establish that measures based on the exercise of discretion in the economic policy context are in truth individual measures, since the Court has consistently held that individuals should not be able to use Article 173 to challenge 'true' Regulations, that is abstract, normative measures. It defined such measures in Cases 16 and 17/62 *Confédération Nationale des Producteurs de Fruits et Légumes* v. *Council* ([1962] ECR 471) as being 'essentially of a legislative nature, . . . applicable not to a limited number of persons, defined or identifiable, but to categories of persons viewed abstractly and in their entirety'. The Court then went on apparently to conflate the question of whether a measure is individual or general with the question of individual concern, as discussed in the previous paragraph; however, in reality, the Court has not always consistently applied this test, and in some cases has additionally imposed a test which looks at the terminology of the measure rather than the persons affected by it.

For example in Cases 789-790/79 *Calpak SpA* v. *Commission* ([1980] ECR 1949) the Court held inadmissible a challenge to a Regulation governing the grant of production aid in respect of certain pears in the following terms (at p.1961):

'A provision which limits the granting of production aid for all producers in respect of a particular product to a uniform percentage of the quantity produced by them during a uniform preceding period is by nature a measure of general application within the meaning of Article 189 of the Treaty. In fact the measure applies to objectively determined situations and produces legal effects with regard to categories of persons described in a generalised and abstract manner. The nature of the measure as a regulation is not called in question by the mere fact that it is possible to determine the number or even the identity of the producers to be granted the aid which is limited thereby.'

Thus even where they have been able to establish that the measures affect only small and easily identifiable groups (e.g. the isoglucose Regulations affecting only isoglucose producers, a small class unlikely to grow because of the major investment required – Case 101/76 *KSH* v. *Commission* [1977] ECR 797) or indeed a closed category of persons (e.g. Cases 103-9/78 *Beauport* v. *Council and Commission* [1979] ECR 17 – a measure affecting only sugar refineries which had previously been granted a sugar quota), direct actions to challenge Regulations implementing the policies of the Community have been unsuccessful, even where policies pursued have been manifestly unfair to particular groups and have proved vulnerable to indirect challenge (e.g. Cases 103 and 145/77 *Royal Scholten*

Honig v. *Intervention Board for Agricultural Produce* [1978] ECR 2037 – isoglucose Regulation held invalid for breach of the principle of equality in the context of Article 177 reference).

The exceptions to this are special cases, either where the Commission is involved in the direct administration of Community law as in the *International Fruit Company* case, or where the applicant is in some way specifically identified by the measure. In Case 138/79 *Roquette Frères* v. *Council* the applicant was one of a number of producers named in an annex to a Regulation. The action in Case C-152/88 *Sofrimport* v. *Commission* ([1990] ECR I-2477) was to challenge a Commission Regulation imposing protective measures which restricted the import of Chilean apples into the Community. Applying only the test of individual concern, and ignoring the abstract terminology test elaborated in *Calpak*, the Court held the actions by importers whose apples were in transit when the measure was adopted admissible on the grounds that the enabling Council Regulation which permitted it to control the imports of fruit into the Community required it to have special regard to the interests of importers whose products were in transit. The Court held that since the enabling Regulation gave specific protection to such importers, they must be able to enforce observance of that protection and bring legal proceedings for that purpose. Thus there was a direct link between the substance of the applicants' case and the admissibility of their action. There is a parallel between *Sofrimport* and *Piraiki-Patraiki*, since in both cases specific features in the enabling measures distinguished the applicants from other affected persons.

9.10   Quasi-Judicial Determinations

Special features characterise the Court's interpretation of the standing rules in the context of the involvement of the applicants in procedures before or within the Community institutions which are quasi-judicial in nature.

In the context of competition proceedings, a disappointed complainant may bring an action challenging a Decision granting an exemption or giving negative clearance (Case 26/76 *Metro* v. *Commission* [1977] ECR 1875). Under Regulation 17, provision is made for the participation of complainants with a legitimate grievance in the proceedings; for example, they have a right to be heard which they are entitled to have protected by the Court. Similar considerations apply in the context of state aids. French fertiliser producers who had complained to the Commission about an alleged state aid given to their Dutch competitors by the Dutch Government were held to be individually concerned by a Commission Decision addressed to the Dutch Government terminating the proceedings when the Commission concluded that there was no aid involved (Case 169/84 *COFAZ* v. *Commission* [1986] ECR 391). Even stronger policy considerations speak in favour of the right of action of the beneficiaries of an aid held to be incompatible with the Common Market, and the standing of a beneficiary to challenge a Commission Decision addressed to the Dutch government and requesting it to refrain from granting the aid in question was confirmed by the Court in Case 730/79 *Philip Morris Holland BV* v. *Commission* ([1980] ECR 2671).

The case of anti-dumping proceedings is slightly different since in that context the enabling powers provide for the adoption of Regulations by the Council of Ministers imposing countervailing duties intended to offset the effects of subsidies granted in third countries to imports into the Community. These Regulations are obviously not 'addressed' to particular persons, although clearly some categories of economic actors may be more seriously affected than others. An unqualified application of the principles set out in 9.8 would doubtless lead to unfairness to those affected by anti-dumping duties by excessively restricting the possibility of judicial review of the procedures in question. The Court has proceeded in this context generally by distinguishing between provisions of anti-dumping Regulations which take effect as decisions *vis-à-vis* certain categories of interested parties, and those which preserve a general normative nature. In other words, a Regulation may be of individual concern to certain applicants, whilst still retaining its general normative character.

So far the following categories of applicant have been held to be individually concerned by anti-dumping Regulations:

- producers named in a Regulation (Case 113/77 NTN *Toyo Bearing Co* v. *Council and Commission* [1979] ECR 1185);
- producers who have been involved in the preliminary investigations (Cases 239, 275/82 *Allied Corporation* v. *Commission* [1984] ECR 1005);
- complainants (Case 264/82 *Timex* v. *Council and Commission* [1985] ECR 849).

Generally importers have been refused standing, unless they were in some way linked to the manufacturer or exporter, or if their resale prices had been used by the Commission to construct export prices as the basis for the duty imposed (Case C-157/87 *Electroimpex* v. *Council* [1990] ECR I-3021). An attempt by the applicants in Case 307/81 *Alusuisse* v. *Council and Commission* ([1982] ECR 3463) to establish standing by challenging the general nature of anti-dumping Regulations was firmly rejected by the Court.

However, in a recent case the Court has indicated that it is adopting a more generous approach to the standing of importers. In Case C-358/89 *Extramet Industrie SA* v. *Council* (16.5.1991) the Court held that without losing its normative character an anti-dumping Regulation may individually concern importers. The applicant was able to establish standing by reference to its specific characteristics as not only the major importer of the product subject to the anti-dumping duty, but also its end-user. It was held to be relevant that Extramet's operations were heavily dependent on the imports and were seriously affected by the disputed Regulation, in view of the very small number of manufacturers of the product in question and the difficulty of obtaining supplies from the only Community producer, which was, moreover, Extramet's main competitor in relation to the end product. It would therefore appear that standing to challenge an anti-dumping Regulation can be established if the importer can show that the Regulation has an impact on its vital economic interests.

It remains to be seen whether the Court will extend this more generous attitude outside the anti-dumping field. While the best argument for the Court's restrictive attitude to standing – namely the availability of indirect review via challenge to national implementing measures using Article 177 – retains its force and indeed becomes stronger as the organic connection between the national courts and the Court of Justice becomes ever firmer, other reasons for limiting standing may have lost their force. In particular, the argument that the Court wished to restrict standing in the early days in order to limit vexatious actions and to protect the nascent Community against a flood of actions from aggrieved companies seems unconvincing in the context of a Community which has now achieved standing as a major international actor (see generally Rasmussen, 1980).

9.11   Time Limits

A second important condition for the admissibility of actions under Article 173 is the observance of the time limit of two months from 'the publication of the measure, or of its notification to the plaintiff, or, in the absence thereof, of the day on which it came to the knowledge of the latter, as the case may be'. Details of the application in practice of the time limits can be derived from the Rules of Procedure of the Court of Justice.

9.12   Interim Measures

In appropriate cases, the Court may award interim measures in the context of Article 173 actions under its general power in Article 186 EC. The same conditions of a *prima facie* case and urgency which are applied in the context of Article 169 EC (see 6.12) govern the award of interim measures under Article 173. These have been awarded in a number of cases involving anti-dumping Regulations (Case 113/77R *NTN Toyo Bearing Co* v. *Commission* [1977] ECR 1721) and decisions taken by the Commission under Article 115 EC authorising Member States to exclude imports from the other Member States of third country goods in free circulation (Case 1/84R *Ilford* v. *Commission* [1984] ECR 423 – see 12.12).

9.13   Grounds for Review

There is considerable overlap between the four grounds for review set out in Article 173 (lack of competence, infringement of an essential procedural requirement, infringement of the Treaty or of any rule of law relating to its application, and misuse of powers). Indeed it could be argued that infringement of the Treaty and of any rule of law relating to its application is potentially a catch-all phrase which encompasses not only the written rules of the Treaty and the various provisions adopted thereunder, but also the body of unwritten general principles of law and fundamental rights, which were discussed as a source of law in chapter 5 and must now be applied in practice here.

Lack of competence has rarely been successfully invoked although a recent example is provided by Case C-303/90 *France* v. *Commission* in which France successfully established that the Commission did not have the power to adopt a legally binding implementation measure (albeit one characterised as a 'Code of Conduct') under the legal regime governing the application of the structural funds (Article 130A EC *et seq*.). The cases on procedural requirements are more common, and the Court has held the following requirements to be essential:

–   the requirement to consult the Parliament where required during the legislative process (Case 138/79 *Roquette Frères* v. *Council*);
–   a sufficiently full statement of reasons under Article 190 EC (Case C-358/90 *Compagnia Italiana Alcool* v. *Commission* [1992] 2 CMLR 876);
–   the requirement of a specific legal basis which is an additional feature of the duty to give reasons (Case 45/86 *Commission* v. *Council (Generalised Tariff Preferences)* [1987] ECR 1493).

In contrast, use of the wrong legal basis constitutes an infringement of the Treaty. For examples of those general principles of law which have been used as the bases for challenges to the legality of Community acts, reference should be made to the discussion in 5.5 *et seq*.

The most infrequently applied ground is the misuse of powers, which constitutes the use of a power for purposes other than that for which it was granted, and is based on the French administrative law concept of *détournement de pouvoir*. In Case 8/55 *Fédéchar* v. *High Authority* ([1956] ECR 292) the ECSC equivalent provision was considered by the Court. It held that a measure will not be annulled simply because one of the reasons for its adoption was improper, if the others are legitimate. Nor will a measure be annulled if the improper purpose had no effect upon the substance of the measure.

9.14   The Consequences of Annulment

The consequence of a successful action under Article 173 is a declaration by the Court under Article 174 that a measure is void. A measure may be declared void in part only, provided the offending part can be effectively severed from the rest. In Case 17/74 *Transocean Marine Paint Association*

v. *Commission* ([1974] ECR 1063) an onerous condition in an exemption from the prohibition under Article 85 issued by the Commission was annulled on the grounds that the Commission had failed to give the applicant a sufficient hearing on the matter. The Court used Article 176, which requires the institution whose act has been declared void to take the necessary measures to comply with the judgment of the Court, to refer the measure back to the Commission for consideration. The alternative – entire annulment of the Commission's decision which would have left an earlier exemption standing – might have been too favourable to the applicant.

9.15   Failure to Act: Article 175 (for the terms of Article 175 see 9.3)

Articles 173 and 175 are intended to provide complementary remedies; acting illegally and illegally failing to act should be two sides of the same coin. Non-privileged applicants with limited standing under Article 173 should be unable to sue in respect of a failure to adopt a legislative act which they would be unable to challenge if it were in fact adopted. In contrast, privileged applicants, who are entitled to challenge any reviewable acts should be able to challenge the refusal or failure to adopt any acts which the authority is under a legal obligation to adopt. In the context of such actions, therefore, the latter condition will be the crucial determinant of what constitutes a reviewable omission.

The Court's position on the linkage between the two provisions has been slightly inconsistent. In Case 15/70 *Chevalley* v. *Commission* ([1970] ECR 975), given the applicant's uncertainty as to whether the action in question should be under Article 175 or Article 173, for the purposes of a preliminary investigation of admissibility, the Court held that it was unnecessary to distinguish between the two remedies, since they 'merely prescribe one and the same method of recourse', although the Court has since stated that where proceedings are begun under both Articles the applicant must identify the act which it intends to challenge by means of an annulment action (Case 247/87 *Star Fruit Co* v. *Commission*. On the other hand in Case 302/87 *Parliament* v. *Council (Comitology)* when initially rejecting the Parliament's standing to sue under Article 173, the Court denied the linkage between Articles 173 and 175. The fact that the Parliament has a right of action under Article 175 had 'no necessary link to any right of action under Article 173'.

Article 175 applies to 'pure omissions', not to refusals to act, which are characterised as negative decisions and actionable under Article 173, if at all. The interplay between the two is illustrated by Case 42/71 *Nordgetreide* v. *Commission* ([1972] ECR 105). The Commission refused to amend a Regulation when requested to do so by Nordgetreide. Article 175 proceedings were barred because the Commission's refusal was held to be a definition of its position, and Article 173 proceedings failed because although the refusal to amend the Regulation was in one sense a 'Decision', Nordgetreide would have no standing to challenge the Regulation which was a pure normative act and could not therefore challenge the negative act refusing to amend it. In other words, the link between the two provisions will be operated in such a way as to prevent one provision being used to evade the restrictive conditions applying to the other provision. This was stated expressly by the Court in Cases 10 and 18/68 *Eridania* v. *Commission* ([1969] ECR 459). The applicants had requested the Commission to revoke a certain measure, and when it failed to do so, they started proceedings for failure to act under Article 175. They also started an action for annulment against the act which failed because they did not have *locus standi* to challenge the act. The Court held that Article 175 cannot be used to circumvent Article 173 in this way (at p.483):

'To admit, as the applicants wish to do, that the parties concerned could ask the institution from which the measure came to revoke it and, in the event of the Commission's failing to act, refer such a failure to the Court as an illegal omission to deal with the matter would amount to providing them with a method of recourse parallel to that of Article 173, which would not be subject to the conditions laid down by the Treaty.'

The same point emerges from Case 246/81 *Bethell* v. *Commission* ([1982] ECR 2277); the Court will normally apply the same rules on standing in order to assess whether a non-privileged applicant under Article 175 who does not claim to be the addressee of the act which should have been adopted, can bring an action. Since at the time of the action brought by Lord Bethell, who was seeking to force stricter application of the competition rules in the air transport sector, air transport was not covered by Regulation 17 which provides enforcement procedures for Articles 85 and 86, he had no protected status as a complainant. Conversely, a complainant under the competition, anti-dumping or state aids provisions should be entitled to force the Community authorities adopt a position *vis-à-vis* them which would be reviewable under Article 173, or to obtain the review of a failure to act under Article 175, in particular where the action is brought in order to enforce observance of the complainant's procedural rights. In Case 191/82 *FEDIOL* v. *Commission* ([1983] ECR 2913) a challenge brought by the Community seed crushers and oil processors federation to ensure judicial review of the extent to which their procedural rights, as complainants, to be involved in anti-dumping proceedings had been observed, was held admissible. Although the position of complainants in competition proceedings long remained uncertain, in Case T-24/90 *Automec* v. *Commission* [1992] 5 CMLR 431, the Court of First Instance finally resolved that such a complainant is entitled to the adoption of a reviewable act by the Commission. On the other hand, complainants cannot force the Commission to take a final decision on the application of the competition rules, provided their procedural rights have been observed (Case 125/78 *GEMA* v. *Commission* [1979] ECR 3173).

9.15   Reviewable Omissions

Only the failure to adopt a legally binding act which the authority is under a duty to adopt is reviewable. This can be derived from the unity principle linking Articles 173 and 175, since Article 173 only provides for the review of legally binding acts. Consequently, a failure by the Commission to put a proposal for legislation is not reviewable, since it is only a preliminary act. Similar reasoning can be used to explain the decisions in Case 48/65 *Lütticke* v. *Commission* ([1966] ECR 19) and Case 247/87 *Star Fruit Co* v. *Commission* in which the Court held that individuals could not force the Commission to take enforcement proceedings against Member States. Nothing in the enforcement procedure constitutes a binding reviewable act.

One of the few instances of success is Case 13/83 *Parliament* v. *Council* ([1985] ECR 1513) in which the Parliament challenged the Council's failure to introduce a common policy for transport and its failure to reach a decision on sixteen specified proposals submitted by the Commission in relation to transport, which were required in order to secure freedom to provide transport services. The Parliament failed on the first rather more general allegation: there was no legally complete obligation under Article 74 to introduce a common transport policy. However, it succeeded on the second ground, since the Council was legally required to implement these freedoms, as guaranteed by Articles 75, 59, 50 and 61 EC, within the transitional period.

By the amendments to the European Community Treaty introduced by the Treaty of Maastricht, the legislative and budgetary activities of the Parliament have been brought within the scope of the judicial control of omissions.

9.16   Procedure

The procedure must begin with a formal request to the defendant to take action. It must state clearly what action is required, that it is made within the terms of Article 175, and that the applicant considers the defendant legally obliged to take the action required (Case 25/85 *Nuovo Campsider* v. *Commission* [1986] ECR 1531). The defendant has a period of two months to comply. If that period expires without response or action by the defendant, the applicant may take the matter to the Court within a further two months. This procedure puts the defendant formally in default, and also gives it the opportunity to comply. In a case decided under Article 35 ECSC (the equivalent to Article 175 EC) the Court has held that the preliminary procedure must be initiated within a reasonable time. In Case 59/70 *Netherlands* v. *Commission* ([1971] ECR 639) the action was held inadmissible because of a lapse of eighteen months between a statement by the Commission to which the Netherlands objected, and the Netherlands submitting a formal request for action. A definition of position by the authority terminates the Article 175 action. For example, Case 377/87 *Parliament* v. *Council* ([1988] ECR 4017) concerned an alleged failure by the Council to comply with the budget timetable. The Council acted after the action was brought before the Court, but before the judgment of the Court was delivered. The Court held that once an institution has defined its position, the action cannot continue, as its subject-matter has ceased to exist. In theory, a definition of position which blocks an Article 175 action where the applicant had standing should, according to the unity principle, always be reviewable under Article 173. In practice, distinguishing exactly what constitutes a definition of position is not easy, and consequently proceedings may have to be initiated under both Articles.

Case 13/83 *Parliament* v. *Council* proceeded under Article 175 as the Council's definition of position was held to be inadequate. For the Parliament, which still does not have full status as a privileged applicant under Article 173 even after the amendments introduced by the Treaty of Maastricht, but whose position under Article 175 is identical to the other institutions and the Member States, the difference between what is and what is not a definition of position – a question of fact, not law – could be crucial. In that case the Council failed either to confirm or to deny the alleged failure to act, and failed also to state what measures it proposed to adopt.

In the event of a finding of failure to act, there is no unlawful act for the Court to annul. The Court will make an order under Article 175 with which the institution in default must comply, but there are no further sanctions for non-compliance. For example, although the Court declined to decide the point expressly in Case 13/83 *Parliament* v. *Council*, it is clear that a legislative failure on the part of the Council does not result in the legislative power reverting to another institution which is willing to act. While changes to Article 171 EC introduced by the Treaty of Maastricht institute the possibility of imposing financial sanctions for non-compliance on the Member States, similar changes to the obligations of the Community institutions were not contemplated. However, the institutions remain under an obligation to compensate individuals in respect of unlawful conduct which causes damage, and there are a few, although so far unsuccessful, examples of actions against the institutions in respect of unlawful omissions (e.g. Cases 326/88 and 66/88 *Francesconi* v. *Commission* [1989] ECR 2087 (10.5) and Case C-63/89 *Les Assurances de Credit SA* v. *Council and Commission* ([1991] 2 CMLR 737 (10.8)).

9.18 Indirect Challenge

The availability of indirect challenge to unlawful acts of the Community completes the system of judicial review as described by the Court in '*Les*

Verts'. The objective is to ensure that illegal 'parent' Community acts can be attacked through the medium of implementing Community or national measures. The availability of two avenues for indirect challenge in Community law – Articles 177 and 184 – was emphasised in 9.3 above. Although, where Article 177 is used, the proceedings will begin in the national court, in practice indirect challenge is an instrument of judicial control which lies principally in the hands of the Court of Justice, since it has claimed the exclusive right to decide on the invalidity of Community acts (Case 314/85 *Firma Foto-Frost* v. *HZA Lübeck-Ost* [1987] ECR 4199).

The types of case in which an indirect challenge may occur obviously include actions for annulment, where the basis for the action is the illegality of a 'parent' Community act; in particular, Article 184 provides the opportunity in proceedings brought by an individual against an administrative act in the Court of Justice to challenge a normative act on which the administrative act is based and which is not susceptible itself to challenge by individuals. In the national courts, the alleged illegality of a Community act may form the basis of either the cause of action or the defence in the full range of civil, criminal and administrative proceedings (e.g. action for the recovery of money claimed by the authorities on the basis of an unlawful Community act; defence to criminal proceedings where the national criminal provisions are based on an unlawful Community act).

The Court has sought to keep the two remedies separate. In Cases 31 and 33/62 *Wöhrmann* v. *Commission* ([1962] ECR 501) it held that Article 184 may only be raised in proceedings before the Court in which the allegedly illegal act is relevant. It cannot be invoked in Article 177 proceedings. However, in Case 216/82 *Universität Hamburg* v. *HZA Hamburg-Kehrwieder* ([1983] ECR 2771), the Court explicitly drew a parallel between Article 184 and Article 177 holding that:

'According to a general principle of law which finds its expression in Article 184 of the EEC Treaty, in proceedings brought under national law against the rejection of his application [for duty-free admission of scientific apparatus from the USA into Germany] the applicant must be able to plead the illegality of the Commission's Decision on which the national decision adopted in his regard is based.'

9.19   Article 184: The Plea of Illegality (for text see 9.3)

According to the Court of Justice in Case 92/78 *Simmenthal SpA* v. *Commission* ([1979] ECR 777 at p.778):

'Article 184 of the EEC Treaty gives expression to a general principle conferring upon any party to proceedings the right to challenge, for the purpose of obtaining the annulment of a decision of direct and

individual concern to that party, the validity of previous acts of the institutions which form the legal basis of the decision which is being attacked, if that party was not entitled under Article 173 of the Treaty to bring a direct action challenging those acts by which it was thus affected without having been in a position to ask that they be declared void.'

In view of these conclusions, the Court interpreted the term 'Regulation' as used in Article 184 broadly in order to include within the scope of indirect challenge any normative acts which produce similar effects to Regulations and which are therefore on those grounds not subject to direct challenge. On the other hand, the raising of a plea of illegality does not in any way exonerate the applicant from satisfying the basic conditions − *locus standi*, observance of time limits, reviewable act − which govern the proceedings in which the plea is raised.

Since it would appear that an Article 184 plea is available first and foremost for the purpose of allowing challenges to measures which the applicant could not have challenged by way of an Article 173 action, it follows that Article 184 cannot be used by applicants to challenge individual acts addressed to them in the context of other proceedings; this would in effect do away with the time limits for challenging such acts and would destroy the coherence and certainty of the remedies system under the Treaty (Case 21/64 *Dalmas* v. *High Authority* [1965] ECR 175). There have been no clear statements from the Court on whether or not Article 184 can be used to challenge measures which the applicant *might* have had standing to challenge, for example, by application of the rules of direct and individual concern. Nor has the Court decided the extent to which privileged applicants can rely upon Article 184; the logical extension of its views in *Simmenthal* would appear to be that since privileged applicants have unlimited standing to challenge all reviewable Community acts they should not be allowed the second chance of an Article 184 plea once the time limit for direct challenge has expired. In Case 32/65 *Italy* v. *Commission* ([1966] ECR 389), although the Court did not decide the point, AG Roemer inclined to the view that privileged applicants should be allowed to rely upon Article 184 since at the time when the act was adopted they might not have thought it was unlawful. There are certainly restrictions on the use of Article 184 as a defence in enforcement proceedings. In Case 156/77 *Commission* v. *Belgium* ([1978] ECR 1881) the Commission had brought proceedings under Article 95(2) for failure by Belgium to comply with a Commission Decision of May 1976 which Belgium had failed to challenge directly. The Court refused to allow Belgium to raise Article 184 as a defence. However, there are some differences between the specific nature of enforcement proceedings in the context of state aids which are based in part on the Commission taking enforcement Decisions which the Member State must challenge by annulment proceedings if it objects, and general enforcement proceedings under Article 169, where the onus lies on the Commission to issue a statement of objections and to bring the Member State before the Court. In that context, it might remain possible for the Member State to argue that the policy measure which the Commission is seeking to enforce is in fact unlawful.

The grounds for review under Article 184 are the same as those in Article 173, which is specifically referred to in the terms of Article 184. The effects of a successful indirect challenge are not formally annulment, but for all practical purposes the act must be seen as invalidated and without legal effect.

9.20   The Scope of Indirect Challenge under Article 177

7.7 outlined the powers of the Court of Justice in relation to rulings on validity, and indicated that there is an implicit obligation on national courts to make a reference in any proceedings where there is a doubt about the validity of a Community measure. The scope of judicial review via the national court is, as we have seen, much more generous to the individual applicant. This is an important aspect of ensuring that the European Community is a Community subject to the rule of law, in accordance with the statements of the Court in Case 294/83 *'Les Verts'*.

For example, in contrast to the position under Article 184, it has been made clear that the possibility of taking Article 173 proceedings does not preclude the right to institute an indirect challenge via Article 177 – at least not for non-privileged applicants. In Case 133-6/85 *Walter Rau* v. *BALM* the Court held that a national court faced with proceedings in which a national act implementing a Community Decision is being challenged does not need to ascertain before hearing the case whether an action could have been brought against the Decision under Article 173. It is sufficient that the national conditions for the bringing of annulment proceedings are satisfied. There are two reasons for the Court to take this approach: first, the applicant in the national proceedings is unlikely to have been notified of the measure in question, and thus, secondly, it might not have been aware of the expiry of the time limit under Article 173.

The effects of findings of invalidity under Article 177 have already been discussed in 7.8 above.

Summary

1 The Court of Justice attaches great importance to the system of remedies for judicial review of Community acts under the Treaties, aiming to ensure that the European Community is a Community based on the rule of law.

2 Article 173 provides the mechanism for direct challenge of Community acts, but for individuals the possibility of using Article 173 is restricted only to administrative acts. Legislative acts must be challenged by individuals via direct

challenges to the implementing acts of the national authorities in national courts, and an Article 177 reference on validity.

3 For the Community institutions and the Member States, Article 173 offers a mechanism for maintaining the constitutional checks and balances offered by the separation of powers and functions within the Community, and between the Community and its Member States; the Parliament's right to challenge the acts of other institutions is limited, however, to challenges brought for the purpose of protecting its own prerogatives.

4 A successful Article 173 action requires:

- a reviewable act;
- *locus standi* on the part of the applicant;
- an application within the time limits;
- substantive or procedural illegality on the part of the adopting institution.

5 Article 175 provides a complementary action for failure to act. It has only very rarely been used successfully.

6 A successful Article 175 action requires:

- a reviewable omission;
- *locus standi* on the part of the applicant;
- a failure to adopt an act on the part of the defendant institution which it is under a duty to adopt.

7 Indirect challenge occurs under Articles 177 and 184. Article 184 permits challenges to general Community measures in the context of challenges to administrative measures brought under Article 173. Under Article 177, the Court claims the exclusive right to declare the invalidity of Community measures the legality of which is impugned before the national court.

Questions

1 What is a reviewable act?
2 In what way has the Court influenced the present text of the judicial review provisions (as amended by the Treaty of Maastricht)?
3 How and why has the Court of Justice interpreted the *locus standi* provisions of Articles 173 and 175 in such a way as to restrict the direct access of individuals to remedies in that Court?
4 Why is the Court's interpretation of the *locus standi* provisions more generous in cases involving quasi-judicial determinations by the Community institutions?
5 What is the unity principle?
6 What is the relationship between a reviewable omission and a reviewable act?
7 How does the system of indirect challenge to the legality of Community acts complement the system of direct challenge?

Further Reading

Bradley (1988) 'The variable evolution of the standing of the European Parliament in proceedings before the Court of Justice', 8 *Yearbook of European Law*, 27.
Bradley (1991) 'Sense and Sensibility: *Parliament* v. *Council* Continued', 16 *European Law Review*, 245.

Greaves (1986) '*Locus Standi* under Article 173 EEC when seeking annulment of a Regulation', 11 *European Law Review*, 119.

Harding (1981) 'The Impact of Article 177 of the EEC Treaty on the Review of Community Action', 1 *Yearbook of European Law*, 93.

Hartley (1988), esp. Chs 13 (failure to act) and 14 (indirect challenge).

Rasmussen (1980) 'Why is Article 173 interpreted against Private Plaintiffs?', 5 *European Law Review*, 112.

Rudden (1987) 'Community Blunders', pp.183–221.

Weiler (1989) 'Pride and Prejudice' – *Parliament* v. *Council*, 14 *European Law Review*, 334.

10 Non-contractual Liability and Compensation for Loss Caused by the Community

10.1 Introduction

The framework of rules governing the non-contractual (i.e. tortious) liability of the Community for the acts of its institutions and servants shares both many of the complexities and the policy-oriented nature of the rules governing judicial review. The key provisions are Articles 178 and 215(2) EC.

Article 178 establishes the jurisdiction of the Court of Justice 'in disputes relating to the compensation of damage provided for in the second paragraph of Article 215'. The latter provision sets out the conditions governing non-contractual liability:

'In the case of non-contractual liability, the Community shall, in accordance with the general principles common to the laws of the Member States, make good any damage caused by its institutions or by its servants in the performance of their duties.'

In principle, therefore, the Community must compensate for the damage it causes. Damage may be caused either by an institution (e.g. through a legislative measure, an administrative act or some other action or statement which inflicts loss), or by its servants, in which case the institution will be subject to a form of vicarious liability (e.g. a Community official reveals confidential information about an undertaking to a third party). The nature of the liability (i.e. fault-based or strict liability; nature of the causal link required; scope of damage recoverable) is determined according to principles common to the laws of the Member States, and has been subject to judicial evolution in the hands of the Court of Justice. As a matter of practice, the Community is represented by the institution alleged, directly or vicariously, to have caused the damage, and not always by the Commission, even though the latter institution does have a number of important representative functions (see 3.5).

10.2 The Conditions of Liability

The judicial evolution of the Community's law of non-contractual liability has revealed the following as the necessary conditions of a successful action:

– a wrongful act; there is little indication as yet as to whether and to what extent the Community may be liable for omissions, although in Cases 19, etc./69 *Richez-Parise* v. *Commission* ([1970] ECR 325) the Commission was held liable for the failure to correct the good faith, but incorrect, interpretation it had given to a number of officials regarding their pensions (see also 10.7);
– damage to the plaintiff;
– a causal link between the two.

These conditions will be examined in turn.

10.3   The Requirement of Fault

It is implicit in the Court's case law that fault is a necessary element of liability. The Court was given the opportunity in Cases 9 and 11/71 *Compagnie d'Approvisionnement* v. *Commission* ([1972] ECR 391) to adopt the French doctrine of *'l'égalité devant les charges publiques'* (equal apportionment of public burdens) whereby the state may in certain circumstances be liable even in the absence of fault as a result of the simple fact that policy measures which it adopts may weigh more heavily on some citizens than on others. Since the Court concluded that the measures under challenge in Cases 9 and 11/71, which were intended to offset the effects of the devaluation of the French franc in 1969, and in particular its disruptive effects on the Common Agricultural Policy (CAP), did not in fact impose a burden on the applicants, it was not required to consider this question.

The requirement of fault is an essential element of the non-contractual liability of the Community institutions under the ECSC Treaty regime (see Case T-120/89 *Stahlwerke Peine* v. *Commission* (27.6.1991).

10.4   Wrongful Acts: Vicarious Liability

In the one case in which it has been required to consider the nature of the Community's responsibility for a fault on the part of one of its servants (*faute personnelle*), the Court has given a restrictive interpretation of the extent of Community vicarious liability. Interpreting the equivalent Article 188(2) Euratom in Case 9/69 *Sayag* v. *Leduc* ([1969] ECR 329) the Court held (at p.335):

> 'By referring at one and the same time to damage caused by the institutions and to that caused by the servants of the Community, Article 188 indicates that the Community is only liable for those acts of its servants which, by virtue of an internal and direct relationship, are the necessary extension of the tasks entrusted to the institutions.'

In *Sayag*, a reference for a preliminary ruling from a Belgian court, the question concerned whether a person injured in a traffic accident caused by an engineer employed by Euratom who had been travelling on official business in Belgium in his private car should be suing the engineer personally in the Belgian courts or the Community as vicariously liable in the Court of Justice. The restrictive interpretation given by the Court resulted in the conclusion that the driving of a private car on official business would not fall within the concept of *faute personnelle* except in the exceptional circumstances where the Community would not have been able to undertake the tasks entrusted to it without the official using private means of transport.

10.5   Wrongful Acts: Carelessness within the Commission

One of the most infamous cases concerning the responsibility of the Community, and one of the very few which have resulted in a definitive award of damages, involved a clear case of carelessness within the Commission which was not imputable to any one official, but to the administrative service as a whole (*faute de service*) (Case 145/83 *Adams* v. *Commission* [1985] ECR 3539). Stanley Adams, while working for the Swiss pharmaceutical company Hoffman-La-Roche (HLR), supplied the Commission with documents, on an assurance of confidentiality. The documents showed that HLR was violating Community competition law, and the Commission successfully took proceedings against the company. In the course of the proceedings, the Commission supplied HLR with documents which assisted them in identifying Adams as the informant. Although Adams had left HLR's employment by that time and was living in Italy, he was arrested under the Swiss industrial espionage laws when he returned for a visit. He was held in solitary confinement, unable to communicate with his family, and his wife, who was also interrogated, subsequently committed suicide. He was eventually convicted and given a one year suspended sentence. When he claimed damages against the Commission, it was found by the Court to have violated its duty towards him, in particular when it failed to warn Adams when it discovered that HLR was planning to prosecute him. The damages payable were reduced by one-half in respect of Adams' own contributory fault in returning to Switzerland, which occasioned his arrest.

A less tragic case is Case 353/88 *Briantex* v. *Council and Commission* [1989] ECR 3623) where the Commission was said to have misled the plaintiff into thinking that it could conclude contracts with Chinese companies in the context of an 'EEC-China Business Week', when in fact the Italian quota for the relevant good was already exhausted. The claim failed on the facts, as the applicants were unable to prove wrongful conduct on the part of the Commission. The same grounds were given by the Court for dismissing the application in Cases 326/86 and 66/88 *Francesconi* v. *Commission* ([1989] ECR 2087). This was an attempt to make the Commission liable for failure effectively to cooperate with a Member State and for bad management and supervision of the wine sector following the so-called glycol and methanol wine scandals in 1985-86. The claim, although unsuccessful, raises the possibility of an extension of Commission liability in the context of its cooperative and supervisory roles in relation to the implementation of Community law (see also 10.9).

10.6   Wrongful Acts: Acts having Legal Effects

In practice, the most important category of cases decided by the Court under Article 215 has concerned alleged liability for damage caused by acts which have legal effects such as an illegal refusal to grant an import or export licence, or measures of economic policy which impose more onerous financial burdens on one product than on a competing product, or which discriminate between producers of the same product. In these cases the wrongful act is quite different in nature to, for example, the breach of confidentiality which caused harm to Stanley Adams.

One of the most difficult questions in this context has been that of distinguishing between actions for annulment and actions for compensation; should recovery be governed by the same conditions which govern the annulment of acts with legal effects? If not, what conditions determine the circumstances in which the wrongful and damaging administrative or legislative actions of a Community institution give rise to an action for compensation?

10.7   The Relationship between Annulment and Compensation

The second paragraph of Article 176 EC states that the obligation on the institution whose act has been declared void to take the necessary measures to comply with the judgment of the Court of Justice 'shall not affect any obligation which may result from the application of the second paragraph of Article 215'. This appears to state clearly that annulment actions and actions for compensation are quite separate.

However, in Case 25/62 *Plaumann* v. *Commission* ([1963] ECR 95) the Court linked the two actions together. It will be recalled that in this case a German importer of clementines sought to challenge a Commission decision addressed to Germany, refusing it the right to lower the duty on clementines from 13 to 10%. Holding the Article 173 EC annulment action to be inadmissible on the grounds that the importer lacked *locus standi*, the Court went on to declare an Article 215 action for compensation admissible. However, the action failed on the merits (at p.108):

'It must be declared that the damage allegedly suffered by the applicant issues from this Decision and that the action for compensation in fact seeks to set aside the legal effects on the applicant of the contested Decision.

In the present case the contested Decision has not been annulled. An administrative measure which has not been annulled cannot of itself constitute a wrongful act on the part of the administration inflicting damage upon those whom it affects. The latter cannot therefore claim damages by reason of that measure. The Court cannot by way of an action for compensation take steps which would nullify the legal effects of a Decision which, as stated, has not been annulled.'

This doctrine has since been reversed and there is now no need for an applicant under Article 215 to challenge directly or indirectly, via Articles 173, 177 or 184 EC, the legality of administrative or legislative measures in respect of which it claims compensation. In Case 4/69 *Lütticke* v. *Commission* ([1971] ECR 325), in the context of a claim for failure on the part of the Commission to address a Directive or Decision to Germany requiring it to modify certain taxes which the applicant had to pay, the Court stated (at p.336):

'The action for damages provided for by Article 178 and the second paragraph of Article 215 was established by the Treaty as an independent form of action with a particular purpose to fulfil within the system of actions and subject to conditions for its use, conceived with a view to its specific purpose. It would be contrary to the independent nature of this action as well as to the efficacy of the general system of forms of action created by the Treaty to regard as a ground for inadmissibility the fact that, in certain circumstances, an action for damages might lead to a result similar to that of an action for failure to act under Article 175.'

The clearest statement of the separation of the actions for annulment and compensation came in Case 175/84 *Krohn* v. *Commission* ([1986] ECR 753) where the Court stated expressly that the existence of an individual decision which has become definitive because it had not been challenged under Article 173 was not a bar to the admissibility of a compensation action.

In practice, although annulment, or a declaration of invalidity under Article 177, is by no means a prerequisite of a successful action under Article 215, many actions for compensation are either linked to, or have been preceded by, successful annulment actions or declarations of invalidity (e.g. Case C-152/88 *Sofrimport* v. *Commission* [1990] ECR I-2477 – actions under Article 173 and 215 brought simultaneously; in the isoglucose cases (see 10.8) Article 215 actions were brought at about the same time as actions in the national courts which resulted in references on the validity of the relevant Community acts under Article 177). However, the actual formula for determining the wrongful nature of the act, for the purposes of resolving the claim for compensation is quite different, and in many ways more restrictive, than the criteria which the Court uses to determine the legality of an act for the purposes of annulment or invalidity. It was elaborated by the Court in the first instance in Case 5/71 *Zuckerfabrik Schöppenstedt* v. *Council* ([1971] ECR 975) and it has consistently applied these principles since that time. The *Schöppenstedt* formula, as restated by the Court in Cases 83, etc./76 *Bayerische HNL et al.* v. *Council and Commission (Second Skimmed Milk Powder case)* ([1978] ECR 1209 at p.1224) states that:

'The Community does not incur liability on account of a legislative measure which involves choices of economic policy unless a sufficiently serious breach of a superior rule of law for the protection of the individual has occurred.'

10.8   The Analysis and Application of the *Schöppenstedt* Formula

This formula applies only to legislative measures of the institutions, that is, to those which are of general application and involve an element of discretionary decision-making. Inevitably such measures will impact to varying degrees upon economic actors and, in order to avoid a flood of claims from aggrieved plaintiffs while at the same upholding the constitutional supremacy of the rule of law under the Treaties, the Court has chosen a restrictive definition of wrongfulness. This definition has in turn been applied in such a way as to exclude the majority of claims.

The first requirement is the breach of a superior rule of law for the protection of individuals. This is a reference to the range of general principles and fundamental rights evolved by the Court in its case law. For example, in Case 74/74 *CNTA* v. *Commission* ([1975] ECR 533) the Court held that the abolition with immediate effect and without warning of monetary compensatory amounts (MCA's), used to compensate agricultural traders for fluctuations in exchange rates which made the single pricing system under the CAP unreliable, could constitute a breach of the principle of legitimate expectations which is protected under Community law. In Case C-152/88 *Sofrimport* v. *Commission*, the Court found that importers of Chilean apples which were in transit to the Community had a legitimate expectation that they would be protected against the unfavourable consequences of protective measures against such apples which were introduced by the Community authorities. This was because the enabling Regulation specificially addressed the situation of those whose apples were actually already in transit to the Community, who could not therefore mitigate their loss by arranging for an alternative disposal of the products.

The prerequisite of a breach of a superior rule of law would normally be satisfied by a successful annulment action under Article 173, or a ruling of invalidity under Article 177, although it is arguable that a successful claim for invalidity on the grounds that the wrong legal basis had been used, or that Parliamentary prerogatives had not been observed would not satisfy the requirement that the rule of law which has been breached must be *for the protection of individuals.*

In addition, the breach must be sufficiently serious. This is, in practice, a much more stringent requirement, and in numerous cases the applicants' cases have failed at this hurdle. Cases 83, etc./76 *Second Skimmed Milk Powder* case concerned the Community's attempt to get rid of a skimmed milk powder mountain which stemmed from the overproduction of milk, by passing a Regulation obliging producers of animal feed to purchase skimmed milk powder from the intervention agencies. This had a damaging effect on soya, which was the alternative, and cheaper, source of protein in animal feeds. The result was also that farmers would have to pay more for their feed. The farmers succeeded in obtaining a declaration that the Regulation was invalid on the grounds that it infringed the principles of non-discrimination and proportionality (Case 114/76 *Bela-Mühle Josef Bergman* v. *Grows-Farm* [1977] ECR 1211), but failed in their tort actions because the institution concerned had not 'manifestly and gravely disregarded the limits on the exercise of its powers'.

Applying this formulation to the facts, the Court considered both the range of potential plaintiffs – which was a wide category of persons – and the effect of the infringement in terms of its impact on the price of the products in question, as compared to other factors such as fluctuations in world prices. It found this effect to be relatively small. It summed up the effect of the Community's measures as being within the normal range of risk inherent in activities in the economic sector concerned.

Soon after the *Second Skimmed Milk Powder* case, the Court made its first finding of tortious liability in respect of Community legislative acts. In Cases 64, etc./76 *Dumortier et al.* v. *Council and Commission (Quellmehl and Gritz)* ([1979] ECR 3091) the alleged tortious act was a Council Regulation withdrawing subsidies from the production of quellmehl and gritz, products used in baking which are in part in competition with starch, but leaving the subsidies in place for starch. The measure was declared invalid on a reference for a preliminary ruling (Cases 117, etc./76 *Ruckdeschel* v. *HZA Hamburg St-Annen* [1977] ECR 1753) on grounds of infringement of the principle of non-discrimination, and when the subsidies were restored for the future, but not retrospectively, the producers brought proceedings under Article 215 to claim the losses they had suffered during the period when there were no subsidies. In finding for the applicants, the Court pointed out that the producers were a small and ascertainable class, and that the loss they suffered went beyond the risks inherent in the economic activity in question. This was not the beginning of a radical change in approach, however, for shortly thereafter the Court rejected the tortious actions in the *Isoglucose* cases, reinforcing the perception that its judgments in this field are tempered by policy factors which it does not always make very clear.

In the *Isoglucose* cases, the Court ruled that a levy imposed on isoglucose was unlawful in so far as it amounted to discriminatory treatment of isoglucose producers in comparison to the treatment of sugar producers (Cases 103 and 145/77 *Royal Scholten-Honig (Holdings) Ltd* v. *Intervention Board for Agricultural Produce* [1978] ECR 2037). However, in Cases 116, 124/77 *Amylum and Tunnel Refineries* v. *Council and Commission* ([1979] ECR 3479) and Case 143/77 *KSH NV* v. *Council and Commission* ([1979] ECR 3583), it rejected the Article 215 actions. Neither the ruling of invalidity nor the special facts of the case, which showed that the victims were a very small group, that there was some evidence that the measure was aimed at driving isoglucose out of the market by making it uneconomical to produce and that the levy was so severe that it pushed at least one firm into liquidation, were sufficient for the Court to hold that the violation was sufficiently 'grave and manifest'. In that case, the Court appeared to push the definition of 'sufficiently serious' even further by requiring the Community's actions to be 'verging on the arbitrary'. Unsurprisingly, the *Isoglucose* cases were the subject of extensive criticism, and appear to mark a low point in the Court's unwillingness to interfere in the economic planning of the Council and Commission (Hartley, 1988: 479-80; Rudden, 1987: 183–215).

Although, as can be seen, the Court's case law in this area is uneven, it would appear that two factors are central to its evaluation of the nature of the breach: these are the conduct of the defendant and the effect of breach. If as in Case C-152/88 *Sofrimport* v. *Commission*, the Community 'fails completely' to take into account the interests of a group of applicants which it was specifically mandated to consider 'without invoking any overriding public interest', and the effect of that breach upon a narrowly defined category of economic actors 'goes beyond the limits of the economic risks inherent in the business in issue inasmuch as the purpose of that provision [i.e. the one disregarded by the Commission] is precisely to limit those risks with regard to goods in transit', then the Court will be prepared to make a finding of liability.

The Court repeated both parts of this formula in its most recent finding of tortious liability on the part of the Community (Cases C-104/89 and 37/90 *Mulder et al.* v. *Commission and Council* (19.5.1992). In that case, the loss stemmed from a Council Regulation fixing an exemption from levies on the production of dairy products by reference to the quantities which undertakings had marketed in a given earlier year. The applicants in the case had not marketed any dairy products in the reference year, since they had undertaken not to do so as part of the Community's attempts to reduce dairy overproduction. The applicants were not therefore allocated a 'reference quantity' excluded from production levies. The Court held that the Regulation violated the principle of the protection of legitimate expectations, which was a superior rule of law for the protection of individuals. The breach was also sufficiently serious for the Community to be held liable. However, the Court found that a subsequent amendment to the rules by the Council, which sought to balance the interests of those such as the applicants against the fragile stability of the market for dairy products in the Community, by allocating the applicants 60% of the quantities they sold prior to the period when they did not market milk, constituted a serious consideration of a matter of overriding public interest and did not therefore amount to a manifest and grave violation of its discretionary powers.

An attempt failed to use the *Schöppenstedt* formula in order to claim compensation for loss caused by an allegedly unlawful Directive harmonising national rules affecting the creation of the internal market. In Case C-63/89 *Les Assurances de Credit SA* v. *Council and Commission* ([1991] 2 CMLR 737) the Court held that a Directive harmonising the conditions in which export credit insurance operations could be undertaken, but which did not apply to public sector insurance business, was not unlawful in the sense of giving rise to a claim for compensation. The Court did not accept the argument that the Directive discriminated against the private sector businesses. It held that the Council could validly pass a partial harmonisation measure and possessed complete discretion as to the timetable under which it adopted harmonisation measures.

10.9 Liability in Respect of Other Acts having Legal Effects

The *Schöppenstedt* formula is not used to assess whether individual acts having legal effects can give rise to the liability of the Community. For example, in Cases 5, etc./66 *Kampffmeyer* v. *Commission* ([1967] ECR 245) the Court found that the responsibility of the Commission was engaged by its wrongful and 'improper' application of a safeguard provision allowing protective measures to be taken to prohibit the import of certain agricultural products. The measure in question was a Decision addressed to Germany, annulled by the Court in Case 106 and 107/63 *Toepfer* v. *Commission* ([1965] ECR 405).

In Case C-55/90 *Cato* v. *Commission* [1992] 2 CMLR 459, the applicant sought to argue that the Commission was liable to compensate for loss caused by the approval, by means of a Decision addressed to the UK, of what he considered to be an incorrect implementation of a Council Directive on the awarding of compensation to persons who decommissioned fishing boats. Cato argued that the UK implementing measures placed an excessive burden of proof on the party claiming compensation, and that the Commission should not have approved them. The Court simply referred, without either discussing or disapproving of it, to the applicant's contention that the Commission had committed a sufficiently serious breach of a superior rule of law for the protection of individuals, and was therefore liable to pay compensation, but dismissed the action on the facts for failure on the part of Cato to prove his contentions about the effect of the UK measures. In the event that the Court might hold the Commission liable for its failure adequately to supervise the implementation of Community obligations by Member States, it is arguable that the test to be used is one which should be different from that governing discretionary legislative activities. If the Commission is subject to a duty, in certain cases, to approve by Decision the correct implementation of particular Directives, a failure to fulfil such a duty does not involve a true exercise of discretion. It is in any event unlikely that the Court will encourage the development of a line of cases which seeks to make the Commission responsible for inadequate supervision. It has long been the tendency of the Court to encourage individuals to seek redress in respect of unimplemented or misimplemented Directives from Member States in national courts, and this line of case law was further strengthened by the decision on damages for failure to implement in Cases 6 and 9/90 *Francovich* v. *Italian State* ([1992] IRLR 84).

10.10   The Requirements of Causation and Damage

It is for the applicant to prove causation and damage; the Court does not draw an inference from the fact of unlawful conduct that the unlawful conduct caused the damage (Case 253/84 *GAEC* v. *Council and Commission* ([1987] ECR 123). The Court has not applied a 'but for' test in assessing whether there is a factual causal link between the unlawful act on the part of the Community and the alleged damage. Rather it has tended to focus on the fact that it will always be difficult to prove in a market situation that a legislative or other measure is 'the' cause of any damage due to a reduction of profits, and it has held (e.g. in Cases 64, etc./ 76 *Dumortier et al.* v. *Council and Commission* (*Quellmehl and Gritz*) that the damage must be a sufficiently direct consequence of the unlawful conduct of the institution concerned. This in practice has a tendency to restrict the ability of applicants to recover for losses of profit. For example, in Cases 5, etc./66 *Kampffmeyer* v. *Commission* the applicants had applied for permits to import maize from France into Germany at a time when large profits could be made because of a zero rate of levy. The German authorities wrongfully refused to grant the permit and the Commission upheld the refusal. Those applicants who had already concluded contracts and had to cancel them were held entitled to recover their cancellation fees and loss of profits, but with the latter discounted by 90%, because of the speculative nature of the transactions. Those applicants who had not previously concluded contracts recovered nothing.

In a number of cases applicants have failed to recover damages despite establishing liability in principle, because they have been unable to prove damage. In Case 74/74 *CNTA* v. *Commission*, although they were able to establish that the sudden termination of MCAs engaged the tortious responsibility of the Community, the applicants were unable to establish that the currency fluctuations had in fact caused loss. Similarly, in Case 253/84 *GAEC* v. *Council and Commission*, the Court refused to consider the applicant's contention that a Council Decision authorising Germany to grant state subsidies to its farmers was unlawful because it was unable to prove that the effect of the subsidies had been to cause damage to French farmers through a lowering of prices on the French market because of competition from artifically cheaper German products. Statistics were produced by the defendants to demonstrate that prices in France had already begun to fall before the entry into force of the contested Decision.

The Court also applies the defence of contributory negligence (Case 145/83 *Adams* v. *Commission*) and the duty to mitigate losses (Cases C-104/89 and 37/90 *Mulder et al.* v. *Commission and Council*) in order to restrict in practice the level of damages payable by the Community. In the latter case the Court deducted from the damages payable to the aggrieved dairy producers an amount representing what they would have earned if they had reasonably sought to undertake alternative commercial or agricultural activities during the period when they could not produce and sell dairy products.

Interest can be awarded on damages payable by the Community, since it is in general awarded under the rules common to the Member States (Case C-152/88 *Sofrimport* v. *Commission*).

In each case, the Court states the basis for calculating the damages (e.g. in Case C-152/88 *Sofrimport* v. *Commission* the difference between the price at which the apples were sold after the Court had suspended the protective measures in interim proceedings, and the price the applicants would have got for them had the measures not been imposed), and then sends the parties away to formulate, within a time limit, an agreed amount of damages which they must then communicate to the Court. In the event of a failure to agree, the parties must submit their views to the Court which will itself fix the amount.

10.11 The Problem of Concurrent Liability: National Court or Court of Justice?

Not all actions for loss ultimately attributable to unlawful conduct on the part of the Community can be brought in the Court of Justice. Despite the fact that the Community operates a system of own resources, whereby the levies collected and sums paid by national administrations on behalf of the Community are in truth the Community's own money (see 4.8), the Court nonetheless refuses to consider certain applications for money damages. A distinction must be drawn to this end between what are essentially restitutionary claims, namely actions for restitution of a sum unlawfully levied and sums withheld in breach of an obligation, and actions for unliquidated damages such as loss of profit.

The case law is generally consistent with the Court's persistent encouragement to undertakings to begin their actions against unlawful conduct on the part of the Community by challenging the national implementing measures. For example, it requires actions for restitution of a sum unlawfully levied to be brought against the national authority which levied the sums in the national court, even though the sums in question may have been paid into the Community funds (Case 96/71 *Haegemann* v. *Commission* [1972] ECR 1005). Consequently, it would be wrong for a national court to deny the liability of the national authority, on account of its role as an 'agent' of the Community. In contrast, it would appear that an action for a sum withheld in breach of a lawful obligation can be brought in either the Court of Justice or the national court. Since the case law on this point is mixed, however, prudence would seem to suggest that, unless damages at large in addition to the specified sum are claimed, the national court is a better place to start. Exceptionally, of course, there may, for some reason, be no national remedy; an example would be where there is no legal basis in national law for an action for compensation once the unlawful act has been removed from the field.

Similar considerations would appear to apply where the damage is alleged to have occurred as a result of the withholding of some other administrative act on the part of the national authority (e.g. the refusal of a licence as in Case 175/84 *Krohn* v. *Commission*). In its judgment in *Krohn*, the Court made clear that the Commission was the true author of the unlawful act, and that a national action would not have provided effective protection for the individual concerned against loss, and consequently held the action admissible.

Actions in respect of unliquidated loss, such as the additional loss suffered as a consequence of the unlawful levying of a sum by the national authority, must always be brought in the Court of Justice, *in addition to the national action* (Case 26/74 *Roquette* v. *Commission* [1976] ECR 677).

The case law remains unsatisfactory, therefore, since it is wrong to impose an obligation upon an aggrieved undertaking to choose between the national court and the Court of Justice, or to take two actions where one should suffice. In reality, since the implementation of Community measures is frequently a result of a combination of Community and national action, it is difficult for the victim of the loss always to assess to whom in truth the wrongful conduct is attributable. Cases 89 and 91/86 *L'Etoile Commerciale* v. *Commission* [1987] ECR 3005 provide an example of the restrictive application of the rules on the admissibility of Article 215 claims where the alleged wrongful conduct was a Decision adopted by the Commission which led a national authority to reclaim certain agricultural subsidies. The Court declared the action under Articles 178 and 215 inadmissible. There is a case for allowing an application of the principles of joint and several liability, widely recognised in the legal systems of the Member States, whereby the victim of a tort may sue one of several or joint tortfeasors in respect of the whole of the obligation, leaving the tortfeasors to recover contributions between themselves (see the analysis of AG Van Gerven in Case 201/86 *Spie-Batignolles* v. *Commission* [1990] ECR I-197 where he recognised the wide applicability of the rules on joint and several liability). However, the continuing organic separation of the Court of Justice and the national courts, and the failure to recognise eith that a Community institution may be a defendant in a national court, or that a Member State may be a defendant in the Court of Justice in an action brought by an individual, represent conclusive obstacles to this more equitable solution of the problem (Wils, 1992).

Summary

1 The non-contractual (i.e. tortious) liability of the Community is governed by Articles 178 and 215(2) EC.

2 The basic prerequisites of a successful action are:

   – a wrongful act (i.e. one involving some fault on the part of the Community);
   – damage to the plaintiff;
   – a causal link between the two.

3 The Community can be liable in respect of *fautes de service* (i.e. failures which are imputable to an institution) and *fautes personnelles* (i.e. unlawful acts of officials for which an institution is vicariously liable).

4 Much of the case law of the Court has been concentrated on attempted claims for damages for discretionary legislative acts. The Court applies the rules restrictively in such cases so as to limit access to compensation, although it does not require the applicant to have first successfully challenged the validity of the offending Community act either via an action under Article 173 or an action in the national court and a ruling on validity.

5 To be successful an applicant seeking damages for an allegedly wrongful legislative act involving choices of economic policy must prove a sufficiently serious breach of a superior rule of law intended for the protection of individuals (the *Schöppenstedt* formula).

6 The Court's interpretation of 'sufficiently serious breach' has been particularly restrictive, and the Community's actions must border on the arbitrary before the Court will make a finding of liability.

7 Where the applicant's action consists of a restitutionary claim for money wrongfully paid to or withheld by a national authority acting on the basis of an unlawful Community act, the Court will normally require the applicant to begin the action in the national court. Only actions for unliquidated damages against the Community institutions may be brought in the Court of Justice.

Questions

1 What are the basic elements of a successful damages claim against the Community?

2 What is the difference between a *faute de service* and a *faute personnelle*?

3 Should the Court require an applicant for compensation under Article 215 to challenge first the validity of the act in question?

4 What is the *Schöppenstedt* formula, and how and why has it been restrictively applied by the Court of Justice?

5 Are there any policy factors which link together the successful actions for damages against the Community?

6 In what ways would the application of a doctrine of joint and several liability assist applicants who bring the claims in tort against the Community and the national authorities?

Workshop (for Chapters 9 and 10)

The State of Rubric is the sole source of imports of a rare desert orchid into the EC. The orchid is much in demand for its medicinal properties. Five firms in the EC, including a UK firm Orchids Alive plc, import the orchids from Rubric. The Commission adopts (fictitious) Regulation 6000 of 1992 imposing an additional import levy of 10% *ad valorem* on imports of the orchids, following representations from the World Save the Orchid Campaign. The Campaign produced evidence of the activities of Orchids Alive plc, including allegations about the environmental damage caused to the eco-system in Rubric as a result of the harvesting of the orchids, and of bribery of public officials in Rubric to ensure that other European Community firms do not get access to the supplies there. The firm did not know of the Commission's intention to adopt the Regulation until it was published in the *Official Journal*. It is also known that a consortium of EC-based firms is planning to launch the farming under glass of the orchids within the EC, and that a group of officials within the Directorate-General of the Commission which was responsible for the Regulation has a financial interest in the venture.

Advise Orchids Alive plc as to which court or courts it should bring an action in, and assess its chances of obtaining the following forms of redress:

1. annulment of the Regulation, or a declaration of invalidity;

2. recovery of the additional import levy paid to the UK customs authorities;

3. compensation for the loss of profits on long-term supply contracts which it holds within the UK.

Further Reading

Bridge (1984) 'Procedural Aspects of the Enforcement of European Community Law through the Legal Systems of the Member States', 9 *European Law Review*, 28.

Hartley (1988) Ch. 17, 'Community Obligations'.

Wils (1992) 'Concurrent Liability of the Community and a Member State', 17 *European Law Review*, 191.

Part V

The Law of the
Single Market

11 Economic Integration and the Law: an Introduction

11.1 Introduction (see also 1.3)

The European Community is a system of regional economic integration, based on the concept of an 'internal market', that is, an area without internal frontiers where goods, services, persons and capital can move without hindrance. It has also been evolving towards an economic and monetary union, that is an area with a common economic and monetary policy, involving, potentially, a single currency. The form of integration chosen is that of market integration; in other words, a larger trading unit in which market forces operate freely is created out of smaller diverse units. As a result, economies will be encouraged to specialise as they become increasingly interconnected, and they will be encouraged to purchase imports from within the regional trading bloc rather than from outside. Thus systems of regional economic integration are discriminatory *vis-à-vis* the rest of the world, and not automatically compatible with a system which aims at global free trade such as the General Agreement on Tariffs and Trade (GATT).

Countries choose to embark upon economic integration primarily for political and strategic reasons. The creation of the ECSC in the 1950s provides a good example of the influence of strategic reasons, since it involved placing what were the basic instruments of war under supranational control. The EEC itself was created not only with a view to enhancing economic welfare in Europe, but above all as a step towards a larger project of political integration. In Europe, the dominant ideology of the integration process has been to see economic integration not as an end in itself, but as part of a continuing process. That view, although dominant, is not held by all interested parties. UK policy towards Europe, particularly since the early 1980s, has been to stress the role of the European Community as a mechanism for achieving free trade, not as an engine of political change.

11.2 Different Levels of Economic Integration

Economic integration can take different forms, depending essentially upon the degree of openness established towards the partner economies. A *free trade area* involves the removal of customs duties between the participating states, but does not involve the erection of a common al barrier. Thus participating states remain free to fix their own levels in international trade. A free trade area will not lead to the removal of internal borders, as frontier controls will need to remain for the purposes of checking the origin of goods. The additional element of uniform external protection is added in a *customs union*, where the participating states agree upon the establishment of a common external tariff (CET), and embark upon the task of creating a common external trade policy (e.g. on quotas and duty free preferences). The Community is based on a customs union; however, it also goes further in the sense that it is a *common market* in which there are to be no restrictions at all on the movement of commodities (goods and services) or on the free flow of factors of production (labour, enterprise, capital). The 'final' stage of economic integration, in the sense that it is only likely to be achieved by groups of states which have become for all practical purposes a single political entity, is *economic and monetary union*. It is this stage of integration – involving the convergence of national economic policies and a gradual assumption of centralised responsibility for economic policy, leading to the creation of a single currency area – which is envisaged by the Treaty of Maastricht, but that objective is far from being attained at present.

The terms used here are not precise and static economic definitions, but rather descriptions of the types of features typically found in an evolutionary process. Systems of economic integration are rather unstable, and the theory of functionalism (see 1.4) has been used to describe the 'spill-over effect' whereby the attainment of one level of economic integration tends to lead onto the next. For example, there appears to be considerable pressure from within business communities in the European Community for the establishment of a single currency, which will eradicate both the uncertainties of floating (or even partially fixed) exchange rates, and reduce the transaction costs associated with dealing in more than one currency. Thus the perspective of a larger accessible market has sharpened awareness of the potential benefits of economic and monetary union.

Confusion arises in the Community context regarding the terminology of integration and the aims of the Community, because of the apparently interchangeable use of the terms 'common' and 'internal/single' market. In a sense this is not a problem, given the somewhat fluid nature of all the different levels of economic integration, which are subject to influence from external factors such as current political ideologies or the state of the world economy. It was argued by some commentators and politicians after the adoption of the Single European Act (SEA) that resolving merely to complete the internal market by the end of 1992 was a stepping back from the aims of the original Treaty. This fear stemmed from the fact that the definition of an internal market inserted by what is now Article 7A EC (previously Article 8A EEC) makes reference to specific elements of the policy framework created by the original Treaty as goals to be paid particular attention, but omits certain key aspects (e.g. Article 74 *et seq.*

EC – common transport policy). However, Article 7A EC is expressed to be without prejudice to other Articles of the Treaty or, to put it another way, to the continuing work of creating of the common market. In that sense, it may be that the creation of the internal market is a more limited goal, but it is one deemed politically attainable within a defined time span. It represents a break with the somewhat jaded concept of a common market, which had lost some of its political credibility as a realistic objective since it should have been established by 1970, but in fact never was.

Looked at from another angle, the internal market, at least in so far as it is defined in Article 7A, may have significant advantages. This Article refers to an area without internal frontiers. It is the Commission's contention that this is a separate element of the internal market programme which should result in the physical disappearance of internal borders, and that Member States which have not complied with this obligation by December 31 1992 are in breach of the Treaty, and subject to potential enforcement actions. It remains to be seen what legal consequences can be attached to the date December 31 1992 (Schermers, 1991).

A distinction is commonly drawn between *negative* and *positive* integration. Negative integration refers to the removal of existing impediments to trade and exchange, and less complex forms of economic integration consist almost entirely of negative measures. Positive integration relates to

'the modification of existing instruments and institutions and, more importantly, to the creation of new ones so as to enable the market of the integrated area to function properly and effectively and also to promote other broader policy aims of the union' (El-Agraa, 1990: 2).

Increased commitment to positive integration is necessitated by the move towards more complex levels of integration. There are numerous examples of the phenomenon identified by El-Agraa in the Community. For example, it is arguable that there is a need, within the internal market, to create Community-wide basic product standards to which all products put on the market should conform in the interests of consumer and environmental protection. This can be achieved by means of the harmonisation of national laws. A further example is the creation of new centralised policy instruments (Articles 85–90 EC) which enable the Community to restrain or punish undertakings or groups of undertakings which seek to recreate, through private behaviour, the same market segmentation which Member States are prohibited from retaining by the Community's guarantees of free movement (competition policy – see 11.4 on the place of competition policy in the legal definition of a common market).

The difficulty with positive integration lies commonly at the level of decision-making. Reference can be made back to Chapters 3 and 4 for details of the rigidities and complexities of the Community's decision-making process. Only since the adoption of the Single European Act in 1986 has there been a marked acceleration in the legislative activity of the Community. In practice, as we shall see, many of the achievements of the Community are a result of creative interpretations of the outer limits of negative integration by the Court of Justice which have in turn altered conceptions about the types of (positive) harmonising measures which are in fact necessary for the completion of the internal market. In other words, the work of the Court has changed the conventional understanding of the difference between positive and negative integration.

Reference should finally be made to *sectoral integration*. Closer integration in particular sectors of the economy may be achievable only by interventionist policy-making which creates uniform regulatory mechanisms. The principal example in the Community (aside from the specific sectoral treaties) is the agricultural sector, where the various national mechanisms existing to subsidise agricultural activities and the earnings of farmers have, since the early 1960s, been replaced by a unified system of price support and intervention buying where the market price falls below a specified guide price. This is not an example of the free market in operation.

11.3   The Economic Benefits of Integration

Economists are greatly divided on the nature and degree of the economic advantages to be derived from integration. Models of customs unions would appear to show that there should be gains in terms of trade creation, but losses in terms of trade diversion. Trade creation occurs where the source of a particular good is switched to the most efficient source of production within the single trading bloc when customs duties which artificially increase prices are removed; trade diversion arises because the most efficient world producer may be excluded from that trading bloc, and its products may be rendered more expensive than those of the most efficient internal producer because of the effects of the customs duties. However, this theory relies upon a model of a static customs union which ignores factors such as the monopoly power of multinational undertakings, economies of scale, costs of transport and non-tariff barriers to trade erected by nation states and is based upon an unrealistic set of assumptions as to why systems of integration are formed. For example, the illustration of trade creation and trade diversion used here is an argument for global free trade, and against regional systems of integration. Global free trade would be the best way of maximising economic welfare, but in practice it remains unattainable. It follows, therefore, and is indeed undoubtedly true, that states have other reasons for embarking upon integration processes.

Regional integration offers other, dynamic benefits. These include the economies of scale and increased levels of competition which benefit both undertakings and consumers in a larger market, all of which may lead to accelerated restructuring and specialisation of economies. The integrateɹ economic entity may also enjoy increased bargaining power in international trade, enabling better terms of trade to be negotiated with third countries. Finally, the fact of membership of a larger economic entity may make a state a more attractive location for inward investment from strong economies. Enhanced economic integration also leads onto other benefits, including increased political interdependence and increased influence upon global political events.

However, although it may be possible to identify the economic factors which should, in theory, lead to growth resulting from customs unions and other forms of more intense economic integration, in practice these gains are very difficult to quantify. It is almost impossible to separate any additional economic growth which may have occurred in the Member States as a consequence of the existence of the Community from the growth in GNP which would in any case have occurred. Undoubtedly it can be demonstrated that trade within the Community has increased greatly at the expense of trade between the Community and the outside world. This is often given as a reason why the UK, which has a tradition of trading outside Europe, may not have benefited as much from membership of the Community as other countries, since it has lost both the sources of many of its cheap raw materials and the destinations of many of its exports. Furthermore, trade within the Community is dominated by Germany which accounts for over 35% of all exports of manufactured goods within the EC. Germany also runs a large trade surplus with the rest of the Community, since it accounts for only 25% of all imports.

Finally, there is a case for treating the figures associated with anticipated growth from the completion of the internal market with a certain scepticism. The possibility of increasing Community GDP by up to 5% as a result of eliminating the 'costs of non-Europe' (i.e. the costs resulting from the failure to complete the internal market) is naturally beguiling. In practice, however, the calculations do not take into account the costs associated with industrial restructuring, shifts in patterns of employment and other regional effects of the creation of a larger market. The argument that the internal market cannot be regarded as complete until it incorporates also a full 'social dimension' will be considered further in Part VI of this book.

Despite these doubts it cannot be denied that membership of the Community continues to be viewed as an attractive proposition for non-Member States. It must be assumed therefore that they envisage deriving economic gains from membership or, perhaps, avoiding losses which might result from non-membership.

11.4 The Role of Law

Law is the principal mechanism available for turning the political and economic aspirations of the integrationists into reality. Integration in

: is, as we have seen, based on Treaties (i.e. it is *prima facie* w), and on the binding secondary legislation passed by ip by Treaties. The system of law set up under the Treaties characteristics which enhance its effectiveness *vis-à-vis* the ~~........ .cgai~~ systems (see Chapter 8). The Community legal order is therefore generally termed supranational rather than international. The key economic law provisions of the Community have an impact within the Member States akin to constitutional provisions. Membership of the Community involves a loss of sovereignty, and the substitution of common political institutions for national political institutions. Key provisions of Community economic law such as those guaranteeing free movement are justiciable before national courts (direct effect), and take precedence over national laws (supremacy). Where the Community has fully exercised an exclusive competence to regulate in the economic domain, in particular in the field of agriculture, the existence of Community legislation will be regarded as precluding national legislation (the pre-emptive effect of Community law). In addition, the Community as a legal order exercising powers in the economic domain claims the legitimacy of adherence to the rule of law. The regulatory activities of the Community are therefore subject to tests of constitutionality and legality under the control of the Court of Justice (Part IV).

Studying the economic law of the Community therefore provides an opportunity to view the operation of the principles considered in Parts II–IV of this book in practice. Weatherill (1992b) provides a good example of the interaction of the institutional and economic law of the Community in an analysis of a decision of the House of Lords (*R.* v. *London Boroughs' Transport Committee, ex parte Freight Transport Association Ltd* [1991] 3 All ER 915). He discusses the refusal of the House of Lords to refer to the Court of Justice questions regarding the interpretation of the scope of certain Community Directives in the transport field which were at issue in a challenge by the Freight Transport Association to the right of the London Boroughs Transport Committee to ban lorries at night in certain parts of London. The House preferred to interpret the Directives without the assistance of the Court; this raises issues of the scope of the obligation to refer under Article 177(3) EC. At issue was also the application of justiciable Community law in the UK (Directives), and the effect of the Community legislation (Directives on Brakes and on Sound Levels) on the ability of the Member States to regulate a particular field arguably already occupied by Community law (in this case the right of a local transport authority to impose a lorry ban in urban areas, and to refuse to give exemptions to lorries which had not had a noise suppressor fitted to their brakes) (the pre-emptive effect of Community law). Weatherill goes on to illustrate how the case reveals other issues not discussed by the House of Lords, such as the nature of the Community's harmonisation programme (should it be aiming for total harmonisation of standards, or only basic minimum harmonisation?), the difficulties of identifying the correct legal base for such measures after the Single European Act and the scope of the

Treaty ban on non-tariff barriers to trade (Article 30 EC) which would be applicable in the event that the Community measures referred to above were held not to have exhaustively regulated the field. These issues are addressed in the following chapters.

The economic law of the Community also has a constitutional significance for the institutions, which are not permitted to act in ways which endanger the unity of the market (Barents, 1990). The fundamental character of the free movement provisions for the Community itself emerges from Cases 80 and 81/77 *Ramel* v. *Receveur des Douanes* ([1978] ECR 927), where the Court indicated that actions by the Community which infringed the free movement rules and

> 'any prejudice to what the Community has achieved in relation to the unity of the market risks opening the way to mechanisms which would lead to disintegration contrary to the objectives of progressive approximation of the economic policies of member states set out in Article 2 of the Treaty.'

In every way the role of the Court of Justice has been central to the evolution of the economic law of the Community. It has passed through a number of distinctive phases 'constitutionalising' the Treaties; it has enhanced the 'instrumentalism' of the Treaties by interpreting broadly the legislative powers of the institutions, and by creating the conditions in which they can best be used; finally, it has been heavily involved in the detailed implementation of the body of economic law which has been passed by the institutions (Easson, 1989).

11.5   The Basic Legal Framework in the European Community

The key to the legal framework of economic law in the European Community is Article 3 EC. As amended by the Treaty of Maastricht, this sets out the activities of the Community; these include:

'(a) the elimination, as between Member States, of customs duties and quantitative restrictions on the import and export of goods, and of all other measures having equivalent effect;
(b) a common commercial policy;
(c) an internal market characterised by the abolition, as between Member States, of obstacles to the free movement of goods, persons, services and capital;
(d) measures concerning the entry and movement of persons in the internal market as provided for in Article 100C;
(e) a common policy in the sphere of agriculture and fisheries;
(f) a common policy in the sphere of transport;

    (g) a system ensuring that competition in the internal market is not distorted;
    (h) the approximation of the laws of Member States to the extent required for the functioning of the common market;
    . . .
    (j) the strengthening of economic and social cohesion;
    (k) a policy in the sphere of the environment;
    . . .
    (s) a contribution to the strengthening of consumer protection.'

Article 3A then goes on to set out the Community's activities in the economic and monetary policy field. Article 6 EC states the important principle of non-discrimination on grounds of nationality within the sphere of Community competence. Article 7 EC sets out the timetable for the achievement of the common market and Article 7A, as noted above, defines the internal market, adding an additional element which does not appear in Article 3(c), namely the elimination of internal frontiers. Part Three of the Treaty elaborates in greater detail the principal activities identified in Article 3, dealing separately with the mechanisms of the customs union, the removal of non-tariff barriers to trade in goods, the elimination of restrictions on the free movement of services, and the free movement of workers, enterprise and capital. Part Three also contains the basic principles of harmonisation policy in the Community, including the principal law-making power, Article 100A EC, and the Community's policies in the fields, *inter alia*, of economic and social cohesion (regional policy), the environment and consumer protection. For the purposes of this book we shall concentrate on free movement of goods alone. This is not only because of the economic importance of trade in goods, but also because the detailed study of one area of Community economic law provides the key also to the study of other fields of economic law, such as the free movement of services, the Common Agricultural Policy (CAP) or competition policy.

    The dominant economic concept in the Community, at least until the adoption of the Single European Act, was the notion of a 'common market'. In Case 15/81 *Schul* v. *Inspecteur der Invoerrechten* ([1982] ECR 1409) the Court stated that the concept of a common market

    'involves the elimination of all obstacles to intra-Community trade in order to merge the national markets into a Single Market bringing about conditions as close as possible to those of a genuine internal market' (para. 31 of the judgment).

Traditionally, the Treaty provided two mechanisms for achieving this: 'provisions . . . relating to "the elimination of barriers" and "fair competition" both of which are necessary for bringing about a single market' (Case 32/65 *Italy* v. *Council and Commission* [1966] ECR 389 at p.405). The programme for the completion of the internal market by the end of 1992 broke away from that traditional framework by emphasising the importance of legislative measures aimed at securing fair competitive conditions.

11.6 Free Movement of Goods in Outline

The principal provisions governing the free movement of goods can be found in Articles 9–36 EC. These provisions have remained unamended since the inception of the Community. The provisions can be divided into two categories: those dealing with the creation of the customs union (Articles 9-29) and those dealing with the non-tariff aspects of trade in goods (Articles 30-36).

Article 9 EC provides that:

'the Community shall be based on a customs union which shall cover all trade in goods.'

The customs union in turn can be subdivided into its external and internal aspects. The external aspect is concerned with the establishment (long achieved) and the operation of the common customs tariff (CCT) (Articles 18–29 EC) and is discussed in Chapter 12. This chapter also reviews briefly the detailed secondary legislation which governs the CCT, which takes the form of directly applicable Regulations. The Chapter concludes with an analysis of the Community's common commercial policy (Articles 110–116 EC). The internal aspect, covered in Chapter 13, can likewise be subdivided into two sections. First, there is the prohibition on tariff barriers and charges having equivalent effect between the Member States (Articles 9–17 EC and second, the prohibition on discriminatory internal taxation contained in Article 95 EC.

The two aspects are closely linked together by virtue of Article 10 which establishes the concept of 'goods in free circulation'. These are goods which have passed the external frontier of the Community, and on which all relevant duties and charges have been levied, and for which customs formalities have been completed. These goods, once within the Community, are, by virtue of the uniformity of external protection offered by the CCT, able to benefit from free movement within the Community. It should be stated at the outset that this linkage is crucial to the successful completion of the internal market. The goal of removing internal frontiers can only be achieved once complete uniformity of external protection has been achieved and the concept of goods in free circulation can be given unqualified application. We shall examine in Chapter 12 the extent to which this is presently the case.

Non-tariff barriers to trade, or, to use the Community jargon 'quantitative restrictions and measures having equivalent effect', are any national measures which tend to restrict interstate trade. These include import prohibitions and quotas, differing product or technical standards, restrictions on advertising and public purchasing policies which favour national goods. The most important provisions are Articles 30 and 34 which prohibit non-tariff barriers on imports and exports and Article 36 which offers the possibility of national derogations from these prohibitions on grounds of public health, public security and other major needs (see Chapter 14).

11.7   The Legal Framework offered by the Single European Act

The internal market programme based on the Commission's White Paper was intended to revitalise the flagging concept of the Common Market. In practice, this involved the adoption of around 300 measures by the Council of Ministers to remove three categories of barriers to trade: physical barriers, technical barriers and fiscal barriers. The degree of openness of the national economies to each other had tended to decrease during the course of the economic recessions in the 1970s and the early 1980s when Member States had become increasingly protectionist. This had led to a proliferation of non-tariff barriers to trade in goods and services which hindered effective exploitation of export opportunities. The Single European Act added, as we have noted, a definition of the internal market, but whether this has some normative effect after December 31 1992 remains uncertain. It also gave the Council of Ministers a number of law-making powers to enable the adoption of the measures deemed necessary in the White Paper to make the internal market a reality. The legislative mechanisms themselves have been amply discussed in general terms in earlier Chapters (especially Chapter 4) and Chapter 15 will concentrate on showing that the internal market programme does not represent a complete break with the past for the Community, but in fact builds upon the earlier work of the Court of Justice in the interpretation of the provisions of the Treaty which guarantee freedom of movement. The discussion in this book will be limited to those areas of legislative activity most closely related with trade in goods, although, of course, the internal market extends to all types of commodities, and is concerned also with the free movement of factors of production.

The key term in the context of the internal market is now 'distortion of competition'. By this is meant the different regulatory regimes which exist in the various Member States which continue to segment the internal market. The differences mean that there is no level competitive playing field for commodities and factors of production which would encourage maximum economic interpenetration. Where distortions of competition in fact discourage interstate trade, there is a case for harmonising national provisions to eradicate them. The nature of that harmonisation and the manner in which mandatory standards of public health, protection of the environment and other public policy interests are to be integrated into Community-wide regulatory regimes will be discussed in Chapter 15.

Summary

1 The Community is a system of regional economic integration based on a customs union and a common market, and aiming at the attainment of economic and monetary union.

2 Although the actual economic gains from European economic integration cannot be proven, static and dynamic customs union theories tend to support the view that the Member States will have benefited from the development of the Community in the economic field. Certainly, membership remains an attractive proposition for outsiders.

3 Law plays a key role in the economic system created by the Treaties, and the basic outlines of the policies to be implemented by law are sketched out in Article 3 EC. Part Three of the EC Treaty contains more detailed rules on free movement, agricultural policy, harmonisation of national laws and competition policy. The economic law of the Community has a constitutional significance both for the Member States and for the Community itself.

4 The Community places an increasing emphasis on positive integration with the programme to complete the internal market, and the Single European Act (SEA) offers the policy instruments to make this possible.

Questions

1 Distinguish between a free trade area, a customs union, a common market and an economic and monetary union. Using the functionalist theory of integration (1.4), explain how one level of integration 'spills over' into the next.

2 What are the benefits of economic integration?

3 What role does law play in the Community's system of economic integration?

Further Reading

Barents (1990) 'The Community and the Unity of the Common Market: Some Reflections on the Economic Constitution of the Community', 33 *German Yearbook of International Law*, 9.

Davidson (1989) 'Free Movement of Goods, Workers, Services and Capital', in Lodge (1989).

Easson (1989) 'Legal Approaches to European Integration: The Role of the Court and Legislator in the Completion of the European Common Market', 12 *Journal of European Integration*, 101.

El-Agraa (ed.) (1990), Ch. 1, 'General Introduction'.

Lintner and Mazey (1991) London, Chs 3 and 4.

Pinder (1991) 'From Customs Union to Single Market', in Pinder (1991).

Weatherill (1992a) Ch. 5, 'Law and the Economic Objectives of the Community'.

Weatherill (1992b) 'Regulating the Internal Market: Result Orientation in the House of Lords', 17 *European Law Review*, 299.

12 The External Aspects of the Customs Union

12.1 Introduction

This chapter covers two topics: a description of the workings of the common customs tariff (CCT), concentrating on basic principles rather than operational detail, and a general analysis of the Community's external trade, or common commercial policy (CCP). The CCT is one of the main tools of an external trade policy which is based on the basic principle of uniformity of treatment *vis-à-vis* third countries, rather than the abolition of barriers and integration of markets. However, the Community is committed to the furtherance of global free trade. Article 18 EC states:

'The Member States declare their readiness to contribute to the development of international trade and the lowering of barriers to trade by entering into agreements designed, on a basis of reciprocity and mutual advantage, to reduce customs duties below the general level of which they could avail themselves as a result of the establishment of a customs union between them.'

Article 110 EC further links together the customs union, the CCP and the pursuit of free trade:

'By establishing a customs union between themselves the Member States aim to contribute, in the common interest, to the harmonious development of world trade, the progressive abolition of restrictions on internal trade and the lowering of customs barriers.

The common commercial policy shall take into account the favourable effect which the abolition of customs duties between Member States may have on the increase in the competitive strength of undertakings in those States.'

It should be noted that these Articles are phrased in terms of encouragement to action, rather than obligation. They do not create justiciable duties on the part of the Member States as a Community to lower their customs barriers towards third countries, but at the most articulate a duty to negotiate in good faith for the achievement of free trade within organisations such as the GATT where it is largely the Community which negotiates and concludes agreements rather than the Member States. The objective is to ensure that the existence of the customs union does not undermine the GATT system. The policies, as formulated unilaterally by the Community or in negotiation with other countries, are concerned principally with ensuring that external trade conditions do not create distortions of competition between the Member States and thus with preventing external factors from damaging the fabric of integration *within* the Community. The interpenetration of the Community market and the world market is clearly not the first focus of the CCT or the CCP. From this focus on preventing distortions of competition follows the link between the internal and external aspects of the internal market stressed already in 11.6. The closer the internal market comes to resembling a market operating under the conditions of a national market for products originating in the Community, the greater is the required degree of uniformity for the rules applying to products originating in third countries imported into the common market. If, for example, technical standards are harmonised in the Community with respect to Community origin goods, their divergent application by Member States to products originating in third countries would partially defeat one of the purposes of such harmonisation; intra-Community controls would still be necessary for third country products, and this in turn would mean that the retention of border controls would continue to inhibit the movement of products of Community origin, even if controls were only exceptionally exercised. In other words, there is little point in seeking to abolish internal frontiers if the level of external uniformity is so poor that they need to be retained for goods coming from elsewhere. The final point of importance is that insofar as the Community can truly claim to be a single trading unit *vis-à-vis* the rest of the world, it is in a stronger bargaining position with third countries, for example when claiming reciprocity of treatment for Community undertakings. This is one of the dynamic benefits of economic integration referred to in 11.3.

It is in order to maximise the level of uniformity of protection and thus to enable the removal of internal frontiers that the work of the Community within the context of the internal market programme has extended also to the external frontiers. Paras. 35–37 of the Commission's White Paper on *Completing the Internal Market* recognises the link between the internal and external frontiers. Successive reports by the Commission have charted progress towards the the uniform management of the external frontiers. The rules discussed in this chapter have been incorporated into a single Community customs code which is intended in future to provide clear and transparent rules for customs administrations and businesses (Regulation 2913/92 establishing the Community Customs Code OJ 1992 L302/1). The Code comes into force on January 1 1994. The Commission has also been developing databases to give the fullest information to the national customs administrations on the appropriate customs treatment of particular imported products.

12.2 The Common Customs Tariff (CCT)

The CCT has been in place since July 1 1968; this was eighteen months before the target date set by the Treaty of Rome itself. The political will of the Member States to make the customs union a reality as soon as possible was expressed in an 'acceleration' Decision taken in July 1966. The CCT comprises three main elements:

- a nomenclature for the classification of goods;
- rules on the valuation of goods;
- rules on the origin of goods.

A definition of the customs territory is also necessary for the operation of the CCT, and this is based on the countries which are from time to time the Member States of the Community (Article 227 EC). The customs territory changed most recently in 1990 with the unification of Germany leading to the incorporation of the former German Democratic Republic into the Community.

The customs union is for practical purposes 'run' by national customs officers, whose task is to apply the Community rules which are most frequently adopted in the form of Regulations. This is an example of the indirect implementation and administration of Community law. The Commission acts in a supervisory capacity, so that it can, for example, take an Article 169 enforcement action for failure by a Member State properly to apply the customs rules or for failure to pay over the customs duties collected, which belong to the Community's own resources. The Commission also exercises implementing powers delegated from the Council, but under a system of 'comitology' (4.7). The Nomenclature Committee is a management committee, and the Valuation and Origin Committees are regulatory committees; the latter two must give favourable opinions before the Commission can adopt implementing measures. The Nomenclature Committee exercises less restrictive blocking powers.

12.3   Nomenclature

Until 1988, the CCT nomenclature was based on the 1950 Customs Cooperation Council Nomenclature Convention. This was the nomenclature used by the Member States before the establishment of the Community, and the Community succeeded to the rights and duties of the Member States (Case 38/75 *Nederlandse Spoorwegen* v. *Inspecteur der Invoerrechten* [1975] ECR 1439). This has been replaced by the International Convention on the Harmonised Commodity and Description and Coding System (OJ 1987 L198/3) which the European Community was involved in negotiating. This Convention is given effect within the Community legal order by Council Decision 87/369 (OJ 1987 L198/1) and Council Regulation 2658/87 (OJ 1987 L256/1). A new nomenclature was needed in order to achieve a common world-wide approach to problems of classification, to develop a more sophisticated system which could be used for statistical as well as customs purposes, and to adapt the earlier classification to technological progress.

Under delegated powers, the Commission may specify the classification heading which applies to a particular good on application by national customs authorities or where the matter is brought to its attention by individual traders. The Commission can act by Regulation, and such Regulations cannot be challenged by aggrieved individuals, since they are not individual measures (Case 40/84 *Casteels PVBA* v. *Commission* [1985] ECR 667 – see also 9.10). The proper means of challenge against customs classification measures is therefore via the implementing decisions of national customs authorities which can be challenged in the national court, which may then make a reference to the Court of Justice on the legality of the underlying Community measure. Despite these implementing measures, however, there remain uncertainties and divergences in the application of the Nomenclature by the national customs authorities, in particular because it is not possible to envisage all the features of products in a written instrument. By Council Regulation 1715/90 (OJ 1990 L160/1) the Community therefore sought to bring about uniformity between the approaches taken by the Member States by regulating the information which customs authorities must provide. This should reduce the need for recourse to the Commission and to the Court of Justice for rulings on what are essentially questions of fact, not law.

12.4 Valuation

Customs duties are generally imposed on an *ad valorem* basis, making it necessary for a uniform system of valuation to be introduced which is not easily susceptible to abuse through the artificial lowering of the 'true' price. The original (1968) valuation system was based on the 1950 Customs Cooperation Council Valuation Convention, to which all the Member States were parties, but this was superseded by an agreement reached under Article VII of the GATT in the context of the Tokyo round of multilateral negotiations in 1979. Council Regulation 1224/80 (OJ 1980 L124/1) now provides for common rules on customs valuation and is based on the GATT Customs Valuation Code. The basic principle is that the value for customs purposes of imported merchandise should be based on the actual value of the imported merchandise on which duty is assessed, or of like merchandise, rather than on the notional value of merchandise of the same national origin or on arbitrary or ficititious values. This is a departure from the use of the notional normal price under the 1950 Convention.

The valuation system provides for five valuation methods which are successively applied to any given imported product until the appropriate method has been ascertained. Where none is found to be applicable, *any reasonable method of valuation* may be resorted to. The five basic methods have regard to:

– the transaction value of the goods (Article 3);

- the transaction value of identical goods (Article 4);
- the transaction value of similar goods (Article 5);
- the deductive value of the goods (Article 6);
- the computed value of the goods (Article 7).

The **transaction value** can only be applied where certain conditions are satisfied. The buyer and seller must not be related, or if they are related, the transaction value must be acceptable for customs purposes; no part of the proceeds of any subsequent sale must accrue directly or indirectly to the seller unless an appropriate adjustment has been made. Transaction value is based on the sale price at the time of entry. In contrast, **deductive value** is based on sale prices after entry, less certain expenses, and **computed value** is based on the costs of production and transport, etc., with an element for profit. Satisfactory documentation must be produced to allow customs valuation, and if this is not available there is likely to be a delay in valuation. National rules on the settlement of disputes apply, with references from national courts to the Court of Justice where necessary in order to settle points of Community law at issue.

There is a considerable body of case law in which the Court has been asked to judge which expenses are to be included in the customs valuation, and which are to be excluded. Goods are valued as if they were delivered to the buyer at the place of introduction into the customs territory of the Community, thus including transport outside the Community, but not inside (Case C-17/89 *HZA Frankfurt am Main-Ost* v. *Olivetti* [1990] ECR I-2301; [1992] 2 CMLR 859). Warehousing costs inside the Community are also excluded (Case 38/77 *Enka* v. *Inspecteur der Invoerrechten* [1977] ECR 2203), as are commission fees paid by an importer to an agent who obtains the goods to be imported from a producer or supplier in a third country, on behalf of the importer. In that case, the price for valuation purposes is the price paid by the producer or supplier to the agent, excluding the commission paid by the importer (Case C-199/90 *HZA Karlsruhe* v. *Hepp* 25.7.1991).

It can assumed that the normal task of the valuation system is to prevent the undervaluation of goods for customs purposes. Case 65/79 *Procureur de la République* v. *Chatain* ([1980] ECR 1345) raises the more unusual problem of how the rules should be applied to goods overvalued for customs purposes. Chatain, the French subsidiary of Sandoz, appeared to have used excessive invoice prices on goods acquired from the parent company, in order to transfer profits to Switzerland and to avoid paying French tax. It was prosecuted for making false declarations and unlawfully transferring capital abroad. The question arose whether the customs authorities were permitted under Community law to reduce the price. The Court ruled that the essential purpose of Regulation 803/68, which then governed customs valuation, was to prevent goods being undervalued, and that Community law could not therefore be used to reduce the value. AG Capotorti came to the opposite conclusion on the basis of a consideration of the relevant multilateral instruments.

12.5   Origin

In contrast to the position with regard to nomenclature and valuation, the rules governing the origin of goods are those put in place when the CCT was first set up in 1968 (Regulation 802/68 JO 1968 L148/1). This is in part because the Community legislation here is autonomous, there being no international agreement on this matter in 1968. The Regulation applies to the free movement of goods within the Community, and to non-preferential external trade. Other rules contained in specific external trade measures govern preferential trade, and these are often stricter. The right of the Council to derogate from the general rules was definitively established by the Court in Case 385/85 *SR Industries* v. *Administration des Douanes* [1986] ECR 2929).

There are particular rules for some agricultural products; for example, fish are classified as free from duty if they were 'taken from the sea' by vessels registered in a Member States and flying its flag. This phrase generated an intriguing case. In Case 100/84 *Commission* v. *UK* ([1985] ECR 1169) the British and Polish trawlers involved in joint fishing operations in the Baltic sea must have thought that they had found an ingenious way of evading the CCT. The British trawlers cast empty nets into the sea which were taken over by Polish trawlers. The Polish trawlers then trawled the nets, but did not take them on board. The ends of the nets were then passed back to the British trawlers and the fish were landed on to the British trawlers. The question arose as to when the fish were 'taken from the sea', for the purposes of deciding whether they were to be treated as British in origin. The Court concluded that the decisive act was that of locating the fish and separating them from the sea by netting, an act which was undertaken by the Polish trawlers. Consequently, the fish were treated as Polish, and liable to CCT.

The normal rule for non-agricultural products is that goods wholly obtained or produced in one country are considered as originating there; goods produced in two or more countries are regarded as originating in the country in which the last substantial process or operation that is economically justified is performed. This was defined in Case 41/75 *Überseehandel* v. *Handelskammer Hamburg* ([1977] ECR 41) as giving the product resulting from the operation 'its own properties and a composition or its own, which it did not possess before that procees or operation'. Change in tariff classification is a guide, but not decisive. Value added in the course of such an operation is also an important criterion. The rule is illustrated by Cases 34 and 114/78 *Yoshida* ([1979] ECR 115 and 151) which concerned the incorporation of Japanese-made sliders into slide fasteners in the Netherlands. It was held that the sliders were only an element in the completed product, and that the price of the sliders was hardly decisive in determining the final price of the slide fasteners. Consequently, the finished products were held to be of Community origin.

A more recent case addressed the problem of the assembly of individual components. In Case 26/88 *Brother International* v. *HZA Giessen* ([1989] ECR 4253) the Court held that the assembly of products may be sufficient to confer Community origin, but only if it constitutes a decisive stage of production. For example, it must require a skilled workforce, or specially equipped premises. Otherwise, the Court will also look at the additional value. In that case, 10% was held to be insufficient.

The operation of origin rules is clearly of considerable importance to multinational enterprises which seek to shift the various stages of production of finished products around the world in order to take advantage of cheap labour, favourable origin rules and preferential tariff treatment, as well as in order to shift profits to low tax economies (cf. Case 65/79 *Chatain*). In *Brother International* it was held that the fact that the assembly of a product is transferred to another country does not automatically raise the presumption that it has been transferred solely for the purpose of avoiding unfavourable origin rules, unless the transfer coincides with the entry into force of those rules, in which case the manufacturer must show other valid reasons for the transfer. The burden of proving origin lies on the importer, although a Member State may not require from importers more information about the origin of goods than they may reasonably be expected to know.

12.6   Harmonised Customs Legislation: Community Competence

It was stated at the outset that rules on nomenclature, valuation and origin are an indispensable element of the CCT. Surprisingly, the Treaty does not explicitly provide for the adoption of uniform rules on these matters, although without such rules the CCT would not in practice provide uniform external protection, and 'tariff-shopping' would be a common practice. Article 27 EC merely provides that:

> 'Before the end of the first stage, Member States shall, in so far as may be necessary, take steps to approximate their provisions laid down by law, regulation or administrative action in respect of customs matters. To this end the Commission shall make all appropriate recommendations to the Member States.' .

This provision is clearly insufficient to achieve the requisite level of harmonisation to make the effective functioning of the CCT a reality. Case 8/73 *HZA Bremerhaven* v. *Massey Ferguson* ([1973 ECR 897) established clearly both the case for harmonised customs legislation (as opposed to simply relying on the international customs instruments to which all the Member States were party), and also the necessity to have recourse to the residual law-making power in Article 235 EC as the legal basis for the Regulations deemed necessary to introduce uniform external protection. Article 100 EC – the only general harmonising provision then available – permitted only the adoption of Directives, not Regulations, and these are not suitable legal instruments for the level of unifomity in practice required. The Court accepted the use of Article 235 in that case as the legal basis for Regulation 803/68 on customs valuation (the predecessor of Regulation 1224/80), thus recognising the principle that Article 235 may be used where powers exist elsewhere in the Treaty, but are insufficient to achieve the Community objective in question.

However, the more recent trend has been towards adopting harmonised customs legislation, as well as other measures concerned with external trade policy, increasingly on the basis of Article 113 EC alone. This provision empowers the Council to give effect to the CCP through measures adopted by a qualified majority. The case law of the Court has shifted towards reducing the scope for application of the general law-making power in Article 235 in favour of stressing the availability of specific law-making powers (Case 45/86 *Commission* v. *Council (Generalised Tariff Preferences)* [1987] ECR 1493). The degree of discretion to choose Article 235 left to the Council in the early case law is now no longer allowed.

12.7   The Exclusive Nature of the CCT

The CCT provides for uniform tariffs in all 12 Member States. Consequently, it would be contrary to the system established by the CCT for the Member States to be permitted unilaterally to impose additional tariffs, or charges having equivalent effect to customs duties ('CEEs') on imported products. In Cases 37 and 38/73 *Sociaal Fonds voor de Diamantarbeiders* v. *NV Indiamex* ([1973] ECR 1609) the Court considered the validity of contributions to the Belgian Social Fund for diamond workers, payable by importers of rough diamonds and calculated on the basis of the diamonds imported. The Court held that although no specific mention is made of CEEs in the provisions dealing with the CCT, that does not mean that they are not prohibited. In fact they are at variance with the objective of the CCT which is to create uniformity of protection, and are therefore prohibited. The Court held (at p.1622) that the CCT:

'is intended to achieve an equalisation of customs charges levied at the frontiers of the Community on products imported from third countries, in order to avoid any deflection of trade in relations with those countries and any distortion of free internal circulation or of competitive conditions.'

Difficulties arise in practice with applying these principles to health inspections carried out at the Community's frontiers with the outside world, and to charges levied for such inspections. Satisfactory common rules for these are still being evolved, and in the interim Member States have been able to carry out, and charge for, inspections which would be compulsory in intra-Community trade and would be carried out on the basis of harmonised rules (Case 70/77 *Simmenthal* v. *Italian Finance Administration* [1978] ECR 1453). The fees charged can even exceed those carried out for similar inspections on Community goods, in order to avoid more favourable treatment of imported goods (Case 30/79 *Land Berlin* v. *Wigei* [1980] ECR 151). Even where the inspection undertaken is not one uniformly undertaken by all the Member States it may still be charged for, at least in so far as the charge corresponds to the cost of the inspection (Case 1/83 *Intercontinentale Fleischhandelsgesellschaft* v. *Freistaat Bayern* [1984] ECR 349). The Community is now moving towards harmonised veterinary checks and health inspections at the external frontiers (see Council Directive 90/675 OJ 1990 L373/1).

The Court has also been called upon to address the possible application of Article 95 EC in the external trade context. Article 95 prohibits discriminatory internal taxation; the question arose in Case 193/85 *Cooperativa Co-frutta* ([1987] ECR 2085) whether Article 95 applied to measures which discriminate against products from non-Community countries. It appeared from Case 148/77 *Hansen* v. *HZA Flensburg* ([1978] ECR 1787) that Article 95 was to be interpreted strictly as not applying to third country products, since they are not explicitly mentioned. However, in *Co-frutta*, which concerned an Italian tax on the consumption of fresh bananas which was imposed on bananas originating in Colombia and imported into Italy via Benelux, the Court held that Article 95 precludes the charging of a consumer tax on certain imported fruit where it may protect domestic fruit production. Such a tax may not be imposed on goods which are in free circulation – that is goods which have been imported into another Member State from a third country – which must be assimilated in all respects to goods originating in the Community. On the other hand, the position was recently clarified in respect of goods imported *directly* from third countries into the Member State where the tax is imposed. In Cases C-228, etc./90 *Simba SpA* v. *Italian Minister of Finance* (9.6.1992), which concerned the same Italian tax on bananas, the Court held that Article 95 does not apply to goods imported *directly* into the Member State where the tax is imposed, and that the application of such a tax is not incompatible with the general principles governing the Common Commercial Policy. It may, however, conflict with arrangements made on the basis of international agreements which the Community has formed with particular third countries, in which case the individual instruments must be scrutinised. The question then arises whether those agreements contain measures which are justiciable in national courts at the instance of individuals (see Case 104/81 *Kupferberg* [1982] ECR 3641 and 8.8). If the provisions of the agreement are justiciable, then they will prevail over conflicting national legislation.

12.8   CCT: Exemptions or Reductions

The Council has powers under Article 28 (unilateral measures) and Article 113 (bilateral or multilateral measures) to establish exemptions from or reductions of the CCT. The most important examples include:

- generalised tariff preferences for certain goods originating in developing countries, in particular those ACP (Africa-Caribbean-Pacific) countries linked to the Community through the Lomé Convention;
- 'duty free' goods, that is small quantities of goods in travellers' personal luggage intended for personal use;
- certain educational, scientific and cultural materials, imported for commercial purposes. Since Case 294/81 *Control Data* v. *Commission* ([1983] ECR 911) the Commission can no longer have a blanket policy of refusing duty-free import for computers, since it must give reasons for each refusal explaining why a particular good does not satisfy the criteria established by the Council;
- inward processing; customs duties may be reimbursed or not levied where goods are imported simply for the purposes of processing followed by re-export.

12.9 Evidence of the Right to Free Movement for Goods in Free Circulation

This has traditionally been provided by appropriate documentation. Community provisions have for some time provided for a Single Administrative Document to simplify arrangements. Uniformity now also exists in relation to transit across the Community. A single measure (Council Regulation 2760/90 OJ 1990 L262/1) was introduced to cover external transit (transit across the Community for third country goods not in free circulation) and internal transit (transit by Community goods or goods in free circulation). This avoided the need for repeated inspections at internal frontiers. The system provided for goods to be sealed and accompanied by an appropriate declaration. The declaration and the seal were all that needed to be inspected at the each frontier. When internal frontiers have been eliminated altogether, however, transit documentation will no longer be necessary, as movement within the Community will be akin to movement within an existing national market.

12.10 The Common Commercial Policy (CCP)

Article 3(b) EC provides for the establishment of a Common Commercial Policy ('CCP'). Aside from the contribution to global free trade highlighted in Articles 18 and 110 EC, the only statement regarding the objectives of the CCP is that it is to achieve the application of 'uniform principles', in a non-exhaustive list of areas contained in Article 113 EC. It covers:

'changes in tariff rates, the conclusion of tariff and trade agreements, the achievement of uniformity in measures of liberalisation, export policy and measures to protect trade such as those to be taken in the event of dumping or subsidies.'

Thus there is no definition of a CCP in Article 113, only examples of what it includes. In *Opinion 1/75* [1975] ECR 1355, an opinion adopted on the basis of Article 228 EEC, the Court indicated that the CCP would contain the same elements as the external trade policy of a state. It elaborated upon this point in *Opinion 1/78* on the international agreement on natural rubber negotiated under the aegis of the UNCTAD (United Nations Conference on Trade and Development) ([1979] ECR 2871), when it stated that the CCP may include trade regulation as well as trade liberalisation measures. The Court held (at p. 2913):

'Although it may be thought that at the time when the Treaty was drafted liberalisation of trade was the dominant idea, the Treaty nevertheless does not form a barrier to the possibility of the Community developing a commercial policy aiming at a regulation of the world market for certain products rather than at a mere liberalisation of trade.'

The CCP also comprises rules which protect the Community's markets against dumping and illicit commercial practices by third countries. The extent of the defensive measures which the Community may take against damaging commercial practices such as dumping are derived from the GATT, and are given concrete form in Regulation 2423/88 on dumping (OJ 1988 L209/1) and Regulation 2461/84 which deals with combatting other illicit commercial practices (OJ 1984 L252/1). In other words, the Community is permitted under international trade law to impose, and in fact does impose, restrictions on imports which abuse the right to free trade.

12.11   The Implementation of the CCP

The Community may have recourse to unilateral, bilateral and multilateral measures to implement the CCP. Unilateral measures will be adopted under Article 113 which provides for the Commission to submit proposals, which the Council may adopt by a qualified majority. In practice, although it is not obliged to do so, the Council does submit many proposals for consultation by the Parliament and the ECOSOC. The new Community Customs Code provides an example of a unilateral Community measure within the context of the CCP. Bilateral and multilateral trade measures will take the form of international agreements and are also envisaged in Article 113. As amended by the Treaty of Maastricht, Article 113(3) provides:

'Where agreements with one or more States or international organisations need to be negotiated, the Commission shall make recommendations to the Council, which shall authorise the Commission to open the necessary negotiations.

The Commission shall conduct these negotiations in consultation with a special committee appointed by the Council to assist the Commission in this task and within the framework of such directives as the Council may issue to it.

The relevant provisions of Article 228 shall apply.'

Article 228 EC lays down the details regarding the conclusion of international agreements, where it is the Council which acts on behalf of the Community. Normally the Council acts by a qualified majority, unless it is a field where internal rules would require unanimity, or the agreement in question is an association agreement involving reciprocal rights and obligations, common action and special procedures, governed by Article 238 EC. The parallelism between internal and external powers and procedures means that in areas covered by the CCP under Article 113, a qualified majority will suffice. Agreements under Article 113(3) do not require consultation of the Parliament; however, where Parliamentary consultation, cooperation or co-decision is mandated in the internal field, the Parliament is required to deliver an opinion before an international agreement can be concluded in this field. Association agreements require the assent of the Parliament.

The CCP confers exclusive competence on the Community to conclude international trade agreements. This was conclusively established by the Court in *Opinion 1/75* on the draft understanding on a local cost standard in relation to exports on credit terms, drawn up under the auspices of the OECD. In practice, many international trade agreements are concluded using a so-called 'mixed agreement', whereby both the Community and the Member States participate. In the case of the natural rubber agreement (*Opinion 1/78*) it was accepted that although the issues covered by the agreement fell within the scope of the CCP, it was the Member States which would bear financial responsibility for the implementation of the agreement, and so they must be allowed to conclude the agreement alongside the Community.

The CCP should have been completed by the end of the transitional period (1.1.1970). In practice it was not. For example, there are not yet comprehensive and uniform rules on imports from third countries. Some Member States continue to impose quotas on the import of certain goods from certain third countries, particularly in the sensitive markets of textiles and clothing, consumer electronic goods and agricultural goods. The Member States do not have a uniform view on the extent of the desirable liberalisation of trade, and consequently it has proved difficult to secure agreement on the substitution of national import restrictions with Community import rules.

Consequently, although the Community competence is exclusive it has not been fully exercised and the CCP is incomplete. Since a first Decision adopted in 1969 (Decision 69/494 JO 1969 L326/39 – renewed annually thereafter, most recently by Council Decision 92/397, OJ 1992 L220/33), the Member States have been able to extend, with the Council's authorisation, national commercial policy measures which are not contrary to the CCP. This structure of authorisations was held in Case 174/84 *Bulk Oil* v. *Sun International* ([1986] ECR 559) to justify the restrictions imposed by the UK Government on exports of oil to certain third countries, since Regulation 2603/69 on common rules for exports (JO 1969 L324/25) which creates the principle of freedom of export does not provide an exhaustive set of rules extending to all products.

As regards rules on imports, the CCP comprises rules derived from three sources. First, there are the Community's unilaterally adopted rules on imports, which are based on Regulation 288/82 (OJ 1982 L35/1). This provides that imports into the Community are free from restrictions but applies only where more restrictive rules are not applicable. Thus, for example, imports from the state-trading countries in central and eastern Europe were long restricted and excluded from the benefits of trade liberalisation, but these restrictions were dropped in the wake of the establishment of official trade relations between the Community and COMECON in 1988 and the collapse of the communist regimes. Special rules also apply to imports of textiles, which are in part governed by multilateral international agreements. This is the second source of the CCP. The Community also has bilateral agreements with many European and non-European agreements which govern trading relations with those countries.

The third source of the rules on imports are unilateral rules maintained in place by the Member States under the authorisation system referred to above. For example, although in principle quotas on imports should only be imposed by the Community, in practice, national quotas are still used, although they are gradually being dismantled.

Moreover, there are no restrictions on the imposition of trading rules other than quotas (measures having equivalent effect to quantitative restrictions – MEEQRs) on imports from third countries. In Case 86/75 *EMI* v. *CBS* ([1976] ECR 871) the Court held, when considering the version of the common rules on imports then in place, that there is no obligation on the Community to extend to trade with third countries the binding principles which facilitate interstate trade within the Community, in particular the prohibition on MEEQRs contained in Article 30. The principle of mutual recognition of technical standards does not apply to third country goods. Thus while there is a presumption that a good validly produced and marketed in one Member State may be marketed in the other eleven Member States without having to comply with local technical standards, unless there are overriding public policy interests which mandate the imposition of local standards (see 14.8), the standards under which third country products are produced and marketed are not recognised. Such a product must comply either with the standards imposed by at least one Member State or with harmonised Community standards, where these exist. Even where an agreement between the

Community and a third country contains what appears to be a prohibition on MEEQRs on trade in goods, this does not necessarily have the same meaning as it does in internal trade. This is because the object of such an agreement – in Case 270/80 *Polydor* v. *Harlequin* ([1982] ECR 379) the free trade agreement with Portugal then in force – is not to create a single market, but to liberalise certain aspects of trading relations.

The Agreement to create a European Economic Area (EEA), concluded between the Community and the EFTA countries is a significant departure from this principle. Here the intention is in fact to assimilate trade relations with these third states to trade relations within the Community, and the Agreement is structured with this in view although the arrangement does not extend to creating a full customs union. However, as the Court made clear in particular in its first Opinion under Article 228 on the compatibility of the EEA Agreement with the system of Community law (*Opinion 1/91* [1992] 1 CMLR 245), novel arrangements such as the EEA intended to accommodate countries which desire closer trade relations with the Community without the burdens of full membership must not be allowed to damage the fabric of the Community's legal order, in particular the principle of the uniform application of Community law. Nothing short of full accession, therefore, can bring all the benefits of the internal market.

12.12 The Incomplete Nature of the CCP: The Possibility of Protective Measures

There is evidence even within the Treaty itself of ambivalence about the feasibility of creating a CCP. Article 115 EC provides:

'In order to ensure that the execution of measures of commercial policy taken in accordance with this Treaty by any Member State is not obstructed by deflection of trade, or where differences between such measures lead to economic difficulties in one or more Member States, the Commission shall recommend the methods for the requisite cooperation between Member States. Failing this, the Commission may authorise Member States to take the necessary protective measures, the conditions and details of which it shall determine.

In case of urgency, Member States shall request authorisation to take the necessary measures themselves from the Commission, which shall take a decision as soon as possible; the Member States concerned shall then notify the measures to other Member States. The Commission may decide at any time that the Member States concerned shall amend or abolish the measures in question.

In the selection of such measures, priority shall be given to those which cause the least disturbance to the functioning of the common market.'

However, the interpretations of this Article given by the Court of Justice have gradually increased the restrictions upon the autonomy of the

Member States, in that it has stressed that Article 115 is a derogation from an exclusive if incomplete CCP, and as such must be interpreted strictly. The basic principles were stated in Case 41/76 *Donckerwolcke* v. *Procureur de la République* ([1976] ECR 1921).

Donckerwolcke imported from Belgium into France consignments of synthetic fibres which had been imported from Syria and Lebanon into Belgium. Customs duties and other formalities had been complied with in Belgium and therefore the goods were in free circulation. Consequently, the documents supplied by the Belgian customs authorities stated the origin of the goods to be the Belgo–Luxembourg Economic Union. The French customs authorities considered that Donckerwolcke had made a false declaration of origin and thus had evaded the requirement of an import licence, which was required for such importations. The applicants lodged an appeal against the heavy penalties which were imposed upon them, and the appellate court referred questions to the Court of Justice regarding the compatibility of the French law with the CCP. The Court stressed the incomplete but exclusive nature of the CCP, and acknowledged that there remained, between the Member States, differences in commercial policy capable of bringing about deflections in trade and of causing economic difficulties. It was these problems which Article 115 was designed to alleviate. However, as an exception to the principle of free movement, the derogation in Article 115 must be strictly interpreted, and the actions of a Member State required, in such a case, *prior* authorisation from the Commission. Since the Member States could be authorised under Article 115 to maintain in force import restrictions, it followed that they were entitled to continue to demand declarations of actual origin in order that they could operate the import restrictions effectively.

Under the terms of Article 115, the derogation may only be used to protect national commercial policy measures 'taken in accordance with this Treaty'. This includes not only national commercial policy mesures explicitly authorised by the Council under Decision 69/494 and its successors, but also national measures which are taken in implementation of the Community's own CCP. In 12.13, it will be seen that the CCP itself has tended, until very recently, to perpetuate at Community level measures which are apt to maintain in place the divisions between the Member States. Authorisation under Article 115 normally has two stages; at the first stage, a Member State may institute 'intra-Community surveillance', allowing it to monitor the flow of trade through a system of declarations of origin and import licences. When the Commission is satisfied that the conditions in Article 115 are satisfied it may authorise protective measures, such as the right to refuse import licences. The authorisation required can only be given if the Commission has taken into account that Article 115 is a derogation from the principles of free movement, and must therefore be narrowly interpreted. The measures taken must be subject to the principle of proportionality: that is, they must correspond to a real need, they must be necessary to achieve the end in question, and they must be no more restrictive than is necessary for that purpose. In other words, the measures taken must be those which cause least disturbance to the common market. The Commission must give reasons for its authorisation Decision.

A frustrated importer will be able to challenge the Commission's authorisation Decision (which will be addressed to the Member State) if, for example, it has already applied for an import licence when the Decision is taken. In such a case it is directly and individually concerned by the Decision within the meaning of Article 173 EC, as part of a closed class (see 9.8). If, on the other hand, the importer is not so identified, it will have no standing to sue, even if it has complained previously to the Commission about its difficulties in relation to imports, thereby identifying itself as having a particular concern (Case 206/87 *Lefebvre Frère et Soeur* v. *Commission* [1989] ECR 275). In that case, only an action in the national court against implementing measures is possible.

In Case 29/75 *Kaufhof* v. *Commission* ([1976] ECR 431) the Court annulled a Commission Decision authorising Germany to exclude certain tinned green beans from China, which a German importer had applied to import. The Court held that Article 115 was to be strictly interpreted, and that the Commission must review the reasons put forward by the Member State in order to justify the measures of commercial policy which it wished to introduce. The Commission should also take into account the size and significance of the threatened imports, at least when considering whether the authorisation should apply to transactions which had already commenced. Case 1/84R *Ilford* v. *Commission* ([1984] ECR 423) shows the readiness of the Court to order interim measures suspending an Article 115 authorisation Decision, in that case because it was not clear that there was in fact a measure of Italian commercial policy to protect.

When enforcing the measures of commercial policy authorised by the Commission, the Member States may impose penalties for failure to disclose the necessary information, but these must be proportionate to the administrative nature of the offence (Case 212/88 *Levy* [1989] ECR 3511).

12.13 The Problem of Quotas

Community competence under the CCP includes the right to regulate Community trade relations with third countries through the imposition of quotas or quantatitive restrictions on imports, at least in so far as this is compatible with principles of international trade law contained in the GATT. The Community also gives duty free quotas to certain third country goods under the preferential trading regimes which apply between the Community and certain developing countries under the Lomé Convention. In practice, Community quota systems have traditionally been little more than an aggregation of the existing national quota regimes, with Community quotas frequently divided into national sub-quotas and the divisions between the Member States maintained in place through frequent recourse to Article 115. Turning national quotas into Community quotas has given them a camouflage of acceptability, creating the veneer of a common policy where in fact no uniformity exists. For the national sub-quotas are not in fact mere devices of administrative convenience required for the effective implementation of a CCP measure, but represent the reality of the measure – the maintenance of national interests. In a series of judgments the Court has gradually gone behind the camouflage of acceptability and has begun to break down the practice of national sub-quotas within Community quotas.

Case 218/82 *Commission* v. *Council* ([1983] ECR 4063) concerned the quota system in place for preferential imports of rum from the Carribean under the Second Lomé Convention. For historical reasons, the UK was allocated two-thirds of the total quota and was instructed by the implementing Regulation to take steps to ensure that the volume of rum imported did not exceed its domestic consumption requirements. The Commission challenged this Regulation before the Court arguing that this was tantamount to an export ban in internal trade, which is prohibited by Article 34 EC. The Court rejected the Commission's interpretation of the provision on the facts, but indicated that if it had amounted to an export ban it would have been incompatible with the system of the Treaty. The Council cannot legislate to abrogate the principle of the free movement of goods, and thus the division of a Community quota into national sub-quotas is permissible only if it does not hinder the free movement of goods.

Subsequent judgments have built on this assessment: in Case 288/83 *Commission* v. *Ireland* (Potatoes) ([1985] ECR 1761) the Court held that Ireland could not unilaterally ban imports of potatoes originating in non-Member States which were in free circulation in the UK, by relying on the quota system. Nor could Italy unilaterally impede the export to Germany of frozen beef imported under its quota (Case 199/84 *Procuratore della Repubblica* v. *Migliorini and Fischl* [1985] ECR 3317). In both cases, an Article 115 authorisation would be required.

Surprisingly, however, in Case 59/84 *Tezi-Textiel* v. *Commission* ([1986] ECR 887), the Court appeared remarkably supine in the face of the continued existence of national sub-quotas. In that case, the Commission had authorised the Netherlands not to permit the importation of cotton trousers originating in Macau and in free circulation in Italy. The Decision was taken in order to allow the Netherlands to protect the quota allocated to the Benelux countries within the context of the Community quota for such products under the Regulation on textile imports then in force. The Court held that although the Regulation, which governed the import into the Community of textiles from third countries which were signatories of the international Multi-Fibre Agreement, was a 'step towards a common commercial policy based, in accordance with Article 113(1), on uniform principles,' it did not completely eliminate existing disparities between the Member States with respect to conditions of importation. Against the advice of its Advocate General, AG VerLoren van Themaat, the Court held that the division of the Community quota into national sub-quotas was permissible and that the use of Article 115 to protect these sub-quotas is also allowed, so long as uniform conditions of importation do not exist.

Since that time, the range of circumstances in which it would be permissible for national sub-quotas to be retained has come under attack before the Court. In Case 51/87 *Commission* v. *Council (GSP)* ([1988] ECR 5459) the dispute concerned the Regulations governing the Generalised System of Preferences (GSP) which established the duty-free quotas for imports of industrial goods and textiles from certain developing countries during 1987. These Regulations are adopted on an annual basis, and until 1987 had always contained fixed national sub-quotas. In its proposal for an industrial products Regulation, the Commission argued that national sub-quotas were no longer necessary and that they jeopardised the unity of the customs union in the Community's relations with third countries. The Council nevertheless enacted the Regulation with sub-quotas. For the textiles Regulation, the Commission accepted the principle of sub-quotas, given the sensitive nature of the products in question (see *Tezi-Textiel*), but proposed that the quotas should not be fixed and that a mechanism for the transfer of unused shares should be instituted at Community level. The Council rejected this and enacted a Regulation with fixed national quotas, and no transfer mechanism. The Commission successfully challenged both Regulations before the Court, arguing that the frameworks it had proposed should have been used. The Court considered that the Council had provided no reasons for continuing to use the sub-quota system for industrial products, fifteen years after it was first introduced, and that a sub-quota system has the disadvantage of increasing not decreasing distortions and deflections of trade since it encourages importers to seek indirect ways of importing into the desired destination Member State. For textile products the Court accepted the principle of national sub-quotas, but agreed with the proposal for a transfer mechanism which could, like the Community quota for industrial products, easily be administered by the Commission using the resources of new technology. Both Regulations were therefore annulled for breach of the Treaty.

Since 1989, the annual Regulations have started to take account of the changes required by the judgment. The Regulations for industrial and agricultural products (the latter was surprisingly not challenged by the Commission in 1987) are now based on Community quotas, but the textiles Regulations have continued to use national sub-quotas (see now Council Regulation 3917/92, OJ 1992 L3961/1 on the GSP for industrial products for 1993 which is based on fixed duty-free amounts).

The gradual dismantlement of national sub-quotas is only one part of the equation; the second part is the continued use of Article 115 EC. It had been hoped that the Treaty of Maastricht would see the abolition of Article 115. In fact, its text was only slightly amended to remove any possibility that Member States might take unilateral protective measures.

It remains an unresolved question whether, notwithstanding the provisions of the Treaty of Maastricht, recourse to Article 115 is legally permissible after January 1 1993 and the abolition of internal frontiers in accordance with Article 7A EC. In practice, the onus lies upon the Commission to exercise restraint in the use of Article 115, and in its Fifth Report on the Implementation of the White Paper on the Internal Market (Com (90) 90) the Commission commented upon the fact that recourse to Article 115 was now at a lower level. Nonetheless, the *Official Journal* continues to provide examples of Article 115 authorisations (e.g. Commission Decision 91/18 OJ 1991 L12/29 allowing certain Member States to continue apply intra-Community surveillance in particular to imports from countries in the Far East), and textiles continue to be one of the areas in which this Article is most frequently used.

Summary

1 The Common Customs Tariff (CCT) is the main policy instrument of the Common Commercial Policy (CCP), under which the Community has exclusive competence to regulate external trade relations. The Community has an obligation to contribute to global free trade.
2 The operation of the CCT is dependent upon the existence and uniform enforcement of common rules on the classification of goods, on customs valuation and on origin.
3 Community competence to adopt harmonised customs legislation has been based on Article 235 EC, and, more recently, Article 113 EC.
4 Member States may not unilaterally impose charges having equivalent effect to customs duties on imports from third states which destroy the uniformity of the CCT.
5 The CCP is based on Article 113; it is to be based on 'uniform principles' and measures are adopted by the Community acting unilaterally, or in bilateral or multilateral cooperation. So far it remains incomplete. In practice, national commercial policies continue to play an important role in framing the conditions in which goods are imported into and exported out of the Community.
6 So long as the CCP remains incomplete, Member States will retain the right under Article 115 EC to take protective measures against imports of third country goods in free circulation in other Member States. This possibility undermines the ability of the Community to create a single internal market, since this must cover both Community and third country goods.
7 As an exception to the principle of free movement, Article 115 must be narrowly applied by the Commission, and the Court has restricted its use, particularly in the context of quota systems.

Questions

1 In what way do the objectives of the CCT and CCP differ from the objectives of the Community rules which govern the operation of the internal market?

2 What contribution does the Community's legislation on classification, valuation and origin make to the effective implementation of the CCT?

3 To what extent do the CCT and the CCP exclude the imposition of unilateral trade measures by the Member States?

4 Is the continued application of Article 115 consistent with the objective of completing the internal market?

5 What steps has the Court taken to emphasise the exclusive nature of the CCP? Is the decision in *Tezi-Textiel* a retrograde step, or is it justifiable?

Workshop

'Trade in Turtles' (Teenage Mutant Ninja (or Hero) Turtles) merchandise is now a multi-million, multinational operation.'

In response to heavy pressure from an organisation representing the interests of parents, concerned that an average of 5–10% of parental income is being spent on 'Turtles' merchandise, the Commission adopted (fictitious) Regulation 7000/92 banning the import of all 'Turtles' merchandise from third countries into the EEC during the three months leading up to Christmas 1992. The UK, in addition, banned imports of 'Turtles' merchandise already in free circulation in the other Member States into the UK.

Would it be legitimate for the Commission and the UK government to act in this way? Outline the remedies which would be available against the Commission and the UK government to (a) an importer of 'Turtles' goods from Taiwan into the European Community and (b) an importer of 'Turtles' goods from Italy into the UK.

Further Reading

Burrows (1992) 'The risks of widening without deepening', 17 *European Law Review*, 352.

Cremona (1990) 'The Completion of the Internal Market and the Incomplete Commercial Policy of the European Community', 15 *European Law Review*, 283.

Eeckhout (1991) 'The External Dimension of the EC Internal Market – A Portrait', 15 *World Competition*, 5.

Green, Hartley and Usher (1991), Chs 1 and 2.

O'Keeffe (1992) 'The Agreement on the European Economic Area', *Legal Issues of European Integration*, 1/92, 1.

Oliver and Yataganas (1987) 'The Harmonised System of Customs Classification', 7 *Yearbook Of European Law*, 113.

Pinder (1991) 'From Common Tariff to Great Civilian Power', in Pinder (1991).

Schueren (1991) 'Customs Classification: One of the Cornerstones of the Single European Market, but one which cannot be exhaustively regulated', 28 *Common Market Law Review*, 855.

Usher (1986) 'The Single Market and Goods Imported from Third Countries', 6 *Yearbook of European Law*, 159.

Voorst and Van Dam (1988) 'Europe 1992: Free Movement of Goods in the Wider Context of a Changing Europe', 25 *Common Market Law Review*, 693.

13 The Internal Aspects of the Customs Union

13.1 Introduction

This chapter examines the prohibitions on fiscal barriers to intra-Community trade in goods which apply under the European Community Treaty. There are two types of fiscal barriers: tariff barriers (Articles 9–17 EC) and systems of discriminatory taxation (Article 95 EC). The two prohibitions are mutually exclusive, but complementary in the sense they are both concerned with fiscal obstacles to trade. A charge is either a customs duty or a charge having equivalent effect to a customs duty (CEE), or it is part of a system of internal taxation which may be discriminatory. In Case 57/65 *Lütticke* v. *HZA Saarlouis* ([1966] ECR 205) the Court held (at p.211):

> 'Articles 12 and 13 on the one hand and Article 95 on the other cannot be applied jointly to one and the same case. Charges having an effect equivalent to customs duties on the one hand and internal taxation on the other hand are governed by different systems.'

The Treaty provides for an absolute prohibition on customs duties and CEEs. The Court has elaborated a comprehensive definition which is qualified by few exceptions. Many of the cases are, however, concerned with the borderline between Articles 12 and 95, in particular in the context of taxes which are imposed on all goods, but are reimbursed in full or in part in respect of domestically produced goods. The Treaty does not prohibit systems of internal taxation. It requires them, however, to be neutral in their treatment of imported and domestic goods in order to avoid distortions of competition within the market; it is therefore the concept of 'discrimination' which is the key to the application of Article 95.

13.2 The Nature and Scope of the Prohibition on Customs Duties and CEEs

The prohibition on customs duties and CEEs between the Member States is a 'fundamental principle of the Common Market' (Cases 80 and 81/77 *Ramel* v. *Receveur des Douanes* ([1978] ECR 927 at p.945). The prohibition is stated clearly in Article 9(1) EC:

'The Community shall be based on a customs union which shall cover all trade in goods and which shall involve the prohibition between Member States of customs duties on imports and exports and of all charges having equivalent effect.'

The Member States committed themselves in Article 13 EC to the progressive elimination of customs duties and CEEs, in accordance with a timetable contained in Article 14 EC. Customs duties were eliminated as between the original Six from July 1968, eighteen months ahead of schedule. Customs duties between the existing Member States and new Member States have likewise been eliminated in accordance with timetables contained in the various Acts of Accession. The end of 1992 marked the conclusion of the transitional period bringing Spain and Portugal fully into the customs union. Customs duties on exports and CEEs on exports were prohibited as from the end of the first stage of the transitional period (31.12.1961). Article 9(2) EC extends the protection of these prohibitions to goods originating in the Member States and to goods in free circulation (see Chapter 12).

New customs duties were prohibited from the inception of the Community (and subsequently for the new Member States from the moment of accession) by the standstill clause in Article 12 EC:

'Member States shall refrain from introducing between themselves any new customs duties on imports or exports or any charges having equivalent effect, and from increasing those which they already apply in their trade with each other.'

It is this provision which gave the Court of Justice the first opportunity to espouse the principle of the justiciability of Community obligations in national courts. It will be recalled that it was Article 12 which the Court was called upon to interpret in Case 26/62 *Van Gend en Loos* v. *Nederlandse Administratie der Belastingen* ([1963] ECR 1). The Court held that the aggrieved importers must be able to rely upon Article 12 in the Dutch courts in order to argue that an increase in customs duties after the entry into force of the Treaty resulting from the reclassification of goods under a new tariff heading carrying a higher tariff rate was prohibited and could not be enforced. The requirement under Article 13(2) that existing CEEs should be abolished has also been held to be directly effective, as from the end of the transitional period (1.1.70) (Case 77/72 *Capolongo* v. *Azienda Agricolo Maya* [1973] ECR 611).

The prohibitions in Articles 9–16 EC bind the Member States unconditionally. According to the Court in Cases 90 and 91/63 *Commission* v. *Luxembourg and Belgium (Dairy Products)* ([1964] ECR 625 at p. 633) 'any possible exception, which in any event must be strictly construed, must be clearly laid down'. There are no general exceptions allowable in the public interest such as those set out in Article 36 EC which permit derogations from the prohibition on non-tariff barriers to trade (Articles 30 and 34 EC). The only possible exceptions are those concerned with charges for services to importers and exporters which the Member States may legitimately impose and charges for inspections prescribed by Community law. The prohibitions also bind the institutions themselves. In *Ramel*, a Council Regulation which authorised the Member States to impose charges on intra-Community trade in wine was held invalid on the grounds that it was incompatible with the principles of the customs union, although it was adopted within the context of the Common Agricultural Policy (CAP) and the common organisation of the market in wine.

It might have been thought that more than twenty years after the expiry of the original transitional period the prohibition on tariff barriers would be of largely historical interest. There are indeed now very few cases in which customs duties *per se* are at issue. An exception is Case C-343/89 *Witzemann* v. *HZA München* ([1990] ECR I-4477) in which the Court held that it was not permissible for Germany to impose customs duties on imports of forged money from Italy. Repressive measures against the crime of forgery, which are, of course, permitted in such circumstances, represent the only penalty which Member States can impose. In contrast, a steady stream of cases on CEEs continues to reach the Court.

13.3 The Scope and Nature of CEEs

In Case 24/68 *Commission* v. *Italy (Statistical Levy)* ([1969] ECR 193 the Court elaborated a definition of a CEE which has since become standard. For example, in Case 132/82 *Commission* v. *Belgium* ([1983] ECR 1649) it held (at p.1658):

> 'according to the established case law of the Court, any pecuniary charge, however small and whatever its designation and mode of application, which is imposed unilaterally on goods by reason of the fact that they cross a frontier and which is not a customs duty in the strict sense, constitutes a charge having equivalent effect within the meaning of Articles 9, 12, 13 and 16 of the Treaty, even if it is not levied by the State.'

It is the fact that a charge has been imposed as a result of goods crossing a frontier which makes it a CEE; it does not actually have to be imposed at the frontier. Thus charges made in the context of customs clearance occurring in special warehouses in the interior of the country fall within the prohibition (Case 132/82 *Commission* v. *Belgium*).

The definition set out above must not, however, be regarded as exhaustive. In a recent case, the Court held that a charge imposed on goods entering a particular region of a Member State was a CEE. In Case C-163/90 *Administration des douanes* v. *Legros* (16.7.1992) the Court condemned a charge imposed by the French customs authorities on goods entering Réunion, which as a *Département outre mer* (DOM) is part of Metropolitan France and therefore of the Community, although it is situated in the Southern Hemisphere. Since the charge was imposed only on goods imported into the DOMs, and not on goods produced there, the Court refused to classify it as part of a system of internal taxation. Moreover, even though it was imposed also on goods originating in other parts of France, and could not, therefore, satisfy the definition set out above, the Court held that it was a CEE. It argued that such a regional charge would represent just as serious an obstacle to intra-Community trade as a tax imposed at a frontier, and that it should be classed as a CEE because it damaged the 'unity of the Community customs territory'.

The fact that the charge is not imposed for the benefit of the State, or that it has no discriminatory or protectionist effects, is irrelevant. There is no *de minimis* rule; even though the charge may be so small that it does not lead to an increase in prices, the prohibition still applies. As the Court has argued (e.g. Case 18/87 *Commission* v. *Germany (Live Animals)* [1988] ECR 5427), even small charges constitute obstacles to free movement which are 'aggravated by the resulting administrative formalities'. In other words, it could be suggested that the Court has been encouraging the Member States to reduce the inspections and checks that they make at frontiers, many of which have, in the absence of Community harmonisation, been permitted under the health exception in Article 36 EC, by preventing them from charging for such formalities. Member States are less likely to maintain in place bureaucracy at the frontiers if it is not self-financing.

The absence of equivalent or competing domestic goods is likewise irrelevant to the existence of a CEE. For example, in Cases 2 and 3/69 *Sociaal Fonds voor de Diamantarbeiders* v. *Brachfeld and Chougol Diamond Co* ([1969] ECR 211) a charge imposed by Belgium on all imports of diamonds was held to be a CEE, even though it was intended for social purposes (to provide social benefits for diamond workers) and despite the absence of a Belgian diamond industry which might benefit from the imposition of the charge.

13.4 The Prohibition on CEEs on Exports

In Case 7/68 *Commission* v. *Italy (Treasures)* ([1968] ECR 423) the Court held that a tax imposed on the export of artistic, historical and archaeological treasures from Italy infringed Article 16. The Court did not admit an exception on the grounds of the sensitivity of the articles in question – they were classed as 'ordinary' (i.e. consumer) goods – or on the grounds of public policy. The Court has also condemned internal charges as CEEs on exports if they fall more heavily on exports than on domestic products (Cases 36 and 71/80 *Irish Creamery Milk Suppliers Association* v. *Ireland* [1981] ECR 735). However, the imposition of a charge on domestic goods alone, and not on imported goods, is permissible under Articles 9–16 EC, provided the proceeds of the charge are not used to finance activities incompatible with Community law, such as a 'Buy National Campaign' (see 14.6).

13.5   Exceptions to the Prohibition

There are three situations in which a charge will fall outside the prohibition on CEEs. These are set out in Case 18/87 *Commission* v. *Germany (Live Animals)* in the following terms ([1988] ECR 5427 at p. 5440):

> 'the Court has held that . . . a charge escapes . . . classification [as a CEE] if it relates to a general system of internal dues applied systematically and in accordance with the same criteria to domestic products and imported products alike . . . if it constitutes payment for a service in fact rendered to the economic operator of a sum in proportion to the service . . ., or again, subject to certain conditions, if it attaches to inspections carried out to fulfil obligations imposed by Community law.'

A charge which is classified as part of a system of internal taxation will, of course, be subject to scrutiny under Article 95. The latter two exceptions are considered here.

13.6   Fees for Services Performed

Services may only be charged for if they provide a tangible benefit to the importer (e.g. a storage service). In Case 24/68 *Commission* v. *Italy (Statistical Levy)* the Court held that a levy on all imports into and exports from Italy, used to finance a statistical service for the benefit of importers and exporters, was in breach of Articles 9–16, as the advantage to importers was so general and uncertain that the charge could not be considered a payment for services rendered. Member States certainly may not charge for undertaking actual customs formalities. Community law requires customs posts to be open for a minimum of ten hours per day. In Case 340/87 *Commission* v. *Italy* ([1989] ECR 1483) Italy sought to justify its charge for customs formalities as covering the cost of the services performed by customs staff for the four hours per day during which customs posts are required to be open which exceed the normal working hours of civil servants in Italy (six hours per day). The argument was rejected by the Court.

Member States may charge for carrying out customs formalities on an importer's own premises, but fees must be calculated in relation to the cost of the service, not the value of the goods, and must not exceed the cost (Case 170/88 *Ford España* v. *Spain* [1989] ECR 2305).

13.7   Inspections

Health and safety inspections on imported goods may be legitimately be undertaken under Community law. Although *prima facie* non-tariff barriers to trade, such inspections will normally fall under Article 36 EC which permits derogations on health grounds from the prohibition in Article 30 EC, unless they are carried out with a protectionist motive in mind. Such inspections are regarded as being carried out not for the benefit of the importer, but for the benefit of the public in general (Case 39/73 *Rewe-Zentralfinanz* v. *Landwirtschaftskammer Westfalen-Lippe* [1973] ECR 1039). They cannot therefore be charged for under the principles governing services rendered set out in 13.6. Inspections may only be charged for in three sets of circumstances: first, where the same inspection is undertaken on domestic products, in which case the same fee must be charged in respect of imports (e.g. Case 50/85 *Schloh* v. *Auto Controle Technique Sprl* [1986] ECR 1855 – a justified test of the roadworthiness of imported vehicles, imposed also on domestically produced vehicles); second, where the inspection is mandatory under harmonised Community rules on the health and safety of products; and third, where they are part of a multilateral and international system intended to promote the free movement of goods.

For example, in Case 18/87 *Commission* v. *Germany (Live Animals)* the Court held that Germany was permitted to impose fees for inspections of imported live animals under Directive 81/389, which introduced harmonised arrangements for such inspections in the Member States. The Court dismissed the Commission's contention that since the fees themselves were not harmonised (the Member States had been unable to agree upon this point), the inspections could not be charged for. The Court rationalised the fee as 'the financially and economically justified compensation for an obligation imposed in equal measure on all the Member States by Community law'. Under the same principles, fees may be charged for inspections undertaken by the Member States in pursuance of international agreements by which the Community is bound or to which all the Member States are parties and which encourage the free movement of goods (Case 89/76 *Commission* v. *Netherlands* [1977] ECR 1355). For example, in Case C-111/89 *State of Netherlands* v. *Bakker Hillegom* ([1990] ECR I-1735) it was held that the Netherlands was justified in imposing charges for field inspections of plants carried out under an international convention intended to encourage the free importation of plants into the country of destination by establishing a system of inspections in the exporting state, recognised and organised on a reciprocal basis. The reason for permitting such charges is that they tend to discourage recourse by importing Member States to unilateral inspection measures which would be permissible under Article 36, and that therefore they promote the free movement of goods. Charges may not, however, be imposed simply because an inspection is expressly *permitted* under Community law, but is not mandatory (Case 314/82 *Commission* v. *Belgium* [1984] ECR 1543).

Where a charge may be imposed, it may not be higher than is necessary to cover the cost of the inspection (Case 46/76 *Bauhuis* v. *State of Netherlands* [1977] ECR 5). To enable this to be accurately assessed, there needs to be a link between the amount of the fee and the actual inspection. Thus, the Court held in *Bakker Hillegom* that the fee may not be calculated according to the weight of the products or the invoice value of the products, but rather according to factors such as the duration of the inspection, the number of persons required, and the cost of materials used.

Particular difficulties arise in charging for inspections which are carried out on all products, but where the cost is imposed only on exported products. For example, in the Netherlands, field inspections of plants are carried out on all products, but the cost is charged on a proportionate basis only to the 75% of products which are exported. The remaining 25% of the cost is borne by the state, and is not charged to the products intended for the home market. In *Bakker Hillegom* the Court held that such a charging structure would amount to a CEE on exports if the products intended for the home market derived any benefit from the inspection which they were not charged for.

13.8   The Distinction between CEEs and Systems of Taxation

Only a 'genuine' taxation system falls outside the prohibition in Articles 9–16, and is subject to scrutiny instead under Article 95. According to the Court in Case 90/79 *Commission* v. *France (Levy on Reprographic Machines)* ([1981] ECR 283 at p.301), a genuine tax is one relating

'to a general system of internal dues applied systematically to categories of products in accordance with objective criteria irrespective of the origin of the products.'

For example, in Cases 2 and 3/62 *Commission* v. *Belgium and Luxembourg (Gingerbread)* ([1962] ECR 425), the Court held that a 'compensatory' tax on imports of gingerbread, allegedly to offset the high domestic price of rye, an ingredient of gingerbread, caused by a national price support system for rye, was not a 'genuine' tax, but a CEE governed by Article 12. This is an example of a general principle expounded in Case 132/78 *Denkavit Loire* v. *France* ([1979] ECR 1928), whereby if a charge is to be treated as part of a system of internal taxation, it must be imposed according to the same criteria on domestic and imported products. For example, it must be imposed at the same stage of marketing, and by the same taxation authorities. In Case 29/72 *Marimex SpA* v. *Ministero delle Finanze* ([1972] ECR 1309) an Italian 'veterinary inspection tax' imposed on imported meat, live and dead, to ensure that it conformed to Italian health standards was held to be a CEE. Although similar domestic products were also subject to inspections and taxes, they were imposed by different bodies under different criteria.

If a tax is part of a general system of internal dues, it will be irrelevant that there is little or no domestic production of a particular product (e.g. cars produced in Portugal – Case C-343/90 *Dias* v. *Director da Alfandga do Porto* 16.7.1992). However, even though such a tax may not fall within Articles 9–16, it will still be subject to scrutiny for discrimination under Article 95.

In the case of one category of tax imposed on both imported and domestic products, the Court has been required to consider not only the relationship between Articles 9–16 and 95, but also Article 92 EC which concerns the compatibility with the common market of state aids paid to undertakings. This is where the proceeds of the tax are used to benefit the domestic product only. In Case 77/72 *Capolongo* v. *Azienda Agricolo Maya* ([1973] ECR 611) the Court held that a charge imposed by Italy on all egg boxes, intended to finance the production of paper and cardboard in Italy, was a CEE, as it was intended exclusively to benefit the domestic product. However, in subsequent cases, the doctrine was refined, and in Case 105/76 *Interzuccheri ApA* v. *Ditta Rezzano e Cavassa* ([1977] ECR 1029) the Court set out three conditions which must be satisfied before a tax (in that case a levy on sales of sugar whether imported or domestic, to benefit the domestic sugar industry in the form of subsidies to beet producers and sugar-processors) will be a CEE, rather than part of a system of taxation subject to scrutiny under Article 95, or an aid to domestic producers subject to Article 92. The conditions are:

– The charge must be exclusively for the financing of activities which for the most part benefit national products subject to the charge.
– The imported product subject to the tax and that benefiting from it must be identical.
– The burden imposed on the national product must be completely compensated.

A charge which does not satisfy these criteria, but involves, for example, only a partial reimbursement of the burden of the tax on the domestic product will be discriminatory under Article 95, and/or subject to scrutiny by the Commission as a state aid under Article 92 (Cases C-149 and 150/91 *Sanders Adour SNC* v. *Directeur des services fiscaux des Pyrénées-Atlantiques* (11.6.1992)). The tax does not as a consequence of such a finding have to be completely abolished, but it does have to be rendered neutral as regards the basis for imposition and reimbursement. For example, as 13.11 shows, it can be altered to use facially non-discriminatory criteria (e.g. it is imposed by reference to certain production methods which are typically national) which in practice benefit domestic production. Such taxes are capable of justification despite their discriminatory *effect* on the grounds that they serve some overriding and legitimate national policy interest (e.g. the protection of vulnerable regions, or the promotion of specialist regional products). This line of case law demonstrates that the Court implicitly recognises the dual purpose of taxes both to raise revenue for the State and also to pursue wider economic, social, political, cultural or environmental goals through redistributive policies. Finally, as the Court stated in Case C-343/90 *Dias* v. *Director da Alfandga do Porto*, the fact that part of a system of taxation is discriminatory does not make the whole system contrary to Community law. The Member State will only be required to change the system of taxation in respect of those products which are discriminated against.

13.9   The Basic Prohibition in Article 95

Article 95 provides two bases for assessing the discriminatory element in systems of taxation. It states:

'No Member States shall impose, directly or indirectly, on the products of other Member States any internal taxation of any kind in excess of that imposed directly or indirectly on similar domestic products.

Furthermore, no Member State shall impose on the products of other Member States any internal taxation of such a nature as to afford indirect protection to other products.

Member States shall, not later than at the beginning of the second stage, repeal or amend any provisions existing when this Treaty enters into force which conflict with the preceding rules.'

The essential purpose of Article 95 is not to engender a principle of equivalence in national taxation regimes. This would be impossible given the diversity of national regimes which continue to exist since the Member States retain fiscal autonomy as regards the raising of revenue and the use of taxation as an instrument of redistributive policy. Taxation must, however, be neutral and the Treaty restricts the prohibition to measures which are discriminatory in form or in effect, provided normally in the latter case that there is a protectionist effect in addition. As the Court put it in Case 127/75 *Bobie* v. *HZA Aachen-Nord* ([1976] ECR 1079 at p.1086), Article 95

'seeks to ensure, by means of the prohibition which it lays down, that an importing Member State does not, by means of internal taxation of imported products and similar domestic products give domestic traders preferential treatment as compared with their competitors from other Member States who sell similar products on the market of that State.'

As Article 95(3) indicates, the prohibitions in Articles 95(1) and (2) are unconditional and capable of judicial enforcement in national courts.

Indeed both paragraphs have been held to be directly effective: Case 57/65 *Lütticke* v. *HZA Saarlouis* – (Article 95(1); Case 27/67 *Firma Fink-Frucht GmbH* v. *HZA München Landsbergerstrasse* ([1968] ECR 223) – Article 95(2).

13.10   The Differences between the Two Paragraphs in Article 95

Article 95(1) applies where there are 'similar' imported and domestic products. Similar products must be taxed equally, unless there are compelling economic policy reasons for differentiating between them, and the policy of differentiation is in any case applied indistinctly to national and imported products. Article 95(2) is broader, using a more general criterion of indirect protection afforded by the domestic taxation system. The goods in question, while not necessarily similar, must still be in competition with domestic products, even if this is partial, indirect or potential. Goods in competititon may be taxed differently, so long as the taxation does not have a protective effect. The element of protection is assessed on the basis of a broader economic measurement of the impact of the taxes.

Goods may be 'similar' if, for example, they are in the same classification category for tax, tariff or statistical purposes, although this point is not decisive. Rum and whisky have been held to be similar, although they are in separate categories (Case 169/78 *Commission* v. *Italy* [1980] ECR 385). A broad economic approach is required to the question of similarity; Case 243/84 *John Walker & Sons Ltd* v. *Ministerium for Skatter og Afgifter* ([1986] ECR 875), concerning the question whether fruit wines and whisky are similar, offered a range of objective criteria, such as origin, method of manufacture and alcohol content, and subjective criteria, such as whether the goods are capable of meeting the same need from the point of view of consumers. These are used together in the assessment of 'similarity'. Here, whisky was held not to be similar to fruit wines, as it has twice the alcohol content.

Many different alcoholic drinks, although not similar, have been held to be in competition. For example, in Case 170/78 *Commission* v. *United Kingdom* ([1983] ECR 2265) the Court had to consider whether wine and beer are competing products. The Court held that in fact they are, at least as regards certain categories of light and cheap wine, in respect of which the degree of product substitution with beer is potentially highest. It can, however, be difficult to assess whether products are in competition on the basis of consumer habits, since these may themselves have been formed by discriminatory national taxation structures. In Case 356/85 *Commission* v. *Belgium* ([1987] ECR 3299) the Court confirmed that beer and wine are in competition, when it was called upon to examine the Belgian VAT regime under which wine (not produced in Belgium) was taxed at 25%, while beer (which it does produce) was taxed at 19%.

13.11   Eliminating Discrimination and Protection: the Problem of National Fiscal Autonomy

The Member States are not precluded by the absence of similar domestic products from imposing taxation on imported products. In Case 27/67 *Firma Fink-Frucht GmbH* v. *HZA München Landsbergerstrasse* the Court was asked to consider a turnover equalisation tax imposed on sweet peppers imported from Italy, although no similar or comparable domestic products existed. It held ([1968] ECR 223 at p.231):

> 'Article 95 is intended to remove certain restrictions on the free movement of goods. But to conclude that it prohibits the imposition of any internal taxation on imported goods which do not compete with domestic products would appear to give it a scope exceeding its purpose. Internal taxes, and turnover tax in particular, are essentially fiscal [i.e. revenue-raising] in purpose. There is therefore no reason why certain imported products should be given privileged treatment, because they do not compete with any domestic products capable of being protected. Where such a tax is imposed at the import stage, even on products which do not compete with domestic products, its purpose is to put every kind of product, whatever its origin, in a comparable fiscal situation in the territory of the state imposing the tax. It must therefore be concluded that Article 95 does not prohibit Member States from imposing internal taxation on imported products when there is no similar domestic product, or any other domestic products capable of being protected.'

A fortiori systems of domestic taxation which do protect domestic products are liable to strict scrutiny under Article 95. For example, in Case 112/84 *Humblot* v. *Directeur des Services Fiscaux* ([1985] ECR 1367) a French car tax which imposed much higher levels of taxation on cars over 16 CV was condemned by the Court. There are no French cars over 16 CV. The Court pointed out that the effect of the tax was to reduce the competition faced by French cars, and could not therefore be regarded as neutral, even though it was not imposed using a criterion overtly based on nationality. On the other hand, in Case C-132/88 *Commission* v. *Greece* ([1991] 3 CMLR 1) the Court upheld a taxation system which imposed much heavier burdens on cars with engines above 1800 cc, even though no cars produced in Greece had engines above 1600 cc, because it found that the tax did not have a protectionist effect.

Tax regimes which are, however, effectively protectionist have in some circumstances escaped condemnation under Article 95, provided they are operated in a non-discriminatory way. For example, in Case 21/79 *Commission* v. *Italy (Regenerated Oil)* ([1980] ECR 1) it was held that tax concessions must be extended to non-domestic products, even though this may make controls upon their operation more difficult. In Case 148/77 *Hansen* v. *HZA Flensburg* ([1978] ECR 1787), which concerned a

German regime of tax relief available in respect of spirits made from fruit by small businesses and collective farms, the Court addressed the reasons why certain types of tax regime which implicitly benefit national products may be compatible with Article 95. It held (at p.1806):

> 'At the present stage of its development and in the absence of any unification or harmonisation of the relevant provisions, Community law does not prohibit Member States from granting tax advantages, in the form of exemption from or reduction of duties, to certain types of spirits or to certain classes of producers.
>
> Indeed, tax advantages of this kind may serve legitimate economic or social purposes, such as the use of certain raw materials by the distilling industry, the continued production of particular spirits of high quality, or the continuance of certain classes of industry such as agricultural distilleries.'

The only requirement is that the preferential system must be extended without discrimination to spirits of the same class coming from other Member States. Regional policy objectives cannot be pursued through measures which differentiate explicitly between products according to whether they originate in a particular region. Such a measure may not be classed as part of a system of internal dues at all, but as a CEE prohibited by Article 13(2) (Case C-163/90 *Administration des douanes* v. *Legros*).

Case 46/80 *Vinal* v. *Orbat* ([1981] ECR 77) demonstrates the 'chicken and egg' problem of permitting taxation regimes which benefit national products in the interests of regional or social policies. Under the Italian tax regime, alcohol of agricultural origin was taxed less heavily than chemically-based alcohol, which is not produced in Italy (because of the heavy tax?). Although the system was clearly discriminatory in that it taxed similar products differently, and also protectionist in the sense that no domestic products fell into the higher tax band, it nonetheless escaped condemnation by the Court. It was not directly discriminatory on the basis of nationality, as non-domestic alcohol of agricultural origin benefited from the tax concession. The Court held that 'the system of taxation pursued an objective of legitimate industrial policy' compatible with Community principles, namely that of ensuring a reasonable level of employment in certain areas, and of ensuring the survival of agricultural distilleries.

13.12   The Basis for Fiscal Comparisons

Fiscal comparisons undertaken to identify the presence of discrimination are generally straightforward where the products in question are the same. For example, in Case C-327/90 *Commission* v. *Greece* (12.5.1992) the Court condemned a system of taxes on private vehicles under which imported vehicles were taxed using a calculation based on a notional value of the vehicles, while vehicles produced in Greece were taxed using a calculation made on the basis of the real price of the vehicles at the factory gate. The basis of the assessment of the tax must be the same for imported and domestic products. Nor may national products be advantaged through the operation of administrative instructions regarding the functioning of the taxation system, even if the relevant legal measures are themselves formally neutral.

Assessment of the taxation levels imposed on competing products are more complex. In Case 184/85 *Commission* v. *Italy* ([1987] ECR 2013), the Court was asked to assess whether a tax on the consumption of bananas was discriminatory. It held that bananas are not similar to table fruit produced in Italy (apples, peaches, apricots, mandarins, etc.), but are in at least partial competition with them. The Commission was able to demonstrate that the tax level on bananas was nearly half the price on importation, and the Court agreed that the tax was discriminatory.

In general, however, the Court does not make clear statements about the criteria which it prefers to use in fiscal comparisons. Problems are particularly acute in the case of alcoholic drinks where at least three possible bases for comparison exist. Conventionally, alcohol is taxed according to either volume, value or alcoholic strength. A tax on volume may need to be adjusted in the light of the differing levels of consumption of various alcoholic drinks, to ensure that beer drinkers do not make an excessive contribution to tax revenues. Taxes on alcoholic strength may also be adjusted in the light of legitimate health concerns about the effects of stronger drinks. In Case 170/78 *Commission* v. *UK*, the Court refused to state a preference for the basis of fiscal comparisons, holding that regardless of which approach was used the conclusion must be reached that there were substantially different tax burdens on the two competing products – beer and light, cheap wines. No one method is capable of yielding reliable results on its own, but rather each will give 'significant information' allowing the assessment of the tax system. Ultimately, the Court's conclusions as to whether the system is legitimate will depend upon the weight given to each criterion and its assessment of the degree of national fiscal autonomy permitted in the pursuit of legitimate public policy goals such as combating alcoholism. However, the effect of the UK tax system was, the Court concluded, to stamp wine with the hallmark of a luxury beverage.

13.13   The Recovery of Unlawfully Levied Charges and Taxes

In accordance with the principles governing domestic remedies for breach of Community law (8.17), unlawfully levied charges and taxes must be reimbursed to aggrieved importers and exporters. In Case 199/82 *Amministrazione delle Finanze dello Stato* v. *SpA San Giorgio* ([1983] ECR 3595), the Court reiterated the well-established point that national remedies for breach of Community law must be both the same as those available for breach of equivalent domestic prohibitions, and also not such as to render the enforcement of Community law impossible in practice. The Court also stated that national authorities are permitted to apply national principles of unjust enrichment in order to justify not reimbursing some or all of the tax, in the face of evidence that the burden of the tax has been passed downstream to its customers by the claimant. However, the authorities are not entitled to assume that this has happened (Case 104/86 *Commission* v. *Italy (Repayment of Illegal Taxes)* [1988] ECR 1799).

Exceptionally, in Case C-163/90 *Administration des douanes* v. *Legros*, the Court placed a temporal limitation upon the recovery of the regional tax unlawfully levied by the DOM authorities in Réunion. Only those importers who had already brought actions for reimbursement were held entitled to claim. Special circumstances surrounding the uncertain status of the French overseas departments within the Community customs territory, and the conduct of the Community institutions which had tended to indicate to the parties concerned that these regions were not at present covered by the prohibition in Article 13(2), justified this departure from general principle.

Summary

1 There are two types of fiscal barriers to trade covered by the European Community Treaty: Articles 9–16 EC prohibit the imposition customs duties and charges having equivalent effect to customs duties on imports and exports of goods between the Member States; Article 95 prohibits discriminatory internal taxation.

2 A CEE is a charge imposed by virtue of the fact that goods cross a national or regional frontier, which has the effect of damaging the unity of the market. Systems of internal taxation are coherent and 'genuine' systems of internal dues which, where they are discriminatory, have the effect of creating distortions of competition and obstacles to economic interpenetration. Articles 9–16 and 95 set up separate but complementary systems of control governing these two forms of fiscal barrier.

3 The prohibition on customs duties and CEEs is a fundamental principle of the common market, subject to very few exceptions. Only services rendered to importers and exporters, inspections prescribed by Community law, and inspections carried out under multilateral arrangements which facilitate the free movement of goods may be charged for.

4 Systems of internal taxation established by Member States which are discriminatory in effect if not in form may be permitted provided they facilitate the achievement of a legitimate socio-economic goal such as the elimination of regional economic disparities.

5 The prohibitions in Articles 9–16 and 95 are directly effective, and charges and taxes wrongfully levied may be recovered by traders, in application of the principles of adequate domestic remedies.

Questions

1 What factors distinguish a customs duty or CEE subject to Articles 9–16 from a system of internal taxation, subject to scrutiny under Article 95?

2 Has the case of *Legros* led to an expansion of the notion of a CEE?

3 What types of charges may legitimately be imposed on goods when they cross national frontiers?

4 In what ways is Article 95(2) broader than Article 95(1)?

5 Why was Italy permitted to maintain a system of internal taxation which imposed heavier dues on chemically produced alcohol than on alcohol produced from agricultural sources?

6 What difficulties face the Court of Justice when it seeks to assess the impact of the systems of taxation which the Member States operate in respect of alcoholic drinks?

Further Reading

Barents (1986) 'Recent Case Law on the Prohibition of Fiscal Discrimination under Article 95', 23 *Common Market Law Review*, 641.

Danusso and Denton (1990) 'Does the European Court of Justice look for a protectionist motive under Article 95?', *Legal Issues of European Integration*, 90/1, 66.

Easson (1984) 'Cheaper wine or dearer beer? Article 95 again', 9 *European Law Review*, 57.

Green, Hartley and Usher (1991), Chs 3 and 4.

Lonbay (1989) 'A review of recent tax cases – wine, gambling, fast cars, and bananas', 14 *European Law Review*, 48.

14   Non-tariff Barriers to Trade in Goods

14.1   Introduction: The Nature of Non-tariff Barriers to Trade in Goods

While the Community succeeded in removing the tariff barriers to trade in goods between the Member States, as well as most of the more visible non-tariff barriers (quotas or quantitative restrictions and import licences) by the end of the 1960s, it did not succeed in eliminating the many other non-tariff measures which have just as much influence on the national segmentation of the Community market. Almost any regulatory divergence between two national markets represents a potential hindrance to trade. The most obvious obstacles are state aids to industry (subject to separate regulation under Articles 92 and 93 EC), public procurement restrictions favouring national suppliers and divergent product and technical standards, but included also are divergent retail market rules (e.g. advertising rules, shop opening hours, product licensing, price regulation), and even divergent labour market regulation measures which restrict the production or marketing of goods. Differences in the rules which govern the operation of the market in goods within the various Member States interfere with the creation of a level competitive playing field within which market forces may operate and market integration can occur 'naturally'.

All these types of measures are categorised under the EC Treaty as 'measures having equivalent effect to quantitative restrictions' (MEEQRs), and are prohibited by Articles 30 and 34 EC, subject only to exemption under certain derogations laid down in Article 36 EC. They also fall under the category 'technical barriers to trade', as defined by the Commission's White Paper on *Completing the Internal Market*, and are therefore subject also to scrutiny at Community level in the context of the '1992' harmonisation programme. The discussion in this chapter will indicate the strength of the contribution made by the Court of Justice in relation to the elimination of non-tariff barriers to trade in goods.

14.2   Basic Principles

Article 30 provides:

'Quantitative restrictions on imports and all measures having equivalent effect shall, without prejudice to the following provisions, be prohibited between Member States.'

The timetable laid down in Articles 31–33 provided for the removal of such measures by the end of the transitional period. This is supplemented by Article 34 which states:

'Quantitative restrictions on exports, and all measures having equivalent effect, shall be prohibited between Member States.

Member States shall, by the end of the first stage at the latest, abolish all quantitative restrictions on exports and any measures having equivalent effect which are in existence when this Treaty enters into force.'

Article 36 provides for derogations from these prohibitions in the following terms:

'The provisions of Articles 30 to 34 shall not preclude prohibitions or restrictions on imports, exports or goods in transit justified on grounds of public morality, public policy or public security; the protection of health and life of humans, animals or plants; the protection of national treasures possessing artistic, historic or archaeological value; or the protection of industrial and commercial property. Such prohibitions or restrictions shall not, however, constitute a means of arbitrary discrimination or a disguised restriction on trade between Member States.'

The direct effect of these provisions has not been in doubt since the end of the transitional period and was stated expressly by the Court in relation to Article 30 in Case 74/76 *Ianelli and Volpi SpA* v. *Meroni* ([1977] ECR 557) and in relation to Article 34 in Case 83/78 *Pigs Marketing Board* v. *Redmond* ([1978] ECR 2347).

These provisions, like those governing the customs union, bind the institutions as well as the Member States, and the institutions are not therefore free to authorise otherwise unlawful Member State actions, except to the extent that they are expressly or implicitly authorised so to do by other provisions of the Treaty. For example, in Case 9/73 *Schlüter* v. *HZA Lorrach* ([1973] ECR 1135) the Court accepted the legitimacy of the system of monetary compensatory amounts, intended to offset the effects of exchange rate fluctuations in the context of fixed agricultural prices, as being less damaging to the interests of the Community than the alternative – namely the diversion of trade which would occur as a result of monetary movements.

14.3   State Measures

Articles 30–36 are concerned with *state measures*. Consequently, they do not apply to the obstacles which individuals place in the way of economic integration, such as refusing to buy or sell imported goods, or refusing to deal with undertakings from other Member States, but such conduct might fall foul of other rules in the Treaty, in particular the rules on anticompetitive and monopolistic conduct (see Case 311/85 *Vereniging van Vlaamse Reisbureaus* v. *Sociale Dienst van de Plaatselijk* [1987] ECR 3801). However, individuals are not wholly free to act in breach of these provisions. For example, an undertaking might find itself unable to rely upon provisions of national intellectual property law which have the effect of segmenting the Community market, such as provisions on the scope of trademark or patent protection against imports of goods from other Member States. It may not make use of provisions of national law incompatible with Community law in order to exclude such imports (see 14.17). Case C-47/90 *Delhaize* v. *Promalvin SA* (9.6.1992) illustrates how Article 34 may be used in litigation between two private parties. Delhaize ordered a quantity of Spanish wine from Promalvin, which in turn ordered a similar quantity from an exporter. When the exporter reported that it was unable to supply the wine because of a Spanish restriction on sales of wine in bulk, which had the effect of securing a competitive advantage for bottling enterprises established in Spain, Delhaize sued Promalvin in the Belgian courts, seeking an order that it should fulfil its contract. The Belgian court referred to the Court of Justice the question of the compatibility with Article 34 of the Spanish restriction (see 14.11).

The concept of a state measure has been broadly interpreted by the Court. It includes the measures of a professional body which lays down the rules of ethics applicable to the members of a profession and has a committee upon which national legislation has conferred disciplinary powers that could involve the removal from the register of persons authorised to exercise the profession in question (Cases 266 and 267/87 *R.* v. *Pharmaceutical Society of Great Britain, ex parte Association of Pharmaceutical Importers* [1989] ECR 1295). Also covered are the actions of a company limited by guarantee charged with the task of organising a 'buy national' campaign, which is subject to instructions from and funded by government (Case 249/81 *Commission* v. *Ireland (Buy Irish)* [1982] ECR 4005). Finally, in *Buy Irish* the Court also made it clear that the measures in question need not be binding; the activities of the Irish Goods Council in promoting Irish goods had a potential effect on imports from other Member States which was 'comparable to that resulting from government measures of a binding nature', and Article 30 covers all measures which are 'capable of influencing the conduct of traders and consumers'.

14.4 Quantitative Restrictions

Quantitative restrictions are 'measures which amount to a total or partial restraint of, according to the circumstances, imports, exports or goods in transit' (Case 2/73 *Geddo* v. *Ente Nationale Risi* [1973] ECR 865). Thus they are measures capable of limiting imports to a finite quantity, including zero, and include import bans (Case 34/79 *R.* v. *Henn and Darby* [1979] ECR 3795 – ban on imports of pornographic material into the UK) and import licences (Case 124/81 *Commission* v. *UK (Imports of UHT milk)* [1983] ECR 203).

14.5   MEEQRs on Imports and Early Views on the Scope of Article 30

An early view on the precise scope of Article 30 came from the Commission in Directive 70/50 (OJ Spn Edn. 1970, p17), issued at the conclusion of the transitional period. The Directive divides national measures restrictive of trade into two categories: those which discriminate overtly between imported and domestic products, and those which are indistinctly applicable to all products.

Article 2(2) lists as falling under the prohibition in Article 30 in particular the following discriminatory measures:

'measures which make imports or the disposal, at any marketing stage, of imported products subject to a condition – other than a formality – which is required in respect of imported products only, or a condition differing from that required for domestic products and more difficult to satisfy. Equally, it covers, in particular, measures which favour domestic products or grant them a preference, other than an aid, to which conditions may or may not be attached.'

Article 2(3) lists numerous examples of the types of measure covered including measures which control the prices or profit margins in respect of imported products alone, which require imported products to be marketed via a national agent, and which restrict the access of imported products to the national market.

Indistinctly applicable measures are also confirmed as subject to the prohibition in Article 30, but only subject to certain qualifications. Article 3 provides:

'This Directive also covers measures governing the marketing of products which deal, in particular, with shape, size, weight, composition, presentation, identification or putting up and which are equally applicable to domestic and imported products, where the restrictive effect of such measures on the free movement of goods exceeds the effects intrinsic to trade rules.
This is the case, in particular, where:

– the restrictive effects on the free movement of goods are out of proportion to their purpose;
– the same objective can be attained by other means which are less of a hindrance to trade.'

It should be noted that this is merely the view of the Commission, reached without assistance from case law of the Court. Although binding on the Member States, as a supplement to or explanation of Article 30, it has not restricted the Court in its development of the meaning of Article 30. In fact, the Court has on a number of occasions made use of Directive 70/50, although in other respects its case law does go beyond the definitions proposed by the Commission.

In Case 8/74 *Procureur du Roi* v. *Dassonville* ([1974] ECR 837) the Court formulated a definition of measures having equivalent effect to quantitative restrictions. The case concerned criminal proceedings in Belgium against a trader who acquired a consignment of Scotch Whisky in free circulation in France, and imported it into Belgium without being in possession of a certificate of origin from the UK customs authorities. This was a violation of Belgian customs requirements, the UK at that time not being part of the customs union. Dassonville prepared his own certificate of origin and was prosecuted for forgery. The Court of Justice, on a reference from the Belgian court, held (at p.852):

'All trading rules enacted by Member States which are capable of hindering directly or indirectly, actually or potentially, intra-Community trade are to be considered as measures having an effect equivalent to quantitative restrictions.'

This is, of course, an extremely broad definition, and potentially catches all forms of economic regulation adopted by the Member States. It has, however, acquired the status of a classic statement of the scope of Article 30, and has been repeatedly cited by the Court as justifying its decisions in subsequent cases. It covers rules governing the circumstances in which goods are produced and marketed as well as rules prescribing standards or contents requirements to which goods must conform. It even extends to rules principally concerned with the supply of services which also affect the supply of goods. For example, in Case 45/87 *Commission* v. *Ireland (Dundalk Water Supply)* ([1988] ECR 4929), the Court held that Article 30 applied to a clause in a public works contract concerning the supply of water which required a certain type of pipe to be used, namely one which complied with an Irish Standard. The Court confirmed the general applicability of Article 30 to all measures which might impede imports of goods. The Court has also held that there is no *de minimis* rule in the context of Article 30. No matter how slight the potential effect of the trading rule on interstate trade, it will still be caught by Article 30 (Case 177/82 *Van De Haar* [1984] ECR 1797).

In the context of *Dassonville* itself, the Court was concerned with a measure which expressly distinguished between imports and domestic products. There was therefore no doubt as to the effect that such a measure was capable of having on imports. The next section will consider the relatively uncontroversial application of the *Dassonville* test to discriminatory measures.

14.6   Article 30 and Discriminatory Measures

The case law of the Court has provided a wealth of examples of the application of Article 30 to such measures:

—   origin marking: in Case 113/80 *Commission* v. *Ireland (Souvenirs)* ([1981] ECR 1625) the Court condemned the requirement that non-Irish souvenirs be marked 'foreign';
—   inspections or checks: in Case 4/75 *Rewe Zentralfinanz* v. *Landwirtschaftskammer Bonn* ([1975] ECR 843) the Court held that Article 30 applied to an inspection of imported apples designed to control a pest called San José scale; in Case 42/82 *Commission* v. *France* ([1983] ECR 1013) Article 30 was held to cover excessive delays in customs clearance, resulting from systematic checks of wine to ensure that it complied with quality standards;
—   discriminatory purchasing requirements: Article 30 covered a requirement that all importers of oil into Ireland purchase 35% of their requirements of petroleum products from the Irish National Petroleum Co. at a price to be fixed by the Minister (Case 72/83 *Campus Oil Ltd* v. *Minister for Industry and Energy* [1983] ECR 2727);
—   discriminatory public procurement measures: Article 30 may restrict the use of regional policy legislation which is linked to the procurement of goods by public bodies; it was held to cover the requirement under Italian law that all public or semi-public bodies buy a fixed quota of their supplies from companies operating in the *Mezzogiorno* (Case C-21/88 *Du Pont de Nemours Italiana SpA* v. *Unità Sanitaria Locale No. 2 di Carrara* [1990] ECR I-889);
—   'buy national campaigns': Case 249/81 *Commission* v. *Ireland (Buy Irish)*; however, in Case 222/82 *Apple and Pear Development Council* v. *K.J. Lewis Ltd* ([1983] ECR 4083) the Court acknowledged that a carefully formulated promotion campaign which draws attention to the qualities of typically national varieties of goods and organises campaigns to promote the sale of such goods, will be compatible with Article 30 provided that it does not discourage the purchase of imported goods or disparage the qualities of such goods in the eyes of consumers;
—   discriminatory rules on the granting of compulsory licences for the exploitation of patents. In Case C-30/90 *Commission* v. *UK* [1992] 2 CMLR 709, the Court held that it was incompatible with Article 30 for the UK to treat a situation in which the demand for a patented product was satisfied by imports as being the same as a situation in which a UK patent was not being sufficiently exploited, and to conclude that both were suitable cases for the grant of a compulsory licence on the patent in question.

It should be noted that any of these measures may potentially be justified under the derogations from Article 30 contained in Article 36 (see 14.14).

14.7 Article 30 and Indistinctly Applicable Measures

One way of applying the prohibition in Article 30 to indistinctly applicable measures would have been to develop a theory of indirect discrimination. Whereas, in the case of measures which formally differentiate between domestic and imported products, it is acceptable to assume that there is a negative effect on interstate trade, the Court could have required proof, in the case of measures which treat domestic and imported products facially equally, that the marketing and sale of imported products is *in fact* thereby rendered more difficult. In the context of the right to equal pay for men and women, laid down in Article 119 EC, the Court has elaborated such a theory, holding that measures which disproportionately affect one sex (e.g. measures denying pay increases to part time workers, who are predominantly female), require justification in the light of some overriding legitimate objective (Case 170/84 *Bilka-Kaufhaus* v. *Weber von Hartz* [1986] ECR 1607).

In one category of cases, namely those involving state price-fixing, the Court does appear to have adopted this approach. In the case of Dutch legislation imposing minimum prices for gin, the Court held that Article 30 would apply to a rule establishing a minimum price which was fixed at such a level as to have an adverse effect on the marketing of imported products, in so far as it prevented them from taking advantage of a competitive lower price undercutting the price of domestic products (Case 82/77 *Openbaar Ministerie* v. *Van Tiggele* [1978] ECR 25). Equally, maximum retail prices may be discriminatory on the same grounds, if they restrict the sale of higher price (higher quality?) imported goods (Case 65/75 *Tasca* [1976] ECR 291). To judge whether price regimes are justified, the Court looks to see if they have been formulated entirely according to national production criteria, and without regard to the conditions of importers. For example, in Case 188/86 *Ministère public* v. *Regis Lefèvre* ([1987] ECR 2963) the Court was asked to scrutinise French legislation which imposed maximum retail prices for sales of beef and veal. It was based on a flat rate sum for retail margin (held acceptable) and a flat rate sum for transportation costs (held unacceptable as it discouraged the retailer from obtaining supplies from distant wholesalers).

An indirect discrimination argument can also be used to justify condemning the use of so-called 'grandfather clauses' in the public procurement field. In Case 45/87 *Commission* v. *Ireland (Dundalk Water Supply)* the Court held that Article 30 caught a provision in a scheme inviting tenders to augment the drinking water supply of Dundalk which required the asbestos cement pressure pipes to be used in the contract to be certified as complying with an Irish standard. In fact, only one manufacturer, an Irish one, had been so certified, and it is obviously indirectly discriminatory in the sense of being more onerous to require the non-national tenderers for a public works contract to comply with specifically national requirements. Such a condition therefore requires justification. A similar analysis can be applied to Case C-18/88 *RTT* v.

GB-INNO (13.12.1991) where the Court applied Article 30 to a requirement that telephone equipment be approved by a public body before being
connected to the network. Such a condition is again clearly more onerous
for a non-national supplier.

However, the indirect discrimination approach is not the one which the
Court has generally applied to indistinctly applicable measures, and
Green, Hartley and Usher (1991: 57) have suggested that price control
measures, in particular, should be regarded as a special case. In fact, the
Court's general approach to such measures is based on an analysis of
restrictions to trade and obstacles to attaining the unity of the common
market, rather than on the concept of discrimination. It was first
articulated clearly by the Court in Case 120/78 *Rewe-Zentrale AG* v.
Bundesmonopolverwaltung für Branntwein (Cassis de Dijon) ([1979]
ECR 649).

A German law prohibited the marketing of liqueurs with an alcoholic
strength of less than 25%. This made it impossible for the plaintiff to
import a consignment of Cassis de Dijon, a French liqueur with a strength
of between 15–20%, into Germany. The liqueur could therefore not
compete with the stronger, and more expensive, German equivalent.
There were no restrictions on the production and marketing of the
weaker liqueur in France. The German Government claimed that the
fixing of minimum alcohol contents had two functions:

–   it avoided the proliferation of alcoholic beverages on the national
     market, in particular alcoholic beverages with a low alcohol content;
     the Government argued that such products may more easily induce a
     tolerance towards alcohol than drinks with a high alcohol content;
–   it protected the consumer against unfair practices on the part of
     producers and distributors of alcoholic beverages consisting of
     lowering the alcohol content in order to obtain a competitive
     advantage in price.

The Court of Justice considered that the restriction on trade stemmed
from the disparity between the French and German legislation on
liqueurs. It concluded that in principle, there is no valid reason why,
provided they have been lawfully produced in one of the Member States,
alcoholic beverages should not be introduced into any other Member
State. The only exception to this principle, termed 'mutual recognition', is
where the disparities result from national provisions which are recognised
as being necessary in order to satisfy certain 'mandatory requirements'.
These mandatory requirements are in essence public policies concerning
inter alia the protection of public health, the effectiveness of fiscal
supervisions, the fairness of commercial transactions and the defence of
the consumer (*Cassis de Dijon* contained a non-exhaustive list which has
since been extended).

Applying the principle of mandatory requirements, sometimes termed
the 'rule of reason', to the measure in question, the Court used a
proportionality test. It looked to see, first, whether the justifications

raised fell within the concept of mandatory requirements; second, whether there was a serious and coherent national policy actually being operated; and third, whether the mesures adopted were reasonably necessary to pursue the policy operated, and whether they were proportionate to the aims. As regards the argument on health put forward by the German Government in *Cassis de Dijon,* the Court held that there was in fact no coherent public health policy being pursued through the ban on low alcohol liqueurs, since in practice a whole range of alcoholic beverages of varying alcohol contents was available in Germany. It also concluded that a ban was a disproportionate way of protecting the consumer against unfair practices. A system of labelling could have achieved the same effect in a less restrictive way.

It should be noted that in *Cassis de Dijon* the Court of Justice strictly overstepped its mark as the court of interpretation within the meaning of Article 177 EC. It left no discretion to the national court, but rather dealt comprehensively with all issues of application of the law itself. In later cases, where the application of Article 30 to certain types of national trading rules has not seemed so self-evident, the Court has not been so unambiguous in its rulings, and has deliberately left issues to the national court to decide, including, in some cases, issues of proportionality. This has in turn created significant difficulties for national courts when applying the Court's case law in practice.

14.8   The Case Law since *Cassis de Dijon*

Read together, the *Dassonville* formula on the scope of Article 30 and the *Cassis de Dijon* approach to indistinctly applicable measures seem to allow the imaginative trader to challenge virtually any national rule which governs the development, production or marketing of goods, forcing the state in each case to come up with a convincing policy-based justification for the rule. From *Cassis de Dijon* itself, and in particular from the mutual recognition principle, it is possible to articulate something close to a presumption that where the importing state imposes stricter contents requirements on products than the exporting state, this will require justification on grounds of the mandatory requirements. For example, the permitted contents of bread in the Netherlands (Case 130/80 *Keldermann* [1981] ECR 527), the permitted ingredients of pasta in Italy (Case 407/85 *Drei Glocken USL* [1988] ECR 4233) and the permitted ingredients of sausages in Germany (Case 274/87 *Commission* v. *Germany* [1989] ECR 229) have all come under challenge. Closely related are attacks on denomination requirements, such as the German *Reinheitsgebot* which restricted the use of the term 'Bier' to beverages containing only certain ingredients (barley, hops, yeast and water) (Case 178/84 *Commission* v. *Germany (Reinheitsgebot)* [1987] ECR 1227) and the reservation of the denomination 'jenever' in the Netherlands only for gin with a minimum alcohol content of 35%, where the Belgian equivalent with 30% alcohol had been lawfully marketed in Belgium (Case 182/84 *Miro BV* [1985] ECR 3731).

Similar considerations govern rules regarding the presentation of products. In Case 261/81 *Rau* v. *de Smedt* ([1982] ECR 3961) the Court held that a Belgian law requiring margarine to be packed in cube-shaped boxes, allegedly introduced in the interests of consumers in order to enable them to distinguish margarine from butter, fell within Article 30. Also covered was a UK requirement that all clothing and textiles indicate the country of origin (Case 207/83 *Commission* v. *UK (Origin Marking)* [1985] ECR 1201). The reservation of certain types of container for particular products likewise falls *prima facie* within Article 30: Case 16/83 *Prantl* ([1984] ECR 1299) concerned bulbous-shaped bottles from Italy, which closely resembled the German *Bocksbeutel* which is reserved under German law for a quality wine from a particular region of Germany; the Italian bottles themselves were also traditional to Italy. The Court held that the restriction fell within Article 30.

All these cases provide good examples of the mutual recognition principle in operation. Each measure held by the Court to fall within Article 30 may be saved under the 'rule of reason', by application of the mandatory requirements, or under the derogations in Article 36 (see 14.13–14.15) However, if the measure is not saved, the Member State will be precluded from prohibiting the marketing of goods lawfully marketed in another Member State which is assumed to have sufficient but different, and possibly lower, standards of food or beverage purity, or product presentation. Market integration is led by the demands of consumers and the responses of traders to those demands, and it requires regulatory authorities, perhaps, to consider more thoroughly the precise form by which goals such as consumer protection and public health are pursued. However, a Member State is not precluded from insisting on the continued application of higher standards for national products marketed at home. In Case 237/82 *Jongeneel Kaas* v. *Netherlands State* ([1984] ECR 483) a Dutch regulation concerning the permitted ingredients of cheese which was applicable only to cheese produced in the Netherlands was permitted under Articles 30–36.

The *Dassonville* formula as interpreted in *Cassis de Dijon* also has the effect of bringing a range of measures concerned with the circumstances in which products may be marketed within the scope of Article 30. For example, a number of cases have addressed the problems raised by bans and restrictions on advertising. In Case 286/81 *Oosthoek's Uitgevers-maatschappij BV* ([1982] ECR 4575) a Belgian manufacturer of encyclo-pedias who offered a free dictionary as a purchase incentive was prosecuted for breach of Dutch legislation which restricted the freedom to offer or give free gifts within the framework of a commercial activity. The Court held that the measure was covered by Article 30, concluding (at p. 4587) that:

'Legislation which restricts or prohibits certain forms of advertising and certain forms of sales promotion may, although it does not directly affect imports, be such as to restrict their volume because it affects marketing opportunities for the imported products. It cannot be ruled out that to compel a producer either to adopt advertising or sales promotion schemes which differ from one Member State to another or to discontinue a scheme which he considers to be particularly effective may constitute an obstacle to imports even if the legislation in question applies to domestic products and imported products without distinction.'

In similar terms the Court applied Article 30 to a Luxembourg law controlling the supply of information to consumers concerning sales promotions (Case C-362/88 *GB-INNO-BM* v. *CCL* [1990] ECR I-667) and a French ban on mentioning the word sugar or its characteristics in advertising of a synthetic form of sugar (Case C-241/89 *SARRP* v. *Chambre syndicale des Raffineurs et conditionneurs de sucre de France* [1990] ECR I-4695). The Court held that if publicity has to be changed according to the country a product is marketed in, this would have the effect of making imports more difficult. Finally, the Court has applied Article 30 to a ban on door to door sales of encyclopedias, citing *Oosthoek* in concluding that Article 30 does apply to rules which deprive a trader of a method of marketing whereby he realises almost all his sales (Case 382/87 *Ministère public* v. *Buet* [1989] ECR 1235).

14.9   The Limits of Article 30

In the light of the foregoing, it would seem that Article 30 is potentially applicable to any national law which regulates the economy in a manner which differs from other Member States. Applying the *Dassonville* test – which looks for actual or potential restrictions on interstate trade – simply by using a 'disparities' analysis places no sensible limits on the scope of Article 30, and gives the trader, who objects to a domestic measure, perhaps on grounds unrelated to its impact on the pattern of interstate trade, the opportunity merely to point to disparities in national rules across the Community in order to trigger the application of Article 30 and to require the Member State to justify its rules.

In principle, the Court has shown itself willing to accept the argument that some rules governing the economy are more intimately connected with the pattern of interstate trade than are others. For example, in Cases 266 and 267/87 *R.* v. *Pharmaceutical Society of Great Britain, ex parte Association of Pharmaceutical Importers* the Court accepted arguments based on figures demonstrating how a ban on pharmacists substituting (often cheaper, often imported) pharmaceutical products with the same therapeutic effect for the branded products prescribed by the doctor had had a dramatic effect on importations of pharmaceutical products. While acknowledging a residual uncertainty about the causal link between the ban and the sales of imported products, the Court in effect presumed that such a ban, although applicable equally to domestic and imported products, must fall within Article 30 (for the justification of this measure on health grounds, see 14.15).

Equally, in a series of cases beginning with Case 75/81 *Blesgen* v. *State of Belgium* ([1982] ECR 1211), the Court has shown itself prepared to hold that certain types of marketing restrictions have an insufficient connection with the pattern of imports to fall within Article 30. *Blesgen* concerned the compatibility with Article 30 of a Belgian law which prohibits the selling and stocking of spirits in places where alcoholic drinks are sold for consumption on the premises. It should be noted that Belgium produces beer in large quantities, and not spirits, and that the effect of the law is to encourage the consumption of beer rather than spirits in cafés and other drinking establishments. The alleged purpose of the law was to combat alcoholism. Instead of holding that the measure fell within Article 30, but was justified on health grounds, the Court referred to Commission Directive 70/50 and the formulation regarding indistinctly applicable measures in Article 3. It held that certain trade rules will fall within Article 30 only if their effects on trade exceed the effects intrinsic to such rules. It then went on (at p.1229):

'That is not however the case with a legislative provision concerning only the sale of strong spirits for consumption on the premises in all places open to the public and not concerning other forms of marketing the same drinks. It is to be observed in addition that the restrictions placed on the sale of the spirits in question make no distinction whatsoever based on their nature and origin. Such a legislative measure has therefore in fact no connection with the importation of the products and for that reason is not of such a nature as to impede trade between Member States.'

The judgment of the Court of Justice encountered criticism for its failure to apply the *Dassonville* test and then to use the rule of reason in order to allow justification on grounds of mandatory requirements.

However, the Court of Justice has repeated this reasoning in a number of subsequent cases; for example, in Case C-69/88 *Krantz* v. *Ontvanger der Directie Belastingen* ([1990] ECR I-583) it held that a national law permitting tax authorities to seize goods found on the premises of a tax-payer and to hold them against tax debts, even if the goods originated in another Member State, had an effect, if any, upon imports which was too uncertain and indirect to justify the application of Article 30. In Case C-23/89 *Quietlynn Ltd* v. *Southend BC* ([1990] ECR I-3059), national legislation prohibiting the sale of sex articles from unlicensed sex establishments was held to fall outside Article 30. It did not constitute an absolute prohibition on such products, and was merely a 'rule regarding their distribution, regulating the outlets through which the products may be marketed'. Similar arguments prevailed in a case on use restrictions, Case 148/85 *Forest* ([1986] ECR 3449), concerning French legislation establishing quotas for the milling of wheat for human consumption. There was no restriction on the import of flour and no direct restriction on the import of cereals for milling, but, since it limited output, the legislation did indirectly limit imports. The Court concluded that the measure fell outside Article 30, holding (at p.3475) that:

'such a system of quotas at the level of flour production in fact has no effect on wheat imports and is not likely to impede trade between Member States.'

It is clear, therefore, that the Court does accept that there are limits to the applicability of Article 30, and that it does not believe that potentially every national rule should require justification under what would in effect be a constitutional rule guaranteeing freedom of trade and limiting the regulatory autonomy of the Member States.

The particular difficulties are encountered in a series of cases in which the Court has not specifically stated that the measure falls outside or inside Article 30, but has left the national court to assess the measure in the light of its objective and the necessity and proportionality of that objective. Green, Harley and Usher (1991: 64) point out that there is a category of cases in which the Court appears to apply the proportionality test not, as in *Cassis de Dijon*, in order to ascertain whether a measure which falls within Article 30 is saved by application of the mandatory requirements, but in order to assess whether it is a sufficiently restrictive measure for it to fall within Article 30 in the first place. These cases concern measures, like that in *Blesgen*, which are not directly related to the question of importation at all.

The approach was outlined in Cases 60 and 61/84 *Cinéthèque* v. *Fédération Nationale des Cinémas Français* ([1985] ECR 2605). In that case, the Court was asked to assess the compatibility with Article 30 of French legislation prohibiting selling or hiring of video cassettes of films within one year of the film receiving its performance certificate. Although intended to encourage attendance at cinemas, and although equally applicable to domestic and imported films, the Court held that potentially the measure fell within Article 30. It held (at p.2626) that such a system of rules

'does not have the purpose of regulating trade patterns; its effect is not to favour national production as against the production of other Member States, but to encourage cinematographic production as such. Nevertheless, the application of such a system may create barriers to intra-Community trade in video-cassettes because of the disparities between the system operated in the different Member States and between the conditions for the release of cinematographic works in the cinemas of those States. In those circumstances a prohibition of exploitation laid down by such a system is not compatible with the principle of the free movement of goods provided for in the Treaty unless any obstacle to intra-Community trade thereby created does not exceed that which is necessary in order to ensure the attainment of the objective in view and unless that objective is justified with regard to Community law.'

In the event, the Court held that a national system such as that in force in France was so justified, even though it does have the effect of screening off the national market.

The Court applied similar reasoning in the first Sunday Trading case, a reference from the Cwmbran Magistrates' Court on the compatibility with Article 30 of sec. 47 of the Shops Act 1950 which prohibits Sunday trading in England and Wales, subject to certain rather absurdly framed exceptions (Case C-145/88 *Torfaen BC* v. *B & Q plc* [1989] ECR 3851). The point should be made that Article 30 has been used by traders objecting to the application of the Shops Act as just one of several means of resisting the application of legislation to which they have long objected. In that context, the invocation of Article 30 is considered by some to be an abuse of that provision (e.g. Steiner, 1992; Diamond, 1991). The Court first assigned the case to the category of cases which are not immediately concerned with the imports, and do not have the effect of making the marketing of imported products more difficult than the marketing of domestic products. It recalled its judgment in *Cinéthèque* in order to hold that such measures, nonetheless, may be incompatible with Article 30 unless justified. The rules must pursue an aim which is justified with regard to Community law, and the effects of such national rules must not exceed what is necessary to achieve the aim in view. The Court left it to the national court to decide these questions, although it indicated that it thought the Shops Act should be regarded as a component of the national rules governing hours of work, and, as it had previously held in an earlier case (Case 155/80 *Oebel* [1981] ECR 1993), such rules form a legitimate part of national economic and social policy which is consistent with the objectives of the Treaty.

It will be seen that the approach taken in *Cinéthèque* and *Torfaen* is closely related to that taken in *Blesgen*. The Court also makes reference to the test suggested by the Commission in Directive 70/50 in those cases. The difference appears to be that in *Torfaen* at least, the Court left more discretion to the national court, and it has been the exercise of this discretion that has caused so many problems in the UK in the context of Sunday trading.

For example, when *Torfaen* itself returned for decision before Cwmbran magistrates, they concluded that the essential objective of the Shops Act 1950 is to preserve the special nature of the English and Welsh Sunday, and that the effect on intra-Community trade of the restrictions in sec. 47 was not therefore excessive in view of that objective ([1990] 3 CMLR 455). On the other hand, in *B & Q plc* v. *Shrewsbury and Atcham Borough Council* ([1990] 3 CMLR 535), on appeal from magistrates to Shrewsbury Crown Court against a conviction under sec. 47, the judge applied the *Torfaen* test and concluded that sec. 47 could not be applied to trade which consisted in large measure of imports. He held that the objective of sec. 47 is that of protecting workers who did not want to work on Sundays and that this could be achieved in a less restrictive way. Sec. 47 was therefore disproportionate, and B & Q's appeal against conviction was upheld.

The problem of the diversity of approach resulted from the conviction of the courts that the question of the proportionality was a question of fact on which the opposing sides could adduce evidence. This obviously made it extremely onerous for a local authority to enforce sec. 47 by way of criminal prosecution, since it would be faced with a battery of evidence in each case from the traders that imports were in fact being affected, and that the regulatory approach taken by sec. 47 was excessively restrictive. Hoffmann J. appeared to solve that problem in *City of Stoke-on-Trent* v. *B & Q plc* ([1990] 3 CMLR 31) by treating the issues which went to the question of proportionality as matters of 'judicial notice', that is, presumed knowledge as to local customs, local history, social mores, etc. Although he held that the aim of the Shops Act was to protect those who did not wish to work on Sundays, he concluded on the basis of his assessment of proportionality that sec. 47 was not incompatible with Article 30. That case was subsequently appealed by way of leapfrog direct to the House of Lords, and the issue referred once more to the Court of Justice (Case C-169/91 *City of Stoke on Trent* v. *B & Q plc*).

However, it became clearer when the Court subsequently decided two cases on Sunday employment (rather a different issue to Sunday *trading*), referred by courts in France and Belgium, that it may be prepared to adopt a stricter approach to the assessment of proportionality. In Case C-332/89 *Criminal Proceedings against Marchandise* [1991] ECR I-1027 and Case C-312/89 *CGT* v. *Conforama* [1991] ECR I-997, both decided by the Full Court, the Court appeared to decide the proportionality points itself. It held that a restriction on the employment of workers on a Sunday pursues a legitimate goal of socio-economic policy under Community law, that it is a matter to be resolved by the Member States at the current point of European integration, and that the restrictive effects on trade of such measures do not appear to be excessive having regard to the aim pursued.

In Case C-169/91 *City of Stoke on Trent Council* v. *B & Q plc* [1993] 1 All ER 481, the Court followed the approach which it took in *Conforama* and *Marchandise*, concluding that although *prima facie* the porportionality point was one to be decided by the national court, it could nonetheless be decided by the Court of Justice itself, in the interests of the uniform application of Community law, in circumstances where it possessed sufficient information to be able to assess the effect of the disputed legislation on the pattern of trade between Member States. The Court did not draw the distinction proposed by the defendant company between Sunday trading and Sunday employment legislation; B & Q had argued that the English rules governing the former were incoherent and therefore disproportionate, and altogether different from the French and Belgian rules on Sunday employment.

There thus appear to be three categories of cases involving indistinctly applicable measures:

– those in which the Court accepts without question the impact of the measure on imports (e.g. composition requirements), and where the measure will only be saved by reference to the mandatory requirements (*Cassis de Dijon*);
– those in which the Court accepts itself that there is no link with patterns of intra-Community trade, and therefore holds that the measure falls outside Article 30 (*Blesgen; Quietlynn*);
– a grey area in which the Court accepts a link, albeit relatively indirect, between the measure and patterns of intra-Community trade, but allows derogation on the basis of the proportionate pursuit of legitimate socio-economic goals such as the regulation of the labour market, or the promotion of culture (*Cinéthèque, Torfaen, Conforama*). This appears to be rather different to allowing derogation on grounds of the mandatory requirements. Here the uncertainties result from the difficulties for national courts in assessing the proportionality of measures of socio-economic policy. Given existing variations in perceptions of the appropriate scope of the judicial role, it is to be anticipated that national and regional variations in the application of Community law will result from such an approach.

14.10   Assessment of the Case Law of the Court

It is one thing to categorise the cases according to this schema, but it is quite another to identify some sort of principled basis for distinguishing between the different types of cases. Given that the definition of MEEQRs in *Dassonville* continues to underlie the whole body of case law, and that it is sufficiently broad to encompass any type of potential restriction stemming from disparities in national legislation, there is a great deal of uncertainty at present in the application of Article 30.

It is for this reason that a number of authors (White, 1989; Mortelmans, 1991; Steiner, 1992) have suggested abandoning the *Dassonville* test as a catch-all test for indistinctly applicable measures, or at least supplementing it with some alternative means of identifying those disparities in national rules which have a truly restrictive effect on trade between Member States. To Steiner, this amounts to revitalising that element in the *Dassonville* formula which talks of 'restrictions' on trade. White has argued (in a personal capacity, but this is also a view he has put forward as agent for the Commission in a number of cases) that the mischief aimed at in Article 30, as interpreted in *Cassis de Dijon* is

'the application by a Member State to products legally produced and marketed in another Member State of its national rules relating to the characteristics required of such products on its territory (which therefore prevents this product from benefiting in the importing Member State from the advantages arising out of its production in the different legal and economic environment prevailing in the other Member State)' (White, 1989: 247).

On his argument this should exclude from Article 30 the rules relating to the circumstances in which goods may be sold or used, providing imported goods enjoy equal access to the market with national goods. Mortelmans, while broadly in sympathy with the approach taken by White, adds an extra element to enable the identification of the damaging disparities: measures with a territorial element, which restrict sales only a fixed location such as *Quietlynn* or *Blesgen* are not damaging to interstate trade in the same way as general measures such as *Oosthoek* and *Buet*. Weatherill (1992c) likewise distinguishes between the different categories of case which potentially fall within Article 30, arguing in favour of a more nuanced application in so-called 'equal burden' cases. These are cases in which the effect of the measure attacked is not to impose a dual burden on the imported product, as do, for example, disparities in composition requirements or technical standards. In cases such as *Torfaen*, it is the existence of the rule on Sunday Trading, not the fact that it may differ from rules in other Member States which may possibly reduce the volume of interstate trade. He offers two possible solutions: either Article 30 can be restricted to 'equal burden' measures which genuinely partition the market, such as the rule in *Cinéthèque*, or courts, the Court of Justice included, can become more sceptical about the evidence produced by traders concerning the alleged effects of trade of the measures challenged. He points to the fact that in *Quietlynn* the Court seemed prepared to discount evidence produced in the national court concerning patterns of interstate trade.

Two Advocates General have also lent weight to the argument that the *Dassonville* formula alone is an insufficient basis for the application of Article 30. In differing from the Court of Justice in the interpretation of the French legislation at issue in *Cinéthèque*, AG Slynn concluded that Article 30 was only applicable to indistinctly applicable measures which require a 'producer or distributor to take steps additional to those which he would normally and lawfully take in the marketing of his goods, which thereby render importation more difficult, so that imports may be restricted and national producers be given protection in practice'.

AG van Gerven in *Torfaen* came up with an alternative analysis of the effects of indistinctly applicable measures in which he used the case law of the Court of Justice on the application of the competition rules (Articles 85 and 86 EC) to conclude that only those measures which have the effect of raising the threshold to imported goods and thus of segmenting the Community market should fall within Article 30. However, the effect of his analysis is to argue that there should be a *de minimis* criterion in the application of Article 30, and this has been expressly rejected by the Court in Case 177/82 *Van de Haar*.

On the other hand, other authors do not favour a departure from the existing *Dassonville* test, and indeed criticise the Court for not applying the test itself. Gormley (1989, 1990) has argued for a straightforward, or even mechanical, application of the *Dassonville* formula to national regulatory restrictions, coupled with a willingness to recognise the legitimacy of the exercise by Member States of their 'local police powers', that is their autonomy to regulate local economic life according to established socio-economic traditions and mores, in the form of the mandatory requirements. The difficulty with this approach, which is close also to the one advocated by Arnull (1991), is that it opens potentially all national rules to judicial scrutiny and places a heavy burden on the national court in the assessment of the mandatory requirements. It would appear, for example, from the diversity of approaches taken by the English judges in the Sunday Trading cases that proportionality is not a concept they feel comfortable applying; Hoffmann J. suggested in *City of Stoke-on-Trent* v. *B & Q plc* that it would be more appropriate to the nature of the judicial function for judges to assess only whether a measure is reasonable in the sense of being one which a reasonable legislator would adopt in order to attain the desired, legitimate object.

14.11 Article 34: The Prohibition on MEEQRs on Exports

Article 34 prohibits MEEQRs on exports. For example, in Case 53/76 *Procureur de la République* v. *Bouhelier* ([1977] ECR 197) a requirement in France for watches destined for export to be given an export licence following a quality inspection was held to breach Article 34 as it was not required for watches destined to be sold in France. However, although the Court applies the *Dassonville* formula to MEEQRs on exports, it does not apply it with the same rigour to indistinctly applicable measures.

For example, a ban on the possession of horse meat by manufacturers of meat products, intended to ensure that exports of those products to countries which prohibit the sale of horseflesh will not be affected by the suspicion that horse meat might have been used in their manufacture, was held not to breach Article 34, even though it represented an obstacle to export. Similarly, in Case 155/80 *Oebel* a restriction on night working and delivery hours in respect of bakery produce in Belgium was held to be compatible with Article 34, even though it had the effect of preventing Belgian bakers selling their wares in other neighbouring Member States in time for breakfast. The Court held ([1981] ECR 1993 at p.2009):

'Article 34 concerns national measures which have as their specific object or effect the restriction of patterns of exports and thereby the establishment of a difference in treatment between the domestic trade of a Member State and its export trade, in such a way as to provide a particular advantage for national production or for the domestic market of the State in question.'

Case C-47/90 *Delhaize* v. *Promalvin SA* provides a good example of how the spin-off protectionist effect of a measure restricting imports can benefit the domestic market in a related economic activity, in this case the bottling of wine. The Court held that a Spanish ban on bulk sales of unbottled wine for export breached Article 34, as it protected the operation of Spanish-based bottling firms.

14.12 Exceptions to the Principles in Articles 30 and 34

State measures which breach Articles 30 and 34 may be saved by the exceptions in Article 36, or, if they are indistinctly applicable measures in breach of Article 30, by the operation of the rule of reason outlined in *Cassis de Dijon*, by reference to so-called mandatory requirements.

Article 36 provides an exhaustive list of grounds of derogation which the Court has held must be interpreted strictly, like any other exception from the basic principles of free movement. Moreover, the mandatory requirements cannot be applied to facially discriminatory measures. In Case 113/80 *Commission* v. *Ireland (Souvenirs)* the Court held that consumer protection grounds could not be invoked to justify a discriminatory measure, as Article 36 contains no consumer protection clause.

In this chapter we have treated as two rather different issues the assessment of mandatory requirements in the context of cases like *Cassis de Dijon*, where the measure in question has a clearly burdensome impact upon imported products, and the assessment of the proportionality of legitimate national socio-economic policies in cases such as *Cinéthèque* and *Torfaen*, where the measure has a much more remote impact upon interstate trade. This distinction will be retained in 14.13.

14.13 The Operation of the Mandatory Requirements

Cassis de Dijon itself listed the following as permissible mandatory requirements which could justify the imposition of state measures which have the effect of restricting trade:

- the protection of public health;
- the effectiveness of fiscal supervisions;
- the fairness of commercial transactions;
- the defence of the consumer.

To this list has since been added environmental protection (Case 240/83 *Procureur de la République* v. *Association de défense des brûleurs d'huiles usagées* [1985] ECR 531 (disposal of waste oil); Case 302/86 *Commission* v. *Denmark (disposable drinks containers)* [1988] ECR 4607). It is possible, also, that any measures of national socio-economic policy which have been held to pursue legitimate aims, such as the protection of culture in *Cinéthèque*, and the protection of workers in *Torfaen* and *Conforama* could potentially also fall within the concept of mandatory requirements. Certainly, the mandatory requirements would be held to be legitimate goals of socio-economic policy which could justify the types of indirectly restrictive measures at issue in those cases. Regional policy objectives could probably also be included in this category as could measures to protect disadvantaged groups such as the unemployed or disabled workers.

In *Cassis de Dijon* the Court showed itself prepared to be sceptical about the claims of Member States that particular measures pursued particular aims, and to assess the reality of the policy pursued in the light of the evidence. For a measure to be proportionate it must satisfy a test with three limbs. It must be:

- suitable to achieve the stated aim;
- necessary to achieve the stated aim;
- no more restrictive than is absolutely necessary for the purposes of achieving the stated aim.

In *Disposable drinks containers* the Court referred to the Single European Act in concluding that the protection of the environment is one of the Community's essential objectives, and that a Danish measure making a deposit-and-return system compulsory in order to enforce the re-use of containers for beer and soft drinks was covered by the mandatory requirement of protection of the environment. It also held that the recycling system itself was a proportionate measure for Denmark to adopt. On the other hand, the Court took a different approach to the practice of requiring drinks to be sold only in approved containers, in order to restrict the range of containers on the market and to encourage maximum re-use by allowing consumers to return empty bottles to any drinks retailer. The practice of allowing only approved containers has a strong effect of partitioning off the Danish market against the penetration of new imported drinks, and although drinks could be sold in non-approved containers, a maximum of 3,000 hectolitres per annum was imposed, on the grounds that re-use was less likely to occur in respect of non-approved containers. The Court held that the restriction of the quantity of products to be sold in non-approved containers was disproportionate to the aim pursued, since a system of returning non-approved containers is still capable of protecting the environment.

Measures of consumer protection, in particular those allegedly aimed at protecting consumers against unfair commercial practices are, in contrast, frequently held to be disproportionate by the Court, and indeed, it is arguably one of the most significant contributions of the Court that it has instituted a system allowing 'real' consumer protection measures to be differentiated from those which have in truth a protectionist inspiration. This trend began in *Cassis de Dijon* itself, where the Court held that the ban on the sale of low alcohol liqueurs in the interests of the protection of the consumer against unfair commercial practices was a disproportionate measure, and that the objective could have been achieved by a less restrictive labelling requirement. In similar terms, the Court held in Case

16/83 *Prantl* that labelling was one way of protecting the consumer against confusion resulting from the fact that in both Germany and Italy a particular bulbous shape of bottle is traditionally reserved for wines from a particular region. While Germany might be able to require specific types of labels, it could not prohibit imports of the Italian wines in the bulbous shaped bottles.

On the other hand, labelling itself may be regarded as disproportionate. In Case 207/83 *Commission* v. *UK (Origin Marking)* the Court held that the UK requirement that clothing and textiles indicate their country of origin was a disproportionate measure of consumer policy. The UK government had argued that consumers regard the origin of goods as an indication of their quality. The Court held that the rule merely enabled consumers to assert their prejudices, thereby slowing down the integration of markets within the Community. The quality of goods can just as well be indicated on the goods themselves or their packaging, and the protection of consumers is sufficiently guaranteed by prohibiting false indications of origin.

In Case C-362/88 *GB-INNO-BM* v. *CCL* the Court trenchantly rejected arguments by Luxembourg that its measures restricting the information available to consumers about the nature of special offers for sale were justified, indicating that the measures in fact ran counter to the Community's own consumer policy of promoting information for consumers.

The Court has taken a rather different approach to the assessment of health protection measures, where it has shown more caution before sweeping away national measures by reference to the mutual recognition principle. However, since Article 36 also contains a specific public health exception and it is therefore of no relevance whether a measure is exempted under the mandatory requirements or under that provision, discussion of this point will be covered in 14.15 below.

14.14   Article 36

The burden of proving that a measure is exempted by Article 36 from the application of the prohibitions in Articles 30 and 34 lies with the Member State. However, in enforcement actions under Article 169, the onus still lies on the Commission to prove its case. In Case C-95/89, etc. *Commission* v. *Italy et al.* (16.7.1992) the Court held that the Commission had failed to prove its case of breach of Articles 30–36 in respect of the bans imposed by Italy, Greece and France on imports of cheese containing levels of nitrates within the limits accepted as safe by scientists. Although the three Member States maintained bans, they all provided for the possibility of exemption from the ban on application by a trader, so that new additives could be placed upon the list of those which are allowed. The Court held that the Commission had failed to prove that the systems being operated in any manner which was contrary to Community law, for example, by demonstrating that a request for the inclusion of an additive presented by a trader had been arbitrarily refused.

It is not sufficient for a measure simply to be shown to fall within one of the express exceptions contained in Article 36, viz. public morality, public policy, public security, the protection of health and life of humans, animals or plants, the protection of national treasures possessing artistic, historic or archaeological value and the protection of industrial and commercial property. In order to avoid being categorised as a means of arbitrary discrimination or a disguised restriction on trade between Member States, such a measure must be shown to be part of a coherent policy applying also to domestic products, where appropriate. Clearly, if the objective of a public health policy is to prevent a particular plant or animal disease becoming established within the national territory – a particularly important matter for the Community's island Member States – then a policy which has its main focus at the borders will be permissible. In Case 74/82 *Commission* v. *Ireland (Imports of poultry)* ([1984] ECR 317) an import licence requirement for poultry to prevent the spread of Newcastle disease was held justified on the grounds of the exceptionally high health standards of Irish poultry. In contrast, in Case 40/82 *Commission* v. *UK (Imports of poultry)* ([1982] ECR 2793) an import licence requirement imposed for similar reasons on imports into the UK was held not to be justified. In fact, it amounted to a total ban on imports from six Member States and was not part of a seriously considered health policy, but operated as a disguised restriction on trade. Thus a test close to that of proportionality is imposed in the context of Article 36.

The Court has made it clear that there is no general derogation from Articles 30–36 on economic grounds to protect Member States against the possibly damaging effects of enhanced competition as a result of free trade. In Case 72/83 *Campus Oil Ltd* v. *Minister for Industry and Energy* ([1983] ECR 2727 at p.2752) the Court stated that

'a Member State cannot be allowed to avoid the effects of measures provided for in the Treaty by pleading the economic difficulties caused by the elimination of barriers to intra-community trade.'

The public morality ground has been invoked on a number of occasions. In Case 34/79 *R.* v. *Henn and Darby* it was successfully invoked to justify a ban on the import of pornographic materials which were 'indecent or obscene'. The internal ban operated on the basis of materials being likely to 'deprave or corrupt'. Although the measure was discriminatory, the discrimination was not arbitrary, and did not amount to a disguised restriction on trade, since there was no lawful trade in such goods in the UK. On the other hand, in Case 121/85 *Conegate* v. *H.M. Customs and Excise* ([1986] ECR 1007) the UK sought to invoke the public morality ground in order to justify the seizure by the customs and excise authorities of inflatable rubber dolls and other items of erotica imported from Germany, on the grounds that they were 'indecent and erotic'. Here there was no equivalent ban on manufacture, only restrictions on marketing, and the rule was clearly operating in a discriminatory manner; the public morality exception could not, therefore, be invoked by the UK.

In contrast, the public policy ground has never successfully been invoked. Perhaps this is because the Court fears the potential breadth of this derogation if it is allowed to be exploited. The closest to what might be regarded as a legitimate case of derogation on grounds of public policy, *Campus Oil*, was decided on the public security ground. In Case 7/78 *R. v. Thompson, Johnson and Woodiwiss* ([1978] ECR 2247) the public policy ground was unsuccessfully invoked for the protection of the integrity of the coinage. In Case 16/83 *Prantl* the Court confirmed that a measure cannot be justified on public policy grounds simply because it is reinforced by penal sanctions.

Public security was successfully invoked in *Campus Oil*, which concerned a requirement that all oil importers buy a certain amount of oil from the Irish National Petroleum Company. The public security interest protected was that of guaranteeing the continuity of oil supplies by ensuring the survival of a national oil refinery.

Protection of national treasures has never been used as a ground for derogation, although it was referred to explicitly in Case 7/68 *Commission v. Italy (Art Treasures)* ([1968] ECR 423) as being not a reason to justify a tax imposed on exports.

14.15 The Protection of the Health and Life of Humans, Animals and Plants

In the assessment of the legitimacy of public health derogations, expert evidence will often be important. For example, a state wishing to argue that its stricter health standards are necessary to protect public health will need, in effect, to demonstrate that the standards in other Member States are inadequate. This was precisely what Germany failed to do in Case 178/84 *Commission v. Germany (Reinheitsgebot)* where the Court held that although the drinking habits of the German population might have justified the exclusion of some additives in beer, a blanket ban was disproportionate. Moreover, simply referring to traditional domestic methods of production as an alternative way of producing the goods in question without the offending additives does not represent a sufficient justification under Article 36. In Cases C-13 and 113/91 *Debus* (4.6.1992) an Italian measure prohibited the marketing of beers in Italy with additive levels which were permissible in France, where they were produced. Figures produced by the Commission demonstrated that the additive levels in the imported beer would not lead to the absorption of the additives in quantities beyond those deemed to be safe by the World Health Organisation. The measures could not be justified by reference to domestic methods of production which did not involve the prohibited additive levels, since this would have the effect of privileging domestic production methods and of restricting interstate trade.

On the other hand, in Case 53/80 *Eyssen* ([1981] ECR 409), a Dutch prohibition on nisin in cheese was permitted on public health grounds, although other Member States permitted it, and the scientific evidence was equivocal.

The Court has shown itself consistently prepared to look behind the veneer of national public health policies. In Case 124/81 *Commission* v. *UK (Imports of UHT milk)* the requirement that UHT milk imported into the UK be marketed only by approved dairies or distributors (supposedly to ensure that the milk was free from bacterial or viral infections) which forced imported milk to be re-packaged and re-treated was held not to be justified. There was evidence available that milk in all the Member States was of similar quality and subject to equivalent controls. Case 4/75 *Rewe Zentralfinanz* v. *Landwirtschaftskammer Bonn* provides a contrast to this case. The inspection of imported apples in order to control San José scale – a pest – was held to be justified since a real risk was involved.

Systematic controls in areas of plant and animal health, where uniform Community legislation has been instituted in place of piecemeal national protection, and where the system is based on inspections by the exporting Member State, have been held to exclude the application of systematic controls by the importing Member State (Case 190/87 *Oberkreisdirektor* v. *Moormann* [1988] ECR 4689). However, occasional controls could be justified on the basis of Article 36. This is an example of the uniform or harmonised Community legislation supplanting the use of Article 36 (see 14.16).

Finally, the Court has shown itself to be generally lenient as regards the assessment of national policies concerning medical and pharmaceutical products. In Cases 266 and 267/87 *R.* v. *Pharmaceutical Society of Great Britain, ex parte Association of Pharmaceutical Importers* a ban on substituting medicines for those specifically prescribed by a doctor was held justified on health grounds. The Court was persuaded that psychosomatic reasons may justify insistence on a particular drug to the exclusion of its differently named therapeutic equivalent, although the balance of scientific evidence on this point is not entirely unequivocal. A similar trend is in evidence in Case C-369/88 *Delattre* [1991] ECR I-1487 in which the Court held that the French monopoly which reserved the sale of medicinal products by pharmacists, including products defined as medicines in France but freely available in other Member States, could be justified on health (and consumer protection) grounds.

14.16   No Derogation where Community Legislation has Exhaustively Regulated the Field

In *Cassis de Dijon* the Court referred to the fact that there were no Community rules which governed the composition and marketing of alcholic drinks. In the absence of such common rules, the Member States retain the right to regulate these matters, subject to the application of the rules on the free movement of goods. Conversely, the existence of

Community legislative measures which exhaustively regulate a field precludes the application of Article 30, and recourse to Article 36. This applies to both discriminatory and indistinctly applicable restrictions on trade in goods, as Case 190/87 *Oberkreisdirektor* v. *Moormann* illustrates with regard to health inspections on imports. It is in fact principally in the field of animal and plant health inspections that Community legislation has been adjudged to provide an exhaustive regulatory system (e.g. Case 28/84 *Commission* v. *Germany* ([1985] ECR 3097), although an exceptional example outside this field is offered by the *Dim-dip headlights* case.

In Case 60/86 *Commission* v. *UK (Dim-dip headlights)* ([1988] ECR 3921). In that case, the UK's prohibition on motor vehicles not equipped with dim-dip headlights was condemned on the grounds that the field had been exhaustively regulated by Community law. Directive 70/156, which was introduced in order to reduce hindrances to trade in motor vehicles within the Community resulting from differing mandatory technical requirements, contained an exhaustive list of lighting and light-signalling devices, not including dim-dip headlights. Total harmonisation in this sense not only triggers the pre-emptive effect of Community law (8.12) but also precludes reliance on derogations such as Article 36.

If Community legislation has only *partially* occupied the field, then national regulatory autonomy will continue to prevail. This point is illustrated by the relationship between Directive 65/65 concerning proprietary medicinal products and the free movement rules. As noted above in Case C-369/88 *Delattre* the Member States remain free to define which products are medicines and to regulate their distribution, subject to the rules of free movement of goods. In Case 174/82 *Officier van Justitie* v. *Sandoz* ([1983] ECR 2445), despite partial harmonisation of the permissible additives in foodstuffs, it was held that the Dutch authorities were permitted, under Article 36, to prohibit the sale without prior authorisation of muesli bars to which vitamins had been added, although these were freely available in other Member States.

Article 100A EC provides a significant departure from the principle whereby harmonisation will normally preclude national derogation. Para. 4 provides:

'If, after the adoption of a harmonisation measure by the Council acting by a qualified majority, a Member State deems it necessary to apply national provisions on grounds of major needs referred to in Article 36, or relating to protection of the environment or the working environment, it shall notify the Commission of these provisions.

The Commission shall confirm the provisions involved after having verified that they are not a means of arbitrary discrimination or a disguised restriction on trade between Member States.

By way of derogation from the procedure laid down in Articles 169 and 170, the Commission or any Member State may bring the matter directly before the Court of Justice if it considers that another Member State is making improper use of the powers provided for in this Article.'

It seems rather odd that the safeguard clause in Article 100A(4) was not drafted in such a way as to cover measures taken to protect consumers, but that is the necessary implication of the reference to Article 36 and the listing of the environment and the working environment as the other 'major needs' which can be protected. The expedited enforcement procedures laid down in Article 100A(4) have yet to be tested before the Court of Justice.

14.17 The Protection of Intellectual Property: Special Problems in Applying Articles 30-36

The derogation regarding the protection of intellectual property contained in Article 36 cannot be properly understood without a brief discussion of how Article 30 has been interpreted as applying to national provisions which protect intellectual property, a special subject deserving of detailed attention in its own right (e.g. Marenco and Banks, 1990). The Court has developed an 'exhaustion of rights' doctrine in order to prevent intellectual property rights, and the national legislation which upholds them, being used to segment the Community product market. A patent-holder who has marketed his or her products, or who has consented to them being marketed (e.g. by an agent or licensee), in another Member State will be precluded by Article 30 from relying on domestic legislation which extends patent protection to parallel imports (that is products under the same or a parallel patent imported from overseas) in order to exclude the imports. Thus the patent-holder is precluded from creating differential pricing systems in which the patented product is sold at higher prices in certain Member States, since intellectual property legislation cannot be used to screen off the national market against imports of cheaper patented products bought up by a parallel importer in another Member State (Case 15/74 *Centrafarm BV* v. *Sterling Drug Inc* [1974] ECR 1147).

In Case 19/84 *Pharmon BV* v. *Hoechst AG* ([1985] ECR 2281), the Court limited the scope of what is meant by 'consent' for the purposes of the exhaustion of rights doctrine, concluding that where a compulsory licence has been granted for the exploitation of a patent in a Member State where the patent-holder has never exploited it, this does not amount to the patent-holder giving his or her consent. It remains possible therefore, to use national legislation which is saved by the Article 36 derogation, to restrict imports of the patented product from the Member State where the compulsory licence has been granted into another Member State where patent protection is also held. By according this protection, the Court claims to be protecting the 'specific subject matter' of the intellectual property rights, namely the reward which the patent-holder (or holder of a trademark or a copyrights) should derive from his or her invention, innovation or design.

The Court applies similar exhaustion of rights arguments in respect of trademarks and copyrights.

14.18   The Contribution of Article 30 to the Completion of the Internal Market

The case law of the Court of Justice on Article 30, in particular the mutual recognition doctrine articulated in *Cassis de Dijon*, has made two important contributions to the programme for the completion of the internal market which will be discussed in Chapter 15.

First, the mutual recognition principle has been explicitly adopted by the Commission as the basis for the majority of its harmonisation proposals in the area of the internal market. In its White Paper, the Commission worked on the assumption of the essential equivalence of the legislative objectives pursued by the Member States when they regulate product and technical standards, and argued for a Community legislative strategy which adopted only minimum health and safety standards and left the detailed elaboration of industrial standards to technical standards authorities based at a Community level. This was a departure from the general approach to harmonisation previously applied by the Community, which had sought to regulate in detail all aspects of the products in question. While Community harmonisation measures in the field of technical and product standards are not new phenomena, legislative progress was consistently blocked by the difficulties of achieving agreement on comprehensive lists of standards in respect of a given product using the law-making power in Article 100 EC which requires unanimity in the Council. The new approach was given support in advance of the Single European Act by a Council Resolution of May 7 1985 on technical harmonisation and standards (OJ 1985 C136/1). Subsequently, the Member States, through the adoption in the Single European Act of Article 100A EC as a law-making power in this field, gave the Council of Ministers the appropriate institutional means by which to pursue this strategy. Difficulties with the new approach will be discussed in Chapter 15.

In the form of Article 100B EC the Member States have also given explicit Treaty recognition to the principle of mutual recognition. Acknowledging that not all the legislative business proposed would be likely to be concluded by the end of 1992, Article 100B offered an accelerated mutual recognition process for the period immediately preceding the deadline:

'1. During 1992, the Commission shall, together with each Member State, draw up an inventory of national laws, regulations and administrative provisions which fall under Article 100A and which have not been harmonised pursuant to that Article. The Council, acting in accordance with the provisions of Article 100A may decide that the provisions in force in a Member State must be recognised as equivalent to those applied by another Member State.
2. The provisions of Article 100A(4) shall apply by analogy.'

Article 100B is the result of a failed attempt by the Commission to achieve an automatic process of mutual recognition in the absence of harmonisation. Since, however, like Article 100A itself, it allows Member States to derogate from the measures adopted by the Council by a qualified majority on the grounds of 'major needs' (Articles 100A(4) and 100B(2)), it would not appear in practice that Article 100B takes the process of market integration much further than the position already achieved by the Court of Justice in *Cassis de Dijon*. The effect of that Article may be rather to emphasise the importance which the Member States attached, when they concluded the Single European Act, to the observance of the timetable set out in Article 7A (Ehlermann, 1987: 402).

Summary

1 Articles 30–36 prohibit quantitative restrictions and measures having equivalent effect to quantitative restrictions (MEEQRs) on imports and exports, subject to derogations based on major needs such as health protection.

2 The notion of an MEEQR was defined broadly by the Court of Justice in *Dassonville*, and that definition has influenced the evolution of the case law on Article 30.

3 The application of Article 30 to discriminatory measures which treat imports and domestic products facially differently is relatively unproblematic; such measures may only be justified by reference to Article 36.

4 In *Cassis de Dijon* the Court elaborated its approach to indistinctly applicable measures, using the principle of mutual recognition in order to identify those disparities between the national laws which tend to restrict interstate trade. It developed a doctrine of mandatory requirements in order to allow Member States to continue to apply, for example, important consumer, health and environmental protection policies.

5 The application of the Court's case law on Article 30 causes difficulties in relation to measures which have only a remote or indirect effect upon interstate trade; in these cases, the Court has yet to identify an approach which is doctrinally satisfactory, and which does not place too great a burden on the national courts.

6 Article 34 only applies to discriminatory restrictions on exports. The *Cassis de Dijon* case law does not apply.

7 The Court interprets the derogations contained in the mandatory requirements and Article 36 strictly, as they are exceptions to the fundamental principle of free movement. The Court has been most prepared to accept justifications based on health protection. It has shown a certain scepticism about some elements of national consumer protection policies.

8 The case law on Articles 30 and 36 has made a significant contribution to the evolution of the Community's internal market programme, in particular through the development of the concept of mutual recognition.

Questions

1 What types of barriers does Article 30 apply to?
2 In what ways do the approaches of the Commission in Directive 70/50 and the Court in its case law since *Dassonville* differ on the interpretation of Article 30?
3 What are the mandatory requirements? In what way do they differ from the derogations contained in Article 36?
4 Why does the approach to indistinctly applicable measures taken by the Court lead to uncertainty in the application of Article 30?
5 Has the Court been too strict or too generous in its interpretation of the exceptions to Article 30?
6 In what ways does the interpretation of Article 34 differ from that of Article 30?
7 Identify the contribution made by the Court's case law to the development of the internal market programme.

Workshop

Brian is a manufacturer of power saws in the UK, with plants in England and Northern Ireland. Consider the difficulties which he faces, in the light of Community law:

1 He is required to obtain an import licence to import his saws into Greece. This requirement was enacted by the Greek government to keep a record of imports of power saws following public pressure after a number of 'copycat' Texas chain saw massacres.
2 In Italy he is prosecuted for putting the saws on the market in breach of an Italian law which requires, on safety grounds, that the handles of power saws, both imported and domestic, be made of a special hardened plastic. The only manufacturer of this type of plastic in the European Community is situated in Italy.
3 In Germany, he finds that power saws may only be sold in registered specialised shops. The justification for this requirement is that it protects the existence of small tool shops, and protects the profession of retail tool sellers.
4 He has a plant in Belfast which produces power saws, but he experiences difficulties competing with manufacturers in Ireland in supplying Irish retailers, although his unit costs are smaller, because of a UK law which prohibits on environmental grounds the use of the machines to make power saws for more than ten hours per day.
5 He finds his products subjected to an organised boycott by French retailers whose professional association has issued details of his union-busting tactics in his factories in England.

Further Reading

Arnull (1991) 'What shall we do on Sunday?', 16 *European Law Review*, 112.
Diamond (1991) 'Dishonourable Defences: The Use of Injunctions and the EEC Treaty: Case Study of the Shops Act 1950', 54 *Modern Law Review*, 72.
Gormley (1989) 'Some Reflections on the Internal Market and the Free Movement of Goods', *Legal Issues of European Integration*, 1/89, 9 esp. Part IV.

Gormley (1990) 'Commentary on *Torfaen BC* v. *B & Q plc'*, 27 *Common Market Law Review*, 141.

Green, Hartley and Usher (1991), Chs 5–7.

Marenco and Banks (1990) 'Intellectual Property and the Community rules on Free Movement: Discrimination unearthed', 15 *European Law Review*, 224.

Mortelmans (1991) 'Article 30 of the EEC Treaty and Legislation Relating to Market Circumstances: Time to consider a new definition?', 28 *Common Market Law Review*, 115.

Steiner (1992) 'Drawing the Line: Uses and Abuses of Article 30 EEC', 29 *Common Market Law Review*, 749.

Weatherill (1992c) 'The free movement of goods: a survey of the decisions of the Court of Justice in 1991', 17 *European Law Review*, 421.

White (1989) 'In search of the limits to Article 30 of the EEC Treaty', 26 *Common Market Law Review*, 235, esp. part 2.

15 The Internal Market Project: the Basic Outlines

15.1 Introduction (see also 1.3, Chapter 11 and 14.18)

As will by now be clear to the reader, one of the central preoccupations of the European Community during the period 1985–92 was the completion of the internal market, defined in Article 7A EC (previously Article 8A EEC) as an area without internal frontiers in which goods, services, persons and capital may move without hindrance. While the Single European Act does not in any way detract or derogate from the goals of the original Treaty of Rome, it had the effect of concentrating the effort of the Community upon a particular project – '1992'. The initial success of the internal market project was such that during the late 1980s and early 1990s it dramatically revitalised the fortunes of the European Community; issues such as Economic and Monetary Union (EMU), which had long been abandoned on the back burner of the integration process, were now taken forward as serious and apparently attainable objectives. In addition, the Community has developed a more comprehensive and coherent regional policy ('economic and social cohesion'), in response to the recognition that the economic adjustments caused by a larger market would exacerbate existing regional disparities. The development of these policies is seen by some as a pay-off to the less well-off Member States in return for their willingness to face the rigours of increased transnational competition, and by others as an aspect of the evolving macro-economic competence of the Community. As an international organisation, the European Community also enjoyed a significant resurgence in its standing during this period. However, by late 1992 the failure of the Community to reach a satisfactory agreement with the USA in the context of the GATT Uruguay Round began to throw doubt on the perspective of internal and external economic and political gains flowing inexorably from the internal market project (2.16). Finally, the possibility that the integration impetus had been stretched beyond breaking point by the failure of the fragile compromises reached in the Treaty of Maastricht on Economic and Monetary Union and Political Union to achieve the anticipated support of the citizens of the Community during the ratification process meant that the final period leading up to the 1992 deadline was not filled with as much euphoria as had been anticipated.

This chapter is not, however, principally concerned with the politics of '1992' (Crouch and Marquand, 1990), but with providing an outline of the internal market project as an enterprise in supranational law-making – concentrating in particular on the task for the Community of harmonising national legislation to the extent necessary to create a level competitive field. It begins with a brief summary of the internal market project, as envisaged in the Commission's White Paper, and proceeds via an analysis of different conceptions of harmonisation, with a particular focus on the 'New Approach' to harmonisation which emerged in concert with the shift from the discredited 'common market' to the new conception of the 'internal market', to a review of the particular successes and failures of the project as a legislative enterprise. The chapter concludes with an assessment of the legal significance of the 1992 deadline.

15.2 The Basic Conception of the Internal Market Programme

The Commission's White Paper begins by identifying three types of barriers which form the main obstacles to the achievement of a single internal market:

- physical barriers (i.e. physical controls on persons and goods crossing borders);
- technical barriers (i.e. non-tariff barriers such as product standards, public procurement policies, etc.);
- fiscal barriers (i.e. VAT and excise duties).

This categorisation is somewhat arbitrary and is adopted mainly for convenience. It is not comprehensive; for example, it does not address directly the crucial question of the relationship between the wider and more integrated internal market and the world market. In the absence of progress on improved coordination of external trade policies, is the internal market programme to lead to a European Community which is increasingly isolated from the world market? This might occur if, in order to facilitate internal free movement of its own commodities, the Community needs to place restrictions on the free access of commodities from outside. This is the fear of 'Fortress Europe', but it is not a charge against the Community which has generally been held to be justified (Meessen, 1989). Perhaps more serious are developments in the context of free movement of persons, where a transfer of responsibility for issues of asylum and immigration to intergovernmental structures aligned to, but not within, the European Community itself (Cooperation on Justice and Home Affairs, Title VI of the Treaty of Maastricht) is raising fears that a European Community turning inward in economic recession may become increasingly inaccessible to those outside it; it is possible that the process of economic integration has heightened rather than lessened racial tensions within the internal market (Szyszczak, 1992b).

The extent to which the barriers in each of the three categories have in fact been swept away will be assessed in 15.7 and 15.8 below. Progress is regularly reported by the Commission in its reports on the implementation of the internal market programme (Commission, 1992). The White Paper proposed the adoption of around 300 measures listed in a detailed timetable annexed to the body of the report. By 1990, the Commission had presented all the necessary proposals, and the legislative onus fell principally on the Council and the Parliament. By autumn 1992, over 90% of the proposals had been adopted, but residual difficulties lay still in pressure points such as the abolition of all frontier controls, indirect taxation and company law; this meant that the programme could not be completed in its entirety by the end of the year.

The removal of physical barriers comprises four main elements: the elimination of controls on goods (i.e. checking of documentation, etc.); the total harmonisation of plant and animal health controls; the abolition of controls on road transport (e.g. vehicle checks normally carried out at frontiers to be assimilated into national road safety policies and carried out in the interior of the state); and the abolition of frontier controls on persons. Physical barriers, in particular controls on persons, are regarded as having a special symbolic significance in the context of need for the Community to be a 'People's Europe'.

The category of 'technical barriers' comprises a wide range of potential barriers to trade including:

- technical and product standards;
- national rules on public procurement;
- restrictions on the free movement of persons, services and capital;
- liberalisation of transport policy;
- creating suitable conditions for cooperation between businesses;
- removal of barriers formed by the national basis of laws governing industrial and intellectual property.

As the extensive case law on Article 30 addressed in Chapter 14 shows, technical barriers have long been one of the most pervasive obstacles to the achievement of market integration in the Community. Their importance has been stressed not only by the adoption of a radical approach to MEEQRs in the Court of Justice, but also by other attempts on the part of the Community institutions to speed up the process of removal. Council Directive 83/189 (OJ 1983 L109/8) creates a 'mutual information' system, obliging Member States to notify the Commission of drafts of new technical regulations which they intend to adopt. This has enabled the Commission to maintain a better overview of the state of technical barriers to trade in the Community (see the Commission Report on the use of the Directive in 1990 and 1991: Com (92) 565).

The removal of fiscal barriers requires the Council to consent to a relatively small but highly problematic number of measures aimed at shifting the place of taxation away from the frontier and at achieving the degree of harmonisation of VAT and excise rates required to prevent distortions of competition when internal frontiers are removed.

It is sometimes suggested that the 1992 programme is concerned solely with deregulation and market liberalisation. In one sense, of course, the programme is a form of economic liberalism since it involves the opening up of formerly closed or partially closed markets. Moreover, at the time when the programme was adopted, philosophies of rigorous free market economics were strongly in vogue in many of the governments of the Member States, the UK included. However, the reality of the process of completing the internal market reveals that it as much to do with reregulation (at a Community level) as it is to do with deregulation and the removal of state interference in business. To that extent, therefore, the internal market programme is an assertion of an extended federal competence, since it has involved the Community legislating in many areas which previously the Member States have jealously guarded as their own. The justification for action on the part of the Community is stated in Article 100A: the Community may adopt harmonisation measures which have as their object 'the establishment and functioning of the internal market.' Moreover, by Article 100A(3) the Commission's proposals must be based on high standards of protection in the fields of health and safety, environmental protection and consumer protection. Coupling together the opening of markets with the acceptance that this change should not lead to an abandonment of accepted standards of protection in a market-led 'race for the bottom' means that Community regulation of the basic structures of the market is inevitable. The logic of deregulation argues that European standards should not be set, but national standards retained and competition between those standards encouraged to see what the consumer chooses (i.e. low cost, low quality or high cost, high quality). This approach has not prevailed. It was the realisation that the internal market programme was perceived not only by the Commission but also by other Member States as accepting this expansion in the regulatory role of the Community which perhaps triggered the regrets about the Single European Act which Margaret Thatcher demonstrated in her infamous Bruges Speech in 1988 when she expressed her firm opposition to a federal Europe. The principal mechanism whereby the Community has been able to exercise an incremental accretion of its competence has been the harmonising Directive.

15.3   Harmonisation: Policies and Methods

The harmonisation of laws means the adjustment of diverse legal systems and the creation of a situation of sufficient commonality and unity between the systems to secure a given objective. Harmonisation is a means to an end, not an end in itself. When undertaken with the specific object of the completion of the internal market in view, successful harmonisation can be defined as that which removes the disparities between the national legal systems to the extent necessary to secure the unity of the market. The Directive as a form of Community legislation provides a good mechanism for securing such a goal. It requires Member States to achieve a particular objective, but does not impose substantive or procedural uniformity upon them. It does not rob the national systems of their individuality by requiring total uniformity. This would imply the 'unification of laws', a process which typically occurs within the sphere of international law, when a group of states agree to unify an aspect of their law (e.g. the law of contract, commercial sales or carriage of goods) and agree upon an international instrument (e.g. a convention or a treaty) embodying this uniform law which must then be ratified and adopted internally. Some aspects of the internal market programme do, however, seek to create uniform, or even unique structures. The Commission has sought the adoption of supranational structures for doing business on a Community-wide front ('creating a propitious environment for business cooperation' in Euro-jargon); in that context, the Regulation may be a more appropriate policy instrument than the Directive, since it provides a uniform and mandatory legal framework. Examples of this approach include the Regulation on the European Economic Interest Grouping (Regulation 2137/85 OJ 1985 L199/1) which provides a flexible form of structure for undertakings from the various Member States which wish to cooperate on a crossnational basis, and the less successful progress towards the adoption of a European Company Statute in the form of a Regulation, which has been a Community project for more than twenty years.

Harmonisation is positive integration in practice; it recognises that negative integration in the form of prohibitions upon barriers to trade cannot lead to total market integration, since it cannot always deal with the reasons why Member States might seek to resist the dismantling of certain types of rule which are restrictive of trade, namely the imperative need to protect important interests such as health or the environment. Indeed, the Community's rules on free movement of goods explicitly recognise these interests in Article 36 EC and the mandatory requirements. Harmonisation aims to substitute for national rules harmonised rules which incorporate the interests which require protection.

Before proceeding to examine the harmonisation of laws in practice in the Community, it is necessary to define certain terms which describe different methods of harmonisation. The simplest form of harmonisation is that which is closest to unification, namely the substitution of diverse rules with a **uniform rule**. This form of harmonisation can be termed **total** or **complete harmonisation**. Typically, in the Community context harmonisation of this nature involves Community legislation 'occupying the field' and pre-empting the exercise of national competence. An example of this can be found in Case 60/86 *Commission* v. *UK (Dim-dip headlights)* ([1988] ECR 3921) where the Court found Directive 70/156 on lighting and light-signalling devices for motor vehicles to have exhaustively regulated the field, leaving no scope for the introduction of a different type of lighting device such as the dim-dip mechanism (see 14.16). It is also possible for these types of measures to amount to only **partial harmonisation**; that is, they constitute a uniform rule in so far as they are applicable, but they only partially occupy the field, leaving scope for the exercise of national regulatory autonomy. This was the conclusion reached by the House of Lords, albeit on rather dubious grounds, regarding the scope of the Directives on Brakes and on Sound Levels in *R*. v. *London Boroughs Transport Committee, ex parte Freight Transport Association Ltd* ([1991] 3 All ER 915) (Weatherill, 1992b). Their Lordships concluded that the Brake Directive did not address the issue of the sound levels of braking devices, and that the Sound Level Directive did not address the problem of the sound levels of air brakes. Consequently, this left scope for a local authority to introduce a restriction on lorries which were not fitted with noise suppressors on their air brakes.

Two alternative techniques can be contrasted with total harmonisation: **optional** and **minimum harmonisation**. Optional harmonisation leaves to the trader the choice of whether to comply with the harmonised standards, or with national standards. The advantage of complying with the harmonised standards is that this will open up access to the entire market subject to the harmonisation rules; the advantage of complying only with national standards is that this may be cheaper, and also sufficient in practice if the national standards in question are also recognised in the destination market. In that case, compliance with Community standards is unnecessary. Minimum harmonisation, in contrast, leaves a discretion to the national authorities. The harmonisation measure sets only minimum standards, which are mandatory, but leaves it to the national authorities to choose, if they so wish, to apply stricter standards. Finally, the objective of harmonisation can be achieved by means of **reference to standards** established by standards institutes rather than through the elaboration in the harmonisation measure itself of detailed standards. This can work well in conjunction with a uniform rule which states only the basic minimal prerequisites for a given product, leaving the detailed rules to be elaborated in the work of the standards' institutes. This latter approch is the favoured approach to harmonisation now used in the Community.

15.4   The Progress of Harmonisation in the Community

Harmonisation (or approximation, as it is often termed) of laws has been an objective of the Community since its inception. Article 3(c) EC is unamended since 1957 and calls for the activities of the Community to include:

> 'the approximation of the laws of Member States to the extent required for the functioning of the common market.'

Early Community harmonisation measures in the field of product standards date back to the early 1960s when Directives on food additives were introduced. Subsequently, the Member States in the Council agreed upon a systematic programme for the harmonisation of national laws in the General Programme of May 28 1969 for the elimination of technical barriers to trade that result from disparities between the provisions laid down by law, regulation or administrative action in Member States (OJ 1969 C76/1). Up to 1984, the Council had adopted just over 150 measures, most of which were based on Article 100 EEC, which remains in force now, but is no longer the most important legal basis available. It provides:

'The Council shall, acting unanimously on a proposal from the Commission and after consulting the European Parliament and the Economic and Social Committee, issue directives for the approximation of such laws, regulations or administrative provisions of the Member States as directly affect the establishment or functioning of the common market.'

In procedural terms, two points are of note: the Article requires unanimity in the Council of Ministers, and Parliamentary input is limited to simple consultation. However, the difficulties of achieving the adoption of proposals within the Council have run deeper than basic questions of process, and concern also the methods of harmonisation used. Typically 'old style' harmonisation involved attempts to achieve total harmonisation, although that was only one of several methods of harmonisation envisaged in the General Programme which contemplated the Community also using, for example, the technique of optional harmonisation. Most of the Directives adopted contain minutely detailed technical regulations dealing with every aspect of the product in question, organised around a picture of a mandatory product standard. Consequently a great deal of time was needed for the preparation, adoption and implementation of measures, and reaching a consensus with manufacturers, standards institutes and Member States on what technical specifications should be included in a measure could be a lengthy process. Unfortunately, proposals rarely made use of whatever standards did already exist at European level (the reference to standards approach), and thus no attempt was made to lighten the work of the Community's institutions by diverting some of the load towards the European standards institutes. Proposals often remained on the Council's agenda for a decade or more prior to adoption, or definitive abandonment. Even once adopted, such detailed Directives could present serious implementation problems for the Member States and enforcement problems for the Commission.

Furthermore, it is arguable that measures of 'total' harmonisation such as this risk destroying the benefits of national variety within the Community, and creating excessive uniformity between products. They are also unreceptive to technological change, although some Directives do provide for a rather cumbersome Committee structure working in conjuction with the Commission under which technical standards may be changed in the light of new developments. With rapidly developing products and slow decision-making processes, however, some Directives risked being outdated before they were even adopted. Even so, the Council made insufficient use of the opportunity to delegate powers to the Commission to adapt Directives to technical progress.

These problems stemmed in part from the fact that historically within the Community, harmonisation was seen as a counterpoint to liberalisation. Harmonisation would begin when liberalisation (i.e. through Articles 30–36) would no longer suffice. The *Cassis de Dijon* case law (Case 120/78 *Rewe-Zentrale AG* v. *Bundesmonopolverwaltung für Branntwein* [1979] ECR 649) greatly expanded the scope for liberalisation, of course, and also indicated an alternative way forward for harmonisation which sought to co-opt the liberalising impulse into the harmonisation process.

15.5   The 'New Approach' to Harmonisation

The political will to make real progress towards economic integration, which distinguishes the work on the '1992' programme from other attempts to relaunch the integration process, has been referred to on several occasions in this book. In terms of legislative technique, the harmonisation programme embarked upon also represents a break with the past. The 'new approach' to harmonisation typically rejects 'total' harmonisation in the sense of comprehensive uniform standards, and makes use of elements of optional harmonisation and standards evolved outside the Community institutions. Moreover, harmonisation will only be undertaken where necessary. If mutual recognition will suffice, then harmonisation will be unnecessary. Although termed the 'new' approach, its heritage can be traced to one much earlier Community Directive, concerned with low voltage electrical equipment, which adopted very much the same approach which is now regarded as the most appropriate to the task of completing the internal market.

The principles of harmonisation are stated in the Council's Resolution of May 7 1985 on a new approach to technical harmonisation (OJ 1985 C136/1) (see also 14.18). This provides that legislative harmonisation will be limited to setting out the 'essential safety requirements (or other requirements in the general interest) with which products put on the market must conform'. Technical standards-setting will be delegated to organisations specialised in this work, and remain voluntary, although compliance with a technical standard set by such a body will provide conclusive evidence that a particular product complies also with the essential requirements contained in the Directive, and is therefore to be guaranteed freedom of movement throughout the Community. For this system to work, the essential requirements need to be sufficiently detailed and sufficiently clear to allow them to be applied by the national authorities. Manufacturers may also prove compliance with the Directive by demonstrating that their products satisfy the essential requirements by some means other than by satisfying the technical standards set by the standards institutes. In practice, of course, there will be a great deal of pressure on manufacturers to comply with such standards, as the most cost effective way of achieving free movement.

An example of the 'new approach' in operation is the Toy Safety Directive (Directive 88/378 OJ 1988 L187/1), implemented in the UK by the Toy (Safety) Regulations 1989 (SI 1989, No. 1275). Evidence of the existence of Community-wide safety standards for toys can be seen in the form of the 'CE' mark which is affixed to toys which comply with these standards and which benefit from the right of free movement automatically. Pursuant to the principle that goods in free circulation should be treated in the same way as goods of Community origin, third country products which have been lawfully marketed in one Member States should be able to circulate freely within the other Member States provided they satisfy the essential requirements.

Clearly the new approach has significant advantages. It is much faster and simpler than the traditional approach, enabling the Council to adopt many more sectoral Directives than previously. It avoids excessive standardisation and uniformity, encouraging diversity and competition between traditional methods of manufacture (e.g. different ways of making cheese). New harmonisation Directives are much easier for the Member States to implement, and the Commission's supervisory tasks are made easier. However, it should not be thought that the new approach is entirely without problems.

For example, there are some doubts as to whether there are at the Community level sufficiently coherent consumer and health protection policies to substitute for existing national policies, or whether it is not in fact that the case that harmonisation on the basis of essential requirements is actually detrimental to the interests of the consumer in the sense that it undermines the high safety standards which have been achieved in some Member States. There has been a fear that since harmonisation of essential safety standards is taking place within the confines of what is a market liberalisation programme, consumer safety may be sacrificed in the interests of short-term economic gains as a result of pressure from commercial interests. The structure of the new approach to harmonisation encourages manufacturers to find cheaper and more efficient ways of satisfying the essential requirements, but in practice this approach may undercut the standards already adopted as the result of consumer group pressure, particularly in the more safety-conscious Member States. In such circumstances there may be a conflict between the public interest and free trade.

There may also be problems resulting from the transfer of functions to the standardisation bodies. Under the new approach, the establishing of minimum requirements and the setting of standards have been separated, with the latter function passing to European standards' bodies, of which the most significant are CEN (the *Comité Européen de Normalisation*) and

CENELEC (the *Comité Européen de Normalisation Electro-technique*), which group together the national standards bodies. The standards set by these organisations take into account the current state of technical knowledge, and can therefore be changed without the Directive itself needing to be changed.

Arguably the new approach consists of replacing national legal rules with privately determined Community standards. This raises problems of accountability. CEN and CENELEC are both private associations incorporated under Belgian law; is it permissible (or desirable) for the Community to delegate a power to make standards to such bodies, given that their decisions are not easily subject to judicial control? The mutual recognition approach results in a division of powers between the public and private spheres which may be problematic from the perspective of the protection of individual rights. Furthermore, who controls the standards-setters? The Commission claims that it can ensure that standards conform to the requirements of the individual Directives, and that there is no major problem because the standards are voluntary. This is disingenuous on the part of the Commission. The standards are not easily characterised as justiciable, because they are privately determined, but they are quasi-mandatory because of the legal and factual benefits which they can confer.

Finally, while it may be faster and simpler for the Council to adopt harmonisation measures under the new approach, the actual standards-setting process remains as time-consuming and laborious as ever. It simply now takes place within a private arena, namely that of the European standardisation bodies. As a consequence, legislative stagnation within the Council of Ministers has been replaced by a bottleneck within CEN, CENELEC and similar bodies.

Undoubtedly, the effectiveness of the standardisation element in the new approach to harmonisation will be enhanced by the development of a comprehensive Community policy on standardisation, and the Commission has been working towards this. It adopted a Communication on standardisation in the European economy in December 1991 (Com (91) 521) and on June 18 1992 the Council adopted a Resolution on standardisation calling for the standardisation process to be efficient, transparent and open, resulting in high quality standards which are accessible and capable of transposition at national level (OJ 1992 C173/1).

The new approach to harmonisation is complemented by continued use of the prior notification system under Directive 83/189, which the Commission argues should be strengthened to extend the procedural restraints on Member States before they may adopt such rules.

Finally, without effective transposition, implementation and enforcement of Directives, the gains of the new approach will not be realised. Reference should be made in this context to 6.14, where the problem of non-compliance by the Member States and the attempts which have been made to make the enforcement process more effective and efficient were discussed.

15.6   The Institutional Dimension: Article 100A EC

Article 100A EC provides:

'1. By way of derogation from Article 100 and save where otherwise provided in this Treaty, the following provisions shall apply for the achievement of the objectives set out in Article 7A. The Council shall, acting in accordance with the procedure referred to in Article 189B and after consulting the Economic and Social Committee, adopt the measures for the approximation of the provisions laid down by law regulation or administrative action in Member States which have as their object the establishment and functioning of the internal market. 2. Paragraph 1 shall not apply to fiscal provisions, to those relating to the free movement of persons nor to those relating to the rights and interests of employed persons.'

Para. 3 commits the Commission to respecting high standards of health and safety, environmental protection and consumer protection in its proposals under Article 100A. Para. 4 allows derogation by Member States from measures adopted under Article 100A by reference to 'major needs'. Finally, para. 5 allows for the inclusion in harmonisation measures of safeguard clauses authorising Member States to take derogation measures, subject to Community control, by reference to the non-economic exceptions contained in Article 36.

As a preliminary point it should be noted that when first introduced by the Single European Act, Article 100A made use of the cooperation procedure. As amended by the Treaty of Maastricht, Council/Parliament co-decision applies to measures adopted under this provision. Thus, both before and since this amendment, Article 100A measures have required only a qualified majority in the Council of Ministers. However, there are additional factors which further distinguish this provision from Article 100. First, there is no reference to a 'direct' effect upon the establishment of the internal market. Second, Article 100A envisages the adoption of 'measures' in pursuit of the objectives set out in that provision, whereas Article 100 restricts to the Council of Ministers to adopting Directives. Finally, and in this respect Article 100 is the broader power, Article 100A(2) excludes certain key areas in which harmonisation is necessary for the attainment of the internal market from the application of the provisions of Article 100A(1).

The scope of the exclusions in Article 100A(2) of measures relating to taxes, the free movement of persons and the rights and interests of employed persons has yet to be tested before the Court of Justice. With regard to the latter category of measures, the derogation can be used to exclude some or all of the following three types of measures: those which (a) solely, (b) predominantly and (c) in any way touch upon the rights and interests of workers (Bercusson, 1990: 634). As Bercusson notes:

'to the extent that labour is a factor of production in the establishment of a unified market, most proposals affecting that market will relate to the rights and interests of employees in some way or other. Which of the interpretations of Article 100A(2) is adopted depends upon the vision of the Community held by its author.'

The Commission, at least, appears to favour a restrictive interpretation of these exclusions since it has proposed that Article 100A be used as the legal basis for a Directive which would harmonise national legislation on atypical work (part-time employment, temporary work, and other forms of marginal employment) with a view to eliminating distortions of competition between the Member States (OJ 1990 C224/6). The alternative legal basis for such a measure would be Article 100, and this provision clearly has certain procedural disadvantages from the perspective of the Commission.

For fiscal measures the alternative legal basis is Article 99 EC which likewise requires the achievement of unanimity within the Council of Ministers. This factor is doubtless one of the reasons for the difficulties encountered by the Member States in completing the removal of fiscal barriers within the internal market by the 1992 deadline.

With regard to the free movement of persons, it was clearly the view of the Council of Ministers that Article 235 would be the obvious alternative to Article 100A as a legal basis for measures designed to ensure the completion of the internal market. Indeed in 1990 the Council adopted three Directives guaranteeing the right of residence of students, pensioners, and those with private means using Article 235. However, the Parliament successfully sought the annulment of the Directive on the right of residence for students (Directive 90/366 OJ 1990 L180/30) in the Court, arguing that Article 6(2) EC provides an adequate legal basis for measures which have as their main objective the elimination of discrimination of those categories of economically active persons who fall within the scope of the right to non-discrimination in that provision (Case C-295/90 *Parliament* v. *Council* [1992] 3 CMLR 281).

One issue concerning the scope of application of Article 100A has already been settled by the Court. This concerns the relationship between Article 100A and other overlapping law-making powers. In Case C-300/89 *Commission* v. *Council (Titanium Dioxide)* (11.6.1991) the Commission (with the support of the Parliament) successfully challenged the decision of the Council to use Article 130S EC as the legal basis for Directive 89/428/EEC approximating national programmes for the reduction and eventual elimination of pollution caused by waste in the production of titanium dioxide. The motive of the Court's judgment may have been to protect the integrity and effectiveness of the cooperation procedure, by ensuring that this form of procedure is used wherever measures aimed at the completion of the internal market are adopted, even if they may also have some other purpose (here, protection of the environment), and are thus capable of adoption under another provision of the Treaty (here, what was then Article 130S EEC). However, the effect of the Court's decision is also simultaneously to reinforce the dominance of the Community's internal market objective over its other objectives, and, arguably to destroy the effect of the saving words in Article 100A(1) – 'save where otherwise provided in this Treaty' (Crosby, 1991).

Finally, it should be noted that in the post-Maastricht phase the exercise of powers under Article 100A may be affected by the adoption of the principle of subsidiarity in Article 3B EC. It is possible that the Community would not have found it so easy to justify the extensive legislative activity which has occurred during the period of the completion of the internal market had the doctrine of subsidiarity then been applicable. However, the discussion of the effects of this principle upon the policy-making activities of the Community is reserved for Chapter 16.

15.7 The Main Achievements of the Internal Market Programme

Many of the achievements which the internal market programme has made to the general welfare and standing of the Community will be apparent either from the earlier paragraphs of this chapter, or from discussion elsewhere in this book. These include a revitalisation of the purpose of the Community, a restoration of confidence, the evolution of new legislative methods, the breakdown of the legislative blockage in the Council of Ministers, and the enhancement of the role of the Parliament through the Single European Act which has a resonance outside the limited field of the internal market. We are concerned here with important achievements within the programme itself, of which the most obvious is the relaunch of the harmonisation programme with the 'new approach', particularly in the context of technical standards for products. Of the many achievement outside this field, just two examples are given.

The first concerns the field of services, and is highlighted here although this book has not addressed in any detail the issue of the free movement of services. A considerably enhanced degree of liberalisation has been achieved within the economically vital sector of financial services and free movement of capital, which accounts for over 7% of Community GDP. The 'mutual recognition' approach has proved capable of application not only to goods but also to services. For example, under the Banking Directives, a single banking licence secured in one Member State, under which a bank will be subject to essential supervisory and prudential requirements, will suffice for it to be able to supply services throughout the Community.

A second area of development which should be highlighted is that of public procurement. Despite the sensitive nature of this issue, the Council has reached agreement on an impressive package of measures opening public procurement procedures more fully to competition from other Member States, including, most crucially, procurement in the public services (transport, telecommunications, energy and water distribution). This achievement is even more economically significant, since public procurement accounts for around 15% of Community GDP.

15.8   The Main Failures of the Internal Market Programme

In many respects the main failures of the internal market programme have been entirely predictable since they involve for the most part issues on which the Member States have struggled to reach agreement throughout the history of the Community. For example, one of the most controversial issues has been the problem of creating a VAT system which does not need frontier controls. The intention of the Commission has always been to shift the collection of VAT on goods from the frontier to inland tax offices. Traditionally, VAT has been levied on the destination principle, whereby it is reimbursed by the Member State from which goods are exported, and collected at the frontier by the Member State of import. For the Commission, the best system would be a shift to the origin principle, whereby goods are taxed by the Member State of export, coupled with harmonisation of tax rates to reduce the incentives to subject such a system to fraud or abuse. However, harmonisation of tax rates represents a serious inroad into national sovereignty and fiscal autonomy, and is not something that national politicians can happily contemplate. The same difficulties apply in relation to excise duties traditionally levied on mineral oils, tobacco and alcoholic drinks.

The Commission has succeeded only in achieving moves towards harmonisation of tax rates – painstakingly put in place by the end of 1992 – and the Member States have successfully resisted the immediate introduction of the origin principle. The destination principle will remain in place for a transitional period, but coupled with administrative arrangements to ensure cooperation between the taxation authorities in the Member States. The adoption of the transitional arrangements has also only been achieved in the context of the Member States retaining a considerable margin of discretion in the practical implementation of the changes.

In general terms, the least progress has occurred where Community measures have been aimed not merely at removing restrictions to economic interpenetration, but also at encouraging a positive environment for business cooperation and growth. This is evidenced by a failure to agree upon the Statute for a European Company, more extensive harmonisation of company law and the harmonisation or unification of intellectual property laws.

15.9 The Concept of an 'Internal Market' and the Effect of the Date 31 December 1992

The significance of the concept of an 'internal market' and the effect of the date 31 December 1992 was thrown into sharp relief as the deadline for the completion of the internal market approached with certain legislative tasks remaining incomplete. In that context, it is important to consider the significance of a Declaration attached by the Member States to the text of what was then Article 8A EEC at the time of its adoption. This Declaration, which was attached to the Single European Act, states that while it was the firm intention of the Contracting Parties to take before January 1 1993 all the decisions necessary to complete the internal market, nonetheless 'setting the date of 31 December 1992 does not create an automatic legal effect'.

The status and interpretation of this Declaration are extremely uncertain. While Declarations are not normally considered to be part of Treaties to which they are annexed, it would be unwise to ignore completely what is an expression of will on the part of all the High Contracting Parties at the time when they signed the Single European Act. Yet Toth argues that the Declaration should not be regarded as having any effect (Toth, 1986). A more cautious approach is to accept the force of such Declarations, at least in so far as they are not in conflict with the express words of the Treaty (Schermers, 1991).

The question remains, therefore, whether, in the absence of the Declaration, legal consequences do flow from the passing of the date set for the completion of the internal market. It must be clear, at least, that such consequences, whatever they are, are extremely unlikely to be of the magnitude of those which occurred at the end of the original transitional period for the EEC Treaty, which saw the free movement rules transformed into mandatory dispositions of a constitutional nature. Given the continued applicability of Article 36 and other provisions which reserve public policy, public health and public security derogations for the Member States in relation to the free movement of workers, establishment, services and capital, it cannot have been the intention of the Contracting Parties that the end of 1992 should see an automatic sweeping away of remaining obstacles to trade within the internal market. The existing rules on free movement will continue to apply unchanged. Nor is it feasible to argue that as of January 1 1993 unadopted Commission proposals are deemed to be adopted regardless of their status within the legislative process. This would destroy the institutional balance of the Community.

It remains to be seen whether any significance can be attached to the reference to 'internal frontiers' contained in Article 7A EC. We have considered already the relationship between the internal market and the common market (11.2). During 1992, the Commission clarified its view that the reference to internal frontiers is a new element in the Treaty and argued that this is a straightforward objective which aims to produce a particular result and leaves no margin for discretion. While the Commission's interpretation focused at that stage on the legislative programme needed to secure the elimination of frontiers, and not the effect of failure to achieve that objective, it is arguable from the language it uses that it regarded the guarantee that there will be no more internal frontier controls on goods, persons and services as *capable of judicial enforcement* after the beginning of 1993. In other words, it would appear that national authorities should, by virtue of the pre-emptive effect of directly effective Community law (Case 106/77 *Amministrazione delle Finanze delle Strato* v. *Simmenthal (Simmenthal II)* [1978] ECR 629), lose the power validly to impose and enforce unilateral border controls after that date. This question remains to be determined by the Court.

Summary

1 The central preoccupation of the European Community during the period 1985–92 was the completion of the internal market. This took the form, in large part, of a programme of harmonisation measures aimed at eliminating disparities in national legislation which cause distortions of competition.

2 The Commission's White Paper identifies (1) physical barriers, (2) technical barriers and (3) fiscal barriers as the main types of barriers which impede the completion of the internal market.

3 The Community's harmonisation programme – in stagnation since the early 1960s – has been radically altered by a new approach which involves a minimum level of legislative harmonisation and a maximum level of delegation of powers to standards bodies which elaborate standards which, while not mandatory, nonetheless provide the key to free movement within the Community. Generally, the Community has experienced success in its project to eliminate the barriers identified in the White Paper.

4 There remain doubts about the new approach, in particular in so far as bodies such as CEN and CENELEC, responsible for the elaboration of standards, are not subject to outside control. There are also fears that the minimalist approach may undermine high consumer protection and safety standards in some Member States.

5 Article 100A represents the main law-making power introduced by the Single European Act with a view to the completion of the internal market. The main difficulty with Article 100A lies in the exclusion by para. 2 of certain types of measure from the scope of qualified majority voting.

6 The effect of the date December 31 1992 remains unclear; arguably, Member States are now deprived of the power unilaterally to impose border controls.

Questions

1 Review, from earlier chapters, the developments which led to the adoption of the '1992' programme as the main project of the Community in the late 1980s.

2 What types of barriers does the White Paper envisage the Community eliminating, and how is this goal principally to be achieved?

3 What is the 'new approach' to the harmonisation of product standards?

4 What difficulties remain with this approach?

5 Identify some of the main achievements and failures of the internal market programme.

6 What is the possible effect of the date December 31 1992?

Further Reading

Argiros (1990) 'Consumer Safety and the Single European Market: Some Observations and Proposals', *Legal Issues Of European Integration*, 90/1, 139.

Burrows (1990) 'Harmonisation of Technical Standards: Reculer pour mieux sauter?', 53 *Modern Law Review*, 597.

Commission of the European Communities (1985) *Completing the Internal Market*. White Paper from the Commission to the European Council, Com (85), 310.

Dehousse (1989) '1992 and Beyond: The institutional dimension of the internal market programme', *Legal Issues of European Integration*, 89/1, 109.

Easson (1990) 'The Internal Market and the Elimination of Fiscal Frontiers', 10 *Yearbook of European Law*, 147.

McGhee and Weatherill (1990) 'The Evolution of the Single Market: Harmonisation or Liberalisation?', 53 *Modern Law Review*, 578.

Pelkmans (1986-7) 'The New Approach to Technical Harmonization and Standardization', 25 *Journal of Common Market Studies*, 249.

Swann (1991) 'Creating the Single European Market', in G. Thompson *et al.* (eds), *Markets, Hierarchies and Networks: The Coordination of Social Life*, Sage.

Part VI

The Social Dimension
of the European
Community

16 The Basic Framework of Community Social Policy

16.1 Introduction

The previous chapters on the institutional and substantive law of the European Community have proceeded on the assumption that the Community's central mission is the achievement of economic integration, embodied most forcefully in the project to complete the internal market by the end of 1992. The dominance of this mission is not challenged here. What is questioned is the extent the Community should be seeking to pursue the objective of economic interpenetration principally by applying what Pelkmans (1991: 63) has termed

'rigorous scrutiny of the hindrances to the free movement of goods, services and capital, with a multitude of proposals about the minimum harmonisation needed to achieve such freedoms, complemented by a fairly strict competition policy applied to distortions in product and services markets, with, on the other hand, little or no scrutiny of the economic obstacles to the free movement of workers or massive distortions of competition in the labour markets.'

He concludes:

'How can one speak of a completed internal market if the national regulatory provisions with respect to the labour market are highly restrictive and diverse?'

Against this negative assessment can be placed the declaration of the Summit Meeting in Paris in October 1972, just as the Community moved from six to nine members. The government leaders declared that:

'they attribute the same importance to energetic proceedings in the field of social policy as to the realisation of the economic and financial union and consider it essential to ensure the increasing involvement of labour and management in the economic and social decisions of the Community.'

In similar terms, the eleven Member States which adopted the *Community Charter of Fundamental Rights for Workers* in 1989 asserted their belief that 'in the context of the establishment of the single European market, the same importance must be attached to the social aspects as to the economic aspects.'

Yet despite these commitments, as Pelkmans indicates, relatively little of substance has emerged, although the debate about the extent to which the Community can and should pursue a social policy, as a necessary component of or complement to its primary economic policies, has raged since the very beginning. This chapter seeks to assess whether the Community can in truth be said to have a social policy, and examines the extent of the contribution of law to that policy, in the form of legally binding legislative measures and social rights conferred on individuals. It begins, however, with a brief discussion of whether it is correct in fact to set up a dichotomy in Community policy-making between 'the social' and 'the economic'.

16.2   Social or Economic: Tensions in the Case Law of the Court of Justice

The case law of the Court of Justice has demonstrated that it is not always possible to draw a rigid division between the economic and social facets of the Community. Key issues of social policy have an inconvenient habit of popping up in a wider economic context. For example, in Case 31/87 *Gebroeders Beentjes* v. *Netherlands State* ([1988] ECR 4635) the Court was required to consider the compatibility with Community law of a Dutch measure governing the awarding of public contracts. This measure effectively gave legal force to the inclusion in an invitation to tender of a clause requiring the tenderer to be in a position to employ long-term unemployed persons, a requirement which could have the effect of giving preferential treatment to locally-based firms better able to fulfil the condition. The plaintiffs' tender was rejected by the awarding body on the grounds that they could not fulfil the condition. The questions posed by the referring court sought to establish whether this was permissible under Directive 71/305 which governs the coordination of procedures for the award of public works contracts, and is part of the legislative programme which seeks to liberalise the Community's public procurement market. In the event, the Court held that the Community legislative framework did not exhaustively regulate the awarding of such contracts, and that national legislative competence in this field was not therefore pre-empted. The national authorities remained free to impose substantive and procedural conditions on the award of public contracts, provided they did not infringe the general rules of the Treaty including the free movement of services and the right to non-discrimination on grounds of nationality.

    This case falls into a line of judgments in which the economic freedoms guaranteed by the Treaty have come into potential or actual conflict with local or national social policies. In 14.6, we discussed the requirement in

Italy that public undertakings purchase a certain proportion of their supplies from firms based in the *Mezzogiorno* as an example of a discriminatory measure in breach of Article 30, and not justifiable under Article 36 (Case C-21/88 *Du Pont de Nemours Italiana SpA* v. *Unità Sanitaria Locale No. 2 di Carrara* [1990] ECR I-889). The *Gebroeders Beentjes* judgment has the potential to make it extremely difficult for local authorities in the Community to use policy measures such as contract compliance in pursuit of goals such as positive action in favour of disadvantaged social groups. Such policies risk being discriminatory in effect, if not in form. A requirement that a tenderer employ a certain proportion of local unemployed people on a public works contract may be more difficult for a firm which is not based in the locality to fulfil, since it may prefer to bring its own workforce to perform the contract.

The potential of Community law to disrupt patterns of social regulation is also illustrated by Case C-113/89 *Rush Portuguesa Lda* v. *Office National d'Immigration* ([1990] ECR I-1417). Here the Court of Justice was required to decide whether a situation in which a Portuguese firm was using its own workforce in order to execute a building contract which it had secured in France was covered by the Community rules on free movement of workers or free movement of services. The significance turned in part on the fact that at the material time Portugal was not entirely integrated into the Community as regards the free movement of labour, which was subject to an extended transitional period during which restrictions could continue to be placed on Portuguese workers. No such limitation applied to the provisions on the free movement of services, which came into force in full on the accession of Portugal. In the event, the Court concluded that it was the provisions on free movement of services (Articles 59 and 60 EC) which applied to a situation such as this; freedom to supply services implies the right of providers of services also to move freely within the Member States, on a temporary basis, with all of their staff, who are not thereby classed as migrant workers. This was a welcome decision from the point of view of the free marketeer, since it allows firms from Portugal and other Member States where wages are relatively low to make use of this competitive advantage when securing contracts in other Member States.

Crucially, however, the Court did address also the difficulty which is inherent in this argument, and that is the concern that the liberalised market for goods and services will lead to 'social dumping'. That is the fear that the lower standards of social and employment protection which apply in some Member States will be 'dumped' in those Member States which have higher standards by means of the type of arangement at issue in *Rush Portuguesa*. The effect of this may be to undermine local standards, since local workers could be faced with unemployment if they refuse to match the working conditions of the workers who have been temporarily transferred. In *Rush Portuguesa* the Court held that the Member States are *permitted* (but not obliged) to continue to apply local labour and employment protection laws to the transferred workers, even though their contracts of employment may be governed by the laws of another Member State. However, this possibility will provide little comfort to unions and workers in Member States which decline to make use of it, and prefer to use the pressure of transferred labour in order to force down domestic employment protection standards. In such circumstances, the liberalising tendencies of the Treaty, as interpreted by the Court, may in fact have the effect of causing a deterioriation of the quality of life of workers, which stands in total contradiction to the stated objectives of the European Community. At that point, arguably, the Council comes under a duty to legislate at Community level to resurrect the standards which the Treaty has contributed to dismantling, and indeed the Commission has put forward a proposal for a Directive on the detachment of employees in the context of the provision of services, which would establish a minimum standard of employment protection and working conditions for workers in the *Rush Portuguesa* situation. The guarantee would be mandatory in all Member States (Com (91) 230). It is arguable that the adoption of such a measure is as important as any of the other components of the internal market discussed in Chapter 15, if the Community is to avoid the accusation that the wider market is actually destructive of working standards and therefore 'anti-social'. However, this is one of several social policy proposals which have an internal market dimension which the Council has not so far adopted.

16.3 A Sketch of the Social Policy Competence of the Community

Article 2 EEC in its original form committed the Community to seeking an 'accelerated raising of the standard of living'. The Treaty offered, however, only very limited 'social' (i.e. redistributive and protective) means of achieving this objective, so that it must be assumed that the drafters of the Treaty believed that improved standards of living would flow inexorably from the economic growth which the Community was expected to promote. Article 117 EC, unamended by either the Single European Act or the main body of the Treaty of Maastricht, reiterates the commitment of the Member States to promoting improved living and working conditions, adding rather obscurely, 'so as to make possible their harmonisation while the improvement is being maintained.' It further states:

> 'They believe such a development will ensue not only from the functioning of the common market, which will favour the harmonisation of social systems, but also from the procedures provided for in this Treaty and from the approximation of provisions laid down by law, regulation or administrative action.'

Article 117 is not itself a legal basis for legislation, but it has been used as an aid to the interpretation of other provisions (Case 126/86 *Zaera* v.

Instituto Nacional de la Seguridad Social [1987] ECR 3697). However, in the social sphere, the Court expressed the view that Community competence is subsidiary to that of the Member States. Consequently, while harmonisation in the social field is not as such excluded from the range of Community policy measures, Article 117 embodies the belief which prevailed amongst the Member States at the time when the Treaty was first drafted that there was unlikely to be a need in a common market for social provisions to harmonised and that social policy could therefore remain in the realm of national competence. This belief can be traced back to the views of the Ohlin Committee of Experts which met under the aegis of the International Labour Organisation in 1956 to consider the relationship between the costs of social protection and competitive or comparative advantage between economies in the context of European integration. The essential question before this group was whether the costs of overheads for employers resulting from differing levels of social protection in different countries created serious disparities between the competitive positions of those countries. The Committee envisaged a situation of economic integration where individual countries would retain sovereignty over macro-economic policy including exchange rates, and where they would be free to adjust policies in these areas in order to offset low levels of productivity in international terms. On that basis, the Committee felt that even if wage costs were forced upwards by high levels of social protection for workers, these were only one element determining the overall cost of products. Other factors such as labour productivity, geographical position, natural resources, size of market and availability of technology might be equally significant. Consequently there was no pressing need for general social harmonisation.

There was one exception to the general pattern of endorsement of this approach in the original Treaty. At the insistence of the French delegation, the Treaty incorporated a guarantee of equal pay for men and women, in order to avoid a competitive disadvantage accruing to France which already had such a guarantee in domestic law. However, while the inclusion of Article 119 may originally have been economically motivated, it has been interpreted by the Court, and indeed implemented and expanded by the Council of Ministers via a series of Directives guaranteeing sex equality in employment matters, very much as a 'social' right to non-discrimination. Most significantly, in Case 43/75 *Defrenne* v. *SABENA* ([1976] ECR 455) the Court held that the right to equal pay in Article 119 was directly effective and could be enforced against all employers in national courts. The interventions of the Court and the Council have had a noticeable impact upon the national labour laws, to the extent that the Community's sex equality policy has become its 'flagship' in the social policy field, and has been subjected to detailed analysis on the basis that it might serve as a model for other areas of development (Szyszczak, 1990b).

The original social policy Chapter of the Treaty contained one other provision of significance. Article 118 conferred the task upon the

Commission of 'promoting close cooperation between Member States in the social field', and in Cases 281, etc/85 *Germany et al.* v. *Commission (Migration Policy)* ([1987] ECR 3203) the Court held that Article 118 implicitly give the Commission the power to take binding measures including Decisions with a view to completing the task it had been given, namely to promote cooperation between the Member States (but not to formulate a common policy).

In a linked Chapter, the original Treaty provided for the creation of a European Social Fund (Articles 123–127 EEC) and Article 128 EEC conferred an outline competence upon the Community in relation to vocational training, calling upon the Council to 'lay down general principles for implementing a common vocational training policy capable of contributing to the harmonious development both of the national economies and of the common market.' Vocational training policy has been a surprising success story for Community social policy, but again, like sex equality, it is a field where progress has been driven forward at least in the first instance by the Court of Justice.

In Case 293/83 *Gravier* v. *City of Liège* ([1985] ECR 593), the Court held that Article 128 EEC, read in conjunction with what was then Article 7 EEC (now Article 6 EC), conferred a right to non-discrimination on grounds of nationality on a student who moves to another Member State in order to pursue vocational training course; students on vocational training courses fall within the scope of the Treaty, by virtue of the outline competence conferred on the Council by Article 128, and as such are covered by Article 7. The Court has made a further contribution to the application of Article 128 by construing it as a sufficient legal basis for Community-funded student exchange programmes such as ERASMUS; in such circumstances the Council may not have recourse to Article 235 EC as well (Case 242/87 *Commission* v. *Council (ERASMUS)* [1989] ECR 1425). The unusual feature of Article 128 in its original form was that it required only a simple majority in the Council of Ministers. Not surprisingly, that particular anomaly was 'tidied up' by the Member States in the Treaty of Maastricht, and the new provisions (Articles 126 and 127 EC) now require a qualified majority.

Finally, no enumeration of the social policy competence of the Community can omit reference to the provisions of the Treaty guaranteeing free movement of workers and providing for a system whereby the social security rights of migrant workers are safeguarded (Articles 48–51 EC). However, it would be more faithful to the original scheme of the Treaty to regard these provisions as conferring economic rather than social rights on beneficiaries and these Articles - with their inevitable focus on economically active persons - are in a sense symptomatic of Community social policy generally, which has a general focus on employment and self-employment rather than on wider issues of social justice.

It will be seen from this review that with the exception of Article 128, the Treaty in its original form did not offer any law-making powers specifically aimed at securing the social objectives enshrined in the

Preamble and Article 2, and addressed in more detail in Article 117. Legislation demanded recourse to Articles 100 and 235 EC as legal bases; Article 235, for example, was used in the case of Directive 76/207 which guarantees equal treatment for men and women in the employment field (OJ 1976 L39/40).

16.4   The Ebbs and Flows of Community Social Policy

The evolution of Community social policy can be divided into a number of distinct phases. The early phase has been described as one of 'benign neglect' (Mosley, 1990). Outside the field of free movement of workers, few policy initiatives were taken in the social policy arena. Only following the relaunch of the aims of the Community to include a more explicit social dimension at the 1972 Paris Summit (see 16.1) did the Community move into a more proactive phase of social policy. In 1974 the Council endorsed a Social Action Programme (SAP) (*Supplement EC Bulletin 2/74*) which should have led to a vigorous programme of legislative action aimed at securing full and better employment, the improvement of living and working conditions within the context of the harmonisation of national measures in an upwards direction, and increased participation of the social partners (labour and management representatives) in social decisions of the Community and of workers in decision-making processes within undertakings.

The new policies were never brought to fruition, with only a handful of the proposed measures ever reaching the stage of adoption. The significant success stories of the 1970s were Directives on health and safety at work and sex equality at work, and a limited programme of employment protection Directives. An example of the latter is Directive 80/987 on the protection of workers in the event of the insolvency of their employer (OJ 1980 L283/23). It was the failure of Italy to implement this Directive which gave rise to the litigation in Cases C-6 and 9/90 *Francovich* v. *Italian State* ([1992] IRLR 84) in which the Court held that a Member State may be liable in damages for failure to implement Community law (see 8.19). This is one illustration of the extensive contribution which the Court's case law in the social field has made to evolution of the Community legal order. After 1974, however, a combination of economic recession and a lack of political will in the Council of Ministers destroyed the SAP as the basis for a comprehensive Community social policy.

Some changes were introduced by the Single European Act. 'Economic and social cohesion' was introduced as a Community goal by a new Article 130A EEC, and regional policy has now developed to the extent that the Community has redistributive policies which see 15–20% of Community resources channelled through the so-called 'Structural Funds' (Social Fund, European Regional Development Fund, etc.).

Article 118A gave an explicit law-making power to the Community in the field of health and safety, thus building on one of the successes of the SAP. The desire to involve the social partners in the policy-making process referred to in the SAP likewise lay behind the formalisation of the so-called 'social dialogue' between representatives of management and labour in Article 118B. On the debit side, it must be noted that social policy measures have been largely excluded from the scope of application of Article 100A by the exclusions contained in Article 100A(2) (free movement of workers, rights and interests of employed persons - see 15.6). The 1980s also saw the launch of a more extensive Community vocational training policy building on the initial impetus given by the Court.

In the late 1980s, Community social policy was relaunched for the second time, in the wake of the commitment to the achievement of the internal market. In 1989, eleven of the twelve Member States (the UK dissenting) adopted the *Community Charter of Fundamental Social Rights of Workers*, a declaratory document in which they committed themselves to developing the 'social dimension' of the internal market.

16.5   The Community Charter of Fundamental Social Rights of Workers

The Community Social Charter was adopted following a period during which the Commission, the ECOSOC, the Parliament and successive Presidencies, including those of Belgium and France, vigorously promoted the argument that an increasingly unified Europe should not lack an effective social policy. However, the proposal to put this commitment in concrete form as a statement of 'rights' was gradually watered down until the Charter took the form of a non-binding declaration. Yet even in that form the Charter could not be agreed upon by all Member States. Attached to the Charter was an Action Programme elaborated by the Commission, in which it enumerated the proposals it intended to make with a view to the attainment of the rights set out in the Charter. These include the right to freedom of movement, the right to a fair remuneration for work, the right to adequate social protection and the right to satisfactory health and safety conditions in the working environment. Again it will be seen that the Charter retains the employment-oriented emphasis of Community social policy generally. Nor is there any change in the general emphasis upon social policy as a national responsibility. The Charter stresses the continuing predominance of the several policies of the Member States rather than the collective policy of the Community in the social policy field. Point 27 states:

'It is more particularly the responsibility of the Member States, in accordance with national practices, notably through legislative measures or collective agreements, to guarantee the fundamental social rights in this Charter and to implement the social measures indispensable to the smooth operation of the internal market as part of the strategy of economic and social cohesion.'

In the Preamble, explicit reference is made to the principle of subsidiarity as governing the allocation of responsibility for achieving the goals of the Social Charter. The Commission has made a number of proposals under the Action Programme; that, for the most part, is where progress has stopped. In terms of the degree of implementation which it receives, social policy continues to play the role of 'poor relation', in comparison to the Community's market-oriented projects. The Social Charter did not extend the range of law-making powers available under the EEC Treaty as amended by the Single European Act. Unless measures could be characterised as 'health and safety' (Article 118A EC) or 'non-discrimination' (Article 6(2) EC), unanimity would be required for legislation to be adopted. For this, the political will rarely seems to be available. Moreover, the non-binding nature of the Charter itself is symptomatic of the tendency to continue to use 'soft law' methods of evolving cooperative policies in the social context.

16.6 The Treaty of Maastricht and the Incorporation of the Principle of Subsidiarity

In contrast to the Single European Act, the Treaty of Maastricht seems set to have a much more significant impact upon the development of Community social policy. There are, for example, minor changes to the substantive social policy provisions in the body of the European Community Treaty, such as the replacement of Article 128 EEC with new Articles 126 and 127 EC which provide separate policy objectives for vocational training and general education and give the Community a stronger role in relation to the former than the latter. More impact is likely to flow from two additions to the body of Community law:

−   the conclusion of a Social Policy Agreement (SPA) in which eleven of the twelve Member States have agreed to move towards a more proactive social policy programme based on the Social Charter. The UK opted out of these changes to the social policy provisions and thus forced their adoption through the rather uncertain mechanism of a Protocol whereby all twelve Member States effectively delegate access to the institutions and processes of the Community for the purposes of implementing the SPA between the Eleven. These arrangements may mark the beginning of a 'two-speed' Social Europe;
−   the incorporation of the principle of subsidiarity (1.4) as a general fetter upon Community legislative activity wherever powers are held

concurrently by the Community and the Member States. Social policy is one field of shared competence where subsidiarity seems set to have a significant impact.

The general effect of the SPA is to establish the possibility of more extensive Community law-making in the social policy field. The law-making procedure provided for in Article 189C (cooperation procedure, qualified majority voting) is to be used for the adoption of 'minimum requirements for gradual implementation' in areas such as health and safety, information and consultation of workers and equality between men and women (Article 2(2) SPA). However, Article 2(3) SPA retains 'old style' Council unanimity and consultation of the Parliament for measures taken in fields such as social security and social protection, redundancy protection for workers and representation of the interests of workers. In other words, the SPA is not set to introduce qualified majority voting into the most controversial areas of social policy. Council/ Parliament co-decision is not introduced into the social policy context. Finally, Articles 3 and 4 offer enhanced input into the formulation of social policy for management and labour in the context of the Community social dialogue. However, whatever the content of the measures adopted under the SPA, there remain considerable doubts regarding the legality of the arrangements for two speed Social Europe, particularly in view of the insistence of the Court of Justice in Opinion 1/91 *Re the Agreement on the European Economic Area* ([1992] 1 CMLR 245) that any form of *external* arrangement such as the EEA which the Community enters must not destroy the integrity of the Community's legal order and the uniformity of Community law. It seems that these are precisely the dangers flowing from the *internal* arrangement for differentiated or two speed integration contemplated in this instance (Shaw, 1992). It must also be stated that there will be considerable difficulties in practice in implementing the SPA; for example, at what point does the UK cease being involved in the adoption of a measure, as is proposed in the Social Policy Protocol? Will it, for example, be permissible for the UK Commissioners and UK Members of the European Parliament to be associated with the law-making process in the context of the SPA?

The inclusion of the principle of subsidiarity in Article 3B EC as the principal criterion for determining the appropriate vertical division of powers between the Member States and the Community is likely to have a major impact upon the assessment of the propriety of law-making in the social policy field. Quite possibly, however, the impact will lie more in the realm of the abstract than the practical, since it is difficult to envisage a situation in which the Member States become more reluctant than they already are to legislate in the social policy field!

However, in view of the heritage of the principle of subsidiarity, which lies originally in Catholic social philosophy, it is useful to assess the place of subsidiarity in social policy. In 1.4, subsidiarity was discussed as one of the key concepts of the Community legal order. It has been introduced into the political and legal order of the Community by Articles B TEU and 3B EC. It also appears indirectly in Article A TEU, which provides that the Treaty of Union

'marks a new stage in the process of creating an ever closer union among the peoples of Europe in which *decisions are taken as closely as possible to the citizen*' (emphasis added).

In Article 3B, subsidiarity appears as a fetter on the exercise of Community competence in areas 'which do not fall within its exclusive competence'. The Community shall in future take action

'only if and in so far as the objectives of the proposed action cannot be sufficiently achieved by the Member States and can therefore, by reason of the scale or effects of the proposed action, be better achieved by the Community.'

This appears to create both a sufficiency criterion (the Community institutions must demonstrate that Member State action is not sufficient) and an effectiveness criterion (Community action must be better able to achieve the end in view). However, there is no definitive interpretation of subsidiarity, either as it is defined in the Treaty, or as a political or philosophical principle in general. Consequently, conclusions at this stage need to be tentative. They also need to take into account two separate streams of development:

– subsidiarity as a defining characteristic of the Community's emerging federal system;
– subsidiarity as a possible basis for challenge to the validity of Community legislation before the Court of Justice.

Subsidiarity crystallised as a term describing a particular way of understanding social relations in Papal doctrine during the inter-war years (Wilke and Wallace, 1990; Adonis, 1991; Emiliou, 1992). This postulates the individual as the base unit of society. Wherever possible individual self-determination should be ensured, and only where decisions can be more effectively taken by groups which are subsidiary to the individual (family, community, locality, region, nation state, federal union) should this occur. Within these hierarchies or networks, the collectivity holds a responsibility for the well-being of the individual (the principle of solidarity). In post-war Germany, subsidiarity, although not explicitly adopted in the Constitution or Basic Law, has constituted an underlying theme dominating the evolution of federalism as a way of breaking loose from the shackles of corporatism under national socialism. It protects the autonomy of the *Bundesländer* in a system of cooperative federalism in which the individual states and the federal *Bund* share certain key political powers.

It therefore ignores the rich and complex history of subsidiarity in Continental Europe to view the doctrine simply as a bulwark against an overcentralising Community. Some UK politicians seized on subsidiarity as the basis for arguing for a return of powers from the Community to the Member States. In that context, subsidiarity becomes practically synonomous with national sovereignty. However, it is at least arguable that the logic of subsidiarity may in fact de-emphasise the importance of the nation state, proposing models of decision-making which imply radical decentralisation towards local and regional authorities. In this model, subsidiarity should not simply operate within the Member State–Community axis, but should inform the full range of social and political relations from the local to the transnational.

It is clear, therefore, that socio-political thought about subsidiarity should underlie the exercise of legislative power in an emerging federal European union. What is less clear is whether failure to observe the doctrine of subsidiarity will represent a ground for challenge to the legality of Community measures as a 'breach of the Treaty' within the meaning of Article 173 EC. If the Court were to conclude that the principle is justiciable in the sense that it is capable of forming a general principle of Community law binding upon the legislature, it would need to overcome two difficulties. First, there is the vagueness of the definition contained in Article 3B. Second, there will be the question as to whether the Court should properly intervene in the exercise of discretion on the part of the legislature. For example, in relation to the use of Article 235 EC, the Court has shown no inclination to limit the legislative powers of the Community by strict scrutiny of whether measures are 'necessary' for the achievement of one of the Community's objectives, preferring to accept what has been agreed unanimously by the Member States as a legitimate exercise of competence. In principle, the Court can accept jurisdiction over the doctrine of subsidiarity, since Article 3B is included in the provisions of the Treaty of Maastricht which are subject to the jurisdiction of the Court. However, it seems most likely that it will evolve an abstentionist case law in which it limits itself merely to ensuring that the Community legislature has properly considered the question of subsidiarity, declining to review the content of legislative discretion.

16.7   Subsidiarity and Social Policy

How might the doctrine of subsidiarity exert an influence upon the evolution of social policy? A clear indication is offered by Article 3 EC, as amended by the Treaty of Maastricht. This speaks of the Community making a 'contribution' in areas where the primary competence will continue to lie with the Member States: health protection; education and training of quality; the flowering of the cultures of the Member States; consumer protection. These general statements are fleshed out in the body of the Treaty, which offers, for example, a more specific picture of what types of measures the Community can take. For example, Article 126, which gives the Community for the first time an outline competence in relation to general education (as opposed to vocational training), provides:

'1. The Community shall contribute to the development of quality education by encouraging cooperation between Member States and, if necessary, by supporting and supplementing their action, while fully respecting the responsibility of the Member States for the content of teaching and the organisation of education systems and their cultural and linguistic diversity . . .

4. In order to contribute to the achievement of the objectives referred to in this Article, the Council:

– . . . shall adopt incentive measures, *excluding any harmonisation of the laws and regulations of the Member States*' (emphasis added).

Thus, in some areas of marginal or shared Community competence, the Treaty itself specifically excludes certain models of Community action. Whether such a provision excludes the adoption of harmonisation measures based on the *general* law-making powers of the Community, should the requirements for the application of Articles 6(2), 100, 100A or 235 be satisfied, for example, is not clear; however, some of those provisions require unanimity in the Council, whereas actions based on Article 126 are to be taken by a qualified majority. Scrutiny of harmonisation measures proposed within the context of the internal market programme will be undertaken on an individual basis, in the light of the definition in Article 3B, wherever the substance of the measure falls within an area of competence held jointly by the Community and the Member States. In that context, subsidiarity should not lead to an automatic presumption against the harmonisation of social or employment legislation, but to a consideration of the question raised by Pelkmans (see 16.1) regarding the different levels of scrutiny currently applied to 'economic' and 'social' barriers to market integration. That approach would be faithful to the interpretation of subsidiarity given in 16.5.

The SPA concluded between the Eleven, which contains more general law-making powers in the field of social policy, will also be subject to the principle of subsidiarity. Article 1 SPA makes clear that social policy is shared by the Community and the Member States, and contains a special saving clause in respect of national diversity in employment relations:

'The Community and the Member States shall have as their objectives the promotion of employment, improved living and working conditions, proper social protection, dialogue between management and labour, the development of human resources with a view to lasting high employment and the combating of exclusion. To this end the Community and the Member States shall implement measures which take account of the diverse forms of national practice, in particular in the field of contractual relations, and the need to maintain the competitiveness of the Community economy.'

Article 2(6) of the Agreement also limits the substantive scope of the law-making power established in respect of social policy. It provides that:

'the provisions of this Article shall not apply to pay, the right of association, the right to strike or the right to impose lock-outs.'

Finally, there is evidence in the context of social policy that subsidiarity should indeed be understood as more than just an expression of the appropriate vertical division of powers between the Member States and the Community, and that it comprises a much broader philosophy of decentralisation of policy and decision-making. Article 118B EC introduced the social dialogue into the field of labour regulation in the Community. It provides:

'The Commission shall endeavour to develop the dialogue between management and labour at European level which could, if the two sides consider it desirable, lead to relations based on agreement.'

Articles 3 and 4 of the Agreement between the Eleven on social policy take this much further. Article 3 involves the social partners in the formulation of legislative proposals, and Article 4 makes provision for the social partners themselves to formulate agreements on employment regulation matters to which the Council can then give legal force by way of a Decision adopted by a qualified majority. Involvement will also extend to the post-adoption phase. Under Article 2(4) Member States are empowered to implement social policy measures adopted by the Community by means of binding collective agreements between representatives of management and labour.

Summary

1 In general terms, the Community's social policy is not well developed, even though 'social issues' cannot be rigorously separated from the economic core of the Community.

2 The social policy provisions of the Community were influenced by the view that the harmonisation of social and labour legislation was not needed in a system of economic integration such as that envisaged originally by the Community.

3 Although the Community is committed to social objectives, in the sense of improving the living and working standards of citizens, in reality few effective mechanisms are offered to the Community legislature for achieving these goals by means of social policy legislation. Moreover, the Community has shown a great reluctance to legislate in the social field, in part because the Member States have consistently regarded the field of social policy as a totem of national autonomy and sovereignty.

4 Significant social policy developments have tended to be based upon the Court's broad interpretations of the few social rights contained in the Treaty, such as the right to equal pay, and the right to non-discrimination which extends also to issues of vocational training. However, the Community's social policy is dominated by employment issues.

5 The Community's social policy has evolved through distinctive phases from 'benign neglect' in the early days, via a cycle of hopeful activism followed disillusionment and legislative stagnation. More recently, the Community Social Charter raised hopes of a more activist social policy, but these hopes have not been fulfilled.

6 It is possible that the new social policy provisions concluded outside the framework of the Treaty itself in the Social Policy Agreement attached to the Treaty of Maastricht may offer the first glimpses of effective law-making powers in the social field.

7 The doctrine of subsidiarity has particular resonance in the social policy field, since it is intimately concerned with the socio-political organisation of societies. Its adoption is likely to influence the evolution of Community social policy in numerous ways.

Questions

1 Why is the 'social dimension' of the European Community underdeveloped in comparison to its 'economic dimension'?

2 In what fields has most progress been made in the social policy area? What particular contribution has been made by the Court?

3 Review the earlier chapters of this book in order to identify examples of the Court's case law in the social field making a significant contribution to the evolution of the Community legal order.

4 What will be the principal effect of the application of the doctrine of subsidiarity in the field of social policy?

5 To what extent can the principles of 'spill-over' outlined in 1.4 be used to illustrate the evolution of Community social policy?

Further Reading

Bercusson (1990) 'The European Community's Charter of Fundamental Social Rights for Workers', 53 *Modern Law Review*, 624.

Hepple (1990) 'The Implementation of the Community's Charter of Fundamental Social Rights', 53 *Modern Law Review*, 643.

Mosley (1990) 'The social dimension of European integration', 129 *International Labour Review*, 147.

Shaw (1992) 'Social Policy after the Treaty of Maastricht: A Brief Comment', *Journal of Social Welfare and Family Law*, 255.

Spicker (1991) 'The principle of subsidiarity and the social policy of the European Community', 1 *Journal of European Social Policy*, 3.

Szyszczak (1990b) 'L'Espace Sociale Européenne: Reality, Dreams or Nightmares', 33 *German Yearbook of International Law*, 284.

Watson (1991) 'The Community Social Charter', 28 *Common Market Law Review*, 37.

Bibliography

Adonis (1991), 'Subsidiarity: Theory of a new federalism?', in King and Bosco (eds), *A Constitution for Europe*, Lothian Foundation Press.

Argiros (1990) 'Consumer Safety and the Single European Market: Some Observations and Proposals', *Legal Issues of European Integration*, 90/1, 139.

Arnull (1990a) *The General Principles of EEC Law and the Individual*, LUP/Pinter.

Arnull (1990b) 'Does the Court of Justice have inherent jurisdiction?', 27 *Common Market Law Review*, 683.

Arnull (1990c), 'References to the European Court', 15 *European Law Review*, 375.

Arnull (1991), 'What shall we do on Sunday?', 16 *European Law Review*, 112.

Artis (1992) 'The Maastricht Road to Monetary Union', 30 *Journal of Common Market Studies*, 299.

Barav (1989) 'Enforcement of Community rights in the National Courts: the Case for a Jurisdiction to grant interim relief', 26 *Common Market Law Review*, 369.

Barav (1980) 'Preliminary Censorship? The Judgment of the European Court in *Foglia* v *Novello*', 5 *European Law Review*, 443.

Barents (1986) 'Recent Case Law on the Prohibition of Fiscal Discrimination under Article 95', 23 *Common Market Law Review*, 641.

Barents (1990) 'The Community and the Unity of the Common Market: Some Reflections on the Economic Constitution of the Community', 33 *German Yearbook of International Law*, 9.

Bebr (1982) 'The possible implications of *Foglia* v. *Novello II*', 9 *Common Market Law Review*, 421.

Bebr (1988) 'The Reinforcement of the Constitutional Review of Community Acts under Article 177 EEC', 25 *Common Market Law Review*, 684.

Bercusson (1990) 'The European Community's Charter of Fundamental Social Rights for Workers', 53 *Modern Law Review*, 624.

Bieber (1984) 'The settlement of institutional conflicts on the basis of Article 4 of the EEC Treaty', 21 *Common Market Law Review*, 505.

Bieber (1990) 'Democratic Control of European Foreign Policy', 1 *European Journal of International Law*, 148.

Bieber *et al.* (eds) (1988),*1992: One European Market? A Critical Analysis of the Commission's Single Market Policy*, Nomos.

Bradley (1988) 'The variable evolution of the standing of the European Parliament in proceedings before the Court of Justice', 8 *Yearbook of European Law*, 27.

Bradley (1991) 'Sense and Sensibility: *Parliament* v. *Council* continued', 16 *European Law Review*, 245.

Bradley, (1992), 'Comitology and the Law: Through a Glass, Darkly', 29 *Common Market Law Review*, 693.

Bridge (1984) 'Procedural Aspects of the Enforcement of European Community Law through the Legal Systems of the Member States', 9 *European Law Review*, 28.

Brown (1989) *The Court of Justice of the European Communities*, Sweet & Maxwell (3rd edn).

Burrows (1990) 'Harmonisation of Technical Standards: Reculer pour mieux sauter?', 53 *Modern Law Review*, 597.

Burrows (1992) 'The risks of widening without deepening', 17 *European Law Review*, 352.

Cappelletti *et al.* (1986) *Integration through Law: Part One, Vol. 1, Methods, tools and Institutions*, Walter de Gruyter.

Cass (1992) 'The Word that Saves Maastricht? The Principle of Subsidiarity and the Division of Powers within the European Community', 29 *Common Market Law Review*, 1107.

Cassese *et al.* (1991a) *Human Rights and the European Community: Methods of Protection*, Nomos.

Cassese *et al.* (1991b) *Human Rights and the European Community: The Substantive Law*, Nomos.

Cecchini (1988) *The European Challenge: 1992, the Benefits of a Single Market*, Wildwood House/Gower.

Clapham (1990) 'A Human Rights Policy for the European Community', 10 *Yearbook of European Law*, 309.

Clapham (1991) *Human Rights and the European Community: A Critical Overview*, Nomos.

Collins (1990) *European Community Law in the United Kingdom*, Butterworths (4th edn).

Commission of the European Communities (1985) *Completing the Internal Market*, White Paper from the Commission to the European Council, Com (85) 310.

Commission of the European Communities (1992) *Seventh Report to the Council and the Parliament on the Implementation of the White Paper*, Com (92) 383.

Coppel and O'Neill (1992) 'The European Court of Justice: taking rights seriously?', 12 *Legal Studies*, 227.

Corbett (1989) 'Testing the New Procedures: The European Parliament's First Experiences with its new "Single Act" Powers', 27 *Journal of Common Market Studies*, 359.

Corbett (1992) 'The Intergovernmental Conference on Political Union', 30 *Journal of Common Market Studies*, 271.

Cremona (1990) 'The Completion of the Internal Market and the Incomplete Commercial Policy of the European Community', 15 *European Law Review*, 283.

Crosby (1991) 'The Single Market and the Rule of Law', 16 *European Law Review*, 451.

Crouch and Marquand (eds) (1990) *The Politics of 1992. Beyond the Single European Market*, Blackwell/*The Political Quarterly*.

Curtin (1990a) 'The Province of Government: Delimiting the Direct Effect of Directives in the Common Law Context', 15 *European Law Review*, 195.

Curtin (1990b) 'Directives: The Effectiveness of Judicial Protection of Individual Rights', 27 *Common Market Law Review*, 709.

Cutler *et al.* (1989) *1992 – The Struggle for Europe*, Berg.

Danusso and Denton (1990) 'Does the European Court of Justice look for a protectionist motive under Article 95?', *Legal Issues of European Integration*, 90/1, 66.

Dashwood and Arnull (1984) 'English Courts and Article 177 of the EEC Treaty', 4 *Yearbook of European Law*, 255.

Dashwood and White (1989) 'Enforcement Actions and Article 169 and 170', 14 *European Law Review*, 388.

De Burca (1992) 'Giving Effect to European Community Directives', 55 *Modern Law Review*, 215.

Dehousse (1989) '1992 and Beyond: The institutional dimension of the internal market programme', *Legal Issues of European Integration* 89/1, 109.

Diamond (1991) 'Dishonourable Defences: The Use of Injunctions and the EEC Treaty; Case Study of the Shops Act 1950', 54 *Modern Law Review*, 72.

Docksey and Fitzpatrick (1991) 'The Duty of National Courts to Interpret Provisions of National Law in Accordance with Community Law', 20 *Industrial Law Journal*, 113.

Easson (1984) 'Cheaper wine or dearer beer? Article 95 again', 9 *European Law Review*, 57.

Easson (1989) 'Legal Approaches to European Integration: The Role of the Court and Legislator in the Completion of the European Common Market', 12 *Journal of European Integration*, 101.

Easson (1990) 'The Internal Market and the Elimination of Fiscal Frontiers' 10 *Yearbook of European Law*, 147.

Eeckhout (1991) 'The External Dimension of the EC Internal Market – A Portrait', 15 *World Competition*, 5.

Ehlermann (1987) 'The Internal Market following the Single European Act', 24 *Common Market Law Review*, 361.

El-Agraa (ed.) (1990) *Economics of the European Community*, Philip Allan (3rd edn).

Ellis (1991) *European Community Sex Equality Law*, OUP.

Emiliou (1992) 'Subsidiarity: An Effective Barrier Against "the Enterprises of Ambition?"', 17 *European Law Review*, 383.

Everling (1984) 'The Member States of the European Community before their Court of Justice', 9 *European Law Review*, 315.

Everling (1992) 'Reflections on the Structure of the European Union', 29 *Common Market Law Review*, 1053.

Fitzpatrick (1989) 'The Significance of EEC Directives in UK Sex Discrimination law', 9 *Oxford Journal of Legal Studies*, 336.

Foster (ed.) (1992), *EEC Legislation*, Blackstone Press (3rd edn).

Gaja (1990) 'New Developments in a Continuing Story: The Relationship between EEC law and Italian law', 27 *Common Market Law Review*, 83.

George (1990) *An Awkward Partner: Britain in the European Community*, OUP.

George (1991) *Politics and Policy in the European Community*, OUP (2nd edn).

Gormley (1989) 'Some Reflections on the Internal Market and the Free Movement of Goods', *Legal Issues of European Integration*, 1/89, 9.

Gormley (1990) 'Commentary on *Torfaen BC* v. *B & Q plc*' 27 *Common Market Law Review*, 141.

Grahl and Teague (1990) *1992: The Big Market*, Lawrence and Wishart.

Gravells (1989) 'Disapplying an Act of Parliament pending a Preliminary Ruling: Constitutional Enormity or Community Law Right?', *Public Law*, 568.

Gravells (1991) 'Effective Protection of Community Law Rights: Temporary Disapplication of an Act of Parliament', *Public Law* 180.

Greaves (1986) '*Locus Standi* under Article 173 EEC when seeking annulment of a Regulation', 11 *European Law Review*, 119.

Green, Hartley and Usher (1991) *The Legal Foundations of the Single European Market*, OUP.

Grief (1991) 'The Domestic Impact of the European Convention on Human Rights as Mediated through Community Law', *Public Law*, 555.

Hamson (1976) 'Methods of Judicial Interpretation', in *Proceedings of a Judicial and Academic Conference*, OOPEC.

Harding (1981) 'The Impact of Article 177 of the EEC Treaty on the Review of Community Action', 1 *Yearbook of European Law*, 93.

Harlow (1992) 'A Community of Interests? Making the Most of European Law', 55 *Modern Law Review*, 331.

Hartley (1988) *The Foundation of European Community Law*, Clarendon (2nd edn).

Hepple (1990) 'The Implementation of the Community's Charter of Fundamental Social Rights', 53 *Modern Law Review*, 643.

Hurwitz and Lesquesne (eds) (1991) *The State of the European Community: Policies, Institutions and Debates in the Transition Years*, Lynne Rienner/ Longman.

Jackson (1992) 'Status of Treaties in Domestic Legal Systems: A Policy Analysis', 86 *American Journal of International Law*, 311.

Jacobs and Corbett (1991) *The European Parliament*, Longman (2nd edn).

Jacqué and Wecher (1990) 'On the Road to European Union – A new judicial architecture. An agenda for the Intergovernmental Conference', 27 *Common Market Law Review*, 185.

Kapteyn and VerLoren van Themaat, (1989) *Introduction to the Law of the European Communities*, Kluwer (2nd edn by Gormley).

Keohane and Hoffmann (eds) (1991) *The New European Community: Decisionmaking and Institutional Change*, Westview.

Koopmans (1991a) 'European Public Law: Reality and Prospects', *Public Law* 53.

Koopmans (1991b) 'The Birth of European Law at the Crossroads of Legal Traditions', 39 *American Journal of Comparative Law*, 493.

Kutscher (1976) 'Methods of Interpretation as seen by a Judge at the Court of Justice', in *Proceedings of a Judicial and Academic Conference*, OOPEC.

Lasok and Bridge (1991) *Law and Institutions of the European Communities*, Butterworths (5th edn).

Lenaerts (1991a) 'Some Reflections on the Separation of Powers in the European Community', 28 *Common Market Law Review*, 11.

Lenaerts (1991b) 'Fundamental Rights to be included in a Community Catalogue', 16 *European Law Review*, 367.

Lintner and Mazey (1991) *The European Community: Economic and Political Aspects*, McGraw-Hill.

Lodge (ed.) (1989) *The European Community and the Challenge of the Future*, Pinter.

Lonbay (1989) 'A review of recent tax cases – wine, gambling, fast cars, and bananas', 14 *European Law Review*, 48.

Louis (1990) *The Community Legal Order*, OOPEC (2nd edn).

MacKenzie Stuart (1977) *The European Communities and the Rule of Law*, Sweet & Maxwell.

Mancini (1989) 'The Making of a Constitution for Europe', 26 *Common Market Law Review*, 595.

Marenco and Banks (1990) 'Intellectual Property and the Community rules on Free Movement: Discrimination unearthed', 15 *European Law Review*, 224.

McGhee and Weatherill (1990) 'The Evolution of the Single Market: Harmonisation or Liberalisation?', 53 *Modern Law Review*, 578.

Meads (1991) 'The obligation to apply European law: is Duke dead?' 16 *European Law Review*, 490.

Meessen (1989) 'Europe on Route to 1992: The Completion of the Internal Market and its Impact on Non-Europeans', 23 *The International Lawyer*, 359.

Millett (1989) 'Rules of Interpretation of EEC Legislation', 10 *Statute Law Review*, 163.

Mitchell (1979) 'The Sovereignty of Parliament: the stumbling block that isn't there', *International Affairs*, 33.

Mitchell, Kuipers and Gall (1972) 'Constitutional Aspects of the Treaty and Legislation relating to British Membership', 9 *Common Market Law Review*, 134.

Mortelmans (1991) 'Article 30 of the EEC Treaty and Legislation Relating to Market Circumstances: Time to consider a new definition?', 28 *Common Market Law Review*, 115.

Mosley (1990) 'The social dimension of European integration', 129 *International Labour Review*, 147.

Munro (1987) *Studies in Constitutional Law*, Butterworths.

Nicoll (1984) 'The Luxembourg Compromise', 23 *Journal of Common Market Studies*, 35.

Nugent (1991) *The Government and Politics of the European Community*, Macmillan (2nd edn).

Nugent (1992) 'The Deepening and Widening of the European Community: Recent Evolution, Maastricht and Beyond', 30 *Journal of Common Market Studies*, 311.

O'Keeffe (1992) 'The Agreement on the European Economic Area', *Legal Issues of European Integration* 1/92, 1.

Oliver and Yataganas (1987) 'The Harmonised System of Customs Classification', 7 *Yearbook of European Law*, 113.

Pelkmans, (1986–87) 'The New Approach to Technical Harmonization and Standardization', 25 *Journal of Common Market Studies*, 249.

Pelkmans (1991) 'Towards Economic Union', in Ludlow (ed.), *Setting European Community Priorities 1991–1992*, Brassey's Centre for European Policy Studies.

Pescatore (1983) 'The Doctrine of 'Direct Effect': An Infant Disease in Community Law', 8 *European Law Review*, 155.

Pescatore (1987) 'Some Critical Remarks on the Single European Act', 24 *Common Market Law Review*, 9.

Phelan (1992) 'Right to Life of the Unborn v Promotion of Trade in Services: The European Court of Justice and the Normative Shaping of the European Union', 55 *Modern Law Review*, 670.

Pinder (1991) *European Community: The Building of a Union*, OUP.

Prechal (1990) 'Remedies after *Marshall*', 27 *Common Market Law Review*, 451.

Rasmussen (1980) 'Why is Article 173 interpreted against Private Plaintiffs?', 5 *European Law Review*, 112.

Rasmussen (1986) *On Law and Policy in the European Court of Justice*, Martinus Nijhoff.

Reich and Leahy (1990) *Internal Market and Diffuse Interests: An introduction to EC trade law*, Story Scientia.

Ross (1993) 'Beyond *Francovich*', 56 *Modern Law Review*, 55.

Rudden (1987) *Basic Community Cases*, OUP.

Rudden and Wyatt (1992) *Basic Community Laws* OUP (3rd edn).

Sbragia (ed.) (1992) *Euro-Politics: Institutions and Policymaking in the 'New' European Community*, Brookings.

Schermers (1990) 'The Scales in Balance: National Constitutional Court v. Court of Justice', 27 *Common Market Law Review*, 97.

Schermers (1991) 'The Effect of the Date 31 December 1992', 28 *Common Market Law Review*, 275.

Schermers *et al.* (eds) (1987) *Article 177 EEC: Experiences and Problems*, North-Holland.

Schueren (1991) 'Customs Classification: One of the Cornerstones of the Single European Market, but one which cannot be exhaustively regulated', 28 *Common Market Law Review*, 855.

Schwarze (1986) 'The Administrative Law of the Community and the Protection of Human Rights', 23 *Common Market Law Review*, 401.

Schwarze (1991) 'Tendencies towards a Common Administrative Law in Europe', 16 *European Law Review*, 3.

Shaw (1990) 'European Community Judicial Method: its Application to Sex Discrimination Law', 19 *Industrial Law Journal*, 228.

Shaw (1992) 'Social Policy after the Treaty of Maastricht: A Brief Comment', *Journal of Social Welfare and Family Law*, 255.

Slynn (1992) *Introducing a European Legal Order*, Sweet & Maxwell.

Snyder (1990) *New Directions in European Community Law*, Weidenfeld & Nicolson.

Snyder (1993) 'The Effectiveness of European Community Law: Institutions, Processes, Tools and Techniques', 56 *Modern Law Review*, 19.

Spicker (1991) 'The principle of subsidiarity and the social policy of the European Community', 1 *Journal of European Social Policy*, 3.

Steiner (1987) 'Making the Action Suit the Case: Domestic Remedies for Breach of EEC Rights', 13 *European Law Review*, 102.

Steiner (1992) 'Drawing the Line: Uses and Abuses of Article 30 EEC', 29 *Common Market Law Review*, 749.

Swann (1991a) *The Economics of the Common Market*, Penguin (8th edn).

Swann (1991b) 'Creating the Single European Market', in G. Thompson *et al.* (eds), *Markets, Hierarchies and Networks: The Coordination of Social Life*, Sage.

Swann (ed.) (1992) *The Single European Market and Beyond. A study of the wider implications of the Single European Act*, Routledge.

Szyszczak (1990a) 'Sovereignty: Crisis, Compliance, Confusion, Complacency', 15 *European Law Review*, 480.

Szyszczak (1990b) 'L'Espace Sociale Européenne: Reality, Dreams or Nightmares', 33 *German Yearbook of International Law*, 284.

Szyszczak (1992a) 'European Community Law: New Remedies, New Directions?', 55 *Modern Law Review*, 690.

Szyszczak (1992b) 'Race Discrimination: The Limits of Market Equality?', in Hepple and Szyszczak (eds), *Discrimination: The Limits of Law*, Mansell/Cassell, London.

Temple Lang (1990) 'Community Constitutional Law: Article 5 EEC Treaty', 27 *Common Market Law Review*, 645.

Temple Lang (1991) 'The Development of European Community Constitutional Law', 25 *International Lawyer* 455.

Toth (1986) 'The legal status of the declarations annexed to the Single European Act', 23 *Common Market Law Review*, 803.

Urwin (1991) *The Community of Europe. A History of European Integration since 1945*, Longman.

Usher (1976) 'The Influence of National Concepts on Decisions of the European Court', 1 *European Law Review*, 359.

Usher (1981) *European Community Law and National Law: The Irreversible Transfer?*, Allen & Unwin.

Usher (1986) 'The Single Market and Goods Imported from Third Countries', 6 *Yearbook of European Law*, 159.

Voorst and Van Dam (1988) 'Europe 1992: Free Movement of Goods in the Wider Context of a Changing Europe', 25 *Common Market Law Review*, 693.

Wade (1991) 'What has happened to the Sovereignty of Parliament?', 107 *Law Quarterly Review*, 1.

Wallace (ed.) (1990) *The Dynamics of European Integration*, RIIA/Pinter.

Watson (1986) 'Asser Institute Colloquium on European Law 1985: Experiences and Problems in Applying the Preliminary Proceedings of Article 177 EEC', 23 *Common Market Law Review*, 207.

Watson (1991) 'The Community Social Charter', 28 *Common Market Law Review*, 37.

Weatherill (1992a) *Cases and Materials on EEC Law*, Blackstone Press.

Weatherill (1992b) 'Regulating the Internal Market: Result Orientation in the House of Lords', 17 *European Law Review*, 299.

Weatherill (1992c) 'The free movement of goods: a survey of the decisions of the Court of Justice in 1991', 17 *European Law Review*, 421.

Weiler (1981) 'The Community system: the dual character of supernationalism', 1 *Yearbook of European Law*, 267.

Weiler (1986) 'Eurocracy and Distrust: Some Questions concerning the Role of the European Court of Justice in the Protection of Fundamental Human Rights within the Legal Order of the European Communities', 61 *Washington Law Review*, 1103.

Weiler (1989) 'Pride and Prejudice – *Parliament* v. *Council*', 14 *European Law Review*, 334.

Wellens and Borchardt (1989) 'Soft Law in European Community Law', 14 *European Law Review*, 267.

White (1989) 'In search of the limits to Article 30 of the EEC Treaty', 26 *Common Market Law Review*, 235.

Wilke and Wallace (1990) *Subsidiarity: Approaches to Power-sharing in the European Community*, Discussion Paper no. 27, RIIA.

Wils (1992) 'Concurrent Liability of the Community and a Member State', 17 *European Law Review*, 191.

Winter (1972) 'Direct Applicability and Direct Effect: Two Distinct and Different Concepts in Community Law', 9 *Common Market Law Review*, 425.

Wistrich (1991) *After 1992: The United States of Europe*, Routledge (revsd edn).

Wyatt (1981) 'Following up *Foglia*: Why the Court is Right to Stick to its Guns', 6 *European Law Review*, 447.

Wyatt (1982) 'New Legal Order or Old?', 7 *European Law Review*, 147.

Index